The One Year®
Daily Moments of Peace

THE ONE YEAR®

DAILY MOMENTS OF

peace

INSPIRATION FOR WOMEN

WALK THRU THE BIBLE®

TYNDALE
MOMENTUM™

*The nonfiction imprint of
Tyndale House Publishers, Inc.*

Visit Tyndale online at www.tyndale.com.

Visit Tyndale Momentum online at www.tyndalemomentum.com.

TYNDALE, *Tyndale Momentum*, Tyndale's quill logo, *The One Year*, and *One Year* are registered trademarks of Tyndale House Publishers, Inc. The Tyndale Momentum logo and the One Year logo are trademarks of Tyndale House Publishers, Inc. Tyndale Momentum is the nonfiction imprint of Tyndale House Publishers, Inc., Carol Stream, Illinois.

Walk Thru the Bible and the Walk Thru the Bible logo are registered trademarks of Walk Thru the Bible Ministries, Inc.

The One Year Daily Moments of Peace: Inspiration for Women

Designed by Mark Anthony Lane II

For information about special discounts for bulk purchases, please contact Tyndale House Publishers at csresponse@tyndale.com, or call 1-800-323-9400.

ISBN 978-1-4964-0607-1

Printed in the United States of America

23	22	21	20	19	18	17
7	6	5	4	3	2	1

Introduction

PEACE OFTEN FEELS LIKE an elusive goal in a world that never seems to shut down—or even slow down. Given all the demands on your time, energy, and resources, does your longing for calm, quiet, and stillness ever seem unrealistic or selfish?

If so, Scripture reveals something surprising. The only source of true peace and restoration, it shows us, is God Himself. After the disciples returned from their first ministry tour, they excitedly told Jesus everything they'd seen and done. Given how much work remained, did Jesus send them right back out into the neighboring towns? No. Instead, He told them, "Let's go off by ourselves to a quiet place and rest awhile" (Mark 6:31).

Likewise, this book is an invitation for you to spend a few minutes each day in quiet contemplation, whether it be first thing in the morning, over your lunch break, or just before bed. God made you and me to function best (and be most at peace) when we regularly take time to connect with Him through Scripture and prayer. As God told the Israelites, "Only in returning to me and resting in me will you be saved. In quietness and confidence is your strength" (Isaiah 30:15).

The One Year Daily Moments of Peace can be your means of connecting with God for a few minutes each day throughout the coming year. These devotions are written by women from all walks of life. Each one opens with a story that will encourage you to embrace the peace that is yours when you remember and rest in God's goodness, power, and love for you. Many readings will also point you to practical ways that you can be God's instrument of peace to others.

You can use the prayer at the end of each reading to begin a longer conversation with God about the people and situations He has put on your heart. If you'd like to go deeper with that day's topic, be sure to turn to the Scripture passage referenced in the Deeper Walk section.

This resource from Walk Thru the Bible is designed to ignite passion for God's Word within you as you relax, recharge, and reconnect with Christ, the one who "himself is our peace" (Ephesians 2:14, ESV).

A New Year's Revolution

Let your face smile on us, LORD.
Psalm 4:6

EVERY YEAR I MAKE New Year's resolutions. I resolve to slim down my waistline, beef up my savings, clean my house, read through the entire Bible, and be a better wife, mother, sister, daughter, friend, and worker.

I love the idea of a clean slate, a fresh start, a do-over. Don't you? I think that's why so many of us make New Year's resolutions.

But usually, by February (or even sooner), I have broken one or more of my resolutions—I've eaten too much chocolate; I've spent too much on clothes for the girls; the house is still a mess; I've already gotten bogged down in Leviticus. And I'm not a better anything. So let's not chocolate-coat the truth here: Out of exhaustion and frustration, I throw up my hands and revert to my old ways.

So this year, I have a new idea. I'm not going on a self-help kick, and I'm not going to make resolutions. Instead, I'm going to ask God to make me who He wants me to be. Instead of resolutions, I'm going to ask Him to start a revolution in me.

Our heavenly Father is in the business of do-overs. He gives us a clean slate through Jesus so we can spend eternity with Him. And He'll give us a do-over every day through the confession and repentance of our sins. He is in the business of fresh starts when we eat too much or spend too much or can't make it through Leviticus.

For this new year, I'll ask Him to help me refrain from gossip, love more, root out bitterness, and change whatever else needs to be changed. The revolution has begun. But, Lord, I still need help with the chocolate issue!

As Jesus followers, we know that self-help books and resolutions will not help us make true, long-lasting, living-for-eternity change. But God can help us become the women He made us to be. Ask Him to start a revolution in you.

Steps of Faith

Lord, please start a revolution in me this year. I want to glorify You in all that I am.

Deeper Walk: Psalm 25

Reading Ahead

And the one sitting on the throne said, "Look, I am making everything new!"
Revelation 21:5

I LOVE TO READ—books, magazines, articles on the Internet, whatever. I come from a long line of readers; I like to think it's in my genetic makeup.

I was talking recently with another book lover, and I confessed to the habit of reading ahead at times. My friend laughed and said he couldn't believe I would do that. But when the story's action gets intense or the leading character looks like she might not make it or even if I get bored, I turn to the last few pages of the book. By knowing the end of the story, I can relax and read the rest of the book at a slower pace. That way, I don't miss important details, and I'm not skimming because I'm anxious to know what's going to happen. Also, by knowing the end of the story, I can decide if it's worth the time to keep reading.

Isn't it that way in our lives, too? Sometimes when our stories look scary, we want to close the book out of fear. We want to skim over the slow-going parts, like working a job we don't enjoy. We want to skip painful life chapters, such as going through a divorce. And sometimes, we want to read ahead to discover how everything works out; for example, who our children will grow up to be.

Right now we are living in the middle of God's story. When the action is intense—your husband has been laid off and you don't know how you'll pay the bills; when the plot is heartbreaking—your dad has been diagnosed with a devastating illness; when the story line is exciting—God has called you to another place; in all of these things, we as Jesus followers know how the story ends. We've read ahead. We know the Author's good plan. And we can know that the characters in His story—us—are going to make it through to that happiest of all endings.

Jesus wins! He is coming again to restore all things (see Revelation 21:5), and we are on His winning team.

Steps of Faith

Father, as we live in the middle of Your story, we've read ahead. We know that You have already won the victory, and we praise You.

Deeper Walk: Revelation 21

Who's on the Throne?

Serve only the LORD your God and fear him alone.
Obey his commands, listen to his voice, and cling to him.
Deuteronomy 13:4

As PASTOR KEVIN BEGAN HIS SERMON, I noticed a chair and sofa on the stage that weren't usually there. "Who's on the throne of your life?" he asked.

Pastor Kevin explained that the chair represented a throne—the throne on which only Jesus should be seated. "But sometimes," he said, "we decide that we want to be sitting there instead." He sat down on the chair to demonstrate. "We invite Jesus into our lives, but instead of letting Him sit on the throne, we lead Him over to the sofa—where we've put all the things we love a bit too much—and give Him a little space there."

Pastor Kevin, playing the part of Jesus, sat down on the very end of the sofa, as if he were being squeezed in next to a bunch of other things.

I thought about his illustration and wondered, *Do I have any idols in my heart? Am I giving Jesus His rightful place on the throne of my life? Or am I keeping myself there and offering Him a tiny space on the sofa along with all my other loves?*

It was a powerful, thought-provoking sermon—one that I'll probably remember for a long time. I took some time that afternoon to examine my life and to ask the Lord to show me if there was anything I had put in His place. When He did, I repented and asked for His forgiveness. Then I asked the Holy Spirit to prompt me anytime I was in danger of moving Jesus off the throne and taking His place.

In all our modern sophistication, we may look at the Israelites' worship of idols in the Old Testament and think how ridiculous it seems to bow down to a block of wood. But sometimes we're guilty of worshiping things: homes, cars, money, fame, technology, careers, or physical perfection. Ask God to show you if there is anything in your life that's out of order. Then be ready to obey when He shows you the truth.

Steps of Faith

Lord, You alone deserve to sit on the throne of my life. Please forgive me for the times I've tried to take Your place. Show me if there are any idols in my life. Let me always put You first.

Deeper Walk: Deuteronomy 13

Three Square Meals

When I discovered your words, I devoured them.
They are my joy and my heart's delight.
Jeremiah 15:16

I WAS BABYSITTING FOR my nephews one evening while their parents celebrated their wedding anniversary. As I prepared dinner, I noticed a small photo album on their kitchen counter and casually picked it up to glance through it, expecting to see pictures of my brother's family. Instead I found index cards containing dozens of Bible verses carefully written in my sister-in-law's handwriting. As I read through the Scriptures recorded on the cards, I could tell they addressed particular needs, hopes, and concerns in Melody's life.

"Tell me about this," I said to Melody when they returned home that evening. "I hope you don't mind me looking through it."

Melody didn't seem offended by my nosiness. In fact, she lit up with infectious enthusiasm when she noticed me holding the album.

"That," said Melody, "is three square meals! I've learned that when I 'eat' or meditate on Scriptures that feed my soul's hungers, I'm a more satisfied woman. That makes me a better wife, mother, friend, and employee."

Melody went on to explain that she keeps the album in the kitchen so she can "eat" from it three to four times each day. She said that's the most convenient place for her to read through her chosen Scriptures, meditate on them, and eventually memorize them.

I decided to try Melody's system for myself. And I can attest that nothing I cook up in my kitchen is nearly as satisfying as the words I eat there!

Besides fortifying us against temptation and equipping us to share the gospel, Scripture memorization feeds our hungry souls. For instance, Job said, "I . . . have treasured his words more than daily food" (Job 23:12). We may taste the sweetness of God's words when we read them (Psalm 119:103), but we don't really "eat" them until we meditate on and memorize them. What are some ways you can make dining on God's Word a regular part of your day?

Steps of Faith

Father, I will find Your soul-satisfying words and take them in throughout the day. I know they will become a delight to me and the joy of my heart.

Deeper Walk: Psalm 119:9-16

Nor Does He Sleep

He holds all creation together.
Colossians 1:17

SHE WAS SITTING IN HER CAR SEAT, singing at the top of her lungs: "He is exhausted, the King is exhausted on high, I will praise Him. . . . He is the Rord . . ."

We were on our way home from church that Sunday afternoon and had just sung that song in the service. Of course, our daughter had a few of the words wrong (exchange *exalted* for *exhausted*, and *Lord* for *Rord*).

But her rendition of the song got me thinking. Who would blame God for being exhausted? Just listening to my own prayers would make an ordinary person tired. And He listens to the tiniest prayers of His children all over the world. Just taking care of and providing for my little family is a full-time job. But He takes care of and provides for everyone.

He causes His rain to fall on the evil and the good. He sees everything—all the good deeds and all the sin. He holds the universe in place, and He knits our bodies together. He calls the stars out by name every night, and He gives me every breath I take. He had a plan of salvation for the world from the very beginning, and He has a plan for my four-year-old daughter's life.

What if He decided to chuck it all and take a nap? What if He said, "Whew. I've had enough. These people are wearing Me out. I need a break"?

Scripture tells us "he holds all creation together" (Colossians 1:17)—that means every cell in our bodies and this planet that we live on. It means that every single creature and every single human being depend on Him for survival. And it also means that He knows your name and what each day of your life is going to look like.

Remember, God is never asleep at the wheel. He's in charge of all that's going on around the globe, and He never takes a day off.

Rest in the truth that God is fully aware of all that is going on in your life. He is tireless in His pursuit, protection, and provision for you.

Steps of Faith

Father, thank You that You will never leave us or forsake us. We can relax in the knowledge that You are sovereign over all things, even our very next breath.

Deeper Walk: Colossians 1:15-20

Learn to Say No

For the LORD grants wisdom!
From his mouth come knowledge and understanding.
Proverbs 2:6

ELAINE SET THE STEAMING steaks down in front of the customers. As she turned around, Katie whispered, "Gotta talk to you, okay?"

"Later," Elaine told Katie and headed toward another table to take orders. Katie had cajoled her into covering the rest of her shift on numerous occasions so she could get off early. Elaine had always agreed and stayed late, hoping she would earn enough tips to make it worth her time.

But recently, Elaine's husband, Blake, had told her, "The kids and I want to spend more time with you. Just tell Katie to find someone else to cover her shift next time."

Dashing back to the kitchen, Elaine prayed silently. *Father, Katie has asked me to cover for her so many times that I feel like she's taking advantage of me. Please help me to set healthy boundaries and to say no without feeling guilty.*

About seven, Katie bounced over to her and grinned. "Hey, how about covering for me tonight? I'm supposed to work until ten, but Ron is picking me up at nine."

"I'm sorry," Elaine began. "I can't. I have to get home so I can spend some time with my family before the kids go to bed."

"But I've already made plans . . ."

"Katie, I can't do it. You'll have to find someone else or change your plans."

Katie's face reddened. "I thought you were supposed to be a Christian!" she snapped.

"I am a Christian, but that doesn't mean I can say yes every time. I have a family, and I have responsibilities at home."

Katie stomped off toward the kitchen, and Elaine prayed again.

Thanks, Lord, for giving me the courage to say no.

Because of our desire to be liked and accepted, we may be tempted to say yes whenever someone asks us for a favor. If you have trouble turning down others, ask the Lord to give you the courage to say no when necessary. He will give you wisdom to take on only what is within His will.

Steps of Faith

Lord, give me the wisdom to know when to say yes and the courage to say no to others' requests when You call me to do so.

Deeper Walk: James 1:5-6

Faithful

What sorrow for those who say that evil is good and good is evil,
that dark is light and light is dark, that bitter is sweet and sweet is bitter.
Isaiah 5:20

As EMPTY NESTERS, my husband, Jeff, and I settled into a comfortable routine. When we got home from work, I cooked dinner. After cleaning up the kitchen, we went for a walk, then came back and sat down to watch TV.

But the shows today seem to have few restrictions about what's acceptable and decent and what's not. When I was growing up, the violence was minimal—in *Gunsmoke*, Marshal Matt Dillon shot the bad guy (in self-defense), who was so far away from the camera that you couldn't see his "injuries" clearly. Lucille Ball and Desi Arnaz, who were married in real life, couldn't share the same bed on their show *I Love Lucy*.

One evening Jeff and I started watching a new drama on cable. It featured a dysfunctional family whose lives were rife with adultery, fornication, greed, and deception. Forget faithfulness. It wasn't anywhere to be found. When the characters had a rough day, they went straight for the bottle. If a character was really angry, he shouted or smashed things.

Jeff and I decided to watch something else. We knew that this program didn't reflect the values we believed in. The next day, while looking through the mail, I uncovered a sales flyer from a local Christian bookstore. It featured some interesting films, music, and books that aligned with our values. I decided to check it out.

Our society and the media today try to convince us that the only things of value are material success, physical beauty, and getting ahead. We are bombarded with messages telling us that faithfulness doesn't matter. We hear constantly that it's not important how we get whatever we want, only that we do. Many TV programs, books, and movies glorify sex, violence, and all kinds of corruption. At the Christian bookstore, I found out there are good alternatives. God's values are vastly different from those of this world. He is faithful, and He wants us to follow in the footsteps of His Son, Jesus.

Steps of Faith

Father, thank You for Your faithfulness. Help me to be faithful in all that I think, do, and say.

Deeper Walk: Psalm 18

This Is My Song

The LORD is my strength and my song; he has given me victory.
This is my God, and I will praise him.
Exodus 15:2

WE THINK OF PRAISE SONGS as fairly new in the church, but they're actually as ancient as the parting of the Red Sea. Here are a few I've been studying: Moses' "Song of the Sea" (Exodus 15:1-18); Mary's "Magnificat" (Luke 1:46-55); and Zechariah's "Benedictus" (Luke 1:68-79). These are spontaneous songs of worship, with beautiful poetic language such as "He has filled the hungry with good things" (Luke 1:53) and "The morning light from heaven is about to break upon us, to give light to those who sit in darkness and the shadow of death" (Luke 1:78-79).

Moses' song was sung on the shores of the Red Sea after God saved the children of Israel from the Egyptian army. The Israelites watched as God threw the Egyptians into the sea, where they sank like lead into the depths. The song proclaims the Israelites' faith in God, glorifies Him as Deliverer, and describes in vivid imagery His mighty acts and sovereignty.

Mary's song, "The Magnificat," is a testimony to how God worked in her life personally. And since Mary knew her child would be the fulfillment of God's covenant promises to Abraham, she also magnified Him as Promise Keeper.

Zechariah's song, "The Benedictus," begins, "Praise the Lord, the God of Israel." It announces that salvation is at hand and foretells his own son's role: He, John, would prepare the way for Jesus.

Inspired by these ancient praise songs, I wrote my own: *Lord, there is none like You. Your fingerprints have been on my life since before I was born. You've provided for me as I've stood with my husband on the shores of unemployment. You've delivered my baby from sickness. You've done great things for me personally. I was thirsty, and You gave me Living Water. I was without direction, and You showed me the Way. I was without hope, and You gave me life. You bury my enemies—my sins—in Your sea of mercy, where they sink like lead. Thank You, Lord.*

Do you have a song?

Steps of Faith

Father God, we extol You for all that You are.

Deeper Walk: Exodus 15

The Missing Storyteller

Seek the Kingdom of God above all else, and live righteously,
and he will give you everything you need.
Matthew 6:33

ONE OF THE FIRST THINGS my husband and I did as newlyweds was put a "year at a glance" calendar on our home office wall. We thought it would be great to add in our vacations, important holidays, home improvement projects, and work commitments so we could see our availability throughout the year. We were so proud of ourselves for this plan.

As we added things to the calendar over the first few months of marriage, we slowly became aware of how quickly it filled up. At first, it was fun to be an on-the-go couple with plans and dreams and general busyness. But then one Sunday afternoon, I received a call from the family ministry coordinator at church. I had forgotten that I'd signed up to tell the Bible story in kids' church. I checked the calendar, and "storyteller" was nowhere to be found. "Stain the deck" was Saturday's entry, and we hadn't forgotten to do that. Although we had attended church that morning, I hadn't even thought about children's church. My husband and I were active in our congregation, but our calendar didn't reflect it.

I called my husband in to see. "Honey, there's nothing on this calendar about our church commitments—no Bible study, no small group, no service or ministry time." I looked at him and said, "What were we thinking?"

"We weren't," he replied. "At least not about the most important things. Why don't we fix that right now?"

"Great idea," I said.

Are you too busy for God? Is your life so full of commitments that time spent connecting with God and fellow believers in Bible study and worship gets crowded out or becomes merely routine? Prayerfully examine your calendar and see if it needs a do-over.

Steps of Faith

Dear God, please forgive me when my priorities don't align with Yours. I desire to honor You and worship You with all of my being.

Deeper Walk: Luke 10:38-42

His Kingdom Prevails

Yet what we suffer now is nothing compared to
the glory he will reveal to us later.
Romans 8:18

WHENEVER MY SMALL GROUP MEETS, we start by catching up with one another and reporting how our weeks are going. This week, one young woman began talking about world events. She mentioned various ongoing wars and conflicts, disastrous famines, and natural disasters and wondered aloud if these were the end times. Then she raised a question: What can we do?

For the next half hour, our group thumbed through Scripture and recounted all that we'd been taught about the "last days" before Christ's return. Many of the younger women were fearful about what the future held for their families. A few mentioned storing up food and keeping a survival kit if times got tougher.

Finally our leader, Linda, addressed the group. "It's true that we need to be watchful for the second coming of our Savior. And it's true that times are getting worse and we must be prepared. But we shouldn't worry or be afraid. Our hearts and minds must be centered on God's leading rather than on packing our bags. We are called to remain faithful through the good times and the bad. In these unsettling times, we can't just say we believe; we have to act on our belief, trusting God to lead and provide for us and our loved ones."

God used Linda's calm directive to remind the group that His Kingdom will prevail. His will is going to be accomplished on earth. It's our job to remain faithful to Him, obey His guidance, and be a light to a world in need.

The world is broken and groans with the pains of childbirth—it is pregnant with expectation of the return of Jesus. If we pull back and see things from a Kingdom perspective, everything weaves together into God's big story of redemption. Life's highs and lows combine to create a beautiful tapestry that glorifies God. Before preparing your survival pack, check your heart and perspective. Are they prepared for Christ's return?

Steps of Faith

Lord, times are getting harder, but I know You are in control and already have the victory. Give me eyes to see where You want me to be. Give me strength of heart to be faithful.

Deeper Walk: Romans 8:18-30

Stepping Out

By faith . . . Abraham obeyed when God called him to leave home and
go to another land that God would give him as his inheritance.
Hebrews 11:8

JENNIFER AND MARK SAT AT the kitchen table with the calculator, their household budget ledger, and clumps of wadded notebook paper between them. The baby would only sleep another half hour before demanding to be fed. Mark drummed the table with his pencil, the way he often did when he gave something serious thought. Jennifer bit her lower lip and sat on the edge of her chair, waiting for her husband to put a stop to their dreams.

"Mark, it's okay," Jennifer finally said with resignation. "It just isn't adding up for me to stop working and stay home with Samuel. I understand."

Mark looked up at his wife, startled. He put the pencil down and took Jennifer's hands in his.

"Jennifer, you misunderstood," he said. "I'm not giving our budget a thorough going-over because I don't think we can do this. I'm just determined that we be smart about it."

"You mean you're okay with me staying home with Sam? I'm going to be able to stop working?"

"I believe God laid it on our hearts for you to stay home with Samuel, at least for a while," said Mark. "According to the numbers we're coming up with in our budget, we're just barely going to make it. But, while the facts aren't all in yet, I think this is one of those decisions we need to make on faith, not on the way things appear. We both feel that this is what God wants us to do, so we need to take a step of faith."

Having faith in God is more than just mentally believing He can do what He says He can do. True faith requires taking a step into the unknown, trusting He will walk the new path with you, and letting go of what's familiar and safe. Consider all the steps of faith that women such as Ruth and Mary took at God's invitation. What step of faith is He calling you to?

Steps of Faith

Father, give me the courage to step out in faith when You call me to something new and unfamiliar.

Deeper Walk: Joshua 3:1-17

Faith Trumps Fear

Don't be afraid, for I am with you. Don't be discouraged,
for I am your God. I will strengthen you and help you.
Isaiah 41:10

CHRIS HUNG UP THE PHONE and fought back tears, wondering to herself, *What else can go wrong in my life?* A nurse had just called to inform her that the results of a test from her annual exam were questionable. She had asked Chris to return in two months for repeat testing.

Cold fingers of fear gripped Chris as she considered dealing with yet another crisis. It was less than a year since her husband had left them, and she was just starting to rebuild her life. Only now did she see her children beginning to adjust.

Chris knew she would need prayer to cope with this time of waiting. She called her friend Gail and told her of the recent report. "This would cause me to be anxious under any circumstances. But it's really scary to think of facing illness or treatment now when I'm the sole caregiver for my children."

"It's only natural that you feel worried and afraid, Chris," said Gail. "But I'm going to e-mail you some Bible verses that help me when I'm afraid. Read them often. Ask God to guard your mind and give you peace. We know He is in control and faithful even in this. Remember that His love can cast out fear (1 John 4:18). Let me pray for you right now to be able to release this to God and trust in Him."

Fear can paralyze us—even more so if it creeps in when we are already vulnerable. But God knows our weakness and gives us comfort in His Word. It has been estimated that the Bible says, "Fear not" approximately 365 times— once for every day of the year! How good to know that He promises never to abandon us and to provide strength one day at a time.

We fight fear with faith—holding on to His Word and trusting His love for us.

Steps of Faith

Father, thank You for being our strength and our hope. Help us to trust You when fear closes in. Be our Prince of Peace.

Deeper Walk: Psalm 56:3-11

Always Growing

*I am certain that God, who began the good work within you,
will continue his work until it is finally finished on the day
when Christ Jesus returns.*

Philippians 1:6

"EMMA, THANKS FOR COMING over to help me with this," Mrs. Crawford said. "My daughter says I'll enjoy finding old friends on this site, but I'm still not sure how it works."

"Sure, Mrs. Crawford. I think it's really cool that you want to learn about Facebook. My grandparents don't even have a computer."

"Well, it's important to always keep learning new things no matter how old you are. God has allowed me to live a long life, and I want to use every moment wisely."

"How long have you been a Christian?" Emma asked.

"Well, let's see . . . almost sixty years!" Mrs. Crawford exclaimed. "And you know what? God keeps teaching me new things about Himself all the time. As I grow in my faith, He shows me how much I need Him and how amazing He is. As much as I want to keep up with technology and the world around me, it's even more important to continue growing spiritually. Even if I live to be 105, I'll never know all there is to know about our good God and His ways. Now, how about we finish up my profile, and then we'll get some lemonade and I'll show you the book I'm reading in my quiet time."

No matter how long we have been walking with the Lord, there is always something new He can reveal to us through His Word, prayer, worship, and our relationships with other believers. If you look back at your walk with God ten years, five years, or even one year ago, would you say it looks different today? If you have become stagnant in your relationship with God, ask Him to breathe new life into your walk with Him. His Word is an unending source of truth that can guide you to know Him better. Plug into a Bible study or small-group environment where you will hear solid biblical teaching and find accountability. And know that God promises to draw close to you when you draw close to Him (see James 4:8).

Steps of Faith

Lord, help me always to seek to know You more. Renew and refresh our relationship through Your mercy and grace.

Deeper Walk: 1 Peter 2:1-5

A Request

Every time I think of you, I give thanks to my God.
Philippians 1:3

"WHAT ARE YOU DOING ON TUESDAY?" Kim asked.

"Nothing," I said. Tuesday was my birthday, so I'd planned to take the day off.

"Can you come over and help me organize my scrapbook supplies?"

"Sure." Kim had become precious to me. The times I'd spent hanging out with her had shown me the importance of breaking away from work, parenting responsibilities, and my endless to-do list in order to invest in my relationships with others. We prayed for each other, shared our struggles, and were thoroughly enjoying getting to know each other after years of attending church together. Whether she remembered my birthday or not didn't matter.

On Tuesday morning, Kim called. "Julie's going to pick you up. She's helping too."

"That's great!" I loved Julie—another recent friendship that I hoped to devote more time to.

When Julie arrived, her mom was in the car, "along for the ride." We walked through Kim's doorway to the smell of homemade coffee cake. Within minutes, three other friends showed up.

"Surprise!"

"Happy birthday!"

I just stood there, speechless, floored by Kim's acting skills.

The seven of us spent almost two hours laughing, chatting, and getting even better acquainted. The best part was knowing that even if we had spent the morning organizing scrapbook supplies, I would have enjoyed it because I was with friends.

The endless tasks of adulthood—working, raising kids, keeping a household running smoothly—can make relationships challenging. Treasured moments with the women God brings into our lives help us see the benefits of making time for our sisters in Christ. The apostle Paul thanked God daily for his friends in Philippi. Which friends do you thank God for? Perhaps it's time for you to make some time for them.

Steps of Faith

Lord, You have brought so many precious friends into my life. Help me to start making more time for them.

Deeper Walk: Philippians 1:3-8

All Grown Up

For our present troubles are small and won't last very long.
Yet they produce for us a glory that vastly outweighs them and will last forever!
2 Corinthians 4:17

I GREW UP IN A SMALL TOWN where people were friendly and life was slow. I rode my bicycle to the library, returning home with a basketful of books. I walked to school with my friends and played softball in my backyard. My school friends were also my church friends.

I'm all grown up now, with a husband, children, and responsibilities. We live far from that town, and my parents moved away long ago too. But on a recent family trip, our path led close to my hometown, so I showed my daughters where I grew up.

Seeing my childhood home, my elementary school, and even the old library brought back so many memories. I remembered schoolgirl problems and heartaches, feeling left out and disliked, being unable to do math.

Everything looked so small through my grown-up eyes. I remembered the house feeling spacious, but this house looked tiny. I remembered being able to run forever in our big front yard, but this yard looked cramped and close to the street. My elementary school looked miniscule, with a small playground and tiny desks. But to my little-girl eyes, everything had seemed big—the house, the school, the problems.

I have adult problems now, and some seem overwhelming. But as I looked at my old home, I wondered, *When I get to eternity, will today's big problems look small? Will I look back at these days with a smile, thinking how insignificant these battles were from an eternal point of view? Will it be like looking through the big end of a telescope at a tiny dot?*

The apostle Paul said our problems here are "light and momentary" in comparison to heaven (2 Corinthians 4:17, NIV). It's hard to remember that when you're staring at a large stack of bills and a small bank balance, or when you are waiting for scary test results. But the Owner of eternity, who has overcome the world (John 16:33), can give us an eternal perspective.

Steps of Faith

Lord, please give us an eternal perspective on what we face as we walk through this world. Faithful and True One, remind us of Your promises.

Deeper Walk: 2 Corinthians 4:7-18

Is It Your Home?

The human body has many parts, but the many parts make up one whole body.
So it is with the body of Christ.
1 Corinthians 12:12

FROM THE FIRST SUNDAY Jeff and I attended our church, we felt welcomed. We quickly got to know the other couples in our Sunday school class, and we soaked up our pastor's biblical messages. Before long, we knew we had found our "home."

But some time later, my mother pointed out that we hadn't moved all the way in yet.

"What do you mean we haven't really moved in and made it our home?" I asked my mom. "We've been attending worship services and Bible study for more than a year."

"Do you remember how when you were growing up, I told you and your brothers that you all had house chores to do because it was your home too?" my mom asked. "When it's your home, you pitch in and do your share of the work. What are you and Jeff doing to contribute in your new church home?"

Ouch. She'd made her point. Jeff and I had been living like guests instead of family members. But that quickly changed. We're part of the greeter ministry at our church now, and we're helping others feel welcomed.

In Romans 12, Paul tells the church to act like a family. He exhorts the Christians in Rome to use their various spiritual gifts in service, be devoted to one another, contribute toward each other's needs, practice hospitality, and "rejoice with those who rejoice [and] mourn with those who mourn" (verse 15, NIV). In other words, they needed to invest in one another and in their common goal of spreading the gospel. How do you participate in your church family? Do you have a church home where you invest in others, work toward a common goal, contribute financially, and serve with love? Or are you enjoying the perks of "home" without doing your part? Consider how you can make your church home a sweeter place for others.

Steps of Faith

Father, thank You for welcoming me into Your family. Show me how I can serve in and through my church to make a difference.

Deeper Walk: 1 Corinthians 12:12-27

Life Skills

Teach them God's decrees, and give them his instructions.
Exodus 18:20

I HAVE TWO DAUGHTERS, ages fourteen and ten. When they were little, I didn't take the time to teach them how to pick up their toys, put away their clothes, or help around the house. I thought I was too busy and could do the tasks more quickly myself. My overarching philosophy was that they only had a short time to be children and would have a lifetime to do laundry.

Big mistake! A friend told me recently of all the practical life skills she was teaching her daughters. They can do laundry, clean the house, and prepare meals. They both have a checking account and a debit card. They earn money by doing extra jobs around the house.

I realized that I was in a position to raise adults who wouldn't know how to take care of a home. Adults who couldn't keep a budget, cook a meal, or mow their own grass. Adults who wouldn't realize that working for an employer requires responsibility, organization, and creativity. Adults who wouldn't know how to work "willingly at whatever [they] do, as though [they] were working for the Lord rather than for people" (Colossians 3:23).

Conviction set in. My husband and I had a prayer meeting, consulting with the Lord about how to make changes in our home. We established some jobs for the girls, rules about messes, and a schedule for learning certain duties.

It's been a few months, and while it was difficult at first to right my wrongs, our girls are learning to be skillful, competent people who will be able to take care of themselves and to serve God.

When your children are young, take the time to teach them life skills. Start small and with age-appropriate duties. Don't expect perfection, and apply praise liberally. You'll be raising competent adults who can serve the Lord, their family, and their employers, to His honor.

Steps of Faith

Father, help us to teach our children the life skills they will need to function on their own.

Deeper Walk: Proverbs 20:11; 22:6

Appointment with God

LORD, you know the hopes of the helpless.
Surely you will hear their cries and comfort them.
Psalm 10:17

I'VE NOTICED THAT THE OLDER I GET, the more quickly life seems to move. Now that I have a husband, two children, and a dog, I have a lot more responsibilities than I did when I was younger.

I used to have a set prayer time each day. I'd grab my prayer journal and my Bible and pray for my needs and the needs of others for at least thirty minutes. If I felt led to, or during difficult times, I'd pray more. But now I'm finding it pretty hard to have a consistent prayer life.

I know how important it is to support my husband and children in prayer, but sometimes I get so wrapped up in the day-to-day activities that I completely neglect to utter even a single prayer for my family until I'm ready for bed.

At night when my head hits the pillow, I often realize that I've neglected my daily prayer time. Then I feel guilty about not making it a priority to have that one-on-One time with God.

How can I get back on track to having that consistent daily time with Him?

If you're having trouble maintaining a regular prayer time, confess it to the Lord and ask for His help. Start with an earnest prayer like Psalm 54:2: "Listen to my prayer, O God. Pay attention to my plea." The Lord loves you unconditionally and deeply desires to spend time with you every day. Having a regular prayer time helps to keep the lines of communication open between you and God. You can also ask Him to help you commit to a specific prayer time each day. Then block out that time for God. Mark it on your calendar if you have to, but make it a priority.

Once you have that time set, treat it like you would any other extremely important appointment. Then during your time with the Lord, be faithful to lift up your loved ones in prayer.

Steps of Faith

Heavenly Father, please help me make my time with You my number one priority. I know that spending time with You keeps me on track spiritually, and staying connected with You gives me more wisdom about how to pray for my family.

Deeper Walk: Isaiah 26:8-9

In the Details

Your Father knows exactly what you need even before you ask him!
Matthew 6:8

RECENTLY I FOUND MYSELF walking briskly through the airport, trying to work off some nervous energy. As much as I enjoy traveling, I'd taken this long nonstop flight before and knew it to be a stressful experience. In the hours leading up to it, I'd mentally prepared myself to navigate one of the world's busiest airports and endure a long-haul flight alone.

I wonder how experienced the pilot is, I'd thought hours earlier. *I hope he's competent.*

That thought was still in the back of my mind when I reached my gate and learned that the plane was running late. Joining the crowd in the waiting area, I plopped myself down and struck up a conversation with the uniformed flight attendant beside me.

One by one, other crew members arrived and came over to where we were seated until the entire flight crew, pilot and copilot included, had joined the conversation. They were happy to tell me about their line of work, and since I was well acquainted with our destination, I answered their questions about the area. As the pilot took coffee orders for the crew and insisted I add mine to the list, I thought back sheepishly to my earlier cynicism.

So began the best commercial flight I've ever been on. Other passengers regarded me with growing curiosity as the crew greeted me by name and kept a friendly eye out for me over the hours. Technically, I traveled alone that day, but in reality, I had company nearly from the moment I cleared security until deplaning.

Sometimes it's easy to see God in life's dramatic moments, when the stakes are high and the impossible looms. But He is no less real or evident in the little things. My travel concerns, while not earth-shattering, still weighed on my heart, but God already had the details worked out in a way that surpassed what I could have come up with. Isn't that just like God, to take such an interest in our lives and leave His fingerprints in the details? Only He could orchestrate that level of detail, using the nuance of each moment to show His care and control.

Steps of Faith

Thank You, Father, for the way You show yourself in the details, knowing and arranging circumstances long before they even cross my mind!

Deeper Walk: Psalm 8

In the Congregation

I was glad when they said to me, "Let us go to the house of the LORD."
Psalm 122:1

I'D BEEN TRAVELING AN abnormal amount for business all month. The longer the mayhem of air travel and business meetings and restaurant dining went on, the edgier I became. I realized I was losing focus, perspective, and joy. Being away from my family and home was taking a toll on me. But I had no choice. Or so I thought.

As I settled into my hotel room one Saturday night, I noticed a listing of local churches on the desk. I realized then that while I wasn't able to attend my home church, I could still worship with other believers the next morning. And so I did.

That Sunday I visited a small church tucked away on a forgotten downtown street. I could tell the church had seen better times, but the small congregation gathered there didn't seem discouraged at all. They were focused on worshiping God, encouraging one another, and hearing from God's Word. By the time I left that sweet fellowship, I felt like I was getting back on track. Ever since that morning, I've made a point of worshiping with other believers on Sundays no matter where I am. That weekly time of praising God with others makes a world of difference, and it's worth the effort.

The author of Hebrews warns us not to neglect meeting with other believers (see 10:25). Why such a warning? Because he knew we are prone to do just that. Whether life gets busy, we move to a new town, or we get our feelings hurt, we're all tempted at times not to worship with a family of believers regularly. But it is in the midst of a congregation of worshipers that we are most likely to have our own faith increased, our joy reignited, and our consciences pricked. When we connect with God and other believers in the body of Christ, lives are transformed and ministry is multiplied. Commit today to worshiping with others each week.

Steps of Faith

Father, forgive me for the times I've neglected worshiping You in the company of others. Help me make corporate worship a priority.

Deeper Walk: Hebrews 10:19-25

When Answers Don't Come

All of God's promises have been fulfilled in Christ with a resounding "Yes!"
2 Corinthians 1:20

TEARS FILLED GAYLA'S EYES AS the leader of her prayer group spoke of her daughter's years of rebellion. Ten years passed before God drew her back and restored her to their family. The leader's final comment struck hard. She said, "I have discovered that God doesn't always tell us yes or no when we pray. But sometimes He says, 'I have a better plan.'"

Gayla pondered those words as she considered her own circumstances. Her family had had its share of problems over the last year, causing division and angst in their household. She'd asked God to restore her family, but it hadn't happened. God seemed unresponsive to their circumstances, and she'd begun to lose hope.

God, Gayla prayed, *forgive me for not trusting Your goodness and believing that You still hear me, love me, and have a better plan. Thank You for all the ways You sustain and carry me. Help me to be faithful as I wait for You to accomplish Your work in our lives.*

Sometimes our lives seem to be littered with "unanswered prayers"—the healing that didn't happen, unreconciled relationships, the home that was foreclosed, the great job that eludes us. Even in those times of waiting or closed doors, we can know God has a better plan because we know His character. He is good, wise, loving, merciful, and compassionate. He is the One who has "a future and a hope" for us (Jeremiah 29:11). His plan is to develop in us the character of Christ and draw us near to Him, however He chooses to do that.

There are times in our lives when we must determine to bow before Him in surrender and run to Romans 11:33, which declares, "Oh, how great are God's riches and wisdom and knowledge! How impossible it is for us to understand his decisions and his ways!"

Steps of Faith

Father, help my unbelief. Give me the faith to trust You even when the answers don't seem to make sense.

Deeper Walk: Psalm 86

Time Out

Don't reject the LORD's discipline, and don't be upset when he corrects you. For the LORD corrects those he loves.

Proverbs 3:11-12

MY GRANDSON JACOB WILL be turning thirteen soon, and he's growing up to be a fine young man. He loves playing hockey, does his homework before he goes outside to skateboard with his friends, and makes his bed in the morning without being asked. But when he was younger, he was a real handful.

One afternoon, I was getting ready to play a game of Old Maid with Jacob and his older brother, Chase, when Jacob pitched a fit. I told him that if he chose not to behave, he would have to sit on "the naughty step." The naughty step was the bottom step of our staircase, which led from the family room to our second floor.

As I brought the cards to the kitchen table, Jacob's little temper got the best of him, and he wound up on the dreaded naughty step. He popped up several times, defiantly announcing, "I don't want to thit on the naughty thtep!" (As a four-year-old, he still had his cute little lisp.)

After I had replanted Jacob's bottom on the step a few times, he knew I wasn't giving up. So with a scowl on his face, he sat on the naughty step and watched as Chase and I played Old Maid just a few feet away. Finally, when Jacob was sufficiently repentant, I invited him to join us at the table.

After I tucked my two sweet grandsons into bed that night, I thought about how God has to discipline us from time to time. I thanked Him for loving His children enough to bring discipline into our lives.

Discipline: It's not pleasant, and sometimes it really hurts. We may pout and whine and wonder what we did to deserve such treatment. But God's ways are always good, and He knows what's best for us. He loves us too much to let us get away with destructive or just downright bad behavior. Next time you feel that God is bringing discipline to your life, ask Him, *Lord, what do You want me to learn from this? Help me to heed the voice of the Holy Spirit and to obey quickly.*

Steps of Faith

Father, thank You for embracing me as Your beloved daughter. And thank You for Your loving discipline that teaches me to walk in Your ways.

Deeper Walk: Hebrews 12:3-13

Sabbath Rest

Observe the Sabbath day by keeping it holy, as the LORD your God has commanded you. You have six days each week for your ordinary work, but the seventh day is a Sabbath day of rest dedicated to the LORD your God.
Deuteronomy 5:12-14

WHEN MY CHILDREN WERE LITTLE, I looked forward to a simple Sunday afternoon ritual all week long. After church and a lunch of grilled cheese or PB and J, my husband would put the kids down for a nap, and I'd head to the local bookstore.

As soon as I walked through the heavy wooden doors, I was met with the sweet, rich smell of paper and coffee. After browsing a bit, perhaps picking up a book or magazine I might want to buy, I'd order a latte and settle myself at one of the café tables. After spending some time digging into my bookstore finds, I'd get out my weekly journal and jot down answers to a few questions: "What went well this week?" "What should I try differently next week?" and "What did God teach me this week?" My musings weren't life changing, but they did help me decide what was effective and what wasn't in my busy schedule as a working mom, as well as reminding me of the ways God had shown up in my life over the past seven days.

Celebrating the Sabbath, I've come to believe, doesn't mean just going to church. It is an invitation from God to sit with Him and tarry a bit so that He can speak to our hearts and recharge our bodies. At other seasons in my life, I've done that by taking a walk around my neighborhood, soaking in a bathtub, or even trying out a new soup recipe. The setting is less important than acknowledging my need for rest, purposefully stepping away from unfinished chores, and opening my heart to God's still, small voice.

Steps of Faith
Father, thank You for designing the Sabbath so that my body gets the rest it needs and my soul has time to rest in You.

Deeper Walk: Mark 2:23-27

Improvise

This is my command: Love each other.
John 15:17

My husband and I don't get a lot of time to ourselves, so when my parents offered to take the kids for a night, we were ecstatic. The only problem was that we didn't have enough cash for a "real" date, so we improvised.

"What about going for a walk around the mall?" Kevin asked.

"That's not a bad idea," I said, "but the mall will probably be pretty busy tonight." The thought of walking through a crowded mall on a weekend didn't sound too appealing.

"What about taking Buford [our Boston terrier] for a walk in the park instead? It's free, and there shouldn't be a lot of people there right now," Kevin said.

"Sounds perfect!" I replied enthusiastically. The three of us were out the door in minutes.

"This was a really good idea," I said to Kevin as we strolled along the path. "I was thinking of something a bit more romantic—probably without Buford—but this is nice."

"It's good to be able to talk without the kids interrupting, and we can just enjoy being together," my husband said with a smile. "When we get home, maybe we can watch that movie you rented for us."

"Sounds like a great idea," I said as I squeezed my husband's hand. I silently thanked God for parents who love our kids and are willing to give us an occasional break.

Spending one-on-one time with your spouse is such an important aspect of your relationship. If you want to be creative or frugal when it comes to dating, there are fun things to do that don't cost a fortune. Just ask for God's guidance on finding inexpensive activities. James 1:5 promises, "If you need wisdom, ask our generous God, and he will give it to you. He will not rebuke you for asking." Prioritizing alone time with your spouse will help strengthen your relationship, and you'll make some great memories as well.

Steps of Faith

Father, please help me nurture relationships with my loved ones. Give me creativity and the desire to keep my relationships growing.

Deeper Walk: Proverbs 3:5-10

Pleasing People or God?

I'm not trying to win the approval of people, but of God.
If pleasing people were my goal, I would not be Christ's servant.
Galatians 1:10

THE YOUNG PASTOR'S COMMENTS gripped Kayla's heart. She was thankful for his transparency as he acknowledged his personal struggle with the desire to win people's approval. Then he shared what God was teaching him about overcoming his people-pleasing tendencies. He closed with a final powerful comment: "I may not be who you think I am, but I am who God says I am."

Kayla recognized this battle as one she had fought most of her life. She also was a people pleaser. She needed to make sure everyone was happy, she pursued peace at any cost, and she fretted often over what people were thinking or saying about her. The result was that she was often anxious, irritable, and tired of trying to influence attitudes and actions that she had no control over. She wanted victory over this weakness.

As the sermon ended, Kayla prayed, *God, help me stop being consumed with pleasing those around me. Let me believe what You say about me in Your Word. Teach me how to please You most of all.*

Many women can identify with Kayla's insight. Our natural role as nurturers and relationship builders can get out of balance. If our need to please others consumes us, it will drain our confidence and steal our joy. We will second-guess ourselves much of the time. Worrying about what others think of us can even rob us of opportunities to do big things for God. Moses, Jeremiah, and Esther all dealt with this, and Paul counseled Timothy regarding timidity and fear of man (see 2 Timothy 1:7). The cure is to choose pleasing God over pleasing people, knowing that He can direct our paths and give us wisdom in our relationships.

Steps of Faith

Lord, Your will for us is always perfect. Free us from fear of what others think of us and give us faith to walk in obedience to Your plans. Thank You for Your presence and power to overcome our weaknesses.

Deeper Walk: 1 Thessalonians 2:4

I Met Jesus

Be sure to fear the LORD and faithfully serve him.
Think of all the wonderful things he has done for you.
1 Samuel 12:24

WHEN I WAS GROWING UP, I thought God was angry and vengeful. I pictured Him sitting in a rocking chair in heaven watching me as one would observe a bug—not only with some curiosity but also with a measure of distaste. When I did anything wrong, whether accidental or intentional, I thought God would grab His giant cosmic flyswatter and smack me down—*hard*. Then He would go about His business, not paying any attention to me until I did something that captured His (negative) attention again.

I didn't know that God had an interest in me personally. I thought He only cared about me following His rules exactly and never falling off the tightrope of good works and perfect behavior. I'd never even heard of grace or mercy, let alone experienced them.

My dad expected me to toe the line, and when I veered one iota to the left or the right, I was punished. There was no room for grace or mercy—only perfection and blind obedience to a father who was always ready to issue another indictment of my less-than-perfect behavior.

But then I met Jesus. And I learned that God isn't always mad at me; He actually loves me. I had such an intense spiritual hunger that I devoured the entire Bible in about ten weeks. I know now that I'm supposed to fear God in a healthy way and not be terrified of Him like I was of my own earthly father. It's good to know we have a heavenly Father who is all-powerful, yet is also full of grace and mercy and loves His children passionately.

The Bible teaches that there is no condemnation in Christ (Romans 8:1). Yet some believers have a distorted view of God. They forget about His unconditional love, mercy, and forgiveness when they mess up. If you struggle with this, ask God to help you develop a healthy fear that manifests itself as reverent awe and worshipful respect.

Steps of Faith

God, help me to know You as You really are—a powerful, holy, loving God who has plans for my good, not for disaster, to give me a future and a hope (see Jeremiah 29:11).

Deeper Walk: Jeremiah 29:11-14

Letting Go of the Controls

For wives, this means submit to your husbands as to the Lord.
Ephesians 5:22

VALERIE CHECKED THE PRICE on the red two-wheeler. "This is a great deal. I'll have to talk to Jason before I buy it, but I think I've found Kyle's birthday gift."

"I thought you managed your family's finances," Kendra said.

"I still pay the bills, but we work out the budget and decide on big purchases together now."

"What changed?" Kendra asked.

"After the couples' conference at church, Jason felt convicted to take a stronger leadership role in our family, including how we spend money. I'll admit I was unsure about this at first. Then God convicted me. I said I managed the budget because I'm a numbers person. In reality, I just liked being in control of the checkbook—among other things."

Kendra lowered her voice. "I know how much you love systems. Are you afraid this will mess up yours?"

"I was at first. Then I realized that God has a system too—one that puts Jason in the lead position in our home. Jason is really trying to be a good example for our boys, and all he asks when it comes to money is that we make decisions together. I believe I'm honoring and obeying God when I do that."

In a society where men are sometimes portrayed as lazy or brainless, it's easy to forget that God calls men to be loving, responsible leaders in their homes. While women are perfectly capable of taking the lead, our families benefit from fatherly leadership. Does this mean that we surrender complete control of our finances, how the kids will be raised, and spiritual matters to our husbands? If we look at God's plan, this clearly isn't the case. When Paul writes in Ephesians 5:24 that "wives should submit to [their] husbands in everything," he goes on to paint a beautiful picture of the loving partnership that takes place when the husband is leading in a Christlike manner and the wife esteems and empowers her husband to reach his spiritual potential.

Steps of Faith

Father, sometimes it's hard to let go of the need for control. You created biblical roles in marriage for our joy and benefit. Help me to be the kind of wife that my husband loves to lead.

Deeper Walk: Ephesians 5:22-31

Me? On Mission?

*Pray that the Lord's message will spread rapidly and
be honored wherever it goes, just as when it came to you.*

2 Thessalonians 3:1

JANNA WAS THOROUGHLY enjoying her church's missions conference. As she listened to foreign and home missionaries share how God was working and recount some of the difficulties they faced, she admired the sacrificial commitment of these special servants. Yet she also felt uneasy. During a coffee break, she voiced this unrest to her friend Alecia.

"I love what I'm learning about missions. But I feel so small and inadequate—as though my life is having so little impact. And I don't have the resources to really help or the freedom to participate even in a short mission trip."

Alecia said, "There's a lot we can do at home. Prayer support is a huge need for these workers. Get on their e-mail lists for current information. We can also offer hospitality through our homes or by providing a meal when they return. We can send them encouraging notes and let others know of their needs. God has planted you where you are for His purposes, and He will use you right where you are."

As Alecia talked, Janna became excited as she began thinking of the ways she could come alongside these precious workers.

Beginning with the New Testament book of Acts, Christians were called to be witnesses (Acts 1:8). But they were to do it on both home and foreign soil. Paul's letters tell us of his missionary journeys and his dependence on those who remained behind to provide and pray. He made it clear that even those who did not go were considered vital contributors to the work of spreading the gospel. Through giving, praying, encouraging, and even sending, all of us have both the calling and the blessing of participating as Kingdom builders in the body of Christ.

Steps of Faith

Lord, it is a humbling thought that You have entrusted us with the work of sharing the gospel. We ask for laborers for the harvest. Protect and provide for Your servants, wherever they are planted.

Deeper Walk: 2 Thessalonians 3:1-5

What's on Your Bucket List

Hope deferred makes the heart sick, but a dream fulfilled is a tree of life.
Proverbs 13:12

"WHAT'S ON YOUR BUCKET LIST?"

I stopped at the question as I was scrolling through my social media news feed. I hadn't given it much thought, but for some reason, this day, I decided to indulge myself.

I made out my list: travel to Alaska, volunteer as a Salvation Army bell ringer during the Christmas season, hike the Appalachian Trail, take my husband to Walt Disney World for a second honeymoon, and sing on Broadway.

Then I dug deeper: pay off my mortgage, have a stronger marriage, see my grandchildren all saved and serving God, live in a way that represents Christ well.

All of those desires are reachable (except perhaps for Broadway). So I asked myself what was keeping me from pursuing them. *Nothing*, came the simple answer. I could chase all those dreams right now. I may not book a flight for Alaska today, but I can start saving money for it. I'm not in shape to hike the Appalachian Trail, but I can begin walking my neighborhood's bike path. I can't force my grandchildren to love God, but I can model what that looks like. I can carve out couple time for my husband and me to reconnect. I can pay a little extra each month toward my mortgage. I can contact the Salvation Army and get the details about volunteering—I can even buy a bell and practice ringing it at home!

I have a choice: I can look at my dreams and sigh that I can't fulfill them. Or I can realize that I may not achieve them right now, but I can enjoy the process of working toward them.

"A dream fulfilled is a tree of life," wrote Solomon in Proverbs 13:12. When we take even baby steps to pursue our dreams, those first steps plant within us hope and anticipation for what is to come.

As you consider your bucket list, in what ways can you begin pursuing those desires and water that anticipation in your heart and spirit?

Steps of Faith

Jesus, thank You for giving me aspirations. May I focus with anticipation and purpose on fulfilling those life-giving dreams, and may I never grow weary of looking forward to those things I can't experience right now.

Deeper Walk: Psalm 37:3-4

Losing a Spouse

*Then you will experience God's peace, which exceeds
anything we can understand. His peace will guard your
hearts and minds as you live in Christ Jesus.*

Philippians 4:7

FAYE POKED AROUND IN the cupboard for a mug, chose one, and poured herself some coffee. She sat at the table, staring at the steaming cup before her.

This was Harold's mug, the one he always used, and this was the chair he always sat in at breakfast. She ran her fingers lovingly over the seat and remembered the many mornings she sat across from him. Tears trickled down her cheeks.

"Oh, Harold," she cried, "why did you have to leave me? Why did you have to die?" She buried her head in her arms and wept.

Words she'd heard at the memorial service crept into Faye's mind: "God blesses those who mourn, for they will be comforted" (Matthew 5:4).

"Oh, I wish," she moaned. "But I need help now!"

Spying Harold's Bible sitting on the window ledge where he always left it, Faye picked it up and leafed through the pages. "I waited patiently for the LORD," she read, "and He turned to me and heard my cry for help. He brought me up from a desolate pit, out of the muddy clay, and set my feet on a rock" (Psalm 40:1-2, HCSB). As she continued to read, a quiet peace replaced the anguish she'd been feeling. *Lord,* she prayed, *please show me what to do to heal this pain.*

A few minutes later, she was on the phone with her friend Lucy. "I need to talk," Faye said. "Are you busy?"

The loss of a spouse is one of the most difficult traumas a person will ever experience, but the grief is part of the healing. A new widow shouldn't be surprised if emotions of anger, depression, and guilt surface frequently. She will find needed comfort by looking to God for strength, reaching out to friends for help, and finding ways to express her feelings. "God is our refuge and strength, always ready to help in times of trouble" (Psalm 46:1), and He promises to give us peace when we ask.

Steps of Faith

Lord, hold those who are mourning close and help them heal. Give them peace and strength and friends to listen.

Deeper Walk: Psalm 40

Fretting Over Others' Sin

Don't worry about the wicked or envy those who do wrong.
Psalm 37:1

THE CLOCK READ 5:30 A.M. Outside, the neighbor's dog had been barking for thirty minutes. *Surely they can hear him!* I thought. *Doesn't it occur to them the barking might be bothering people?*

As I lay in the dark, I realized I was angrier about my neighbor's irresponsibility as a pet owner than I was about being woken. Though I tried to pray, my mind was distracted with thoughts about how this same dog had bitten three people on our street, my husband one of them. The owners had not kept their aggressive dog contained, and he had threatened us many times. They had been fined and written up by animal control. Now they were putting him outside at all hours to bark! By the time I pulled out of my driveway later that morning, I had gotten so worked up that I was sick to my stomach.

Several mornings later, I awoke at 3:30 a.m. to more barking. As I began to stew, I felt the Lord prompting me to read Psalm 37. I opened my Bible and read about the futility of getting agitated over others' sin and the need to trust God when it seems others are getting away with wrongdoing. "Stop being angry! Turn from your rage! Do not lose your temper—it only leads to harm" (verse 8). Instantly convicted, I released my neighbors' thoughtlessness into God's hands, asked forgiveness for my wrong attitude, and asked Him to help me sleep despite the noise. Within minutes the dog grew silent, and I drifted back to sleep.

People will do wrong and seem to get away with it. God promises, however, that He is just and that He will take care of His beloved. Fretting or growing bitter over how others behave or how they treat us only leads to evil. Trust God to deal with others. Release them into His capable hands. Then thank Him for the grace He's shown you for your mistakes.

Steps of Faith

Lord, help me not to carry the burden of judging others' sin. Thank You for the mercy and grace You've shown to all of us.

Deeper Walk: Romans 12:17-21

Grace at Home

From his abundance we have all received one gracious blessing after another.
John 1:16

As MOST MOMS DO, I check the pockets of my husband's and children's pants and jackets before running them through the wash. One day I found a few dollars and some loose coins with a receipt or two wadded up, adding interest to the hunt.

A *yellow receipt?* I thought. No, not a receipt. A speeding ticket. Written across the top was the name of my oldest daughter. Internally, I fumed. I stormed up the stairs to her room. She wasn't there. I looked at the ticket again, noting the day, time, and place. Something seemed familiar. Then I remembered. Ashley must've gotten this ticket when she was driving home from work to get changed and go to our church for her sister's recital.

The night before, my women's small group had discussed grace. I thought about Ashley and the job she worked to help fund her college education, and how she'd always been conscientious in supporting her younger sister.

Ashley turned the corner and found me sitting on her bed with the ticket. I stood up, hugged her, and said, "Please be careful. You are precious. It doesn't matter to me if you show up a few minutes late, as long as you arrive safely."

"You're not mad?" she asked.

"No, I'm not mad. I know you work hard and are responsible. We'll have to take care of this ticket, but in the future please slow down."

It's sometimes easiest to lash out and punish those we love the most—our families. We accept shortcomings from friends and acquaintances much more easily—giving grace generously, sometimes even when we've been severely wronged. Within your family, serve each other and prayerfully extend grace in certain "undeserving" moments. Let the world see what grace looks like when it looks at your family.

Steps of Faith

Father, heighten my awareness in those moments when I need to give grace to my loved ones. Thank You for the grace You have lavished on me.

Deeper Walk: Matthew 18:21-35

Let Them See the Truth

Pride leads to conflict; those who take advice are wise.
Proverbs 13:10

"How did the bus trip go?" My mobility teacher opened my file.

I swallowed the lump in my throat. "The driver didn't appreciate me asking him to announce my stop. Thankfully, someone else rang the bell, and I recognized a landmark; otherwise I would've missed it."

"Did you have the white cane out?"

Oh yeah, that. I'd been visually impaired since birth, but only recently had a mobility teacher advised me to use a white cane while traveling by bus and crossing busy intersections. Even though I understood the purpose—to show bus drivers and motorists that I didn't see well—my pride kept me from using it. After a lifetime of overcoming my limitations, I did not want to appear weak, no matter how many times my teacher repeated, "Quit worrying about what people think."

"I thought I could get by without it," I admitted.

"Try it next time and see what happens."

Begrudgingly, I did. When I extended the cane and made my way past a group of people, they scattered like a flock of birds. At least it felt that way. And when I boarded the bus holding the universal symbol of visual impairment, the driver was eager to help. I forced myself to stop assuming that people saw me as helpless. In reality, I was simply letting them see the truth.

From that point on, my bus trips doubled as an exercise in letting go of my pride.

I've since learned that the apostle Paul didn't try to hide his thorn of weakness. Instead, after wrestling with God over it, begging Him to remove it, he finally accepted it as a reminder of God's strength, to the point where he learned to glory in it.

Why is it so hard for us to let people see our frailties? Paul's words encourage me to humbly embrace my weaknesses, seeing them as opportunities to let His strength shine.

Steps of Faith

God, You created me as I am for a purpose. Pull me back when my pride prevents me from letting people see the truth. May my weaknesses reflect Your strength.

Deeper Walk: 2 Corinthians 12:7-10

From the Mouths of Children

O Father . . . thank you for hiding these things from those who think themselves wise and clever, and for revealing them to the childlike.
Matthew 11:25

As a parent, I am responsible for raising my children in the ways of the Lord. That being said, God has worked through our daughters to bring about spiritual growth in my own life. Who is teaching whom?

Our younger daughter is eleven, and she and I are going through the exact same spiritual issue at the same time. Both of us have been betrayed by a friend, both of us have not received an apology, both of us are hurt, and both of us have allowed a root of bitterness to grow up in our lives. And the only ones being hurt by our bitterness are ourselves.

We've talked about this issue a lot, but I could only advise her to pray about it. She can't seem to get over it.

One night, my oldest daughter (she's fifteen) said, "Why don't you both think of one nice thing about the person who hurt you? You don't even have to say it. You can just think it. And that will be a start toward healing because you will think of other nice things to say about her."

I was so amazed . . . and convicted! I had been praying for months that God would help me release my hurt and bitterness. And from the mouth of my child came His answer. So I tried it, and long story short, it's working. The root of bitterness is beginning to die out because I'm no longer feeding it the rottenness it needs to grow. I don't know if I can be best friends with this person again, but I can now relate to her in a godly way that is honoring to the Lord.

God wants parents to teach their children about Him, to take them to church, to make God moments with them, and to help them see Him in the everyday. He wants us to showcase His love and follow in Jesus' footsteps. So while you're teaching your children about the Lord, let them know how it pleases Him when we love and serve others. And don't be surprised if He teaches you something through them!

Steps of Faith

Father, I love teaching my children about You. But I also love how You teach me through them. Thank You, Father, for these precious gifts.

Deeper Walk: Matthew 21:15-16

What's in It for Me?

People may be right in their own eyes, but the LORD examines their heart.
Proverbs 21:2

WHEN I WAS A KID, my dad volunteered me to sing "special music" with him at our local church. I was mortified. We practiced and practiced, and finally I felt comfortable with the song and with holding my part.

The day came, the service started, and we sang. After the service, as we made our way to the parking lot, I was overwhelmed with the kindest sentiments from my church family. It felt great! I was young, and I didn't really know what being humble meant, so, naturally I wanted more of this great attention.

I sang some more with my dad up through middle school, and then in high school I began singing solos. When I became an adult, I was part of a leadership team that started a church plant.

Because we were a small church without many volunteers, I felt the added pressure of being the only one who could lead worship on the level we wanted to put forth. So I led worship and received a lot of attention.

But then I realized a resentment growing toward my church and fellow leaders. Exhausted and disillusioned, I left that church and became a fly on the wall at a neighboring church where no one knew I could sing.

I had led worship because of what I was receiving from it. Although worship was a good and honorable way to serve my church family, I used it for myself. I led worship not from my heart—a heart centered on Jesus—but from my fallible ego.

It's possible for us to do good things that help others and serve the Lord and still have the wrong motives. Most of the time, we have to meet a higher and higher standard to receive the return that serves those misplaced motives. This cycle of doing more to gain more for ourselves leads to burnout, disillusionment, resentment, and even distance in our relationship with God. Before you lend that hand, step foot on that stage, or volunteer, ask yourself whether you're serving your own interests or God's. Then ask God for a pure heart.

Steps of Faith

God, my desire is to bring You fame. May my life be a reflection of Your goodness, grace, and mercy.

Deeper Walk: Matthew 6:1-18

Pursuing Passion

You must love the LORD your God with all your heart,
all your soul, all your mind, and all your strength.
Mark 12:30

CAROLE'S MIND WAS anywhere but in her Bible study class. She was racing through her mental to-do list, wondering how it could possibly get done and thinking perhaps she shouldn't have even taken the time to attend today. But the voice of Kim, her study leader, finally broke through.

"The Bible clearly teaches that God is to be our primary passion—we are to love Him with all our heart, soul, mind, and strength. We are to have no idols. Most of us believe we do put God first and certainly serve no idols. But is this really so? Is He really our primary passion?"

Carole began shifting uncomfortably as Kim continued.

"Christian women today can easily get caught up in our to-do lists and the demands of life and lose our focus. We can misplace our true passion by trying to please others or chasing affirmation. Perhaps we need to consider what regularly receives the bulk of our time, attention, and resources. If we discover God's percentage of our affection is actually small, we need to make the choice to return to our first love. Remember, you can trust God to faithfully direct your path when you 'seek his will in all you do'" (Proverbs 3:6).

Oh Father, Carole silently prayed, *forgive me for being so distracted. Please restore my passion for You.*

What would misplaced passion look like? It could be revealed by a strong attraction to the culture. It could be reflected in a great concern for physical beauty, a materialistic focus, a loss of hunger for God's Word, and a diminished heart for His kingdom work. It might look like apathy or perhaps a lack of loyalty to the body of Christ, His church.

God is glad to do a heart check if we ask Him. He rejoices to see His children make a fresh surrender to His plans for us.

Steps of Faith

Your loving-kindness, grace, and mercy toward me are without limits, Lord. Help me daily to renew my commitment to seek Your glory and walk in Your ways.

Deeper Walk: Colossians 3:1-4

"I Don't"

Let your conversation be gracious and attractive so that
you will have the right response for everyone.
Colossians 4:6

PLANNING A WEDDING IS a big task, and Julie was taking it on all by herself. She intentionally steered clear of bridal magazines, wedding websites, and Pinterest, knowing the high potential to go overboard with details.

What Julie didn't plan for was the myriad of ideas, suggestions, and outright direction given by friends, family, and in-laws-to-be. In the beginning, Julie nodded to each comment, assuming everyone meant to be helpful. Unfortunately, this nodding came across as a go-ahead for the advice-giving party to start executing their idea. Very quickly, Julie had to learn to say, "No, thank you."

During one family gathering, Julie and her future sister-in-law, Emily, were talking about plans when Emily launched into another idea. Without thinking, Julie blurted out, "Stop. No more ideas. I don't want to hear them." Just then, Julie was called to the kitchen. As she rose from the sofa, she saw Emily slouch and sink down.

The Holy Spirit gave Julie's heart a gentle tug. She knew she'd hurt Emily and needed to make it right.

"Emily, I'm sorry that I dismissed your idea so quickly," Julie said. "I enjoy hearing what you have to say and am so thankful for your willingness to help. I won't implement everyone's suggestions, but I want you to know that I value you and your opinions."

Emily brightened, and the two continued talking—this time about sales at a local discount store.

Since creation, God has made boundaries clear to all of us—from the separation of night from day to the Ten Commandments. Creating personal boundaries requires communication with God—asking Him to reveal appropriate limits—and introspection. Once we are aware of our boundaries, implementing them well honors God. As followers of Christ, it's our job to treat others as we want to be treated. When saying no to others, are you doing so in a way that honors God and builds others up?

Steps of Faith

Father, guide me as I set boundaries. Give me a loving attitude when saying no.

Deeper Walk: Psalm 19:7-11

Encourage One Another

Encourage each other and build each other up.
1 Thessalonians 5:11

JENNA GRABBED HER BIBLE and sat on the sofa. She especially needed this time with the Lord today. She was disturbed by the tense atmosphere in her home lately. Her husband seemed distant, and she didn't know why.

Lord, give me wisdom and discernment, she prayed. *Show me what to do.*

Opening her Bible, she turned to the reading for the day in 1 Thessalonians, chapter 5. Verse 11 got her attention. "So encourage each other and build each other up, just as you are already doing."

She felt God tug at her heart. The verse reminded her of something a speaker had said to her women's group at church. "Often we as women are not meeting our husbands' emotional needs because a man's needs are different from a woman's. A man needs to feel accepted, admired, trusted, and appreciated. If his emotional needs are not being met, he may begin to drift and become more distant."

Jenna read the verse again and then prayed. She knew she hadn't been encouraging her husband by meeting his emotional needs.

When her husband came home that evening, she met him with a kiss. "I really appreciate your working so hard for our family," she said. "I feel so blessed to have a husband who does his best to support us."

New warmth filled his eyes, and he smiled.

"Thanks," he said. "I appreciate that."

That evening they chatted more freely, and a more positive atmosphere began to permeate their home.

Sometimes we're not very good at showing appreciation to our husbands. If you want your marriage to thrive, start using words that show admiration, acceptance, trust, approval, and appreciation. Men are encouraged when their emotional tanks are full. We as wives can fill them and warm up our marriages when we better understand our husbands' needs.

Steps of Faith

Lord, fill my heart with true appreciation for my loved ones. Show me how to encourage my husband so he will feel my love and be all that You made him to be.

Deeper Walk: Romans 15:2-7

Letting Go

It is time to forgive and comfort him.
Otherwise he may be overcome by discouragement.
2 Corinthians 2:7

WHEN I READ THE NOTE, I didn't know how to respond. Never had I expected such a heartfelt apology from this person. I won't pretend that she had nothing to be sorry for; she had done some hurtful things. But God had removed this friend from my life, the experience taught me some things about relationships, and I had moved on. At least, I thought I had.

A sudden rush of mixed emotions hit me as I reread the note—memories of her rudeness, her harsh reaction the one time I gently confronted her, her tendency to belittle me. She might be sorry, but had she changed?

Then I stopped mid-thought. She was asking for forgiveness. I had no idea what triggered her need to make things right. Whether she would treat me differently in the future or not, God was clearly working on this woman's heart. He wasn't asking me to invite her to lunch so we could rekindle our friendship and repeat old patterns; He was asking me to extend His grace to her. I read the note again, and this time I couldn't bear the idea of her suffering in remorse, thinking I was still mad at her.

I immediately sent a reply, assuring her, "I forgive you." And in the process, a weight lifted from my spirit as I truly let go of those memories.

Relationships, whether in friendships or within the family, open us up to a wide range of offenses, from personality clashes to life-changing hurts. Unfortunately, we receive a lot more emotional punches than apologies. Whether that long-awaited "I'm so sorry" comes or not, God calls us to forgive. It helps to know that forgiveness does not require us to renew an unhealthy relationship, deny pain, or justify sin. It means refusing to let an offense take up precious space in our minds anymore, and finding freedom in the release.

Steps of Faith

Lord, when I am asked to let go of something big, sometimes it can be hard to forgive. Reveal the hurts that I need to forgive, whether I hear "I'm sorry" or not.

Deeper Walk: Colossians 3:13

I Am Mephibosheth

Ziba replied, "Yes, one of Jonathan's sons is still alive.
He is crippled in both feet."
2 Samuel 9:3

I'VE BEEN READING THE story of Mephibosheth in 2 Samuel 9, and as God always does when I'm reading Scripture, He's been teaching me that there's deeper meaning to a story than what I first perceive.

At first glance, this is a story of King David being compassionate and kind to the son of his friend Jonathan. Both King Saul and Jonathan had been killed in battle, and after Saul's death, David had taken the throne.

One day David asked Ziba, a servant of Saul's family, if there was anyone left in his family to whom he could show God's kindness and compassion. Ziba told him about Jonathan's son, Mephibosheth, who was lame (verse 3). David then requested to have Mephibosheth brought to him.

In those days, descendants of a fallen king were considered enemies of a new king. Mephibosheth had been in hiding ever since his grandfather died, so when he arrived, he bowed and paid homage to David.

David said, "Don't be afraid! I intend to show kindness to you."

Mephibosheth replied, "Who is your servant, that you should show such kindness to a dead dog like me?" (verses 7-8). But David invited Mephibosheth to dine at his table, as if he were his own son.

And here's what God revealed to me: I am Mephibosheth.

Before Jesus intersected my life, I was a sinner—a sinner in hiding, who was "lame." I could not come into the presence of God without Jesus, who took me from my miserable place of despair. Just like Mephibosheth, I could only fall on my face, prostrate before Him, expecting the worst because I was His enemy. I was a "dead dog"—dead in my sins and hopelessness—without Jesus.

But because of God's compassion, He sent Jesus to ransom me from my sin. By receiving through faith God's gift of salvation, I will eat at His table forever.

My friend, if you are a Jesus follower, join me as we sit at God's table, feasting on the riches of His grace, forever.

Steps of Faith

Father God, thank You for the compassion and kindness You've shown us in Jesus.

Deeper Walk: 2 Samuel 9

Hard Work

A wise woman builds her home.
Proverbs 14:1

ERIN ROSE FROM THE TWIN BED, careful not to disturb her daughter, who had just fallen asleep. She quietly closed the door behind her but was startled when she bumped into her husband in the dark hallway. Quieting his wife with a finger to his lips, Jacob ushered Erin into the family room, where he had turned on soothing praise music.

"You sit here and rest while I get the popcorn and sodas," suggested Jacob, motioning to the sofa. Erin was too exhausted to argue. As she settled on the sofa, her mind returned to the problems of the day. Jacob and Erin had done everything they could imagine to prepare their children— Erin's daughter and Jacob's two sons—for combining their families, but their first trip to visit relatives had created new, unexpected issues. They had just gotten home from the excursion that evening, and Erin felt drained from it all.

Returning to the family room, Jacob set the snacks on the coffee table and sat beside his wife. Erin's tired eyes opened, and she looked at Jacob hopelessly.

"Erin, we certainly have our work cut out for us," Jacob started, "but I'm not worried. I'm willing to work hard to build a strong family that honors God and blesses others. I know you are too. And God will work on our behalf as well."

Erin felt hope return with Jacob's resolve. He was right, of course. They would have to be creative, carve out the necessary time, and doggedly protect what God had put together. But she, too, had a heart to build a strong, unified family.

Building a strong family that honors God is not easy. Parents struggle to balance careers with family priorities, but they must also fight constant encounters with materialism, self-absorption, and other worldly attitudes. Add to that the struggles of blending families, recovering from loss, handling severe illness, or regrouping from financial loss, and the challenge intensifies. But God blesses us when we have the will to keep working toward a godly goal.

Steps of Faith

Father, grant me wisdom and endurance as I invest in the lives of others.

Deeper Walk: Proverbs 31:10-31

Doubt Detour

Come close to God, and God will come close to you.
James 4:8

LAST YEAR, I had a surgical procedure that resulted in much more recovery time than I had anticipated. Rather than being back on my feet in a week as I had expected, there were complications and my body didn't heal for months. During that time, I was unable to do simple things I had previously taken for granted, and I had to rely on my family and friends to help me. I felt weak and frustrated and ultimately depressed.

As I sometimes do when I go through trials, I began doubting God's goodness, His love for me, and, in my darkest moments, even His existence. Instead of seeking Him more during this time, my anger and doubt caused me to withdraw from Him. The Bible seemed stale and my prayers were sparse—nothing more than *Lord, help my unbelief!* As I withdrew and stopped renewing my mind through prayer and Scripture, my doubt became an excuse to indulge in old habits and mind-sets, dealing with my emotions in negative and sinful ways instead of casting my anxieties on the Lord.

Thankfully, even though I wasn't drawing near to Him, He graciously renewed my faith in Him. His kindness led me to repentance. Looking back, I know that time was much harder for me than it should have been because I didn't invite God into my spiritual struggle. Next time, I will remember this lesson and bring my doubts and questions to Him.

Everyone will have doubts at times. Don't be afraid of them, but beware of pulling away from God during those times and using doubt as an excuse to indulge in spiritual laziness. Instead, when you have doubts and questions, press into God. Seek Him through prayer and Bible reading for answers and confirmation of His existence and love for you. He will reward you for earnestly seeking Him.

Steps of Faith

Father, thank You that all truth is found in You. Help me bring all my doubts, questions, and worries to You.

Deeper Walk: Hebrews 11

Morning by Morning

The faithful love of the LORD never ends! His mercies never cease.
Great is his faithfulness; his mercies begin afresh each morning.
Lamentations 3:22-23

EARLY IN OUR MARRIAGE, whenever we sang the hymn "Great Is Thy Faithfulness" in church, my husband and I would grin. We sang just two verses of that song during our wedding; however, my husband insists we sang six or seven! At any rate, we chose to sing that song on that special day because we both had known God's faithfulness in our singleness, and we knew we could depend on His continued faithfulness throughout our marriage.

Twenty-five years later, when I sing the hymn along with the congregation my husband now pastors, the smile remains on my lips, but tears of joy form in my eyes. As we sing, "Morning by morning new mercies I see," I reflect on varied "mornings" of our marriage. There have been nights of restless slumber due to uncertainties, afternoons filled with the angst of teenage drama, days spent in the emergency room, nights ended early by an alarming phone call, mornings filled with the joy of a new baby's cry, and mornings interrupted by special news bulletins reporting national tragedies. When we first said our "I do's," we had no idea of the mercies we would require throughout the upcoming days and years. But for better or for worse, for richer or for poorer, in sickness and in health, God's presence has provided not only cheer and guidance, but also "strength for today and bright hope for tomorrow"—just as the hymn says.

While we may have struggled at times to be true to every vow, God's faithfulness has never wavered toward us. And though the struggles of life can mount, making it difficult to honor our commitments, by leaning on God's enduring faithfulness, we will find strength to remain faithful ourselves. If you're in a season of struggle right now, run to God's throne, where you will find new mercies for every day and in every situation. There you will be fortified.

Steps of Faith

Lord, Your faithfulness and mercy compel me to press on morning by morning, even in difficult circumstances. Thank You for always being faithful to me.

Deeper Walk: Lamentations 3:19-24

Daily Worship

I will praise the LORD at all times. I will constantly speak his praises.

Psalm 34:1

THESE DAYS, I am in a battle season. As the stay-at-home mom of young children, I often feel like I'm in the trenches. My job is wonderful, but sometimes it can be mundane, tiring, and full of little tasks and choices that will cumulatively make a lifelong impact on my kids.

Many days, I have no mental capacity for the deep Bible study I used to love. Sleep deprived, I can barely string an intelligent thought together, much less intercede for others in profound, meaningful prayer. Some days I personally rely on the Holy Spirit's groanings (see Romans 8:26) to cover my own prayer needs, or I cry out short prayers along the lines of "Help!" or "Wisdom, Lord?" or "I don't think I can do this!"

During this season, I've exchanged intense Bible study for short-term studies, and I've learned a surprising new way to prepare for my day: worship.

Remember the ACTS acronym for prayer—adoration, confession, thanksgiving, and supplication? I used to skip adoration, thinking it wasn't as productive as the others. But I've discovered there is a lot of power in simply speaking or singing the truth about God's amazing attributes. It puts my chaotic life in the trenches into godly perspective, and walking in the Spirit has become more effortless. Worship will be a mainstay of my daily devotions from now on, and that's something to praise God about!

In 2 Chronicles 20, when King Jehoshaphat was told a vast army was coming against Jerusalem, he led the people in worship. Jehoshaphat then appointed men to lead the army into battle by singing and worshiping God. When they got to the battlefield, God had already won the battle! If you want to see more victory in your life, try going into each day with worship.

Steps of Faith

You deserve my daily worship, and it helps me center my heart on the truth, Lord. Lead me in worship that glorifies You.

Deeper Walk: 2 Chronicles 20:1-30

He Will Be Found

Can a mother . . . feel no love for the child she has borne?
But even if that were possible, I would not forget you!
Isaiah 49:15

FOR YEARS, Kaylee prayed the same prayer: *God, please provide a husband for me who loves You.* Finally, emotionally exhausted from pouring out her heart to God, Kaylee prayed He'd take away her desire for a husband.

A few months later, Kaylee stopped asking altogether. Instead, she began praying with gratitude and praise. Her heart couldn't bear to hope for the things she'd asked of God; she simply would tell Him that He knew what she'd asked, and she trusted Him with it.

Kaylee began participating in a "Read the Bible in a Year" challenge at her church. She discovered Scripture she'd never heard but that spoke directly to her, like Exodus 14:14: "The LORD himself will fight for you," and Isaiah 49:15, "I would not forget you!"

As she drew close to God, more and more she sought Him in her work, her friendships, and her service. She asked for the awareness of God's Spirit to be heightened within her, and it was. Her heart found opportunities to learn about God and obey Him through mission trips and service projects.

Today, Kaylee is married with two children. Her pursuit of God didn't unlock His favor. Her pursuit increased her faith and her desire to follow where He led, which eventually was right into a classroom in South Africa where her future husband, Jackson, was teaching.

God promises in His Word that when we come close to Him, He will come close to us (see James 4:8). We will find Him when we seek Him with all our hearts (Jeremiah 29:13, NIV). If we pursue God, He will give us even more than we ever thought possible. As you give more of yourself, this "giving away"—through service, devotions, worship, etc.—makes room in your heart for more of God to fill.

Steps of Faith

Dear Lord, draw near to me as I draw near to You. Cause me to identify and obey Your voice as I seek to know You and become more like You.

Deeper Walk: Isaiah 49:8-19

Taking the Time

Children are a gift from the LORD; they are a reward from him.

Psalm 127:3

I SKIMMED OVER MY TO-DO LIST. Was it even physically possible to accomplish everything I needed to get done today?

My four-year-old, Jake, came jumping into the kitchen. "Mom, will you play with me?"

"Ummm . . ." I stalled. "I have some things I need to do this morning, buddy."

"Oh. Okay," he replied.

I returned to my list and heard his little feet shuffle down the hall. My mommy impulse said that my little guy needed some attention. "Hey, Jake!" I called out. "I really want to play with you, so maybe you can help me put dishes in the dishwasher and then we'll play for a while."

Jake grinned and yelled, "Yes!"

Lots of tasks were calling my name, but the thing that mattered most was making time for my little boy. He wouldn't always be there asking me to play, and those tasks would still be there when we were through.

In our task-oriented world, it's easy to put relationships and quality time on the back burner. Yet parents need time with their children to build those trusting relationships that last a lifetime. This means making time together a priority and entering into their children's world by asking questions and engaging in activities that they enjoy. With little ones, this means interacting through play. Simple games and role-playing are great tools for teaching biblical principles. With adolescents and teens, quality time can involve a shared interest or allowing your children to teach you about something they enjoy. As you spend time together, you engage, build trust, and show genuine love for the person God has made your child to be. So often, kids just want their parents to listen. And when parents listen, kids respect them, trust them, and learn to listen to them as well. God has given us the family structure as a means to build His Kingdom and glorify Him. By strengthening our family relationships, we encourage future generations to know Him better and love Him more.

Steps of Faith

Father, thank You for the family You have given me. Bring honor and glory to Yourself through each one of us.

Deeper Walk: Matthew 19:13-15

A Formidable Wall

*Why worry about a speck in your friend's eye
when you have a log in your own?*
Luke 6:41

I FELT A BIT UNCERTAIN when I first visited the women's prison with a group from my church. We had been asked to provide a monthly Bible study and fellowship time for a group of inmates who had made commitments to follow Jesus. The chaplain felt these women needed to socialize with other Christian women from outside the prison before their release dates approached.

As I entered the secure area of the prison that first Sunday afternoon, I assumed the women from my church would serve as mentors to these struggling converts, that we would have much to teach them about God and His holy standards. After all, they had each done something to bring them here.

But when the introductions had been made and we began to sing along with the guitar, I quickly realized that these inmates had a relationship with God that hinged on something beyond my scope of experience. They sang with tears flowing down their cheeks, hands raised in submission, and voices aching with hope. They opened their worn Bibles and listened with an unexpected eagerness to every truth taught. And they thanked us profusely for our time, enthusiastically offering us blessings as we left.

As we drove away that night, the van was silent, until one woman quietly remarked, "The one who is forgiven more, loves more" (see Luke 7:47).

Self-righteousness builds a formidable wall between us and God that must be overcome with humility and poverty of spirit. In Luke, Jesus taught a Pharisee that such self-righteousness can also keep us from loving our Savior with as much abandon and gratitude as one who has appropriately measured her own sinfulness. Perhaps if we rubbed shoulders more often with those who have been forgiven much, we, too, would have a clearer estimation of our own need for a Savior. How can you minister with humility to those most desperate for a Savior?

Steps of Faith

Jesus, I am a sinner in need of a Savior. Thank You for paying for my sins.

Deeper Walk: Luke 7:36-50

On the Other Side

Blessed are those who are generous, because they feed the poor.
Proverbs 22:9

MARCY SEPARATED A cluster of cans and boxes from the rest of her groceries. "Can you bag those separately, please?"

On her way out of the store, Marcy dropped the bag into a collection barrel for the local food bank, wishing she could have afforded more items. A few years ago, she'd waited for holiday food drives to donate anything, seizing the opportunity to clean out her pantry. She'd dusted off cans of lima beans, tossed in boxed mac and cheese that hadn't gone over well with the kids, and convinced herself that someone would probably appreciate the jar of marinated artichoke hearts. She had watched with dismay as mothers paid for groceries with food stamps. *Why don't they just go out and get jobs?* she had wondered.

Then her husband lost his job a month after she'd lost hers. For the first time in her life, she was humbly driving to the food bank, praying that she'd get enough to nourish her family of four until the next unemployment check arrived. She hadn't needed artichoke hearts; she'd needed real food, hopefully something that didn't require extra ingredients or doctoring up.

When circumstances improved, Marcy vowed to give quality donations and contribute year-round. Buying at least one extra can of soup per shopping trip became a new routine. And never again would she make assumptions about those on the receiving end of charity.

God, she prayed as she loaded her groceries into the car, *thank You for using that time to teach me compassion.*

Experiencing personal need has a way of changing our attitudes toward the poor. We understand what it feels like to receive instead of give, and we come to see the recipients as people desperate to provide for their families. Insensitivity is exchanged for Christlike empathy. What a gift it is when God uses hardship to soften our hearts. Ask God to send regular reminders to give as if you or someone you love were on the receiving end.

Steps of Faith
God, prompt me to go beyond halfhearted donations and consider the real people on the receiving end.

Deeper Walk: Proverbs 11:24-25

Unexpected Blessings

Honor your father and your mother so that you may have
a long life in the land that the LORD your God is giving you.
Exodus 20:12, HCSB

FOUR YEARS AGO AFTER a particularly rainy week in February, a giant pine tree crashed through my father's small house. From the back bedroom all the way to the living room—the entire length of the house—the damage was significant and irreparable. Unable to afford rebuilding, my father moved in with my family.

Each day, I prayed for our changing family unit, with the blending of my father into our family's unique dynamic. Just as my husband, Grant, and I had had to talk through and agree on a parenting style of our own, we had to bring my father into that plan and explain our reasoning for why we allowed our kids some things and denied them others. At times it seemed we had to parent my dad on how to parent our kids. And though there were, and still are, times of frustration and confusion, there are many more times of blessing that come from including my dad so closely. Not only do Madison and Taylor get to hear their family history and how God has worked in their grandfather's life, but Dad's mind is continually exercised as he helps the girls with their homework.

At the time, the loss of my dad's house was devastating and traumatic for him, but since he moved in with our family, not only has his "home" been restored, he has enriched our lives with his unique wisdom, skills, and heritage.

Blending families with older adults, like parents or grandparents, can be a bumpy ride. After all, adults do tend to get set in their ways as time goes by. Fortunately, God's ability to work in our hearts doesn't change or stagnate. When God's honor is elevated, growing together as a multigenerational family can be a testimony to His faithfulness over a lifetime.

Steps of Faith

Father God, thank You for my parents and grandparents. Their stories were ordained by You. I seek to honor You by honoring them.

Deeper Walk: Ephesians 6:1-4

Wise Choices

You simple people, use good judgment.
You foolish people, show some understanding.
Proverbs 8:5

WHEN OUR KIDS WERE growing up, my husband, Mike, and I always tried to model responsible behavior in our spending and saving habits. We had a budget and stuck to it. We didn't spend money we didn't have, and if we made a credit card purchase, we paid it off as quickly as possible instead of making minimum payments.

Lately, Mike and I have had frequent discussions about the unwise financial decisions our kids are making—splurging on new cars when their old cars were in perfectly good condition, buying houses that have strapped them financially, and purchasing expensive toys for their kids that we would have considered out of the question when we were younger.

But recently, we were pleasantly surprised when our youngest son told us that he and his wife were attending a seminar at church on finances. After the classes were over, they cut up their credit cards and began paying down the balances. They refinanced their home to obtain a lower interest rate. And our son sold his gas-guzzling vehicle so he could purchase a more practical economy car.

Mike and I are proud of the progress they've made, and we pray for all our children to make wise decisions in all areas of their lives. As parents, we do not like to see our kids shouldering great debts or being enticed by every latest "must-have." Being responsible with our finances is healthy for our marriages and families, and it honors God.

If you are struggling with finances, consider taking a course at a church or speaking with a financial advisor to help you make some changes. Pray for wisdom, and remember that God has provided us all things for His glory.

Steps of Faith

Father, thank You for everything You have given me. Please let me be wise with the resources You have generously provided.

Deeper Walk: Proverbs 9:10-12

My Red Sea Parting

I am as good as dead, like a strong man with no strength left.
Psalm 88:4

THE ALARM CLOCK BUZZED, and I squinched my eyes shut. I didn't want to get up. In fact, I could have slept forever, never facing my insurmountable problems.

But I had to get up, at least for my older daughter's sake. It was a school day.

We had just brought our three-year-old daughter home from a two-day stay in the hospital. She has a neurological disorder, and the doctors had no answers for us. On top of this, my husband's business was failing. And I couldn't seem to get out of bed. I felt like I was standing on the shores of the Red Sea, complete with enemies all around and clouds above my head, and a sea of pain I couldn't cross.

In Exodus 13–14, God had led the Israelites out of Egypt with a pillar of cloud by day and a pillar of fire by night. He led them right to the edge of the Red Sea with the Egyptian army on their heels. They were hemmed in by huge foes on all sides (the army and the sea), and they cried out to the Lord to save them.

So did I. And I felt Him saying to me, *I am with you.*

But Lord, I said to Him, *You know I can't swim. I'm drowning. I can't do this.*

And He said to me, *I know. That's why I'm with you every step of the way, holding your hand, comforting you.*

My depression didn't go away overnight, but God never let me go. He walked me through my own Red Sea, and I didn't even have to swim.

Depression affects many women, and it can be caused by many different things. Difficult circumstances, hormonal imbalances, a major life change, loss—all these and more contribute to the clouds of hopelessness and despair that characterize depression. If you are experiencing depression, seek professional help, reach out to family and friends, and lean on God. He will take your hand and lead you to a place of comfort and refuge.

Steps of Faith
Dear Father, please redeem us from the pit of depression. You are our Healer, the One who lifts our heads (see Psalm 3:3, NIV), and we are grateful.

Deeper Walk: Psalm 88

Living for Eternity

He has planted eternity in the human heart.
Ecclesiastes 3:11

"YOUR LIFE IS ONLY A BREATH. You were made for eternity, and your time on this earth is short. Nothing is guaranteed. So are you living to make every moment count for God's eternal Kingdom?"

The speaker's words resonated in my ears and heart. She had fought cancer at a young age and won the battle, but she came away with a new perspective on life. Her challenge rocked me because of the way I had been living lately. I had recently lost twenty pounds by changing my lifestyle—healthy eating habits and lots of exercise. Those were great things, but my success with my body image had taken over. If I didn't feel thin and healthy, if I ate dessert or skipped a workout, I felt worthless.

I realized my healthy habits had become an unhealthy obsession, more important to me than anything else in my life. Though there was nothing wrong with taking good care of the body God had entrusted to me, I knew that when caring for my body was the most important thing in my life, it had become an idol.

As I left the conference, I asked God to change my heart to reflect His priorities, to put eternity in my mind and heart so I could keep things like my appearance in perspective and use my time and energy to better serve Him.

While it is good stewardship to care for our bodies with healthy eating and exercise, many of us struggle with becoming slaves to our desires for young, fit bodies. If this is a tendency in your heart, ask God to give you His Kingdom perspective in this area. Seek accountability with another woman, and share your feelings about yourself as well as any physical struggles you may have. And pray that God would help you see anything that is getting in the way of your worship of Him.

Steps of Faith

God, You alone deserve my worship and praise. Help me to see myself as You see me, in light of eternity.

Deeper Walk: Job 7:6-8

Praising the Good in Others

Reward her for all she has done.
Proverbs 31:31

SEVERAL YEARS AGO my husband and I brought home a puppy. Soon our lives became consumed with crate training, housebreaking, and teaching simple commands such as "Sit," "Come," "Outside?" and "No bite! No bite! Noooo bite!"

Before we had picked her up, we studied all the manuals, from *Training Your Dog* to *The Complete Idiot's Guide to Positive Dog Training*. And they all said basically the same thing: If you want to train your puppy, give her lots of praise when she does something right. Positive reinforcement is more effective and will emphasize the behaviors you desire her to have.

So we started praising our pup for all the things she did correctly. The results were amazing—she did everything she could to be good.

Not to compare my friends and family with a dog, but they do have some similarities. Whether it's my spouse, my children, my friends, or even my coworkers, people need to hear when they've done something well—just as I love to hear praise for the good things I've done.

We can never overpraise someone when he or she does good things. We have great opportunities to applaud our husbands every time they fill the gas tank, cook dinner, pay the electric bills, throw laundry in the laundry basket, and let us control the remote. We can grow a work colleague's self-esteem when we praise him or her for finishing a big project on time, picking up the workload while we're out of the office, or turning in a quality report. We can strengthen our children's character when we thank them for doing their chores, coming home before a curfew, and not making a total mess of their rooms. Even the most insignificant things are worthy of praise.

Too often we fail to applaud people when they've simply "done their job." Yet we honor God when we praise and uplift those around us. May we always be willing to offer that encouragement.

Steps of Faith

Lord, I know how good it feels when someone recognizes something good I've done. Make me aware of what others do, and remind me to reward their work with praise.

Deeper Walk: Proverbs 10:21; 12:25

Knowing His Will

*For the LORD grants wisdom! From his mouth
come knowledge and understanding.*
Proverbs 2:6

LEAH ATTEMPTED TO stifle the familiar feeling of anxiety threatening to overtake her. She longed to be obedient to God, but sometimes it seemed truly difficult to know His will. She wrestled with so many decisions, and she knew this anxiety could not be His intention for her. Now she had been offered an exciting ministry position requiring increased responsibility and an extra time commitment.

"Oh, God," she cried out, "how can I know what Your will is for me regarding this?" Even as she prayed, she recalled a discussion with her friend Bonnie about seeking God's will.

Bonnie had said, "First I read Scripture and then I pray, asking God to speak and help me hear. Then I ask godly friends for counsel. I see how the opportunity fits with my passion and gifts. I also remember God often calls me to work that requires His power to keep me dependent on Him. I then ask Him to confirm what I'm thinking and hearing."

Leah remembered the words from Psalm 94:19: "When my anxious thoughts multiply within me, Your consolations delight my soul" (NASB). She relaxed, knowing God would show her what she needed to see.

Today's culture offers a multitude of choices. Our lives are bombarded with decisions, from what to eat, wear, and drive, to where we'll live and work, to whom we'll marry. We could become immobilized just anticipating choices and their outcomes. For Christians wanting to serve and please God, making these decisions can be especially difficult. But remember that we serve a God who "is a wonderful teacher" and who gives "great wisdom" (Isaiah 28:29). We can turn to Him through Bible reading and prayer, and He will direct our paths.

Steps of Faith

Father, You are my Wonderful Counselor. Thank You that You will direct my path and order my steps for Your purposes.

Deeper Walk: Proverbs 2:1-6

No

My child, listen to me and do as I say, and you will have a long, good life.
Proverbs 4:10

"JESSICA, I KNOW HOW YOU FEEL, but I'm going to have to say no."

My sixteen-year-old daughter fumed. "But that's not fair! You and Dad told me I could date when I turned sixteen. Patrick just asked me to go to a movie with him."

"Patrick is twenty-one years old. He's old enough to vote, drink legally, and make his own decisions."

"But he's really a nice guy," Jessica insisted.

"He may be a nice guy, but he's too old for you right now."

"Well, Dad is six years older than you!" she replied.

I was tired of arguing, but I stuck to my guns. "Dad and I didn't start dating until I'd been out of college for a year. I had a job, an apartment, and my own car."

"I'm going to call Dad and ask him," Jessica said angrily as she stomped out of the room.

"Dad is still in Sydney on business, and he won't be home for another week. Besides, it's the middle of the night in Australia."

Later, when Greg arrived home from his trip, we talked about the situation between Jessica and Patrick.

"I'm glad you didn't cave under the pressure," Greg said. "I know it's hard, but we can't be afraid to tell our kids no when it's for their own good. You made the right decision, and God will honor that."

Sometimes parents feel that they have to be their children's best friends, and they have a hard time telling their children no. They're afraid their kids won't like them.

But parenting isn't a popularity contest. Many times tough decisions must be made, and sometimes that involves saying no to youthful requests. If you are a parent, pray for wisdom, patience, and the strength to stand your ground when necessary. Choose your battles wisely, and give grace when needed.

Steps of Faith

Father, please give me the wisdom to be a godly influence on the children You have brought into my life. Let me be strong enough to say no when it's necessary.

Deeper Walk: Deuteronomy 6:1-9

Why Me?

Surely your goodness and unfailing love will pursue me all the days of my life,
and I will live in the house of the LORD forever.

Psalm 23:6

DURING MY SOPHOMORE YEAR IN COLLEGE, I was the victim of a hit-and-run accident. I'd been jogging along a trail that cut across a four-way stop. Although I looked both ways, a car seemed to appear from out of nowhere and sped through the stop sign. I was hit on my right side and ended up landing in the gravel several feet away. The driver sped off without even checking to see if I was okay.

The accident broke me physically, and it shook my faith in God. I had the mistaken idea that since I was a dedicated Christian, I wouldn't have to endure certain problems that others faced. But there I was lying in a hospital bed with a fractured pelvis, a broken arm and leg, internal injuries, and contusions everywhere. I had to drop out of school to focus on my recovery. In that moment it seemed as if my dreams for the future just flew out the window.

Every day I wondered, *Why me?* Frankly, I was disappointed with God. But over time, I learned that He is faithful, no matter what we must endure. He is there with us in our darkest moments.

My recovery took a long time, but eventually I was able to walk again. I graduated college and married a wonderful Christian man.

When life doesn't go the way we planned, we can be left with a deep disappointment in God. Although we might think we know the plans God has for us, sometimes we can't see how He will use our painful circumstances for our good. But we can choose to keep our faith and trust God in all circumstances. Although God doesn't promise us a pain-free life, He does promise us that He will always be with us. If you are dealing with disappointment in God, ask Him to help you see your circumstances from heaven's point of view. Keep your faith and stay in the Word.

Steps of Faith

Father, although I don't always understand Your ways, I pray that You will give me confidence to trust that no matter what happens to me in this life, You have eternity in mind.

Deeper Walk: John 16:25-33

Our Economic Refuge

The earth is the LORD's, and everything in it.
The world and all its people belong to him.
Psalm 24:1

ERIN GREETED LUCAS AT the door with a smile and a kiss. She could tell by his hunched shoulders that it had been another frustrating day of job searching. Despite her own rising panic, Erin tried to encourage him. Since being laid off, Lucas had submitted countless résumés, searched job databases, made phone calls, and gone to networking meetings. Despite all his time spent searching, it seemed as if no one was hiring.

Now, several months into his unemployment, Erin was apprehensive about how they were going to continue to pay their bills. She played the what-if game frequently. *What if we have to pull the kids out of their activities? What if we lose the house and cars? What if we end up homeless?*

As her husband plopped onto the couch, Erin brought him some iced tea and began to reassure him that God was in control and would provide. As the words left her lips, Erin was convicted. For weeks she had been battling fear over their situation but had not entrusted her own worries to God. She needed to bring her many fears to the Lord and believe in the words she was saying to her husband now.

As Christians, we say the Lord is our Provider. But do we always believe it? If your financial stability is threatened by a bad housing market or a layoff, do you panic, or do you remember the One who provided all your material blessings? The Lord is your Rock. In times of uncertainty, turn to Him, cast your anxieties on Him, and find your refuge in Him.

Steps of Faith

Dear Lord, I affirm that You truly are in control of all things, but I need Your help remembering that. Help me trust You with my future.

Deeper Walk: Psalm 91

Traffic Jam

Stop being angry! Turn from your rage!
Do not lose your temper—it only leads to harm.
Psalm 37:8

As WORKING PARENTS, Brian and I wake up before dawn to get ourselves and the kids ready on time. While Brian puts our seven-year-old son on the school bus, I put on my makeup and brush four-year-old Kara's hair and teeth. Then Brian leaves for work, and I strap Kara into her car seat and take her to day care on my way to the office.

One morning the traffic was particularly heavy because there had been a three-car pileup on the interstate. People (including me) became impatient as the traffic came to a dead stop. Horns blared and frustrated drivers tried to weave their way around the accident.

Slamming on the brakes, I shouted at a driver who cut in front of me.

"What's the matter, Mommy?" Kara asked from the backseat.

"These people drive like idiots!" I fumed.

I felt the beginnings of a tension headache as I tried to squelch the frustration I felt.

"Stupid!" Kara yelled at a passing car.

Suddenly, I realized that God was showing me that the problem was not the traffic—it was my anger. And Kara was modeling her behavior after mine. I was ashamed.

"I'm sorry, honey," I said to Kara. "Mommy shouldn't talk like that." I knew I had to allow the Lord to help me deal with my anger issues. He had used a traffic jam and a four-year-old to reveal that to me.

Ecclesiastes 7:9 says, "Control your temper, for anger labels you a fool." It's not always a sin to be angry, but Ephesians 4:26 says, "'Don't sin by letting anger control you.' Don't let the sun go down while you are still angry." The next time you find yourself getting angry, ask the Lord to help you handle it constructively.

Steps of Faith

Father, help me deal with anger when it arises. Mold me into the image of Your Son so I can be pleasing in Your sight.

Deeper Walk: Proverbs 15:18; 29:11

Made to Make Him Known

God created man in His own image; He created him in
the image of God; He created them male and female.
Genesis 1:27, HCSB

I HAVE A SUSPICION THAT my nine-year-old son, Cole, will one day be an architect. Why is that? Because he spends every spare moment building things. His building material of choice is LEGOs. We must have thousands of LEGOs all over the floor, in bins, in boxes, even in a dresser drawer that we have devoted to the cause.

One afternoon while we were sorting the mini blocks, I asked Cole, "Why do you like LEGOs so much? Why are they your favorite toy?"

Cole shrugged and said, "I guess because I can use them to build anything I want. I like thinking of new things to make and trying to make them better."

I thought about Cole's answer, and it pointed me to our design as God's image bearers. We are made in the image of our Creator, reflecting the good and beautiful aspects of His character, including His desire to create and transform. That compels us to create too. Of course, we can't create like He can, but whether it's building LEGOs, making a nice dinner, writing a short story, or planting flowers in the front yard, our activities reflect our desire to create and to add beauty and function to our lives.

That night when I tucked Cole in, we read from Genesis 1 about God's creation and how it was good. We marveled at how caring and brilliant God is to make such a variety of animals, so many interesting plants, and such remarkable human bodies. We prayed and thanked God for the fun of building with LEGOs. We thanked Him for making us able to design and enjoy things in this world, and we prayed that He would fill our hearts with a desire to do these things for His glory.

God designed us in amazing, complex ways, with bodies and souls that are made to know Him intimately. He has also given us the ability to work creatively in order to point us toward Himself, the source of every generous act and perfect gift (see James 1:17). Allow your tasks to draw you closer to the One who designed you for Himself.

Steps of Faith

Creator God, Your works are wonderful. Help me to reflect who You are in my life and work.

Deeper Walk: Genesis 1

Who Is He?

Then he asked them, "But who do you say I am?"
Matthew 16:15

I HAVE BEEN A CHRISTIAN FOR MANY YEARS. I've read through the Bible, and I've heard many sermons. And yet, after all this time, Jesus is still teaching me new things—even from Scripture I've read many times before. As I was reading Matthew 16, the Holy Spirit pointed out a new significance to me.

Jesus had recently fed the five thousand, and the disciples had picked up twelve baskets of leftovers. Later "he asked his disciples, 'Who do people say that the Son of Man is?' 'Well,' they replied, 'some say John the Baptist, some say Elijah, and others say Jeremiah or one of the other prophets.' Then he asked them, 'But who do you say I am?' Simon Peter answered, 'You are the Messiah, the Son of the living God'" (Matthew 16:13-16).

Many times we've heard Jesus described as "a great teacher" or "a good man." But Jesus really wanted to know who the Twelve believed He was. And I believe He's asking us the same thing today.

When my husband has been laid off and I don't know how we'll pay the bills, who do I say Jesus is? When my dad has been diagnosed with a life-threatening illness, who is Jesus? When the world looks scary and out of control, who is He to me?

In other words, in the difficult, scary, heartbreaking times of life, what do I really believe about Him? In the good times, it's easy to say who He is. In the hard times, sometimes it's an act of faith and worship to say who He is. And it's a remembering.

Jesus, You are my Provider. You've never let me go hungry. You are my daddy's Healer, Jesus. You will take care of him. And Jesus, You have my world and the whole world in Your hands. I do not need to fear.

My friend, who do you say He is?

When you are facing a hard time, a scary circumstance, or a desperate situation, remember who Jesus is. Remember what you know about Him. He's got you.

Steps of Faith

Jesus, help me to remember in my heart of hearts who You are. You are my Savior, the Son of the living God.

Deeper Walk: Isaiah 40:28-31

A Crisis and a Crossroads

I am poor and needy; please hurry to my aid, O God.
You are my helper and my savior; O LORD, do not delay.
Psalm 70:5

ELI'S PARENTS WERE shocked when they received a call from the high school principal. A teacher had found a sizable bag of marijuana stashed in Eli's locker, and he had admitted to smoking regularly with a new group of friends.

Because of the school's zero tolerance policy, Eli was expelled from school for the remainder of the year. His parents were confused and distraught. Eli was a great student and had never gotten in trouble before. How had their child gone from being a normal, thriving teenager to a juvenile delinquent expelled from school? Where had they gone wrong?

The truth was that Eli had a deep need to fit in, to find friends who would like and accept him. When some kids who liked to party offered him acceptance, even on a shallow level, he responded with loyalty and conformity.

Thankfully, this story has a happy ending. God used the situation to speak into Eli's life. Eli started attending rehab and seeing a counselor, as well as spending time with a Christian college student who had dealt with similar struggles in his past. Even though Eli had gone to church and knew about God, he hadn't realized his sin or his need for a Savior. Now he saw that his deep need for acceptance could only be met by a loving Father, and he submitted his life and desires to what God wanted. Eli began to change from within—a supernatural transformation that only God could have done.

Drug use is an unfortunate constant in a culture seeking relief from all kinds of pain and looking for acceptance wherever it can be found. Yet drugs are just a symptom of a deeper problem. Our kids need a personal relationship with the God who loves them. Ask God to put a teen on your heart, and pray for him or her regularly—that God would intervene in his or her life and be their All in All.

Steps of Faith
God, thank You for accepting and loving us in Christ. Thank You for meeting all our needs in Him. Help me persist in prayer for those who don't know You.

Deeper Walk: Psalm 18

Answering Prayer

Everyone who asks, receives. Everyone who seeks, finds.
And to everyone who knocks, the door will be opened.
Matthew 7:8

I WENT TO THE CONFERENCE with one specific prayer: direction. By the second day, I'd learned a ton, received encouraging feedback on a story I was writing, and was enjoying the time to focus on something besides my busy life. But direction? The closest I'd come was an idea that would require more transparency than I was ready for, and the sense that my days of writing in one particular area were over.

As I got ready for day three, I felt discouragement set in. Once again, I sent up a prayer for clear direction in my writing life. That's when a thought stopped me:

You have *been receiving direction.*

Had I?

Maybe you don't see it as an answer because it seems scary or because it isn't what you hoped for.

Hadn't I prayed expecting God to answer? What had I meant when I prayed for direction? Did I want God to give me a glimpse of His next step for me, or did I really only want an exciting connection that I could brag about and see unfold quickly and effortlessly? The ideas that were coming to mind required risks, including waiting on His timing and pulling away from a comfort zone. Did I have the courage to do what He asked? That's when I realized that what I needed most was a willingness to accept and obey the direction He had already given.

The more we grow in our walk with God, the more quickly we call on Him for direction in our careers, ministries, relationships, and family decisions. But what happens when He points us toward the opposite of what we wanted or to something so unexpected that we almost miss it? That's when the truth comes out. Did we want His way, or was there a selfish desire behind our prayer? Are we willing to obey even when His assignment requires more courage than we think we have? Then we must face the challenge of accepting the answer and recognize the surrender involved in receiving His best for us.

Steps of Faith

God, I confess that an agenda often motivates my prayers. Help me let go of my pride-driven goals and truly pursue Your path.

Deeper Walk: Matthew 7:7-11

How Can I Repay?

God saved you by his grace when you believed.
And you can't take credit for this; it is a gift from God.
Ephesians 2:8

JODI OPENED THE DOOR TO FRANCES, who stepped around the toys littering the entryway. Bouncing one baby on her hip, Jodi closed the door before the other baby could crawl out.

"You certainly have your hands full now that these two are crawling," commented Frances. She clapped her hands playfully and reached for the baby in Jodi's arms.

The baby easily left her mother's embrace and grabbed hold of Frances. Meanwhile, Jodi lifted her teetering son into her arms and beckoned Frances to follow her.

"Frances, you've done so much for me," Jodi began. "Are you sure you want to take the twins again today?"

"I remember what it was like as a young mom," Frances replied. "And I had a mom living close by who helped out. You don't have that. Besides, I love taking the babies for a stroll around the park."

Jodi gathered things into the diaper bag, but she felt the familiar guilt surfacing as she prepared to send her babies off with Frances for the afternoon. How could she ever repay her? The older woman must have sensed Jodi's hesitance because she put down the baby and wrapped her arms around the young mom.

"Jodi," she whispered, "I know how hard your days can be, and I just want to show you a little grace. God has blessed me with time and energy to spare. It's my pleasure to share it with you."

Grace is given with enthusiasm, goodwill, and no strings attached. The gracious giver has an abundance to offer, and the recipient stands in humble need with no way to repay. Have you ever been the recipient of such grace? You have if you've come to Jesus, broken and desperate for forgiveness and mercy. To our great relief, God, who is rich in every resource, graciously gives love, mercy, restoration, peace, and more. Praise your gracious God today. You cannot repay Him, but you can sing His praises.

Steps of Faith

Father, thank You for graciously giving me all I need for life. Thank You for fresh starts, new hope, and abundant joy, all gifts of amazing grace!

Deeper Walk: Ephesians 2:1-10

In His Timing

Wait patiently for the LORD. Be brave and courageous.
Yes, wait patiently for the LORD.
Psalm 27:14

AN EXCITING JOB OPPORTUNITY CAME available only to be put on hold for what seemed like forever. How could this happen? I needed the funds and résumé credit that the job would provide. I felt let down, like God had dangled the answer to a prayer in front of me only to snatch it away.

Despite my confusion, I made up my mind to wait on His timing. If the opportunity had truly come from Him, He would make it happen when it was supposed to.

During the months of waiting, a family crisis came out of nowhere and monopolized my days. Every now and then, that job came to mind. I resented that it had been replaced by a trial. *You trust His timing, remember?* I reminded myself. *If you had that job in addition to all that's going on, would you have it in you to do your best? God isn't holding out on you.*

Sure enough, I received the long-awaited call when I expected it least and needed the lift most. It was time to move forward. Best of all, now I had the time and stamina required.

A month later, my ability to trust God was put to the test again with a different set of circumstances. Once more, I had to make up my mind to wait on Him, knowing that He was at work even in the delay.

"Wait for the Lord." It sounds so simple until we have to do it. Whether we are suffering from an illness, needing deliverance from an unfair situation, waiting for a phone call that could change everything, or praying for Him to work in the heart of a wayward child, the timing can feel like forever. In Psalm 27, David cried out to God as he waited on Him, recalling His history of faithfulness, reviving his trust in the process. What are you waiting on God for today? Take some time to trace God's track record in your own life, just as David did.

Steps of Faith

God, I confess that I can be so impatient. Help me trust You more fully as I wait for You to move.

Deeper Walk: Psalm 27:7-14

Golden Apple Friend

Timely advice is lovely, like golden apples in a silver basket.
Proverbs 25:11

YEARS AGO, a dear friend gave me a pretty little book titled *Apples of Gold*. Filled with Scriptures, wise sayings, and sweet sentiments, this classic book takes its name from Proverbs 25:11, which asserts that "a word fitly spoken is like apples of gold in a setting of silver" (ESV).

As I thumbed through that book recently, I found it both fitting and precious that the friend who gave it to me still faithfully speaks good things into my life. Vivian prays for me, encourages me to act wisely, reminds me of biblical truths, gives me godly perspective on my situations, and comforts me when I'm weary. She also asks me the tough questions, holds me accountable to promises I've made to God, and helps me examine my ways honestly in light of His Word.

Holding the little book covered in shimmery gold fabric, I realized that Vivian is indeed a golden-apple friend. She lives hundreds of miles away from me now, so she's not the friend with whom I go to the mall or out to lunch. But she is the friend who has spoken the most good into my life. I treasure the copy of *Apples of Gold* that she gave me years ago, but I treasure the golden-apple words she has spoken into my life even more.

Do you have a golden-apple friend, one who consistently speaks good things into your life? If you do, thank God for her today. But if you don't have a godly friend who encourages you spiritually on a regular basis, ask the Lord to help you be such a friend to someone else. In Luke 4:22, when the people heard Jesus speak gracious words, their hearts were stirred. Gracious words—the right words spoken at the right time—still have that effect on people. Consider how you can speak more graciously to your friends.

Steps of Faith

Father, thank You for the friends who have consistently and graciously spoken truth to me. Help me be such a friend to others.

Deeper Walk: Ephesians 4:29

Through His Eyes

Your unfailing love, O Lord, is as vast as the heavens;
your faithfulness reaches beyond the clouds.

Psalm 36:5

"COLIN, DO YOU REMEMBER the older man you held the door open for at church last week?" I asked my twelve-year-old son.

"You mean the man with the walker?" he asked.

"Yes. I just wanted to tell you that I'm so proud of you. It was really sweet and thoughtful for you to help him so patiently. You're developing into a very kind young man, and God is pleased with that."

Colin smiled. "Whenever I see someone who has some kind of disability, it makes me think of you. I know how hard it is for you when you have to ask someone for help."

I felt tears welling up in my eyes. Colin was referring to my left arm, which had been amputated at the elbow after an automobile accident four years ago. While most boys his age didn't have to think about much other than sports and homework, Colin had a lot of responsibilities to deal with to help me out.

Colin hugged me. "It's okay, Mom. I don't mind helping you. I know that's what God wants me to do."

As Christians, we have a responsibility to help others in need. In Matthew 10:42, Jesus said, "If you give even a cup of cold water to one of the least of my followers, you will surely be rewarded."

Those of us who have suffered can understand how much something simple, like helping a person in need, can make someone else's day.

Try to imagine what life must be like for people in difficult circumstances. Pray that God will help you to reach out to others, show them how much God loves them, and remind them that He is with them in the midst of their suffering.

"I have told you all this so that you may have peace in me. Here on earth you will have many trials and sorrows. But take heart, because I have overcome the world" (John 16:33).

Steps of Faith

Father, please help me see others through Your eyes. Let me develop a heart of love and compassion so I can become more like Jesus.

Deeper Walk: Lamentations 3:31-33

Digital Idolatry

They worshiped their idols, which led to their downfall.
Psalm 106:36

STACY FRANTICALLY FELT around in her purse for her phone. She knew how to get to her destination, but after road construction made her take a detour, she was suddenly lost in an unfamiliar part of the city. As she stopped at a red light, she turned her purse upside down, emptying it. No phone. Panic set in. She must have left it at home, and now she had no GPS. No way of calling or texting someone to ask for directions. As the light turned green, unsure of which way to go, she pulled into a parking lot. *Lord, I'm lost. Please help me.*

Stacy hadn't realized how dependent she had become on her technological network. GPS, the Internet, her cell phone, and e-mail—all resources she went to first when she had a problem or question, or even if she was lonely or bored. It had been a while since Stacy had felt she needed God like this. In fact, if she were honest, the amount of time she spent plugged in had even encroached on her daily devotional time. *Lord, has technology become an idol for me?* Even as she prayed, she knew it had.

Peace began to replace Stacy's fear. Looking around her, she saw a familiar street. If she headed north on that street, she would be able to find her way. Relieved, she pulled the car back onto the road and thanked God for helping her and reminding her to trust in Him more than technology.

How many times a day do you update your Facebook status, check your e-mail, or go to the Internet to find the answer to a question? Do you feel you have to stay connected through texts and phone calls? Do you share the same passion for staying connected with God? Anything done in excess could signal a problem. Try unplugging for a few days and see what it reveals about your heart.

Steps of Faith

Lord, thank You for the gift of technology. Help me use it in moderation and not put it before You in my life.

Deeper Walk: Proverbs 3:5-8

Dare to Be Labeled

I am not ashamed of this Good News about Christ.
It is the power of God at work, saving everyone who believes.
Romans 1:16

MARILYN TOOK HER leftover spaghetti out of the microwave and stepped aside so the woman behind her could use it.

Cindy, Marilyn reminded herself as the pretty blonde prepared her lunch. It was Marilyn's third day working at the bank, and she was still learning her coworkers' names.

Marilyn overheard Cindy's conversation with one of the tellers.

"I miss Scott, but I don't miss his roommate Jeff at all," Cindy said.

"Was Jeff the one who was really religious?"

"Annoyingly so! He actually offered to pray with me the night that Scott and I broke up."

Marilyn stared into her plastic bowl, stirring her noodles with a fork. If she stopped to pray, her bowed head would alert Cindy that she was one of those "annoyingly" religious people too.

God, please forgive me if I pray without bowing my head. Cindy is a supervisor, and I've already seen her pattern of singling out people she doesn't like. I can't afford to offend her.

Marilyn's cheeks burned as if Jesus were sitting across the table. Who would she rather offend—God or a woman who didn't fear Him?

Lord, what am I thinking?

Marilyn bowed her head and thanked God for her food as she did before every meal.

Stories of Christians suffering for their faith, and biblical accounts of those who paid an agonizing price for proclaiming Christ, can make our avoidance of ridicule seem pitiful. Still, the fear of being labeled or snubbed by neighbors, fellow employees, and even family is very real. It often takes verses like Mark 8:38 to wake us up: "If anyone is ashamed of me and my message . . . the Son of Man will be ashamed of that person." Suddenly the idea of standing out as a follower of Christ pales in comparison to being ashamed of Him.

Steps of Faith

Lord, how many times have I claimed to be devoted to You only to have my actions prove otherwise? Help me to never again be afraid to let others see who I belong to.

Deeper Walk: Mark 8:34-38

Balm

The LORD helps the fallen and lifts those bent beneath their loads.
Psalm 145:14

AFTER DROPPING HAYLEY OFF at the nursery, I followed Joey as he ran toward his Sunday school class, where his teacher stood at the door.

"Hi, Joey," said Miss Sherri, folding him in her arms. "You're such a good hugger! Tommy is here, building a wall with those big blocks." Joey zipped into his class without a backward glance.

"Have fun!" I called. To Sherri, I said, "Sorry I'm late. I never seem to make it on time."

"No big deal. I know it's difficult doing everything on your own. How are you?"

"Tired," I said. "So tired. My house is a mess, and I'm stressed at work. I never seem to get caught up on anything. I don't know how I'm going to keep going."

"But you will, Abby. You're doing great! It must be discouraging seeing things undone, but you're giving your children much more than a perfect house or neatly folded laundry could—you're providing financially for them, raising them in a loving home, and teaching them about God. Way to go."

Her words felt like a balm. "Thank you. You have no idea how good it is to hear that."

"It's true. And you know what else? The Lord is watching over you. He will give you the strength you need to keep going."

Single motherhood is one of the toughest roles there is. Carrying the load of both parents can make a woman weary, discouraged, fearful, and depressed. If you are a single mom, remember that God has not forgotten you. You and your children are precious to Him. Go to Him and let Him wrap you in His arms. He will carry you. He is your Rock, your Fortress, and your Deliverer. If you know a single mom, encourage her today, and make a point to reach out to her regularly.

Steps of Faith

Lord, my strength comes from You. Fill me with Your presence so I can live for You even when my circumstances are difficult. Thank You for being with me.

Deeper Walk: Psalm 62:1-2

The Buffet

The LORD will guide you continually,
giving you water when you are dry and restoring your strength.
Isaiah 58:11

MY HUSBAND, Dave, and I promised his parents that we would visit them during our kids' spring break. So we packed our suitcases, got in our SUV, and made the four-hour trip to their house.

We arrived just in time to drop off our luggage and go out to dinner. They suggested a buffet restaurant so everyone could find something they liked.

Although I'd been trying to watch my weight, I caved under the pressure of being overly hungry and having too many choices. Pretty soon, a spoonful of this and a small serving of that added up to a plate that was nearly overflowing.

Halfway through the meal, I knew I couldn't possibly finish everything unless I stuffed myself to the point of discomfort. *Lord, why did I do this to myself?* I asked silently.

Then I saw a parallel between my overstuffed plate and all the things I had taken on in my life. I worked full time, and our three children were each involved in sports, music lessons, and the student ministry at church. I also led a women's Bible study. There was just too much going on, and we were all paying for it. Again, I thought, *Lord, why did I do this to myself?*

I left the rest of what was on my plate and pushed it away, and I decided to do the same with my schedule. I needed to submit my time to the Lord and ask for His help in managing our busy lives.

Women today seem busier than ever. Whether we're single, stay-at-home moms, or working moms, we all pile our plates high and end up on overload—feeling overwhelmed, exhausted, and frustrated. If you have taken on too much, take time to stop and reevaluate your activities and your schedule. Submit your time to the Lord and ask Him where to cut back so you can live a life of peace and balance.

Steps of Faith

Father, *"teach me to do your will, for you are my God. May your gracious Spirit lead me forward on a firm footing"* (Psalm 143:10).

Deeper Walk: Psalm 25

More than Having Fun

Don't look out only for your own interests, but take an interest in others, too.
Philippians 2:4

I WAS DISAPPOINTED when I had to miss the women's brunch. For months, we had been collecting gently used clothes, shoes, and accessories—not so we could have our own clothing exchange or sell the items to build the retreat scholarship fund, but so we could give it all away to women who needed clothes far more than we did. Women recovering from addiction, abuse, and other difficult circumstances were invited to be fed, entertained, pampered, and assigned a personal shopper to help them choose a complete outfit. Once every woman had something, the rest was up for grabs. Friends who attended said it was the best event ever—that seeing those women uplifted moved them to tears. I had skipped retreats and events before, but this was one that left me thinking, *I totally missed out.*

Since then, our women's ministry has made it a priority to reach beyond ourselves, planning events that are about more than just fun and fellowship.

Right now, we are passionate about supporting a local ministry that helps those caught up in prostitution. We still have time for fellowship, but our luncheons, teas, and retreats have a purpose—showing the love of Christ to those who desperately need it.

As Christian women, we look forward to retreats where we can laugh ourselves silly, cry our eyes out, and laugh some more before eating too much chocolate and staying up late chatting with our "sisters." And our Bible studies offer opportunities to grow and address our issues in a biblical way. But what about the world outside our Christian bubble? When do we apply what we learned in those weeks of soaking up God's Word and pass on the love that we have received? As we are learning, growing, and fellowshipping, how can we also shine Christ's light on hurting hearts that have no idea how much they ache for Him?

Steps of Faith

Lord, thank You for creating us with such a huge capacity for enjoyment and relationships. Show me how to take what I have gained beyond my spiritual community.

Deeper Walk: Hebrews 6:10

The Setup

Keep watch and pray, so that you will not give in to temptation.
For the spirit is willing, but the body is weak!
Matthew 26:41

I TRY TO STAY AWAY FROM SHOPPING MALLS. They are, as they say, a hotbed of temptation for me. Of course, it's not a sin to buy a new purse or pair of shoes if needed, but I'm prone to whip out my credit card for these alluring items and buy things I don't have money for.

So when I needed to purchase a wedding gift recently, I purposefully asked my husband to do it for me. Aware of my resolution to stay away from this particular brand of temptation, he gladly said that he would go to the department store and buy the gift for me. But when he had to leave on an unexpected business trip, I had to go to the mall myself.

Sure enough, the entrance to the department store landed me in the women's shoe department. I should have walked past the colorful flats, leather boots, and pretty pumps, but instead I found myself meandering through tables of footwear and picking up shoes to try on. Just as I was searching for a sales assistant, I saw my friend Michelle.

"I see I'm just in time," Michelle said as she reached for the red pump and two black flats I carried. I grinned and handed over the patent leather temptations.

"Yes, you are," I admitted. "Thanks for agreeing to meet me here. Accountability may be tough on the ego, but it's definitely better for my wallet and my marriage!"

God always provides a way of escape from our temptations, and mine even took me to lunch that day to celebrate a little victory.

Are you setting yourself up for failure by surrounding yourself with temptation? First Corinthians 10:13 assures us that God provides a way out of every tempting situation, but we can sabotage His provision when we don't heed our own weaknesses. When you do have to enter tempting situations, fortify your personal resolve with prayer, memorized Scripture, and accountability.

Steps of Faith

Lord, help me be honest enough about my own weaknesses to seek the accountability and prayer support that I need. I want to please You in all my actions, attitudes, and words.

Deeper Walk: 1 Corinthians 10:6-13

Speak Up!

Speak up for the poor and helpless, and see that they get justice.
Proverbs 31:9

SEVERAL YEARS AGO, as my first child got older, I started asking God how I could use writing to serve Him. As a stay-at-home mom, I found myself with the blessings of extra time and flexibility.

God led me to a local ministry that spoke up for and helped women and girls in some of the hardest places and darkest situations in the world. My heart broke when I learned about girls discarded from temporary marriages in Mali, AIDS orphans in China, the rape and abuse of Sudanese women and girls in displaced persons camps, and the infanticide of baby girls in India. I wasn't in a life season that allowed me to go across the globe to serve, and I didn't have the resources to do so. But I could be a voice and advocate for them here in the United States.

Living in poverty in remote places and usually deprived of an education, these women and girls can't speak up for themselves. They don't have laptops or smart phones to make known the abuses and oppression they endure. But I do. I began researching potential grant opportunities for the ministry. I also wrote a post on their website highlighting stories of abuse and redemption. I told others about what the ministry was doing and how they could help. These were small ways I contributed to helping these women, requiring just a few hours each week, but God used my efforts to transform their lives and mine.

There are a lot of hurting people in the world that we never know about because they have no media, no resources, no voice. How can people help them if they don't know what's happening? There are many Christian ministries that carry the light of Jesus to the hungry, to the poor, and to abused and exploited girls and women, transforming their lives by providing basic necessities and education. These ministries need advocates to help raise awareness and funding. Will you be a voice for them?

Steps of Faith

Lord, open my eyes to the world's suffering. Show me how I can speak up for those in need.

Deeper Walk: Psalm 72:12-14

Spring Cleaning

She watches over the activities of her household and is never idle.
Proverbs 31:27, HCSB

CAITLIN GAVE HER DAUGHTER one more push on the swing and rejoined her friend Amelia on the park bench. Amelia had pulled a spiral notebook from her large bag and was writing in it.

"What are you doing?" asked Caitlin.

Amelia looked up, excitement and determination on her face. "I'm writing out my plans for spring cleaning," she said.

"Wow! You're actually going to spend a week cleaning your house?" Caitlin asked. "Cleaning out closets and cabinets and the refrigerator?"

"That's right," responded Amelia with a chuckle. She put her notebook down and turned toward Caitlin. "I've actually been praying about this," she said, more seriously.

Surprised but curious, Caitlin waited for her friend to explain.

"I've read several books lately about home keeping and organization," continued Amelia, "and while I don't want to be obsessive about this, I do see the benefits of keeping an orderly home. Then yesterday when I was reading my Bible, I was drawn to Proverbs 31. I know the woman's accomplishments described there seem unattainable, but when it says that she watches over her household and isn't idle, that just spoke to me. What I gained from it is that she makes her home a true haven for her family, and even for other people. I want that kind of home . . . so I'll have to get busy and make one!"

In Luke 10:38-42, Jesus prioritized time spent at His feet over time spent in the kitchen, but He wasn't saying we shouldn't be good stewards of our homes. Obviously Mary and Martha kept an orderly house: They were able to invite Jesus and His disciples into their home more than once. What are some things you can do to make your home a haven for ministry and hospitality?

Steps of Faith

Father, I know a spotless home is not the goal, but a serviceable one surely is. Help me make my home a welcoming place where I can serve others in Your name.

Deeper Walk: Proverbs 31:10-31

The Best Lifeline

Let us come boldly to the throne of our gracious God. There we will receive his mercy, and we will find grace to help us when we need it most.
Hebrews 4:16

I STILL REMEMBER THE day Facebook buzzed with the Gambrell family's terrible news. Early that morning Sarah posted that she was taking her four-year-old son, Parker, to the emergency room with a high fever and achy legs. By noon her Facebook updates included a request for prayer as she headed to a large children's hospital where they would perform extensive tests on her son. By evening, Sarah had ceased updating her Facebook status, but her husband, Jeff, notified friends that Parker had been diagnosed with leukemia. All in the space of a day's updates, the family had entered the storm of their lives.

Friends began to message friends asking each other for details, inquiring about the young family's needs, promising support. Careful observation of the remarks revealed both a contagious reality check of "This could be us!" and a determined drive to serve this family with a fierce outpouring of love. Within days of the diagnosis, fund-raising efforts were coordinated, gift baskets were delivered, meals were lined up, and gift cards were sent to the family. Sarah and Jeff's church stepped in like true brothers and sisters, insisting that the young couple rely on them for the duration of the storm.

Two years later, I asked Sarah what actions had ministered to her most. She said that prayers alone had seen her through. And while she had appreciated every mention and promise of prayer, the petitions offered by friends holding her hands had been her lifeline.

Often when we are called upon to navigate stormy waters with a loved one, we feel helpless and alone. But James said in his epistle that prayer is a sure go-to when someone is in distress. Do you know someone awaiting medical treatment, living with chronic pain, battling disease, or wiping her child's feverish brow? You could pray for her right now. If you sense God's prompting, go to her and pray in person, providing the extra comfort of your companionship.

Steps of Faith
Father, make me more sensitive to the needs of those who are hurting. Show me how I might minister to them.

Deeper Walk: James 5:13-18

Respect

The wife must respect her husband.
Ephesians 5:33

FOR THE FIRST SEVEN YEARS OF my marriage, if my husband made mistakes or didn't meet my expectations, I made it known and treated him like a child. I figured that if I didn't "tolerate" behavior I didn't like, then he would change. Forgot to take the trash out? No mercy! Late from work and forgot to call? How rude and inconsiderate! The house a mess and the kids unfed while you play computer games? I don't think so! My tone and body language were accusatory, dismissive, even scornful.

We went to a lot of marriage conferences and read many marriage books. I heard the "Wives, respect your husbands" message many times. My heart remained hard, though, and I argued that surely the Bible didn't mean for me to give respect to someone who hadn't earned it.

Thankfully, God didn't give me over to my hard heart. Instead, through marriage counseling, mentoring, and Bible study, I began to see that respecting my husband doesn't mean approving of bad behavior. It means communicating my hurts and needs with gentleness instead of nagging, criticizing, and belittling. It means speaking humbly and being vulnerable when my feelings are hurt instead of going on the attack. It means focusing on the good instead of the negative I see in him. After all, I'm still a work in progress myself. Today we communicate very differently, and I have seen a beautiful peace in our family as a result.

No matter what we say or how we say it, we can't change our husbands. Only the Holy Spirit can. Some of us are tearing down our houses with our own hands (see Proverbs 14:1) through the way we treat our husbands. God says to respect them, just as He says to "[think] of others as better than yourselves" (Philippians 2:3).

Steps of Faith
Father, show me where I'm being disrespectful and help me honor You by honoring my husband.

Deeper Walk: 1 Peter 3:1-2

Faith in Action

Faith shows the reality of what we hope for;
it is the evidence of things we cannot see.

Hebrews 11:1

LOOKING THROUGH HER BANK STATEMENT, Beth couldn't help but think that if she didn't pay her tithe, she'd have enough money to provide better day care for her son. She really wanted Jack to be in a better environment, but she couldn't afford to do it all. She was tempted to cut down on the amount she normally gave to her church or stop paying it for a time.

After a few days of praying and asking God for direction, she sensed Him leading her to step out in faith by enrolling her son in the better day care while continuing to pay her tithe.

For a month or two, Beth struggled to make ends meet. But she refused to quit tithing. As the weeks went by, Beth found different ways of cutting expenses and stretching her gas and food money a little further. Trusting that God would provide for her was one of the hardest things Beth had ever done. It required a step of faith she'd never taken before. But she kept at it. And she kept praying.

Over time and in small ways, Beth kept cutting expenses. After a while, she became comfortable within the constraints of her budget. Soon, she received a promotion and pay raise at work. Thankful, Beth increased her tithing accordingly and began a savings fund for the extra money. Jack would need to go to college one day, and saving now would help him get there.

God is faithful and keeps His promises to His people. Obeying Him when we don't see how it's going to work takes a tremendous amount of faith. In your busy schedule today, when you think you don't have time to drop off extra clothes at the shelter or take food to someone in need, trust that God will give you the time and resources to do all that He calls you to do.

Steps of Faith

Father, I trust You to be there for me when I don't see a way. I pray that You would help me to do what I need to do, as well as what You call me to do.

Deeper Walk: Matthew 14:22-33

Back Home

Be strong in the Lord and in his mighty power.
Ephesians 6:10

KATE SAT BETWEEN HER MOTHER and younger sister in the pew, trying to focus on the sermon. It felt so strange to live with her parents again, listening to her sister Megan chatter about community college life, helping with dishes as she had as a teenager, and riding to church in Mom and Dad's van. Instead of sharing a bedroom with Megan, she shared her childhood bed with her two-year-old daughter, Jacie. Instead of lecturing her about grades and curfews, her parents awaited her updates on Dave, who had just been deployed to Afghanistan. As much as she loved her family, she had been totally unprepared for how difficult it would be to move back home. They got along great, but some days she felt like she was fourteen again, like when Dad playfully but firmly pushed her feet off the couch. She fought annoyance when they offered parenting advice or when she couldn't find privacy. But what would she do without them?

Thank You, God, that I have loving parents to turn to right now. I could be like my friend Beth, raising two kids alone in military housing with no family close by. Give me the patience and courage that I need while I wait for my husband to come home.

As wars rage around the world, more and more women are left behind while their husbands serve overseas. For some, this means living as a single parent, caring for children and household responsibilities alone. Other women find themselves back in their childhood bedrooms, fighting mixed feelings of gratitude and temporarily lost independence. All of this is compounded by constant uncertainty.

Take some time to pray for, call, or plan an act of service for a woman who is fighting her own battle while her husband fights far away. If you are a military wife, consider beginning or joining a Bible study specifically for military wives.

Steps of Faith

Heavenly Father, prompt me to help military wives, and remind me to pray for them.

Deeper Walk: Ephesians 6:10-18

A House of Light

*Your light will shine out from the darkness, and
the darkness around you will be as bright as noon.*
Isaiah 58:10

SEVERAL YEARS AGO, my husband and I took a vacation to the North Carolina coast, where we visited some of the lighthouses that have dotted the shoreline for more than one hundred years. I was pregnant at the time, so I wasn't interested in climbing the two hundred plus steps inside the lighthouse towers. Still, their history was fascinating.

All constructed in the 1800s, the lighthouses were built to warn the sailors in approaching boats of the dangerous shoals and shifting sandbars that line the coast. At least one of the lighthouses has been moved in the last decade to save it from erosion, and each lighthouse has its own story. I imagined the lighthouse keepers living close by so they could light the beacons at night to guide boats away from danger. Were they lonely? Did they feel the weight of their responsibility?

As Jesus followers, we are a light to the world. We are to warn people that they are approaching the deadly shoals and shifting sands of time and eternity. We are to let His light shine through us like a beacon to those who don't know Him. As His light bearers, we each have our own story. We can tell others how He rescued us from the dangerous waters of our sin. We can tell how He protected us from a serious crash on the rocks of bad decisions. We can tell how we were drowning and He offered us the lifeboat of His forgiveness.

We are His lighthouses to guide people safely home.

Jesus said we should not hide His light in us under a basket, but let it shine for all the world to see. People are looking for the true Light, and they will be drawn to it. Be a house of light.

Steps of Faith

Jesus, You are the true Light. You have come to rescue people from the darkness. Help us to be beacons for You.

Deeper Walk: Matthew 5:14-16

Not Abandoned

Pure and genuine religion in the sight of God the Father means caring for orphans and widows in their distress and refusing to let the world corrupt you.

James 1:27

WHEN MY DAD DIED OF a sudden heart attack, my mom was thrust into widowhood.

Although my mom walked a very hard road, my husband and I were there to support her. We helped her sift through the details of the funeral, navigated her through the insurance maze, and notified friends and loved ones of our loss.

I recently learned that widows in other countries sometimes have a very different fate. On top of the grief of losing their husbands, these women can face devastating hardships because of social stigmas.

Gospel for Asia reports that in South Asia, it is not uncommon for a woman to be blamed for her husband's death. "For some widows, the humiliation starts when she is stripped of her colorful clothing and forced to wear a white sari signifying her new status as a widow. Her glass bangles, which previously let the world know of her marital status, are smashed into thousands of tiny shards. Her life will now be controlled by her eldest son. If she is lucky, she'll get a tiny corner of his house in which to sleep. More often, though, she is sent out of the family home and ends up working for a few cents a day at a temple or begging on the streets."*

But with the help of various Christian organizations, widows in these countries are receiving the skills and tools they need to earn a living, such as a sewing machine and vocational training. They are also receiving the Good News of Jesus Christ and learning about His love for them.

Widows and orphans hold a special place in Jesus' heart. He brought a widow's son back to life in Luke 7:11-17. He noticed the poor widow who put her two coins into the Temple collection box in Mark 12:42. And just as Jesus poured out His love toward widows, we must do the same. Be prayerful about how you can help someone in need today.

Steps of Faith

Father, give me a tender heart toward hurting people. Show me what You want me to do to help.

Deeper Walk: Psalm 71

---

* Gospel for Asia Australia, "Pray for South Asia's Widows," accessed May 2, 2017, http://www.gospelforasia.org.au/pray/widows/.

Do You Tweet?

Teach us to realize the brevity of life, so that we may grow in wisdom.

Psalm 90:12

CLAIRE PARKED HER CAR IN the garage and checked her cell phone before going into the house. Three new e-mails since she left work. Tossing the phone in her purse, she decided to answer them later. For now, she had to fix dinner for Brandon and the kids.

Later that evening, after Chloe and Michael finished their homework, Claire just wanted to sit down and relax.

Brandon called to her from the den. "Hey, honey, come and watch this new program with me."

"Not right now," Claire replied. "I have to answer a few e-mails. I'll be down in a little while."

After logging out of her e-mail account, Claire decided to check her Facebook page. As she scrolled through the postings, she thought, *I don't know why I spend so much time reading this stuff. Most of what people say is really not that important. How earthshaking is it to read that one of my coworkers just finished Chinese takeout?*

Next, Claire checked her Twitter page. She sent out a final tweet for the day, then went to the den to join Brandon. But the room was dark and he had already gone to bed.

Another day was over, and Claire had wasted a good part of it checking e-mail, Facebook, and Twitter.

Oh, Lord, she prayed, *I'm sorry. I blew it again. Technology can be a blessing, but today it was a big time waster. Please help me use my time more wisely tomorrow.*

Technology has changed the way we do business, shop, communicate, and live our lives. Some people who are technologically savvy may spend far more time with their devices than they do talking and building relationships with real people.

If you think you may be spending too much time with your electronics, pray for wisdom and ask God how He would have you bring balance to your life.

Steps of Faith

Lord, thank You for the blessing that technology brings to our lives. Please give me wisdom, and help me use it according to Your will.

Deeper Walk: James 1:5-6

Making a Difference

Encourage each other and build each other up, just as you are already doing.
1 Thessalonians 5:11

ONE MORNING A YOUNG WOMAN I'm mentoring and her two preschoolers stopped by. While the children played with the toys we keep in the family room for our grandchildren, Emily and I headed to the kitchen for some iced tea and grown-up conversation.

"How did you do it?" Emily asked. "You had four kids—I only have two, and I can barely keep on top of things. I feel like all I do is clean up messes, change diapers, and wash endless loads of laundry."

I smiled. "I remember feeling overwhelmed every now and then when my kids were little."

"Sometimes I envy my friends who went back to work after their kids were born. They bring home a paycheck and get to talk to other adults on a regular basis, and they're doing something besides wiping runny noses and breaking up fights over a toy."

I stopped Emily and said, "I understand how you feel, but don't be deceived into thinking that what you're doing isn't important. You're doing something incredible—raising your kids. You teach them about Jesus, you and Derrick take them to church every week, and you spend time with them. It's the best job in the world, though it's probably the toughest job in the world, too. And you're making such a difference in your children's lives."

Emily looked out into the family room at her children and smiled. "You're right," she said. "Thanks for encouraging me."

Sometimes women get discouraged and bogged down in the details of daily life. But the influence moms have on their children is enormous. If you feel that you're being pulled in all directions and no one seems to notice everything you have to do, remember that we serve "the God who sees" (Genesis 16:13). Whether you're a stay-at-home mom or a working mom, you are making a difference for the next generation. And the Lord will see.

Steps of Faith
Lord, help me encourage mothers and let them know how valuable they are in the lives of their children.

Deeper Walk: 2 John 1:6

He's in Love All Right!

Those who exalt themselves will be humbled, and
those who humble themselves will be exalted.

Luke 14:11

WHEN I WAS IN COLLEGE, I was interested in a young man in my physics class. Brian was popular, handsome, and athletic—and I thought that if he would just ask me out for a date, my life would be perfect. One day, he asked me to join him at a nearby coffeehouse, and I was ecstatic. But instead of it being the perfect evening I had envisioned, Brian spent the entire time talking about himself. He had just been chosen to be captain of the football team, he excelled in snowboarding and mountain biking, he had taken several international trips, his parents were going to give him a brand-new BMW for his next birthday . . . and on and on he went. Suddenly, I wasn't so impressed with him.

I'm sure I'm not the only person who has had an encounter like this. Often, people can be so busy talking about themselves that they don't bother asking you anything about your likes, interests, family, and career.

In Luke 14:7-11, Jesus explains why trying to impress others has a major potential to backfire. In this parable, He instructs us on humility and how we should act by taking "the lowest place at the foot of the table" (verse 10). By doing so, God may honor you and recognize you for putting others before yourself.

Instead of trying to make yourself look good, point out the good things in your friends, family, and coworkers. Listening to other people is an easy way to make them feel important. You can identify humility in someone when you leave a conversation feeling like he or she took a real interest in you. Find ways to help and serve other people. It will keep you from focusing only on yourself by reminding you that other people have very real needs in their lives too.

Steps of Faith

Father, let me always be willing to put others before myself and to serve others out of love and obedience to You.

Deeper Walk: Luke 18:9-14

Take Time to Listen

My sheep listen to my voice; I know them, and they follow me.
John 10:27

OVER STEAMING CUPS OF TEA, Jan and I got caught up on our news. Then I asked this question: "I tell God all my requests, but sometimes I wonder if He's really there. I mean, how do you know He is? It's not like He says anything back."

Jan answered, "Good question. You said that you tell God your requests. Do you do any listening?"

"Listening? Hmmm. Well . . . no, I guess not."

"I'm just starting to understand its importance in prayer. I used to talk the whole time."

"But isn't that what we're supposed to do? Otherwise, we'd just be sitting there, right?"

"Prayer is, at its heart, a conversation. We praise and thank God and share our requests with Him. But we're also supposed to listen. To be quiet and let Him speak."

"Out loud?"

"Well, not usually, but in your heart and mind. It helps to be actively listening. Read a passage from His Word and let it soak in as you sit. Ask Him to show you what He wants you to see in it and how to apply it to your life."

"Okay, I'll try that, though I'm not always good at sitting still."

"Me neither! But we can't expect to hear God if we're doing all the talking. When we are quiet and wait on Him, we are in a better position to hear from Him."

We encourage children to sit and be quiet, but sometimes we don't give ourselves the time to do the same. In order to hear the voice of God, we need to allow Him space and time in our lives to speak. Meditating on Scripture—letting it percolate in our hearts—can quiet us and help us focus. The Bible shows God speaking in different ways. Don't miss His voice, however it comes to you.

Steps of Faith
Father, help me be quiet and listen. Open my heart to hear Your voice.

Deeper Walk: 1 Kings 19:1-18

Sabbath Prep

The seventh day is a Sabbath day of rest dedicated to the LORD your God.
Exodus 20:10

A COUPLE OF YEARS AGO, I realized I was running myself ragged seven days a week. My husband works for a church, and Sundays were anything but restful for us. I remember sitting in worship one Sunday with my mind whizzing away. *I need to talk to this person. I need to get a meal to that person. I need to check on this or that.* The Holy Spirit revealed my own sin to me—I wasn't setting apart the Sabbath; I was treating it like any other day.

So my husband and I brainstormed ways we could make Sunday different. We started by doing as much as we could on Saturday—cleaning up, ironing and laying out clothes, prepping breakfast, and setting out Bibles and teaching notes. We also prepared our hearts for worship—going over our children's Sunday school lessons with them, praying for the upcoming services, and listening to praise music while getting ready on Sunday morning. We resolved not to talk shop too much while at church—no hunting people down to ask questions that could wait until Monday or jotting down reminders during the service. These little things really paved the way for a more intentional time of worship and a more restful Sabbath. And we start the week more refreshed and focused after simply enjoying the Lord's Day.

God created the Sabbath for the benefit of His people, to remind us that in Him we have eternal rest from our sin. Every Sunday, we have the opportunity to put aside worldly cares, focus on worshiping Him, and rest in the knowledge that He has promised eternal rest in His presence. By preparing our hearts and schedules, we can set apart Sunday as a day of worship and rest, to the glory of God.

Steps of Faith

God, thank You for offering the rest that our souls long for. Help me set apart a day for You.

Deeper Walk: Matthew 12:1-8

Perfect Peace

I am leaving you with a gift—peace of mind and heart.
And the peace I give is a gift the world cannot give.
So don't be troubled or afraid.
John 14:27

AS MARY DROVE TO THE HOSPITAL, she fought the urge to fear the worst. She'd received a call from her husband's boss saying that there had been an accident. Mary's frantic mind began to fill in the missing pieces. Perhaps Jack had fallen from the scaffolding on the building he was examining. Perhaps he'd experienced a heart attack. Or maybe he'd been in a car accident between job sites.

But as Mary drove past a small church nestled beneath a grove of trees, she noticed a simple sign in the parking lot. It read, "His peace trumps your understanding." Mary read the words aloud and then remembered a corresponding Scripture in Philippians 4:7. She recited the familiar verse to herself several times as she drove on. When she parked her car at the hospital, Mary felt God giving her the peace He promised.

Lord, I don't know what I'm about to walk into, but You do, Mary prayed. *I will simply trust You. Please guard my heart with Your peace so I can handle whatever lies ahead.*

It's easy to have peace when we feel we have everything under control, when all is going smoothly. But when we can't see what lies ahead or when we don't know all the details of our current struggle, things become more unnerving. And when our problems seem out of our control or the crisis is intensifying, it's easy to lose our calm.

But God promises that those who keep their minds focused and dependent on Him will have perfect peace. While we may think we need all the facts and background information, God just asks us to trust Him with the details. He can give peace that is better than any measure of our own understanding.

What dilemma have you been trying to solve? What fear have you been wrestling? No matter what it is, trust Him, and He will give you peace that surpasses all understanding.

Steps of Faith

Father, sometimes I want more information, more control, or more input. But I know that what I really need is to trust You so I can have peace.

Deeper Walk: Philippians 4:4-9

Sing!

I will shout for joy and sing your praises, for you have ransomed me.
Psalm 71:23

MY HUSBAND DOESN'T SING IN CHURCH. Apparently, someone once told him, "You can't carry a tune in a bucket." So rather than offend the ears of everyone around him, Bill chooses to stand respectfully and worship in silence, occasionally raising his hands as he is led by the Spirit.

When I was growing up, I took piano lessons and flute lessons, and I sang in the chorus at school. Bill and I provided our three children with lessons in piano, violin, and flute, and all three can carry a tune. But Bill never had music lessons or sang in a chorus. Even if he knew how to read music, I'm not sure he could reproduce the proper notes. Some people refer to this as "tone deafness."

In spite of his lack of musical ability, Bill and I love listening to music, and a few nights ago we attended a concert. The musician is an incredible guitarist, and he also sings pretty well. On the way home we talked about the performance, and Bill said, "I really wish I could sing."

We were silent for a few minutes, and then he turned to me and asked, "Do you think I'll be able to sing when I get to heaven?"

"Absolutely!" I said. We all will, and we'll be singing on key to give glory to the God of the universe. But for now, God doesn't care that Bill doesn't sound like Andrea Bocelli or have perfect pitch like worship leader Travis Cottrell. God doesn't care that the sounds coming out of our mouths aren't perfect, but when the praise that comes from our hearts is genuine, He's delighted.

A. W. Tozer said, "I cannot sing a lick but that's nobody's business. God thinks I'm an opera star!"* So sing your heart out. God is listening.

Steps of Faith

"I give you thanks, O LORD, with all my heart; I will sing your praises before the gods. I bow before your holy Temple as I worship. I praise your name for your unfailing love and faithfulness" (Psalm 138:1-2).

Deeper Walk: Psalm 96

---

* A. W. Tozer, *Tozer on Worship and Entertainment*, comp. James L. Snyder (Camp Hill, PA: WingSpread Publishers, 2006), Kindle edition.

A Changed Life

Anyone who belongs to Christ has become a new person.
The old life is gone; a new life has begun!
2 Corinthians 5:17

PATTY AND ED'S YOUNGEST SON, Cody, was a handful. He went through a phase where he hated school, and his attendance record clearly showed it. In his frustration, Ed quipped that if Cody could earn frequent-flier points for being in detention, their entire family could circle the globe.

Cody was caught with alcohol and drugs during his teen years, but he was unrepentant. And though Patty and Ed tried to enforce appropriate consequences, nothing worked.

But something happened during Cody's senior year. One evening he told his parents he was going out with his friend Todd the following night, and no one was going to stop him because he was eighteen. Patty and Ed begged God to prevent that from happening. The next day Cody wound up with a bad stomach virus and decided to stay home.

That night Todd got behind the wheel of a car after he'd been drinking. He lost control of the vehicle and caused a crash that killed a pregnant woman and her two-year-old daughter. Now he was facing felony charges for vehicular manslaughter that would most likely result in his imprisonment.

After this, Cody began to realize how many times his parents' prayers had been answered in spite of his rebellion. He began going back to church, and soon he surrendered his life to Christ.

During the difficult years, Patty and Ed had wondered if God heard their prayers, but He heard—and He changed their son.

When a loved one has wandered far from God, change and restoration might seem too much to hope for. If we have prayed for someone for years without seeing results, we may be tempted to lose heart and give up. But remember the story of the Prodigal Son in Luke 15:11-32. Although he left his father's home in rebellion, he came home a changed man.

If you know someone who needs change in his or her life, be diligent in prayer. Know that God hears and that it is His desire to save and restore.

Steps of Faith
Father, thank You for Your faithfulness. I entrust my loved ones to You and ask that You draw them close to You.

Deeper Walk: 2 Corinthians 5:16-21

Taking Out the Trash

My guilt overwhelms me—it is a burden too heavy to bear.
Psalm 38:4

AT CHURCH ON A RECENT SUNDAY, our pastor took the pulpit, and all eyes were on him. Expectant, we waited for him to begin his sermon.

Then we saw three deacons walking down the middle aisle of the sanctuary, each pulling a large, clean rolling trash can.

Pastor Scott began by asking if any of us were hauling around any sins—sins that we had already confessed to Jesus and repented of. The trash cans illustrated the heavy burden of carrying around sins that Jesus had already forgiven.

"He has removed our sins as far from us as the east is from the west," Pastor Scott read from Psalm 103:12. "'I—yes, I alone—will blot out your sins for my own sake and will never think of them again,'" he continued (Isaiah 43:25). "'I have swept away your sins like a cloud. I have scattered your offenses like the morning mist. Oh, return to me, for I have paid the price to set you free,'" he finished (Isaiah 44:22).

The image of the trash cans really struck me. I was still carrying around sins that I had confessed to Jesus. I was living with regret over sins He had forgotten—that thing I didn't do that I should have done, that thing I said that was better left unspoken, and that sin that still makes me wince when I think of it. My garbage can was stuffed full of dirty, nasty old sin that had already been forgiven.

My daughter, your sins are forgiven, I felt God telling me.

Thank You, Jesus. I'm leaving this old trash can on the side of the road. I'm not going to let myself be weighed down by these sins that You have forgiven. Thank You for dying for me and for Your forgiveness and resurrection.

Do you have sins that you are hauling around? If you have asked His forgiveness, believe that you are forgiven. He says you are clean. Leave your trash can by the wayside and follow Him.

Steps of Faith

Jesus, thank You so much for the forgiveness of sins You accomplished for us through Your death on the cross. Help us to leave them behind, because You have.

Deeper Walk: Isaiah 43

Don't Give Up!

*Keep on loving others as long as life lasts, in order to
make certain that what you hope for will come true.*
Hebrews 6:11

WHILE GROCERY SHOPPING one Saturday, I couldn't resist stopping at a display of little ceramic pots that looked like the bottom half of a decorated Easter egg. Each came with a large soil "tablet" and a tiny packet of seeds. Longing for some sign of spring, I bought two for my windowsill.

At home I added water to the tablets, which made the soil expand. Once I'd fluffed it with a fork, I had enough dirt to fill each little container. Next I planted about half the seeds, careful to water the pots without flooding them.

For a couple of weeks, I tended those little ceramic eggs. Nothing happened. Did I plant too many seeds? Water too much or not enough? Maybe the light wasn't as good as I thought. One night I considered dumping the soil and filling each planter with jelly beans or a votive candle instead.

Amazingly, when I looked again the very next evening, I saw seven tiny sprouts where I had seen only soil the night before. Finally, the promise of spring right before my eyes! How glad I was that I had held out for one more day.

Too often my prayer life is like my experience with those pots. For years I have been praying for a loved one, and I haven't yet seen his heart soften toward God. It's easy for me to ask: Are my prayers not getting through? Are they making any difference? Can't the Lord give me a hint that *something* is happening?

I don't have all the answers, but those little plants remind me that the seeds we plant in the hearts of others through prayer and loving actions will not lie dormant indefinitely. Though I cannot see it, I am confident that the Lord is gently inviting my loved one to turn to Him. In the end, you and I cannot force anyone to come to Christ; our only responsibility is to faithfully water those seeds with prayer, loving actions, and the Good News of the gospel.

If you, too, have been longing and praying for someone you love to come to Christ, remember: The seeds that you planted may be sprouting below the surface. Leave them to God's care, knowing that He alone can bring growth and vitality to what appears fallow and lifeless.

Steps of Faith

Creator God, I praise You as the source of all life—both physical and spiritual. May I remain a faithful partner in Your saving work through my prayers and loving deeds for others.

Deeper Walk: 1 Thessalonians 5:14-18

Easter

The LORD laid on him the sins of us all.
Isaiah 53:6

WHEN I WAS A LITTLE GIRL, I loved Easter Day. My mama always bought me a new dress and new shiny shoes, usually white patent leather. Our family went to church, where we learned about Jesus' sacrifice and His resurrection.

After lunch, Daddy would hide Easter eggs—those colorful marshmallow ones that were individually wrapped in cellophane—in the yard for us (they tasted really nasty, by the way). My sister and I would race around the yard, looking under bushes, in tree forks, in the taller grass, and on the porch. After our baskets were full of those treasures, Daddy would hide them for us over and over again.

Later in life, when I gave my heart to Jesus, I also got new clothes, the "clothing of salvation" (Isaiah 61:10). No longer do I wear the "filthy rags" of my own acts of righteousness (Isaiah 64:6); *He* is my righteousness. I don't have to look for the world's cheap treasures among the bushes and the grass; I have eternal treasure because of what Jesus did on the cross.

Today, Easter has special meaning for my own little girls. Their heavenly Daddy has provided the "clothing of salvation" for them, too, through His sacrifice.

This Easter, reflect on the Cross and what Jesus did there. Because of our sin, the One who walked on water walked up the hill of Calvary, carrying our cross. The One who "measured off the heavens with his fingers" (Isaiah 40:12) allowed His hands to be pounded with nails. The One who is limitless stepped into human flesh and allowed that flesh to be beaten, broken, and hung on a cross. Through His sacrificial death and His resurrection, He has given us an eternal home, access to the Father, and a new life. Let us never take it for granted.

Steps of Faith

Jesus, thank You for what You did for us on the cross. You paid our sin debt— which we could never pay—and we are eternally grateful.

Deeper Walk: John 19

The Sword of the Spirit

*Put on salvation as your helmet, and take the sword of
the Spirit, which is the word of God.*
Ephesians 6:17

WHEN MY SON JOSH WAS A PRESCHOOLER, the latest episode of *Bibleman* seemed to play on constant repeat in our VCR (well, except when Josh replaced it with the latest VeggieTales video).

Josh loved to wear his miniature purple cape—just like Bibleman's—and run around slashing everything in sight with his foam sword. When my parents visited, Josh was waiting at the front door so that as soon as Grandpa walked in, he could engage him in battle.

As silly as my little boy's play sometimes got, those videos helped him understand why the apostle Paul referred to Scripture as the sword of the Spirit. Josh, too, could fight evil—whether the temptation to sin or to cower in fear—using the passages he learned at Sunday school, at his Christian preschool, or around the dinner table.

How often I need to remember this too! It's no kids' cartoon or fairy tale: God gave us His Word as a weapon to fight the evil one, who often harasses us by whispering, "Did God really say . . . ?" (Genesis 3:1). In fact, Scripture is the only weapon Jesus used when tempted by the devil in the wilderness—and He brandished it so successfully that Satan had to flee!

So when you're discouraged or feeling trapped today, remember that God knew you would face trouble and temptation in this world. That's why He gave us His Word. If you're not sure where to look for guidance, seek a key word in the Bible's index—or search for it online. Then use those passages just like Josh used Bibleman's sword—relentlessly and mercilessly against your foe.

Steps of Faith

Father, thank You for giving me Your Word, such a potent weapon against evil. May Your Spirit speak words of direction, encouragement, and victory through it whenever I need them today.

Deeper Walk: Matthew 4:1-11

The Gain of Giving

God bought you with a high price. So you must honor God with your body.
1 Corinthians 6:20

ELLEN SAT ACROSS FROM her college roommate in a booth at a local coffee shop, catching up about Mandy's mission trip to Guatemala.

"When I gave up my spring break to go to Guatemala, I had no idea that I would actually feel more refreshed at the end of the week than I would have if I'd gone to the beach," said Mandy.

"Well, you certainly look great," Ellen replied. "But I thought you were doing physical labor, digging for water and such. Aren't you exhausted?"

Mandy chuckled. "Well, we actually used machinery to 'dig' for the water, but, yes, it was hard work. When I wasn't involved in digging the well, I was playing with the children or walking with the women to the closest water source. So truthfully, it was an exhausting week."

Ellen looked pensively at her friend as she continued sharing. Ellen had been sensing God's call to serve a two-year missionary term after graduating college but had wondered if postponing graduate school that long would be wise. After hearing Mandy's report on her short-term mission trip, Ellen felt confirmation that the price of putting off grad school would be minimal compared to the eternal impact of obeying God's call.

"I thought I was making such a sacrifice," Mandy said as the two gathered their things to leave, "but in the end I gained more than I gave."

True sacrifice doesn't consist of self-deprivation for no purpose. Jesus showed us through His death on the cross that sacrifice costs a great deal but ultimately yields something of great value. Jesus' death, a painful and humiliating price paid by the One who owed absolutely nothing, achieved for us peace with God and eternal life.

If God is asking you to make a sacrifice for His Kingdom, you can know for certain that He will bring great gain from the price you pay.

Steps of Faith

Father, I can't always see the benefit of the sacrifice You call me to, but I can trust You to bring good from it in the end.

Deeper Walk: Philippians 2:1-11

The Guide

Lead me by your truth and teach me, for you are the God who saves me.
All day long I put my hope in you.
Psalm 25:5

WHEN WE MARRIED TWENTY YEARS AGO, Don and I went to Europe for our honeymoon. Our trip coincided with a visit to his company's headquarters in Switzerland.

We decided to map out our own trip, rent a car, and drive through the countryside, stopping at little inns along the way. No planned group trip for us!

When we landed in Frankfurt, I was immediately struck by every difference. The air smelled different. The customs were different. The language, food, money, and street layouts—all different.

We learned the hard way that if you didn't get your money converted at a bank before Friday's closing time, you were without cash for the weekend (this *was* twenty years ago). Some places wouldn't take a credit card, and no amount of pleading and flashing of the plastic could gain us access to a cash-only inn.

When ordering at a restaurant, we could only point at menu items hoping they were something we would want to eat. Loud talking and pantomimes didn't help anyone understand us. We vowed to learn to speak German and French fluently as soon as we got home.

We also got hopelessly lost a few times. No amount of logic or intellect could help us figure out the street layouts. I actually said to my husband, "We're lost! Our families will never see us again!"

We needed a guide. And in our daily lives, here on earth, we need the Guide. Our earthly currency of sin and selfishness will never gain us entry into God's Kingdom. Our logic can't help us become more Christlike. Our language of busyness and materialism is not the King's language of love and sacrifice.

Listen to God, our everlasting Guide. He is trustworthy and true, and you'll never lose your way. Depend on Jesus—our source of salvation is also our road map. He will help us navigate the confusing paths of this life until we are safely home with Him.

Steps of Faith
Lord, thank You for guiding us through this life to live with You forever.

Deeper Walk: Isaiah 58:8-12

Heart of Worry

Worry weighs a person down.
Proverbs 12:25

I FEEL LIKE A LITTLE KID, I thought to myself. *It's just a trip to the dentist.* I was very nervous about my dental checkup, mostly because I suspected I had a cavity. No one likes pain, and my checking account couldn't take a big hit either. I was tempted to fret and fear and even cancel the appointment. But that would just be avoiding the issue and risking my tooth getting even worse.

Lord, I am so anxious right now, I prayed in the waiting room. *You tell me that I'm not supposed to worry about anything, and that everything will be used for my good and Your glory. Please help me look at this from Your perspective. Remind me that You are with me and You will take care of me.*

Sure enough, I did have a cavity. But I tried to have a good attitude—I didn't complain about the cost, and I went the extra mile to be kind to the dental staff who were caring for me. Only God knows how He will use a little trial like a cavity in the grand scheme of things, but I do know that He calls me to be obedient in the little things—including not worrying about the details of life.

Worry is one of those things that we're tempted to downplay because it doesn't seem to hurt anyone or cause any trouble. Yet Jesus died for all our sins—including worry. When it surfaces, ask God to replace your fear with a deep, abiding trust in Him. Meditate on Scriptures that address your worry triggers, and live in the peace of knowing that our good, wise, infinite God loves you and cares for you. He is with you during difficult times when things may look hopeless.

Steps of Faith
Lord, calm my fears and help me live in the truth of Your promises and Your presence.

Deeper Walk: Psalm 13

Blissfully Unaware

The LORD himself watches over you!

Psalm 121:5

"THE ONLY WAY OUT OF Chicago traffic is the Rapture," joked Aimée, a youth leader, looking out the bus window at the gridlock. The teenagers who filled the bus were far less concerned with the delay or the rain. Laughing and talking with their friends, they were heading downtown for a fun activity for the day.

Assigned to help lead the trip, Aimée was sitting across the aisle from Rick, another youth leader. As she did a final check on her supplies, Aimée heard an earsplitting wail above the teenagers' chatter. It was clearly distinct from the familiar wail of emergency vehicles or the harsh drone of a storm siren. This sound was piercing. And then it clicked: the Chicago tornado sirens.

Aimée was still listening intently when she looked over at Rick. "Is that . . . ?" she said.

He gave a subtle shake of his head. "But let's stay calm until we know for sure. No need to worry everyone at the moment."

Aimée tried to play it cool, nervously waiting for the teens to notice. But aside from the casual "Hey, what is that sound?" they never did. Even as the bus made its way further into the city, with the siren echoing off the tall buildings and further distorting its unnerving wail, the teens remained blissfully unaware of what the sound indicated.

Only when they reached the destination and the staff rushed the teens into an interior hallway did they realize something was amiss. The teenagers had only ever heard traditional storm sirens and had no frame of reference for the noise designed to stand out from the everyday sirens of a city.

As everyone huddled in the concrete hallway, waiting out the worst of it, Aimée took a moment to breathe a prayer of thanks. So many times, she knew, God had watched over her—and not just from storms—when she had been unaware of His protection.

Steps of Faith

Lord, thank You for the way You protect me in life. Help me be mindful of all that You do to keep me from harm.

Deeper Walk: Psalm 18

Tears

You keep track of all my sorrows.
You have collected all my tears in your bottle.
You have recorded each one in your book.

Psalm 56:8

WE WERE BUILDING A house in a new neighborhood, and I was delighted to learn that there would be four kids next door who were all close in age to our three kids. My youngest, Andrew, and my next-door neighbor's youngest, Allen, quickly became best friends. The boys spent time playing basketball and baseball, sledding down the hill in the backyard after snowstorms, and sliding down the dirt piles on the vacant lot across the street. Andrew wore out more shoes and jeans than I could count.

Two years later, when Andrew was eight, I had to tell him that Allen and his family were moving away. I knelt by his bed, and we prayed that God would find a new friend for Andrew. He cried harder than I had ever seen him cry, and then he said, "Now I won't have anyone to play with." It broke my heart to see my sweet son so inconsolable.

Over the years, I comforted our children over things like the loss of a friend, someone's hurtful comment, the death of our beloved Doberman, and a serious relationship that didn't last.

In my own life, I've shed many tears over people's careless remarks, my own experiences with being jilted, the death of a loved one, an argument with my husband, losing my best friend to cancer, and many other painful events.

Although I have no idea how many tears I've cried, God knows. He records each one in His book. And just as He is there to record each tear that falls, someday He will be there to wipe away every tear (Revelation 21:4).

Shedding tears is part of the human experience. And whether the tears you have cried were due to deep hurt, a loss that seemed too painful to bear, or pure joy, God notices each one. The next time you doubt God's love for you, remember that the Creator of the universe—the One who created you—is keeping track of all your sorrows, and He's counting each one of your tears.

Steps of Faith

Father, You care about me so much that You know every tear I have ever shed, and You record each one. Thank You for loving me and for never leaving me.

Deeper Walk: Luke 7:36-50

A Badge of Love and Beauty

He has sent Me . . . to give them a crown of beauty instead of ashes.
Isaiah 61:1-3, HCSB

"OH, MOMMY," SAID MY DAUGHTER, "your scar looks bad. I'm so sorry." She was looking at the four-inch scar on my back from melanoma.

Several years ago my dermatologist told me to visit her every six months because I have several moles. At first I kept my appointments like clockwork, but then I got busy with my life. The months became years, and her warnings became a faded memory.

The only way to explain what happened next is God. He practically pushed me to go see her. When she saw my back, she knew right away that I had melanoma. During the surgery, her assistant kept apologizing about the big scar I would have, how they could laser it to make it look better, how her own vanity would cringe at a scar that size. But I don't see my scar as something ugly; to me, it's a badge of love and beauty, straight from God. It's a visible illustration of His love and care for me.

There is Another with scars. His hands were scarred for me, because of me. Every day, I'm touched by those badges of love on His hands and blown away by His amazing love—love greater than all my sin. His scars—scars that can't be lasered off or covered up—are also an illustration of His deep love for me.

So now, on days when I wonder if God really loves me or cares about me or even likes me, I just look at my scar and remember how He showed His love for me that day in the doctor's office. And I look at His scars and remember how He showed His love for me on the cross.

Examine your life for badges of love and beauty from the Lord. You may not have a physical scar, but if you look deep enough, you can find a rescue or a provision or a God-appointment that affected you profoundly. He can make beauty from ugliness, so look for it in the big stuff and the everyday ordinariness of your life.

Steps of Faith

Abba Father, You can make beauty out of ashes. Help us look for all the ways You show us Your love.

Deeper Walk: Isaiah 61

Crossing the Uncrossable

*The people left their camp to cross the Jordan, and the priests
who were carrying the Ark of the Covenant went ahead of them.
It was the harvest season, and the Jordan was overflowing its banks.*

Joshua 3:14-15

WE HAVE A CREEK IN OUR BACKYARD. It's about five feet wide and two feet deep, and it's usually very quiet and placid. We've seen small fish, turtles, ducks, cranes, and coyotes in its waters.

But when it storms, the water rises, and the creek becomes turbulent and angry looking. The water has spilled over the banks a few times and even came within five feet of our house once during a one-hundred-year flood.

So when I read this passage of Scripture from Joshua, I can sort of understand what the Israelites were facing. But it's easy to gloss over phrases like "overflowing its banks" (or "at flood stage" as the NIV says) when you're just reading words on a page.

Recently, a coworker showed a group of us pictures of the Jordan River "at flood stage." He said that during this time of year, the river could be up to a mile wide and twelve feet deep, and it moved very swiftly. Imagine what the Israelites saw: rushing water, deep and angry looking, as far as the eye could see. They faced an uncrossable barrier.

Why did God bring them to the Jordan River during the harvest season, when it floods? After all, they had been wandering in the desert for forty years. Surely He could have led them to the Jordan when it was easier to cross, right?

God wants to be our Deliverer. He wants to make the impossible possible, the uncrossable crossable. He wants us to follow Him, to trust Him when our need is great. Left to our own devices, we take the path *we* think is best or try to find our own solutions.

But when we see Him and trust Him as the God of the impossible, the outcomes point to Him. When we are at the end of ourselves and He delivers us, He gets the glory—not us or our own capabilities.

When you're faced with a seemingly impossible situation or circumstance, cry out to God. Trust Him and watch to see what He does.

Steps of Faith

Father, help us to step out in faith and see You as our Deliverer when we see the impossible. You are still the God of the miraculous.

Deeper Walk: Hebrews 11

The Invaluable Assistant

Whenever we have the opportunity,
we should do good to everyone—especially to those in the family of faith.
Galatians 6:10

I STOPPED BY THE BOUTIQUE AFTER work to pick up a unique gift for my precious administrative assistant. Darlene is truly a treasure—always one step ahead of me, polite and professional, and fun to work with. So when Administrative Professionals Day comes around, I try to do something special to express my appreciation to my invaluable assistant.

Just as I headed toward the cashier with Darlene's gift, I ran into Susan, a friend from church, who was browsing through the greeting cards. We chatted for a few minutes, and then I completed my purchase and left. As I got into my car and fastened my seat belt, it occurred to me that Susan serves me as an administrative assistant too. Susan doesn't work in my office; she works at my church as our children's ministry assistant. Thanks to Susan, I have the supplies I ask for each Sunday when I go into the first-grade Sunday school classroom where I teach. She orders and distributes the curriculum, mails the postcards I write to my absentees, and helps me register for training opportunities. Susan helps me succeed at my job on Sunday mornings just as Darlene does for me Monday through Friday.

I waited in my car a few more minutes until I saw Susan leave the shop. Then I headed back in to buy gifts for Susan and the other ministry assistants at church.

Administrative Professionals Day is celebrated in the United States on Wednesday during the last full week of April. If your church employs administrative or ministry assistants, prayerfully consider how you could encourage them on this special day. While your pastors may already provide a gift or special lunch, it's certainly appropriate for members of the congregation to show their thankfulness as well. After all, a church's administrative professionals really serve more than just the ministry staff. Consider giving a card or gift to thank them for their faithful service.

Steps of Faith

Father, bless those who serve our church in administrative roles. Their work is easy to overlook but necessary for the building of Your Kingdom.

Deeper Walk: 1 Corinthians 16:15-18

Not My Way

The LORD has told you what is good, and this is what he requires of you:
to do what is right, to love mercy, and to walk humbly with your God.
Micah 6:8

FROM A YOUNG AGE, I LEARNED TO BE SELF-RELIANT. When the adults in my life weren't there for me, physically or emotionally, I survived by taking care of myself. This quality was something I prided myself in for a long time because it made me feel strong and capable. When I became a Christian, though, I learned that God wanted me to trust in and depend on Him.

Surrendering my self-reliance has been one of the hardest things about my walk with Christ. Unlike Hezekiah or Jehoshaphat or others in the Bible, I have a difficult time asking God for help instead of trying to deal with my circumstances on my own.

Over the years, as God has dealt with various sins in my life, I am always brought back to this theme of self-reliance. My sins are mostly the result of me trying to handle things my way instead of looking to God—overeating to deal with my stress, procrastinating because I don't know where to start, letting resentment creep in rather than speaking the truth in love to a fellow believer. Every time I realize my sin, I come to the same crossroads of pride and humility. Will I insist on continuing to do things my way because I like being in control, or will I humble myself and admit that God's way is better? Thankfully, as I get older, God continues to sanctify me through His power, and I submit to Him more and rely on myself less.

If you're stuck in a sinful pattern, ask God to show you how His way is better and to give you the grace to repent. To truly repent of sin, we must admit we've been doing things our own way and humble ourselves before God by embracing His way. Otherwise, we'll continue going in circles rather than living victorious lives marked by God's power and freedom.

Steps of Faith

Lord, I confess that I lack the wisdom and knowledge to guide my own life, but You are trustworthy. I humble myself before You now, knowing that Your way is best.

Deeper Walk: James 4:1-10

Ready-Made

Let the children come to me. Don't stop them!
For the Kingdom of God belongs to those who are like these children.
Luke 18:16

EVER SINCE MY CHILDREN WERE YOUNGER, I assumed they would get married someday and start their own families. But when our son Ryan began dating a young woman he had known for a couple of years, Mike and I were concerned because Lisa had a three-year-old son. We talked to Ryan about some of the issues that might be involved in taking on a ready-made family. We knew that marriage can be a challenge in the best of circumstances—let alone when children are in the mix from the beginning.

Not only that, but little Lucas was deaf, so his needs were much greater than if he had been born with hearing. He could be difficult to deal with at times because he simply couldn't communicate. We put in our two cents' worth of advice, but though Ryan was still young, he was a grown man.

Though we had our concerns at the start, God made clear that Ryan and Lisa were a perfect match. As Lisa walked down the aisle, tuxedo-clad Lucas beamed from ear to ear. When the pastor pronounced the couple man and wife, Lucas stood up on the steps of the altar and threw his hands in the air to show all in attendance that he was overjoyed.

Over time, Lucas became more proficient in sign language, and Ryan learned it as well. Lisa is a wonderful young woman and a strong Christian, and Ryan is a great husband and father.

Ryan and Lisa recently celebrated their fifth anniversary, and Lucas got a cochlear implant that now allows him to hear. He adores Ryan and imitates everything he does. That sweet little boy has won a special place in our hearts, right alongside our other grandchildren. We thank God for bringing Lisa and Lucas into our lives.

Many children today are from blended families, and they might have more than the traditional two sets of grandparents—in addition to half-siblings, stepsiblings, and other relatives. If you're part of a blended family or have loved ones who are, pray that there will be unity and that God will be glorified in each relationship.

Steps of Faith

Father, be glorified in my family's relationships. Help us to be obedient to Your Word.

Deeper Walk: Luke 18:15-17

Suffering

Here on earth you will have many trials and sorrows.
John 16:33

HEATHER WAS A BRAND-NEW CHRISTIAN, and she was excited about Jesus. She had just begun reading the Bible, and I was privileged to mentor her. One morning she stopped by after dropping off her kids at school. Before I had a chance to turn off the TV in the family room, she noticed a news clip about a devastating earthquake in another country. People were still looking for survivors in the rubble.

"How awful. I'm sure glad we won't have to suffer like that," Heather said.

"What do you mean?" I asked.

"Well, we're Christians. God doesn't want us to suffer."

"Heather, God doesn't enjoy seeing us go through hard times, but Jesus does say that we will have suffering in this world."

"Really? If God is good and He loves us, why would He allow us to suffer?" she asked.

"When Adam and Eve sinned in the Garden of Eden by disobeying God, that changed things," I said. "Now we live in a fallen world, and sin, death, violence, natural disasters, wars, and disease are all part of it. Just because we're Christians doesn't mean we're immune to suffering. But in spite of all the things we may have to go through in our lives, God loves us and promises to be with us in the midst of our pain."

Some people have the mistaken impression that Christians don't have to go through difficult times. Especially in the United States, where we have so much, it can be hard to imagine the living conditions among the poorest of the poor. We don't like to think about the fact that tens of thousands of people die every day from hunger or that natural disasters can affect countless people.

But God has promised to be there with us. Isaiah 43:2 says, "When you go through deep waters, I will be with you. When you go through rivers of difficulty, you will not drown."

Steps of Faith

God, You are my "refuge and strength, always ready to help in times of trouble." Therefore, I will not be afraid (Psalm 46:1-2).

Deeper Walk: John 16:25-33

Put It to Rest

When doubts filled my mind, your comfort gave me renewed hope and cheer.
Psalm 94:19

KATIE GENTLY TURNED ONTO HER BACK. She didn't want to wake John, but she didn't want to get up. She just wanted to go back to sleep. She had been awake since 2:00 a.m., and her mind was racing. For the past hour Katie had wrestled with one worrisome thought after another. Even the smallest problems seemed to loom large in her mind during the middle of the night. She felt the urge to get up and set things right, make some necessary phone calls, balance the checkbook, and check out some information on the Internet. She recognized all of these as irrational thoughts. Still, they fired through her mind rapidly, one anxious thought after another.

Finally Katie remembered some advice she'd heard recently on a Christian radio show. The guest had talked about how Satan uses a tired and unguarded mind to set up land mines of anxiety. Katie recognized that her mind was like an exploding minefield, and she needed to follow the advice given.

Katie tried to relax her body by concentrating on her breathing. Then she began to meditate on God's character by going through the alphabet and naming one attribute of God after another: almighty, beautiful, counselor, deliverer, eternal. Dwelling on Him and resisting the urge to worry about other things, Katie finally drifted back to sleep. Her anxious thoughts had been put to rest.

The Bible says not to be anxious about anything, but to handle all our concerns with prayer. But when anxious thoughts multiply rapidly, it can be a challenge to get our minds calm enough to pray. If anxiety has been robbing you of peace often, it might be wise to consult a Christian counselor. And we all need to learn to recognize anxious thoughts so we can counteract them with truth and sound thinking.

Steps of Faith

Father, I don't want anxiety to rob me of Your peace. Help me guard my mind against anxious thoughts.

Deeper Walk: Psalm 4

Husband Appreciation Day

Love . . . does not demand its own way. It is not irritable,
and it keeps no record of being wronged.
1 Corinthians 13:4-5

SEVERAL YEARS AGO I heard about Husband Appreciation Day, a time for wives to reflect on the various ways their husbands enrich their lives. I love the idea—especially since my husband does so much that I often take for granted, such as taking care of the yard, fixing leaky faucets, and watching sappy romantic movies with me.

I was talking about this "holiday" with an acquaintance, and she said, "What about *Wife* Appreciation Day?"

Taken aback by her tone, I answered, "Wouldn't that be Sweetest Day?"

She snorted in disgust.

"Mother's Day?" I tried again.

"And *they* have Father's Day," she insisted. "Wives make huge sacrifices every day. We have responsibilities too. Many women have a job outside the home *and* a full-time job inside the home. So where's *my* kudos?"

Her give-to-get mentality stuck with me. How many times have I taken that stance in my marriage? The idea is *You do for me; I do for you. Equal. Fifty-fifty. I appreciate you—so where's my appreciation?*

It sounds fair, justifiable. But when I slip into the mentality of *I give, so you'd better pony up and do your fair share*, I do nothing to strengthen my marriage or, frankly, my relationship with God.

The give-to-get argument doesn't hold up against God's standard for love. I shudder to think what would happen if God took that mentality with me. How could I possibly equal giving an only son to die a horrible death for an enemy? Even for a friend? I can never do enough to equal God's blessings. Yet he keeps blessing—whether or not I reciprocate, and despite the unfairness. And God calls me to love my husband exactly as God loves me. With or without an official Wife Appreciation Day.

Steps of Faith

God, I know how self-centered and self-indulgent I can be—playing the mental tit-for-tat game in my marriage. May I always remember how you lavish your blessings on me. Help me do the same for my husband, whether he reciprocates or not.

Deeper Walk: 1 John 4:7-11

Salt and Light

Let your light shine before others, that they may see your
good deeds and glorify your Father in heaven.
Matthew 5:16, NIV

FINISHER MEDAL, CHECK. *Gatorade, check. Thermal blanket, check. Collapse on the ground from exhaustion, check.* Finally, Jessica stood up and began walking toward the park—and away from the finish line of the 2013 Boston Marathon.

A few minutes later, she heard a loud blast coming from where she'd just been. Though she was unsure of what it was, in the pit of her stomach she knew something bad was happening. A second blast confirmed it. Word spread quickly among the people walking along the streets, and before Jessica made it to her friend who was waiting for her a distance from the finish line, everyone around her began running in panic.

The shock and trauma Jessica felt in the coming weeks motivated her to pay more attention to world events, and she wondered if there was a way she could make a difference. When she raised the topic to members of her small group from church, she learned that one of them lived in an apartment complex that also housed several families who were refugees from Sudan.

The group prayerfully decided to have a Kidz Club on Saturdays. When they arrived at the apartment complex with games, balls, crafts, snacks, and a picture story Bible, the curious children couldn't resist. Soon, some watchful parents drew near. Over time, the group gained the trust of many of the refugee families, and God continues to bless this ministry today.

While there is unrest in every corner of the globe, you don't have to travel the world to make a difference. Be on the lookout for opportunities to pour into the lives of people right in your own backyard. Respond to these global issues by sharing God's Word with all who will listen and giving generously to those in need. Pray today that God would reveal a direction for you to take.

Steps of Faith

Dear Jesus, establish my faith so that I may boldly tell others about Your saving grace. Open my eyes to those in need. Show me how and when to give, that I may bring glory to Your name.

Deeper Walk: Ephesians 5:8

Distractions!

I am saying this for your benefit, not to place restrictions on you.
I want you to do whatever will help you serve the Lord best,
with as few distractions as possible.
1 Corinthians 7:35

MANY YEARS AGO, *Leadership Journal* ran a cartoon of Martin Luther sitting in front of a television, holding a remote control and channel surfing. The title offered the comment "If there had been television in 1517," and the punch line was Luther saying, "I ought to write down those ninety-five things I was thinking about the other day . . . naaah . . . let's see what's on the tube." The great Reformer, who is famous for writing ninety-five charges against the church and changing the landscape of Christianity by introducing Protestantism, was procrastinating so that he could watch a little more TV.

Television, video games, social media. They seem like harmless distractions, but they can be empty, time-wasting bunk. Though they may provide a mental break for the moment, when I think of all the other, more significant things I could be accomplishing, I cringe. How much healthier would I be had I taken a walk rather than channel surfed for two hours? How much face-to-face time could I have had with family and friends had I not spent hours on social media—often while sitting next to one of them? How many people did I fail to give a kind word and a smile because I was too engaged with a game app on my phone? How many conversations with God did I miss because I was busy checking how many Facebook likes I received?

When God has called us to do something Kingdom important, that's exciting! Let's commit to avoiding distractions so we don't lose out on opportunities to make a lasting difference in the world and into eternity.

Steps of Faith

Father, I am so easily distracted! When I look at what distracts me, I can't believe what I fall victim to. Make me aware of when I'm losing focus on what's truly important—and give me strength to choose wisely.

Deeper Walk: Hebrews 12:1-2

APRIL 18

"That's My Girl!"

Don't forget to do good and to share with those in need. These are the sacrifices that please God.
Hebrews 13:16

IT WAS FAMILY NIGHT AT OUR HOUSE, so I cooked something special that everyone likes. Then we all watched a movie together. The movie was funny, but I found a spiritual application in it, too. When the middle-school-aged boy in the movie was playing guitar in the school talent show, his mom beamed with pleasure from the audience, yelling, "That's my kid!"

I could relate to the feeling. How many times have I beamed with pleasure when my girls did something good? Because I want the absolute best for them, it makes my heart swell with joy when they shine at something.

So I've been watching for some "That's my girl!" moments at home. "That's my girl!" when my youngest cleaned out the dishwasher without being asked. "That's my girl!" when my oldest made an A in algebra. "That's my girl!" when they help others and volunteer at church.

I've also wondered if God ever sees "That's My girl!" moments in my own life. Do I make Him beam with pleasure? Do I make His heart joyful when I do something that He created me to do? How can I make my Father smile?

I began looking for Scripture about what pleases God. I found that without faith it is impossible to please Him (see Hebrews 11:6, ESV); that God is pleased when we do good and share (see Hebrews 13:16); and He is pleased when we grow in wisdom and knowledge of Him (see Colossians 1:9-10).

So I'm working on pleasing my Father. Through His Spirit and His strength, I want to be obedient and make Him smile. I want Him to say, "That's My girl!"

Just like an earthly parent, God is pleased when we do good things. He is pleased when we are obedient, when we do what He has created and called us to do, when we love others. Look for ways that, with His help, you can make Him smile.

Steps of Faith
Father, we long to please You. Help us to do just that.

Deeper Walk: Colossians 1:9-10

108

Raising Children of Light

Once you were full of darkness, but now you have light from the Lord.
So live as people of light!
Ephesians 5:8

PEGGY LOOKED OUT over the group of young moms and remembered her own days with five little ones. She was thankful for this opportunity to share what God had taught her about passing the baton of truth to another generation. She was also glad to be able to challenge these moms to persevere even when fatigue seemed overwhelming. She spoke with transparency.

"I was raised in a dysfunctional family dominated by divorce and alcohol abuse. Although I was a Christian when my children were born, I didn't know how to raise healthy Christ followers. So I cried out to God to teach me. And He did. He showed me it was about much more than church attendance.

"I filled our house with joyful Christian music and Bible stories, and we celebrated our holidays with a focus on Jesus. We prayed for each other and people outside our family, supported missionaries, and learned to use our abilities to serve others.

"Our home wasn't perfect, but my children understood that Christians should live differently than our culture and think differently than the world-view expressed around us."

When her time was completed, several young moms gathered around her with questions and comments. Peggy knew that God had used her to speak to their hearts.

To raise Christ followers in a world that increasingly believes anything goes and all ways lead to heaven, you need to be intentional. It requires time and planning to teach our children at home and on the road, when we go to bed and when we get up (Deuteronomy 6:7). It also takes discipline to live the Christian life before them. But this is purposeful parenting, and the rewards are eternal.

Steps of Faith

Thank You, Lord, that we don't live our lives in our own power but in the power of Jesus, who gives us His strength to do all things. Grow our children in the grace and knowledge of You.

Deeper Walk: Deuteronomy 6:4-9

Uncomfortable Evangelism

*I fully expect and hope that I will never be ashamed, but
that I will continue to be bold for Christ.*

Philippians 1:20

MY HUSBAND ONCE WENT ON a mission trip with his good friend Steve. On the long flight back, he and Steve were unable to get seats next to each other. Being resourceful, young, and gregarious, Steve told the man seated next to him, "Hey, you can either listen to me tell you about Jesus on the flight home, or you can switch seats with my friend back there in row 20." The man wasted no time gathering his stuff, and my husband and his friend were able to sit together during the flight.

We've often laughed about Steve's unorthodox tactic on that flight, but he is the kind of man who would have joyfully shared the gospel with anyone sitting next to him. He is one of those people whose default is to talk to everyone, from waitresses to homeless guys on the street, about Jesus. For him, it's never a question of whether a person wants to hear about Jesus. He operates fully from the belief that everyone needs to hear about Jesus. And his engaging personality makes him a winsome witness.

I blush to think of "bothering" a fellow airline passenger by trying to tell him or her about Jesus. I'd worry I was making the person uncomfortable. But how can I be more concerned about a little discomfort than whether someone has the joy of knowing Jesus? I have often excused my silence with the rationale that I'm just not gifted with evangelism, but gifted or not, Jesus gave the great commission to all His disciples, including you and me.

Let's face it. The gospel can be uncomfortable. It's radical and outside the box. Jesus challenges people's thinking and the lifestyles they may not want to give up. But we can't let a little discomfort keep us from obeying His call to tell others.

If you shy away from sharing about Jesus, pray for boldness and ask God to go ahead of you, preparing hearts to hear the Good News.

Steps of Faith

Lord, forgive me for being ashamed of the gospel. Show me people who need You. I am willing to be the bearer of Good News to all who need to hear it.

Deeper Walk: Luke 12:8-12

What if It Were You?

Imitate God, therefore, in everything you do, because you are his dear children.
Live a life filled with love, following the example of Christ. He loved us and
offered himself as a sacrifice for us, a pleasing aroma to God.
Ephesians 5:1-2

SHEILA HAD BEEN PRAYING all day about how to approach this conversation with her fifth grader.

"I talked to Alana's mother today. Apparently, some girls in your class are being so cruel to Alana that her parents are considering changing schools."

Sheila watched Justine bite into her toast. Sheila's heart ached for Alana. Their families had been friends since the girls were in the church nursery together.

"They call her names, send nasty notes, and are spreading lies about her," Sheila continued.

"I know," Justine said as she looked at her plate. "It's Casey and Brianna."

Sheila fought to hide her disappointment. "Justine, Alana's mom said you've been unkind lately too."

"Only a couple of times, and I didn't mean what I said to her," Justine stammered. "Casey and Brianna turn on anyone who tries to be friends with Alana."

"That is no excuse to participate in bullying. If those girls were being mean to you, wouldn't you want someone to stand up for you or tell an adult?"

"Yeah, but . . ."

"Do you think this is how Christian friends should treat each other?"

"No." Justine burst into tears. "I don't want Alana to change schools."

"Well, I think you have an apology to make. But first, let's pray about what we can do to help."

Being bullied can leave lasting scars. Sadly, it starts at a young age and can happen anywhere kids congregate, whether it's a large public school, a small Christian campus, a neighborhood, or online. As parents, we can't shield our children from all cruelty or guarantee that they won't hurt others, but we can (and should) take discussions about bullying as seriously as we do other tough talks. As we model Christlike compassion and stress the importance of kindness, our treatment of others can be presented as a reflection of the God we serve.

Steps of Faith

Lord, it breaks my heart when this unkind world rubs off on my children. Give me wisdom as I teach them to embrace compassion.

Deeper Walk: 1 Peter 3:8-9

A Picture of Grace

God decided in advance to adopt us into his own
family by bringing us to himself through Jesus Christ.
This is what he wanted to do, and it gave him great pleasure.

Ephesians 1:5

THE TWO MOMS ESCAPED the clamor of the birthday party and stepped into the kitchen to prepare cake and ice cream.

"I didn't realize Griffin was adopted until today when you told the children the story of how he came to be a part of your family," said Kara. "But your two older children aren't adopted, are they?"

"No, Mandy and Jake are our biological children," said Jenny, reaching into the freezer. "We felt God pulling our hearts toward adoption a few years after Jake was born. Griffin actually spent his first months in a Russian orphanage."

Kara noticed Jenny's eyes glistening with tears. "Are you okay?" she asked.

"Yes," said Jenny with a smile. "It's just that days like today really showcase what God did when He grafted Griffin into our family. If he hadn't been adopted from the orphanage—and many children never are—then he probably wouldn't ever have had a birthday party with cake and ice cream. More importantly, he never would've known a family's love."

Kara smiled, holding back her own tears, and said, "This birthday party just became even more fun. Let's get back out there!"

Adoption is an act of grace. When God grafted us into His family through Jesus' death, He redeemed us from slavery and made us His children and rightful heirs. Our adoption into His family changed everything for us: our spirits, our hearts, our goals, and our destination.

When a family adopts a child and showers him or her with love and acceptance, that child also experiences grace. What a wonderful way to share the gospel—to physically show that child and others the redeeming power of God's love. Whether you were adopted, are the parent of an adopted child, or have the privilege of loving an adopted child, spend some time reflecting on the changes that adoption can make in a life. Then thank God for adopting you and blessing you with all the benefits of His family.

Steps of Faith

Father, as I reflect on the act of adoption, I'm amazed by Your love and grace. Thank You for redeeming me.

Deeper Walk: Romans 8:12-17

Hope in the Midst of Heartache

Your promise revives me; it comforts me in all my troubles.
Psalm 119:50

JESSIE JOINED OUR grief support group at church after her father took his own life. I felt a connection with her because my own sister committed suicide two years before. I greeted Jessie and asked her to help me prepare coffee before the rest of the group arrived. "How have you been?" I asked.

"Some days are better than others," she answered.

"I know what you mean," I said.

"At first, I was mad at God and demanded answers from Him. But now I actually feel relief and gratitude for the fact that He's in control. That's the only way I can survive this, remembering that He's with me and He's just as much in control now as He was before my dad died," she said.

"I don't understand why my sister did what she did," I told Jessie, "and I probably never will. I used to blame myself—what if I had just called one more time? What if I had done this or that? But I've come to realize that I can't change the past. I can't change my sister's choices. But I can do something with the future and use what I've gone through to help other people and glorify God. That's why I'm here tonight, to encourage people in the truth that God doesn't leave us or forsake us, ever."

Jessie had tears in her eyes. She said, "I'm glad I'm not alone—that God is with me and that He's given me people to talk to about my loss and grief."

Those who deal with the loss of a loved one due to suicide may feel shame, bitterness, regret, guilt, and many other emotions, but they may not feel comfortable sharing their pain. If you have lost a loved one to suicide, seek out other believers who can encourage you in the healing process—whether at a support group or in meetings with a Christian counselor—and rest in God's promise to be your peace and comfort. He alone can bring healing and hope in the midst of such heartache.

Steps of Faith
Lord, thank You for being my Healer and Comforter. Please bring healing to the wounded places in my life.

Deeper Walk: 2 Corinthians 1:3-5

A Place to Heal

You must be compassionate, just as your Father is compassionate.
Luke 6:36

KIM SLIPPED INTO THE BACK PEW. God had made it clear that she'd avoided church long enough. She'd opted for trying a new church. So far her kids had been welcomed by a friendly Sunday school teacher, and several ladies had approached her to say hello. But how would they respond when they learned about her recent divorce? Would they swoop in with questions about what happened, whether the divorce was "biblical," and how hard she'd fought to save her marriage? *I'm not ready for that, God.*

Divorce hadn't been her choice. But that hadn't stopped some of her friends from pulling away when she needed them most. She was still reeling from the rejection, and the heartbreak of seeing her husband choose another woman over her and their three children.

The kids and I need a place to heal, Kim prayed silently. *Please make it clear if this is the right church for us.*

Kim opened the bulletin she'd been handed at the door. A weekly calendar caught her attention. "Wednesday, 6:30 p.m. Divorce Recovery." The time was convenient, and she would be driving by the location on her way home from work. If the church had a group like that, she at least had a chance of connecting with people who understood what she was working through. She wouldn't get that by staying home and hiding the truth. She noted the date and time of the meeting in her weekly planner, sensing that God had sent her to the right place.

Divorce affects the Christian community as much as it does the rest of the world. While God desires marriages to stay intact, the sad truth is that many end, leaving at least one spouse in a wilderness of rejection and loss. Then comes the dread of telling other believers, "I'm divorced." How can we create a refuge of healing and grace for those who desperately need it? Offer support by reaching out in friendship, resisting the temptation to judge, and welcoming the wounded as Christ welcomed you.

Steps of Faith

God, give me compassion for those who have experienced the pain of divorce. May I be an example of grace, never judgment.

Deeper Walk: Romans 12:9-13

Anointed to Lead

Lead a life worthy of your calling . . . making allowance for each other's faults because of your love. Make every effort to keep yourselves united in the Spirit.
Ephesians 4:1-3

LAST YEAR MY CHURCH MADE some changes. At my age I have difficulty adapting to change, but nevertheless, I listened to our pastors and elders as they explained their innovative ideas. I know they love the Lord, love our church, and care for the lost, so I try to respect their decisions.

I couldn't really understand why we needed to put the words to the songs up on a big screen in the front of the sanctuary. After all, the words to the songs I like are in the hymnal. And I certainly couldn't understand why we needed to sing new songs. We have plenty in the hymnal we've yet to sing. Changing the offering time to the end of the service didn't bother me, but some of my friends didn't like it. Still, I knew I should hold my tongue, pray for God to bless the leadership of my church, and respond positively.

It's been almost a year since we made those changes. Surprisingly, I like the new way of doing things even better than the old. Some of my friends are still choosing to scowl at the screen rather than sing the words displayed on it, but I'm hoping they'll come around. Meanwhile, I'm praying for our church leaders to continue leading us courageously.

While the leaders of our churches are not perfect, they do deserve our respect. When we treat our leaders with suspicion and disrespect, we draw their attention and energy away from the calling God has given them and tempt them to focus on our behavior and attitudes instead.

Such was the case with the church in Corinth and the apostle Paul. Second Corinthians displays the pain and frustration this congregation caused when they questioned Paul's motives, challenged his calling, and distrusted his efforts. With a mixture of anguish and love, Paul penned 2 Corinthians to regain their trust, exonerate himself, and get the church back on track.

Let's commit to encourage church leaders and their families.

Steps of Faith
Father, help me show the leaders of my church respect and love. Remind me to pray for them often.

Deeper Walk: 1 Peter 5:1-5

Golden Bowls

The earnest prayer of a righteous person has great power and
produces wonderful results.
James 5:16

SEVERAL YEARS AGO I was working through a Bible study on prayer and happened upon an interesting Scripture. The writer of the study pointed out that
Revelation 5:8 refers to "the prayers of God's people" as "gold bowls filled
with incense." Immediately this image resonated with me, and I decided that
I wanted to fill bowl after golden bowl in heaven with prayers for my children.

As the years have passed and my children have grown into young adults,
those prayers have become even more important to me. I feel like my hands
are tied in many ways when it comes to advising, protecting, or aiding them.
But when I'm tempted to worry, I try to pray instead.

If you were to open my kitchen cupboard, you'd find a pink sticky note
hanging noticeably from one of the shelves, just below my stack of cereal
bowls. The note simply says, "Pray." I used to take bowls from that shelf
to feed my children, but now as I take bowls down or stack them up, I am
reminded to pray for my children instead. I may not be able to serve them
by feeding them, but I can serve them for years to come by praying for them.

Our children may leave our nests, but they never leave our hearts.
Unfortunately, it's just as our children are entering the time in their lives
that presents the most opportunities for challenge, change, and trouble that
we must take our hands off and allow them to make their own decisions, find
their own way, and determine their own priorities. But just because we have
less "say" about their lives doesn't mean we have less influence.

When we pray we are petitioning the King of kings. Rather than fret about
your adult children, commit to pray for them consistently.

Steps of Faith

Father, thank You for the gift of prayer. Help me to turn my worries into
prayers so they are more powerful.

Deeper Walk: 1 Samuel 1:26-28

The Best Reward

Don't do your good deeds publicly, to be admired by others,
for you will lose the reward from your Father in heaven.
Matthew 6:1

I HAVE THE BEST JOB IN THE WORLD, in my opinion, but it comes with few accolades. God has called me to be a stay-at-home mom, and I know He is pleased with my work, though most of what I do is unseen and unrecognized by others. I rarely get thanks for the clean underwear that appears in our drawers or for the vacuumed floor. I don't get Employee of the Month awards for kissing boo-boos, or salary raises for teaching Bible verses to my children and training them up in the ways of the Lord.

When I serve in various charitable organizations and ministries, it's a different story. I am recognized and thanked often, and it feels good. It feels so good that I realized recently that the attention I was getting had begun to drive my decisions about what I should be involved in. Because I didn't want to say no to new opportunities, I became overcommitted. For a woman whose job is her home and family, laundry and dishes weren't getting done, I was irritable with my children, and I had little time for my husband. After praying about where the Lord wanted me to serve, I relinquished some of my volunteer positions and the glory that went with them. I had to make tough decisions and disappoint people, but I'm far more blessed knowing I'm pleasing the Lord than I am getting value and recognition from others.

Prayerfully evaluate the commitments you've made to worthy causes. Are you doing any of them because they give you recognition or a sense of value? Jesus taught in Matthew 6:1-4 that we shouldn't practice our acts of righteousness to be seen by people. We need to safeguard our hearts against the pride that can creep in with well-meaning praise from others. Jesus wants us to serve with humble spirits, with hearts that want to please Him.

Steps of Faith

Lord, help me have a humble heart that pleases You. I pray that one day I'll hear You say, "Well done, good and faithful servant!" (Matthew 25:21, NIV).

Deeper Walk: Proverbs 16:19; 29:23

A Crown

*[Jesus] sat down, called the twelve disciples over to him,
and said, "Whoever wants to be first must take
last place and be the servant of everyone else."*

Mark 9:35

MY COWORKER Jill and her husband, Ed, are going through a difficult time. They're caring for Ed's mother, Audrey, who has Alzheimer's. Jill told me about some of the challenges they face each day and how tiring it is being a caregiver. But she wasn't complaining; she was just stating the facts.

Their daily routine includes getting Audrey up in the morning and trying to keep her focused long enough to dress herself properly. Then Jill and Ed drop her off at adult day care so they can go to work at their respective jobs.

Long after most people have retired for the night, Jill and Ed may still be trying to get Audrey into bed. Even after Audrey falls asleep, she may wake up several times before morning. Jill and Ed take turns getting up during the night to take Audrey to and from the bathroom, and sometimes they have to change her sheets in the middle of the night.

As I listened to this sweet, godly woman tell me what her days and nights are like, I was humbled. I was not only aware of Jill's selflessness in the face of some very difficult circumstances, but I wondered if I would have the same Christlike attitude if I were in her shoes. If I had been my mother-in-law's caregiver (she also suffered from Alzheimer's), would I have handled it with such dignity and grace?

Jill said, "I love my husband, so how could I not take care of his mother? Sometimes it's really hard, but my sister keeps telling me that the Lord has a crown waiting for me in heaven."

Selflessness. It's not something we're born with—quite the opposite. We begin life thinking the world revolves around us, and some of us still struggle with that in adulthood. But if we follow Jesus' example, God will be pleased. He is faithful, and He will give us the grace we need to get through each situation.

Steps of Faith

Lord, when You call me to serve, let me do so in a way that will bring You glory. Help me see others as You see them, and remind me that my reward is not here but in heaven.

Deeper Walk: Mark 9:35-37

Pursuing God

I have tried hard to find you.
Psalm 119:10

WHEN I TAUGHT SIXTH GRADE, I was the assistant track coach at our middle school for one season. The school was in a rural area, and many kids on the team came from disadvantaged homes and even had illiterate parents. Because some of these kids had so few opportunities, winning a track race meant a great deal to them.

One eighth grader worked hard all season at the 800 meter. Toward the end of the season, I watched the lanky student run his heart out at a meet and cross the finish line first. As he came off the track, a smile the size of Texas was on his face, and tears streamed from his eyes.

He had given his all and was reaping the benefits of his dedication. He couldn't stop talking about how he "actually did it," and his joy was infectious.

When I read Psalm 119:2, "Joyful are those who obey his laws and search for him with all their hearts," and Deuteronomy 4:29, "If you search for him with all your heart and soul, you will find him," I picture that victorious young boy who gave his all. I remember the many other students who worked diligently during practices and ran so hard at meets that they were sometimes sick afterward from the exertion. As I pursue intimacy with Jesus, I want to hold nothing back, like those passionate students on the track team.

God promises that if we earnestly seek Him, we will be rewarded. Paul compares our spiritual life and pursuit of God to running a race, and he exhorts us to run it diligently. Jesus taught that those who hunger and thirst for Him are blessed. If you feel convicted about being halfhearted in your faith, ask God today to give you a deep desire for Him.

Steps of Faith

Dear Jesus, knowing You is the best reward of all. Help me long for You so much that I can't help but seek You with all my heart.

Deeper Walk: Joshua 24:14-15

Homemade Hospitality

Keep on loving each other as brothers and sisters.
Don't forget to show hospitality to strangers.
Hebrews 13:1-2

As NICOLE WALKED INTO the produce section of the supermarket, she saw her friend Joelle from the church singles' group. "Hey, Joelle! What are you up to?"

"I'm shopping for dinner tonight. I've invited Pastor Daniels, his wife, and their kids over," Joelle explained.

"At your apartment? You're brave hosting the pastor and his family. What are you making—filet mignon?" Nicole asked, only half-joking.

"No, I'm making my famous fried chicken and mac and cheese. I'm keeping it simple, and I figured the kids will enjoy it too."

"Aren't you nervous? I mean, it is the pastor! I'd be intimidated to try to entertain for him and his family," Nicole remarked.

Joelle smiled. "You act like they're royalty or something. They're part of our church family, and I want to get to know them better. Besides, I know I don't have to meet some standard for cooking and decorating perfectly. I'm just going to be myself and share what I have. That's hospitality."

"Wow. That's awesome."

"Hey, why don't you come too?" Joelle asked. "My apartment isn't a mansion, but there's always room for one more. It would be fun and a good chance for you to get to know the Daniels family better too."

"Sure!" Nicole was excited. "I can bring dessert."

"Sounds great. See you at my place at 5:30. And bring some board games if you have them."

Hospitality focuses on serving others by meeting their needs in your own home, at your own cost. It means showing thoughtfulness as you create a welcoming environment where fellowship can flourish. No matter your situation, you can offer hospitality to others even in small ways. Just reach out to them in thankfulness for the kindness God has shown you in Christ.

Steps of Faith

God, thank You for all that I have. Help me share my home and my heart with others so that Your love can be made known in the world.

Deeper Walk: 1 Peter 4:8-11

An Embarrassing Situation

A friend is always loyal, and a brother is born to help in time of need.
Proverbs 17:17

I KNEW GOD WAS LEADING me to make the call, but I didn't want to. I didn't know what to say to someone whose house had been foreclosed. Besides, Terri and I weren't even close friends; we just knew each other from Bible study. Still, I had thought of Terri often over the past few weeks, and I'd noticed her absence from our weekly class. The fact that she had come to mind so often and that her plight had struck a tender chord with me made me believe God was urging me to give her a call, so I did.

"I'm so glad you called," Terri said with surprising eagerness. "I've been so embarrassed by our ordeal—losing the house and moving in with my parents. That's why I haven't been to Bible study lately. I just didn't want to face everyone with my shame."

"You don't have anything to be ashamed of," I countered. In my heart I knew I would probably feel the same way. But I'd never considered that Terri had been staying away from church because of that shame.

We talked for almost thirty minutes. I was sad to hear that some of Terri's better friends had contributed to her feelings of shame and embarrassment by offering unsolicited advice, chiding her for taking out an unwieldy loan, and speaking poorly of her husband. I didn't have any advice to give, nor did I know her husband, so I just listened. In the end, I think that's what Terri needed more than anything.

"Could you pick me up for Bible study next week?" asked Terri just before we got off the phone. "I think I could go if you'd walk in with me."

Whether a friend has struggled financially, lost a job, or filed for bankruptcy, consider her hurt and embarrassment. Pray for her and look for opportunities to tenderly and gently express comfort, support, and grace.

Steps of Faith
Lord, make me sensitive to the hurts of others. Show me how and when to express my concern and love.

Deeper Walk: Psalm 142

J Nanthini

Anyone who welcomes a little child like this on my behalf is welcoming me.
Matthew 18:5

I RECEIVED AN UPDATE from a child sponsorship ministry I was involved with and began reading the letter from Dinakaran, the partnership facilitator at the Compassion center in India where my sponsored child, J Nanthini, lived.

In the letter, Dinakaran said that child labor and early marriage were rampant in the area around the center. Due to poverty, girls were not valued and were even considered a liability. Many children were forced to work in factories, and some were even trafficked for sex.

But thankfully, during the school year, J Nanthini lived in a hostel for girls that was run by a Christian church. The small monthly fee I paid covered the cost of her education, nutritious meals, tutoring, medical checkups, and other basic necessities. The most important thing the children learned about was God's love and His gift of salvation through Jesus. Dinakaran reported that if it were not for the sponsorship ministry, J Nanthini and many other girls at the center would have been married very early and would not have received an education.

I had sponsored J Nanthini since she was seven years old. Now she was twenty and would soon graduate from the program.

I had mixed feelings about her graduation. I was proud of her for working hard in school and learning valuable practical and spiritual lessons. But her graduation meant she would no longer need a sponsor. I would miss exchanging letters and Bible verses with her and receiving the picture updates. I had seen her grow from a cute little girl into a beautiful young woman.

I think I was blessed even more than J Nanthini by our relationship. And when it ended, I decided I would sponsor another child.

Sponsoring a child through a Christian organization like Compassion International or Gospel for Asia is a rich and rewarding experience, for the child and for you. Prayerfully consider sponsoring a needy child.

Steps of Faith

Father, when I see someone in need, help me respond with compassion and the love of Jesus.

Deeper Walk: Matthew 18:1-5

Waiting for an Answer

The LORD is good to those who depend on him, to those who search for him.
Lamentations 3:25

ELAINE KNELT BY HER BED in the early morning light, just as she had faithfully done for many years. She always started her day with prayer and submission to God's will. This morning, however, she only stared at the familiar pattern on the comforter with an empty, lost feeling inside her.

For many months now, Elaine had been asking God to provide a job for her unemployed husband, Greg. When his company downsized, she had unwaveringly begun praying. In a way, Elaine had been excited to see how God would answer and turn their trial into good. Even though Greg had been shaken by his job loss, Elaine had not worried in those first months, confident that God would come through. Now, after eating through almost all their savings and cutting their monthly budget to bare bones, she knew they couldn't survive much longer without losing the house or going bankrupt.

Where was God? Was He hearing her daily prayers? Didn't He appreciate her faith and persistence? Why hadn't there been even one strong job lead for Greg?

Elaine had prayed for many things over the years and had witnessed God faithfully answering her. Now, God seemed so silent that Elaine was tempted to doubt He was ever going to answer. But she pushed her fears and doubts away, knowing that the very fact that she was struggling with those doubts and questions about God's character meant that she should seek Him now more than ever.

Abraham, Sarah, Moses, and Hannah were no strangers to waiting on God to answer prayers and fulfill promises. If you're in the process of waiting to hear from God, you're in good company. Take heart and know that He is good, faithful, and loving. So are His timing and purposes for you. Perhaps His delay is even stretching and refining your faith. As you wait, choose to trust and obey Him. God will bless your faith and obedience.

Steps of Faith

Father, I confess I've doubted You as I've waited for You to answer me. Renew my faith today and help me continue to seek You steadfastly.

Deeper Walk: Romans 8:24-28

A Spiritual Felon

Since our friendship with God was restored by the death of his Son while we were still his enemies, we will certainly be saved through the life of his Son.
Romans 5:10

I AM A FELON.

When I was in third grade, I forged my mother's signature on a math test that received a less-than-acceptable grade. Math was never my strongest subject, and I was probably talking through the lesson when I should have been listening to my teacher.

I was shocked when I received this bad grade and even more dismayed when I saw that it came with instructions from Mrs. Barnes (my teacher) to have my mother sign it.

My friend Lauren told me to sign it myself. So, painstakingly, I traced my mother's signature in my third-grade penmanship.

Mrs. Barnes quickly discovered my fraud, explained to me that it was called forgery, and called my mother. Boy, was I in trouble! My mother was so upset and disappointed with me. Her sadness over what I had done hurt me more than any discipline I could have ever received. And to top it off, I was so afraid the police would come to my house and escort me to jail that I hid under my bed.

A few months later, Jesus knocked on the door of my heart. Until that point in my life, I was also a spiritual felon. I understood what it meant to "hide under my bed" from God. I knew that I had been mean to my sister, that I had scraped my vegetables into the trash after being told to eat them, and that I had even forged my mother's signature. I understood that even if my mother never knew about these things (she always did!), God would still know. I couldn't hide from Him, not under my bed or in my closet or in my heart.

Even though I was God's enemy and had broken His laws, He saved me. He drew me to Himself and convicted this little felon's heart, reconciling me to Himself. Thank You, God, for Your indescribable gift.

As Jesus followers, we are no longer spiritual felons. And if you've never accepted His gift of eternal life, why don't you talk to Him about it now? He has already paid your debt and is waiting for you with open arms.

Steps of Faith
Dear Abba, thank You for paying my debt and calling me Yours.

Deeper Walk: Romans 5:6-11

Sweet Boys

God blesses those who are humble, for they will inherit the whole earth.
Matthew 5:5

AT A PARENT-TEACHER CONFERENCE for my youngest son, I rejoiced over how well he was doing in school, but I walked away just as proud of the character traits his teacher pointed out.

"The other day, one of the little girls was crying, and Nathan got up very quietly, grabbed a tissue from the box, and set it on her desk."

At that time I was suffering the ramifications of another family member's self-centeredness, and I thanked God that my son was known as tender and kind. But would Nathan's sweetness fade as the preteen years set in? I determined to nurture this side of him by setting a good example and stressing the importance of thinking beyond ourselves, presenting sensitivity and thoughtfulness as godly attributes.

Almost two years later, I flopped back on my bed, exhausted from a long week. Nathan walked in. "Are you tired?" He gave me a hug.

"Extremely," I admitted.

"You want to watch a movie?"

"Sure." I expected him to come back with one of his favorites. Instead, he brought a stack of DVDs that he knew I loved. I thanked God that my son's sensitivity seemed to be increasing even more, to the point of recognizing his mom's needs. I prayed that it would continue, not only through his childhood and teen years, but into adulthood as well.

Jesus wept with Lazarus's grieving sisters, stopped to heal the sick, and served His disciples the very night that He faced death. The apostle John set his own fear aside and stood at the foot of the cross as his beloved Teacher was crucified. The apostle Paul prayed for his friends as he sat in prison and wrote on the importance of love. Would we call any of these men of God weak? Their actions as they put others' needs above their own reflect unshakable character and reveal sensitivity as a godly quality. Parents of boys can look to such men as motivation to encourage a tender, unselfish heart, even as they try to build manly strength.

Steps of Faith

Father, thank You for providing such strong examples for us as we try to mold our boys into godly, strong, compassionate men.

Deeper Walk: Matthew 5:1-9

Blending In

*The LORD says, "I will guide you along the best pathway for your life.
I will advise you and watch over you."*
Psalm 32:8

I LEAD A SMALL GROUP OF high school girls, and one night we were discussing ways we could pray for our families. One student, Jessa, asked us to pray for the details of a special surprise she was planning for her stepmom. She was going to have a family photo taken for Mother's Day with all the kids. Jessa said the hard part was coordinating the custody schedules for herself and her siblings with those of all her stepsiblings. They were all with different parents, and she didn't know if there would be a weekend where everyone could be in the same place.

I tried not to let my surprise show as the reality of this sank in. I hadn't realized I would be ministering to kids in blended families. I hadn't considered that all of the girls came from different backgrounds that God used to shape them and bring them where they are today. I now try to be more mindful of each girl's family situation and not make assumptions about what they are dealing with. I also pray that the Spirit would make me sensitive to their needs and show me opportunities to bring God's Word to bear on their lives, right where they are.

Many children and teens are dealing with the fallout of their parents' broken marriages while also trying to adapt to a new, blended family. This combination can prove difficult, but it can also be a training ground where they learn that God is with them and loves them unconditionally. He calls His children to honor Him in all their relationships, even in difficult family circumstances. If you have the privilege of working with students, constantly point them toward the Good News of Jesus' saving love and His power to work in and through every hardship. Help equip them to live out the gospel at home by honoring God in their family relationships.

Steps of Faith
Father, help me find ways to minister to those who need help in their families.

Deeper Walk: Psalm 37:23-24

He Knows

I live with integrity. So redeem me and show me mercy.
Psalm 26:11

MEG'S EMPLOYER HAD AGREED to let her work at home one day a week, and today she was just beginning a writing assignment. It was a blessing not to have to fight the heavy traffic. She could concentrate better when she was at home, away from the office chatter and constant interruptions. Meg asked the Lord to give her wisdom and direction. She was running on fumes and needed His help.

The phone rang, interrupting her train of thought. It was her friend Carly. "I know it's your day to work at home, so can you quit early today?" she begged. "You and I haven't had a girls' day out at the mall for a while."

"I'd love to spend some time together," Meg replied. "But maybe we could try for Saturday instead."

"But you're working at home."

"Carly, my boss expects me to be on the job during the week."

"No one will know if you take off early to do a little shopping."

The offer sounded tempting. But Meg had been talking to Carly about Jesus, and Carly seemed open to hearing about Him. What kind of message would she send Carly by ditching work to go shopping?

"Even if no one at work finds out that I skipped out early, I'll know," Meg replied. "And what's more, the Lord will know."

Carly was disappointed, but she respected Meg's decision. "Okay," she said. "We'll wait until Saturday."

Computers and the Internet have made it possible to stay connected to work from your home. And while telecommuting is a great convenience, there may be temptations to take shortcuts or focus on household duties instead of the job you're being paid to do. But God expects Christians to conduct themselves in a manner that is beyond reproach. If you're telecommuting and tempted to compromise, remember that Colossians 3:23 says, "Work willingly at whatever you do, as though you were working for the Lord rather than for people."

Steps of Faith

Lord, please help me be a woman of integrity. Show me how to conduct myself in a way that brings honor and glory to You.

Deeper Walk: Psalm 84

The Queen

Search me, O God, and know my heart; test me and know
my anxious thoughts. Point out anything in me that
offends you, and lead me along the path of everlasting life.
Psalm 139:23-24

IT HAD BEEN A HEAD-ACHING, bellyaching week, and I was Queen of the Bad Attitude. When I walked into Bible study, I wanted to sit in the back and sulk.

When the teacher started reading Psalm 51, I started tuning out until she said, "I recognize my rebellion."

Rebellion. That word echoed in my brain. Was I rebellious? True, I didn't like having to work part-time now that my husband's hours had been cut back. I made sure everyone around me knew it too: my husband, kids, friends, and coworkers. I realized with a jolt that based on my behavior, my coworkers probably had no idea I was a Christian.

My relationship with the Lord had suffered; I couldn't remember the last time I'd read my Bible or prayed. I was angry and didn't want to acknowledge God. I wanted to turn my back on Him because of all I had given up to go back to work.

Acknowledging the truth felt like a punch in the gut. I wanted to turn my back on God? The Father who loves me, who gave up everything to give me life? The Son who suffered the torture of the Cross and separation from His Father because of my sins, including this rebellion? *God, help me,* I prayed.

There in the back row, this Queen of the Bad Attitude came to the King of kings with a broken and humble heart. I repented and He forgave me, just as He said He would.

Repentance isn't something we like to talk about, much less do. Besides, didn't we already do that when we became Christians? We did, but anytime we have unconfessed sin in our lives, we need to repent of it. With life's demands crowding our schedules, we can easily go through our days without spending time with the Lord or really seeing the sin in our lives.

As you read through Psalm 51, examine your heart. Be open to God's leading. If He shows you something sinful in your life, repent. Ask Him to restore to you the joy of His salvation (verse 12).

Steps of Faith
Father, I repent of my sin. May it never again come between us.

Deeper Walk: Psalm 51

Hi, Good Looking

Clothe yourselves with tenderhearted mercy,
kindness, humility, gentleness, and patience.
Colossians 3:12

CAUGHT UP IN LIVELY conversation with her friends, Julie didn't realize her husband had lagged behind. She looked back and saw Henry following several feet back on the walkway.

I'll bet his knees are hurting again, she thought.

Although she slowed her pace, her friends' children continued to skip along toward the theater. "God, help me be sensitive to Henry's need," Julie whispered.

Her friend Renee hesitated, but Julie knew everyone was anxious to get to the show. "You go on ahead with the kids," Julie said. "I'll wait for Henry. He's having trouble with his knees."

"Are you sure you don't want us to wait?" Renee asked.

"Yes, just save us seats."

Julie hated missing out on the conversation and fun of being with her friends, but she didn't want Henry to feel abandoned. She knew from experience that when his knees began to hurt, he just couldn't keep up, and he was embarrassed when people felt they had to wait for him. Julie strolled back toward him.

"Hi, Good Looking," she said.

Henry laughed. "I think Hobbling Henry would be more accurate."

"Are your knees bothering you again?"

"You don't have to wait. Go ahead. I'll find you."

"We can catch up with them together," Julie said. "I enjoy being with you."

Ministering to someone in pain means being sensitive to their needs so we can help them feel more comfortable physically, emotionally, and socially. Sometimes this requires sacrificing our own desires to accommodate their greater need. Time and again, Jesus showed compassion for those with physical ailments. He asks us to do the same. It's hard to understand how to help someone when we haven't experienced the pain ourselves, but we can seek God's wisdom and discernment about how to be more sensitive in giving assistance.

Steps of Faith

Lord, help me to be sensitive to those in physical pain. Cleanse my heart from selfishness and give me a heart to serve.

Deeper Walk: Luke 10:25-37

More than Just a Job

Seek his will in all you do, and he will show you which path to take.
Proverbs 3:6

WHEN MY COLLEGE-AGED SON needed a job, I expected his search to be difficult. While Christian had three summers of work experience, the economy had tanked, and we lived in a state with one of the highest unemployment rates in the nation. Sure enough, he requested applications only to hear, "We aren't hiring right now." Seeing his willingness to accept anything that provided a paycheck, I found myself praying that he would find not just a job but something that would be a good match for him.

One Sunday night, I attended the weekly prayer meeting at church and mentioned Christian's need for employment. "Have him call my son," one of the women said. "He's head of security at the art museum, and I know he's looking for someone."

With no experience in security, museum work, or even art for that matter, Christian gave it a shot. Not only was he hired, but he also ended up with a boss who was a believer, coworkers who became his friends, and a position that he enjoyed but never would have thought to pursue.

Seeing his employment experience unfold reminded me that God is not limited by the economy, statistics, or even our job histories. This memory continues to inspire me to trust Him more completely with my employment needs.

When we need a job and unemployment rates are high, expecting a position that we feel suited for and would enjoy seems like too much to ask. Shouldn't we be willing to settle for anything? Isn't it challenging enough to trust God to open a door when so many are pleading with Him for the exact same thing? At the same time, we know God has a specific plan for us, and He wants us to talk to Him about it. The most exciting doors seem to open when we risk praying, "Send the job that is right for me," do our part in looking, and relax in His ability to "accomplish infinitely more than we might ask or think" (Ephesians 3:20).

Steps of Faith

Heavenly Father, You know my needs. Help me trust You to point me toward a source of income that I know is from You.

Deeper Walk: Mark 11:21-24

Beyond the Wedding

A man leaves his father and mother and is joined to his wife,
and the two are united into one.

Genesis 2:24

"I'M ABOUT TO HAVE A MELTDOWN," Rachel told her sister Grace. "My dress needs more alterations and won't be ready until two days before the wedding. The florist can't get fresh tulips during the winter months, and we're already a thousand dollars over our budget. This is so stressful!"

Grace told Rachel to take a deep breath. "It's going to be okay. At the end of the day, you're going to be married to an awesome man who loves you and wants to be by your side for the rest of your life. That's what matters!"

"It's just that I've been dreaming of this day for years and want everything to be perfect," Rachel said.

"As hard as we might try, nothing is perfect this side of heaven," Grace said. "Remember what this day is really about. God is bringing the two of you together as one so that you can honor Him. Your marriage points to Him, not to you."

"You're right. It's not really about me. As much as I want it to be a beautiful day, I want it to be a day that honors God even more."

The wedding industry is big business in our culture, and often the significance of the marriage is downplayed by the glamour of the big day. While there is nothing wrong with creating a wonderful wedding experience, Christians have an opportunity to display the glory of the gospel through the wedding *and* the ensuing marriage. If you or a loved one is preparing for marriage, consider ways that Christ can be shared and glorified in the ceremony and celebration. Use the wedding as an opportunity to encourage understanding of the righteousness we receive from Christ, making us pure and spotless before the Father. Remember the reality of the promise that one day Jesus will return to take the church—which Scripture calls His bride—home to heaven to be with Him forever.

Steps of Faith

Jesus, prepare us for the day when You will come back for Your beloved. Help us live in light of that day.

Deeper Walk: Ephesians 5:15-33

God's Grace, Baby Grace

He gives us grace and glory.
Psalm 84:11

GRACE. It's a word we use to describe a ballerina's movements, the way some-one handled a situation, a girl's name, or the beautiful, undeserved gift of God.

At age thirty-eight, I was pregnant and less than thrilled about it. I felt as if I would be almost as old as Abraham's wife, Sarah, when this baby reached teenager-hood. And didn't God know that I had plans for the rest of my life? We already had one daughter, and that was enough. Wasn't it? As the months went on, my selfishness had plenty of time to grow along with my swelling belly.

Our baby girl was born right after my thirty-ninth birthday. As I looked into her sweet little face, all my anxiety, disappointment, and selfishness just melted away. I felt so humbled and ashamed of my nine-month-long bad atti-tude. Suddenly I knew that I had received an undeserved gift from the Lord, and so we named her Grace.

We don't deserve any gifts that we receive from God. Every good thing in our lives, from the very air that we breathe to our families to our salvation, is out of pure love and unmerited favor that He doesn't have to give.

Today, a few years later, I am still convinced that I didn't deserve baby Grace. And as I grow in my walk with Jesus, I know more and more every day that I don't deserve the ultimate gift of grace, His salvation. I didn't earn it, I can't work for it, and I can't pay for it. I am humbled every time I think that He didn't have to do any of it for me. It's just pure goodness from the heart of our purely good God. And I'm going to spend the rest of my life and eternity thanking Him for grace . . . and for baby Grace.

Grace is getting something we don't deserve. We receive grace every day of our lives from our Father. And we received grace when we asked Jesus to save us. Amazing!

Steps of Faith

Thank You for the unmerited favor that You bestow on us every day of our lives and for eternity. You, Lord, are always good and loving, full of grace and truth.

Deeper Walk: John 1:14-17

Not Alone

Rescue me because you are so faithful and good.
For I am poor and needy, and my heart is full of pain.
Psalm 109:21-22

I AWOKE TO LITTLE giggles as my kids brought me breakfast in bed. It was Mother's Day, and my husband did a great job of encouraging our three- and five-year-old sons to make me feel special. As we went out to the van to head to church, we saw our young neighbor, Carrie, leaving for her shift at a local restaurant. I recognized her babysitter's car and knew that her one-year-old boy wasn't going to get to spend the day with his mom because she had to work to support their family. As a single mom, she didn't have much help. Her plight weighed heavily on my heart, and I couldn't stop thinking about her when we went to worship.

After the service, I suggested we eat lunch at the restaurant where Carrie works. She took us to our table, and I told her, "Happy Mother's Day!"

For a second, she looked surprised. Then she smiled. "Jack is too little to know how to say that, so I haven't had anyone say it to me before. Thank you!"

Then I asked Carrie if Jack could come play at our house that afternoon until she got off work. "You could let your sitter go early, and then you can come have dinner with us after you get off work."

At first Carrie resisted, but I think her hunger for friends won out, and she agreed. "You need a special Mother's Day too!" I insisted.

Single moms bear so much responsibility, but one of their most painful realities is loneliness. If you know a single mom, remind her what it feels like to be loved and cared for. Show her that she is not alone; there is a God who will never leave her side. Serve her in practical ways like offering to listen, babysit, or share a family meal. Single moms, like all of us, need to know of the unfailing love of Christ, so be a friend who lives that love out.

Steps of Faith

God, You alone provide perfect love for our lonely hearts. Help us love others as You have loved us.

Deeper Walk: Psalm 118

Gossip Girl

The tongue can bring death or life;
those who love to talk will reap the consequences.
Proverbs 18:21

"EVERY DAY, MELINDA COMES home from school with another story, another morsel of information, about her friends," Sherry admitted. "I'm not sure how to handle it. How did Mom handle it with us?"

I thought for a second. How had our parents handled gossip when we were teenagers? "I just remember Mom telling me, 'If you can't say something nice, don't say anything at all,'" I said.

Sherry laughed. "Yes, the Disney approach to parenting."

As we continued to discuss Melinda's behavior, Sherry decided just to ask her why she talked about other people. Later that night, Sherry called. "First she rolled her eyes. Then she said, 'Who cares, Mom? It's just conversation.' Then she stomped off."

Apparently Melinda didn't see anything wrong with gossip because she hadn't gotten caught and so far it hadn't hurt anyone. Sherry determined to handle it in two ways: First, talk to Melinda about what the Bible says about gossip and how it is disrespectful and hurtful to others; and second, get Melinda involved as a volunteer at the food bank, giving her an opportunity to focus on others in a different way.

Over the next couple of weeks, Melinda began to see that being involved in gossip wasn't a good way to spend her time and energy. Slowly, her interests shifted to getting her friends to donate food to help local families.

Often, kids struggle with gossip and "drama" when they become internally focused and self-centered during their teenage years. Providing opportunities for growth with people in their community can help them focus on serving instead. In addition, talking with them about what the Bible has to say about gossip and the power of words will show them how our words can be used to build others up or tear others down.

Steps of Faith

Dear Lord, I pray that You would guard my speech and help me honor You. Help our family serve You in word and in deed.

Deeper Walk: James 3:5-8

Stepping Out

The LORD will personally go ahead of you. He will be with you;
he will neither fail you nor abandon you.

Deuteronomy 31:8

I WATCHED MY FIFTH-GRADER hug his teacher good-bye, and I knew from the stiffness in his shoulders that he was fighting back tears. My heart broke for him. How could I move him out of this wonderful Christian school and away from the friends he'd known since birth? What was I thinking leaving our church and the friends who had seen us through the darkest trial of our lives? We would be moving closer to family, but we were leaving a lot behind.

As soon as we got through the door of our packed-up house, my son crumpled against me, even with his grandparents and friends from church in the room.

God, is this a mistake? I prayed.

My heart knew it wasn't. I was taking a step of faith, daring to have a fresh start after more than a year of losses. I had prayed too long and hard to start second-guessing God's direction now. As much as I hated the good-byes and seeing my son sad, I knew God would bless our willingness to step out in trust.

Two months later, my son walked into a room filled with kids he had never met for his first guitar lesson. We had seen many blessings in leaving our comfort zone, and now he was taking a step of faith of his own.

When God directs us to make a major life change, it can feel as scary as crossing the Jordan River and entering a foreign land filled with hostile inhabitants. The moment we are about to take that first step forward often triggers second thoughts: *Maybe I heard God wrong. What if this turns out to be a huge mistake?* But if we have sought God and know He is pointing us toward a step of faith, we can also be assured that He will be with us in every change and adjustment. Even in our moments of fear, we will discover great rewards in our willingness to be courageous.

Steps of Faith

Lord, give me courage to follow Your direction, even when it means leaving behind everything familiar.

Deeper Walk: Deuteronomy 31:3-8

The BFFs

Share each other's burdens, and in this way obey the law of Christ.
Galatians 6:2

KATHY AND HER THREE FRIENDS CALL themselves the BFFs—Best Friends Forever. They met while serving in the children's ministry at church. Soon, they started planning family outings, service projects, fund-raisers, and family vacations together.

In 2007, Amanda, one of the BFFs, was diagnosed with cervical cancer. With a dire prognosis looming, the remaining BFFs got to work coordinating various duties—each according to her gifts. Kathy was good at arranging meals, housecleaning, and babysitting, while Sara was better at accompanying Amanda to doctor appointments. Joyce was put in charge of tracking insurance claims. This freed up Amanda's husband to be the emotional support she needed, as well as to maintain his law practice.

When the doctors ceased treating Amanda because of the cancer's growing severity, the BFFs were devastated. But they continued their support network and adapted it to fit the new reality. When Amanda died, because of her family and the BFFs, her children had memory books and a freezer full of meals.

Today, the BFFs honor Amanda often—taking the kids for an afternoon while their dad goes fishing, or celebrating their birthdays.

A crisis can bring out the best in people. You could be someone's reprieve from a burden. In this hurting world, there are abundant opportunities to serve individuals and families in crisis. Ask God to show you how He wants you to serve others in His name. He will place you where someone needs to hear the gospel through your service and your story.

Steps of Faith

Father, show me opportunities that You would like me to respond to. Give me Your supernatural discernment to know when to come alongside someone in crisis.

Deeper Walk: 1 John 3:16-18

Construction Manual

Don't use foul or abusive language. Let everything you say be good and helpful, so that your words will be an encouragement to those who hear them.
Ephesians 4:29

LAST MAY, MY HUSBAND AND I SPENT two weeks building a new railing for our second-story porch. The old one didn't meet the code and was a danger to our toddler. We aren't carpenters, but after much research and planning and many trips to the store, we completed our project. We took pictures and posted them on social media for everyone to see; we were so proud of what we had accomplished.

But it wasn't easy for us to work together on such a lengthy project. My husband would have been fine with a simple railing that went unnoticed. I, on the other hand, was disappointed when after all our work, we had not built the porch railing to shame all porch railings. With such different approaches, we certainly argued some. There were times I was tempted to lose my temper and throw some tools around, and I'm sure he felt the same. However, we finished with a safer railing and no injuries.

When tools are used correctly, they can create objects of usefulness and beauty. The Lord has been teaching me how I'm not always careful with the tool in my mouth—my tongue, which can be used to bless others or to tear them down.

We all know what we're not supposed to say, but on the flip side, there are many ways we can use our tongues to build instead of destroy. Here are just a few: Speak up for the voiceless victims of injustice (Proverbs 31:9). Sing (Psalm 13:6). Laugh (Psalm 126:2). Talk about eternal things (Colossians 3:2). Brag on God (Psalm 71:24). Lovingly confront someone who has hurt you (Matthew 18:15). Search Scripture and see what other ways you can find. Then post your list in a visible place as a reminder to use edifying speech.

Steps of Faith

Lord, I confess that I have used my speech in hurtful ways, and I repent. Teach me to use my tongue constructively.

Deeper Walk: James 3:2-12

God, Please Take Over

Give your burdens to the Lord, and he will take care of you.
He will not permit the godly to slip and fall.
Psalm 55:22

A FEW DAYS AFTER FINISHING a time-consuming step in an overwhelming process, I realized I'd made a mistake. Pointing it out would most likely mean paying more than I could afford to lose.

"Don't say anything," friends said. "They'll never know."

But I knew and God knew.

I turned to the Internet (not recommended when your mind is already creating worst-case scenarios), researching the possible ramifications of speaking up or hiding the information and getting caught. This only fueled my fears.

God, what am I going to do? I want to do what is right, but what will it cost me?

Several sleepless nights later, I had no choice but to give the situation to God. *Please take over, Lord. This feels too big for me. Show me what to do and give me peace with the outcome.*

That's when I finally accepted the answer that had been there all along: *Admit what happened. I've provided for you this far. Do you think I'll stop when you choose to do the right thing?*

When I admitted the truth, I learned that my mistake was less serious than I'd thought and would not cost me a penny. Relief flooded me. But the greatest peace came in knowing that I had handed the situation over to the only One capable of working out the details, including those details that I had messed up.

"Don't worry." We've likely heard those words since childhood, whether we grew up with God in our lives or not. We know worry doesn't help the situation, that it's unhealthy, reflects a lack of faith, and eventually proves to be a waste of time and energy. But when a legitimate concern consumes our thinking, worry seems to be second nature. Putting "Don't worry" into practice comes more easily as we turn our problems—large or small—over to our capable Lord, sensing His reassurance and realizing that our fretting does nothing but rob us of peace.

Steps of Faith

Lord, remind me that worry has never solved any problems. Help me lay my concerns at Your feet more quickly.

Deeper Walk: Philippians 4:4-7

The Widow's Might

There came a certain poor widow, and she threw in two mites,
which make a farthing.
Mark 12:42, KJV

SHE CAME INTO THE TEMPLE COMPLEX, the lowest of the low (a woman *and* a widow), the poorest of the poor. She made her way to the treasury, which was a trumpet-shaped metal offering box. She waited in line to make her gift as others with more money made a show of giving it.

Then she threw in two tiny coins, which were worth very little. Certainly not enough to make a difference to anyone.

She turned away, facing an evening with not much to eat.

But the Master was watching her. He saw what she did. And He knew—He knew that she was poor, that she was a widow, that she gave everything she had. And He talked to the disciples about all the people who had more wealth and were making large gifts. In God's math, Jesus tells us, the widow gave more than any of them because she gave out of her poverty; they gave out of their wealth. She held nothing back; they still had plenty.

I wonder: When I give, do I hold back? Do I give because I have to? Is it a duty or a privilege? An act of obligation or an act of worship? When I serve, do I look for fanfare? Do I pick the glamour jobs? Am I just as happy to change a diaper as I am to serve on the deacon-nominating committee? Do I serve out of gratitude for the Giver? When I share my talents and do what God made me to do, is it about me? Or is it about the One who gave me those talents? Am I noisy with a "look-at-me" attitude, or do I go about quietly, humbly?

I like to think that Jesus provided miraculously for this widow—that someone invited her to dinner that night, or gave her a sack of barley or a jar of oil. We're not told what happened to her, but this brief moment of her life was noticed and recorded for eternity for us to read. She dared to love God, dared to have faith that He would provide, dared to give all. May I do no less.

Steps of Faith

Father, thank You for the truths You share with us in Scripture. Thank You for noticing even the smallest acts of faith and love.

Deeper Walk: Mark 12:41-44

Stop Sin before It Starts

God is faithful. He will not allow the temptation to be more than
you can stand. . . . He will show you a way out so that you can endure.
1 Corinthians 10:13

As I THREW THE CLOTHES INTO THE DRYER, I realized things were too quiet in the rest of the house. I ran into the hallway to see what my four-year-old was doing. "Cole, you know better than that! Stop writing on the wall!" My eighteen-month-old had also used Cole's markers but on a different canvas: her shirt.

As I went to get rags and soap, I saw that our border collie puppy had left another kind of mess for me to clean up.

I felt my internal temperature rising. I was tired of spending so much time cleaning up after everyone else. I felt like yelling at the kids, the dog, or whoever crossed my path next.

Thankfully, the Holy Spirit had been working on me in this area, and I recognized that I was about to lose my temper. I counted to ten and prayed, *Lord, help me glorify You in all things—even in the way I handle a tough day.* I recited the verse I had memorized to help me deal with anger: "Be quick to listen, slow to speak, and slow to get angry. Human anger does not produce the righteousness God desires" (James 1:19-20).

I was still upset, but I was no longer at my boiling point. Instead, I was yielding control to the Holy Spirit.

When temptation knocks at the door, what is your first reaction? If you recognize the temptation and ask God to deliver you, He promises to do so (1 Corinthians 10:13). Prayerfully pinpoint your struggles and use your Bible's concordance or an online search to find verses that address those issues. Memorize several verses you can call to mind when tempted. The psalmist wrote, "I have hidden your word in my heart, that I might not sin against you" (119:11). Jesus used Scripture to resist Satan's temptations in the wilderness (Matthew 4:1-11). This shows us that our best defense against sin is to know God's Word, depend on it, and obey it.

Steps of Faith

Dear Lord, thank You for delivering me and forgiving me of my sins. Please show me areas that I struggle with and empower me to resist temptation.

Deeper Walk: Psalm 119:9-16

When God Is Silent

Point out anything in me that offends you.
Psalm 139:24

STEPHANIE OPENED HER BIBLE and began to read. She had been praying but felt her prayers were bouncing off the ceiling. In fact, for several weeks God had been strangely silent, and she wasn't getting any of the answers she had been seeking. Though there had been dry spells in the past, this period of God's silence was different. She no longer enjoyed her prayer times, and in the past few days she had forced herself to have them, something she had never experienced as a believer.

Following her reading plan, Stephanie read Psalm 139. The last verse stopped her. "Point out anything in me that offends you, and lead me along the path of everlasting life" (verse 24). *God, is there anything in me that offends You?* Before she could finish the prayer, she knew exactly what was offensive to God in her life. She and her boyfriend, Peter, had been increasingly physical. Though both of them loved the Lord, they had been giving in to temptation rather than guarding their purity. It had bothered her, but she had resisted the Holy Spirit's conviction. Her time with the Lord used to be so sweet, but after weeks of hardening her heart to the Spirit, she was finding it difficult to hear Him or sense His presence at all.

Stephanie repented and asked God to show her how to talk to Peter about reestablishing purity in their relationship.

Sometimes it's difficult to pray because we are unmotivated, experiencing difficult circumstances, or just too busy. Sometimes the Lord seems absent in order to teach us to seek after Him with more fervor. There are other times, however, when we have allowed sin to creep into our lives, and it takes precedence over God. If you're experiencing consistent silence when you pray, ask God to show you if there is anything in your life that offends Him; then repent, receive His forgiveness, and enjoy a restored relationship with the God of grace.

Steps of Faith

"Have mercy on me, O God, because of your unfailing love. Because of your great compassion, blot out the stain of my sins. Wash me clean from my guilt. Purify me from my sin" (Psalm 51:1-2).

Deeper Walk: Psalm 139

A Quiet Sanctuary

Search for the LORD and for his strength; continually seek him.
1 Chronicles 16:11

ONE SUNDAY AFTERNOON I headed out for a walk through a nearby forest preserve. As I started out on the limestone trail that circles the lake, I felt my body relax. My mind and heart, which had been on overdrive all week, felt lighter. In this place of calm, I began to pray silently as I watched prairie grasses bend and sway gently in the breeze. Tiny waves lapped the rocky shore. When I passed an inlet, I stopped to listen to a chorus of birds chirping from a small stand of trees growing along the water's edge.

Suddenly a rumble from above interrupted the symphony. I watched as a plane zoomed overhead, its engines drowning out the birdsong. No sooner had its sound faded than another plane emerged from the clouds, filling the air with a familiar rumble. Just twenty-five miles from Chicago's O'Hare Airport, the forest preserve was clearly in one of its flight paths.

Just minutes before, talking with God had seemed easy as I poured out my concerns and sensed Him bringing encouraging Scriptures to mind. Now I simply wanted to finish walking the loop around the lake and head home.

When I got to thinking about how my prayer time was cut short that afternoon, I realized it wasn't all that different from my experience when starting the day with prayer. I am easily distracted. If it's not the hum of a plane engine, it's the sudden thought of a phone call I need to return or the memory of an argument with my husband. Worse, if I don't guard my heart, my prayers can devolve into a laundry list of worries.

Like those approaching planes, my anxious thoughts so easily break the calm sanctuary the Spirit longs to establish in me. However, while I can't alter a plane's flight path, Scripture tells me I can redirect my disruptive musings. I can confess and turn my worries over to the Holy Spirit. I can pray Scripture passages that relate to a concern I have for a family member, knowing God will always fulfill His promises.

Christ is still the Good Shepherd who "lets me rest in green meadows" and who "leads me beside peaceful streams" (Psalm 23:2)—even when I'm not in a secluded (or noise-free) forest preserve.

Steps of Faith
Heavenly Father, when distractions and noise threaten to drown out Your voice today, draw me close and remind me of Your unfailing promises and love for me.

Deeper Walk: 2 Corinthians 1:20-22

Tear-Down Talk

The tongue can bring death or life;
those who love to talk will reap the consequences.
Proverbs 18:21

MY HUSBAND, SAM, AND I SANK into the restaurant booth. We rarely had lunch together, so I was looking forward to it. As we opened our menus, the women in the booth behind us grew lively.

One woman said, "You know, I have a full-time job, but I do all the housework and help the kids with homework. Barry comes home from work expecting dinner when I just got in myself. It's ridiculous!"

"My ex didn't do anything either," said another woman. "His mother coddled him even as an adult. If I asked him to load the dishwasher, he looked like he didn't know what a dishwasher was."

"If I ask Joe, he gets mad," came another voice. "He'll argue until I say, 'Forget it.'"

Just then, the server came to take their order.

Sam looked at me and said quietly, "If those guys could only hear what their wives say about them! I hope you don't talk about me that way to your friends."

I grinned. "Of course not. What could I say? Only that you're a fabulous husband and I feel sorry for all the other wives in the world."

He grinned too. "You've got that right!"

We went back to our menus, but I kept thinking about what Sam had said. Yes, I sometimes unloaded about him to my friend, Carla, but I didn't make a habit of it. Or did I? Hmm . . .

Words have the power to build up or tear down. Sometimes our conversations with friends can turn destructive, and before we know it, we are disrespecting the men we love. We forget that we once vowed to honor them 'til death do us part. Verbal bashing is not only unfair; it also displeases the Lord. Pray that He will help you tell your husband, not your friends, about what's bothering you. Pray that He will help you choose words of life instead of death.

Steps of Faith

Lord, remind me to pour out my frustrations to You. Show me how to honor my husband with my words.

Deeper Walk: James 3:3-12

The Best Gift

Listen to advice and accept instruction,
that you may gain wisdom in the future.
Proverbs 19:20, ESV

THIS BOOK LOOKS PERFECT, Claire thought as she headed for the cashier.

"Hi, Claire," her friend Kristy said as she spotted her. She glanced at the book in Claire's hand. "*Reaching the Heart of Your Teen Girl*. Getting an early start for when Lily reaches her teen years?"

"Actually, I thought I'd buy it for Melissa. I figured she could use some professional insight while she's dealing with the situation with Abby."

Kristy paused and then said, "I know you're concerned about her, but are you sure that's a good idea? Abby tried to commit suicide. Melissa is already beating herself up for not seeing the signs."

Claire felt her cheeks turn crimson. Kristy had a point. What would a book on parent/teen communication say to Melissa? Not only was she working through the devastation of Abby's choice, but her family had received some insensitive comments and intrusive questions that had made her feel worse. Melissa needed a friend, not a gift that suggested she needed some parenting advice.

Claire set the book down. "Maybe I'll give her a call instead and invite her to lunch."

"That sounds like a gift Melissa could use."

When a crisis makes family secrets and hidden problems public, the question of how to help can be complicated. It's tempting to give trite advice, probe for details, or act impulsively. Often what a hurting sister needs most are reminders that she is loved. Sometimes the best help we can offer is a listening ear, a handwritten card, or a warm casserole rather than words of wisdom. Our prayers will also help sustain them. How can you reach out to a friend this week who is living through a painful crisis?

Steps of Faith

God, I never want to hurt a friend who is already overwhelmed. Help me to be sensitive to those who are going through difficulties.

Deeper Walk: Job 2:11-13

Walking in the Word

How sweet Your word is to my taste—sweeter than honey in my mouth.
Psalm 119:103, HCSB

JEAN IS A NO-NONSENSE lady who loves God's Word. We usually meet to walk together once a week before work. Jean is a fast walker, and she makes me kick up my pace so by the time we're done, I am usually breathless and sweaty.

One morning when we met, she issued another challenge for my life: "Erica," she said, "I think we should memorize Scripture together. We can take turns picking passages and then recite them to each other when we meet the next week. That way, we'll be hiding God's Word in our hearts and holding each other accountable at the same time. What do you think?"

At first, it just sounded like one more thing to add to my to-do list. But I knew that memorizing Scripture was important, and it wasn't something I did very often. So I agreed to join my friend in this new discipline of memorizing God's Word. I quickly found that although it took a little work, the benefits were abundant!

So now every week, Jean and I huff and puff and share our verses during our walk, and many times, we share a way that God used that verse in our lives that week. I am so thankful that God showed me how much I was missing when Scripture memory wasn't a part of my life!

Many of us think that Scripture memory is just for children in church, but the truth is that we are all lifelong students of God's Word. It is a precious treasure, and He promises that if we hide it in our hearts, it will aid us in our war against sin. God's Word is also a comfort when we're facing frightening circumstances, a guide when we need His direction, and a guard for our hearts, our mouths, and our lives.

Make time to memorize God's Word, and ask your friend, spouse, or even your child to join you. It will change your life and your outlook.

Steps of Faith

Father, Your Word is a lamp and a light. Thank You for giving us Your Word to teach and guide us. Help us learn to love it more every day.

Deeper Walk: Psalm 19:9-11

Online Attacks

You have been my refuge, a place of safety when I am in distress.
Psalm 59:16

JAMIE STORMED INTO the house, eyes red and nose sniffling. She explained that after a fight with a "friend" at school, this girl had posted an unflattering picture of Jamie on her Facebook page with a cruel comment underneath.

"Everyone has seen it, and I'm so embarrassed!" Jamie sobbed.

Even though Jamie insisted I stay out of it, I wasn't about to let this bullying go unchecked. I called the girl's parents and informed them of the situation. They made their daughter remove the picture and comment, and they completely deleted her Facebook account.

To help Jamie heal, I reassured her that nothing people say or do can change her value as a child of God. I emphasized to her that true friends talk through their troubles and don't get revenge or embarrass one another. I also reminded her that although she is growing up, her dad and I are her protectors and her advocates. We will always be there for her.

In today's day and age, online bullying is becoming more prevalent. Several states are attempting legislation to address this issue, and software companies are developing anti-bullying programs. While these measures can help, parents and educators must be proactive in protecting students. Open conversation is key—making children feel they can report bullying without losing their own Internet privileges has been shown as a leading factor in reporting cyberbullying. Keeping the computer in an open area, creating your own profile on social networking sites, and having access to your kids' passwords will help you protect their online activities. Your kids might not like sacrificing their privacy, but reassure them it is for their safety. Finally, pray for your kids' relationships and online activities—God cares about them and wants to be honored in every aspect of their lives.

Steps of Faith

Dear Lord, protect my children. Give them wisdom and discernment, and help them walk with You.

Deeper Walk: Psalm 16

Wasted Time

*You must love the LORD your God with all your heart,
all your soul, and all your strength.*
Deuteronomy 6:5

RECENTLY OUR PASTOR ASKED us to write down how much time we spent on various activities each day—for example, cleaning, working, playing with the kids, praying, etc. He said that this would help us determine what we value most.

At the end of the week, I realized that I had wasted a good portion of my time doing unnecessary things. On Saturday alone, I'd spent two hours on the computer and a few more at the mall while the kids attended a birthday party. What I hadn't done much of was spending time in the Word with God. I had let time with Him be crowded out until the end of the day, and I only prayed for a few minutes before falling asleep.

On Tuesday afternoon, my six-year-old and I had planned to have some mommy-daughter time. We'd decided earlier in the week to go to the playground together. When I was ready for her after school, she told me that all the neighborhood kids were going to play a game of kickball and asked if she could join them. She'd completely forgotten about our planned time together. I acted like it was no big deal and assured her we could have girl time another day. Then I watched her run off to join her friends. As I stood by the front door watching her, it dawned on me how God may feel when I plan on spending time with Him but then do something else.

Have you ever analyzed how you use your time? Try keeping a journal for a week. Track how much time you spend doing each of your daily activities, and it will show you what your priorities are. Ask God to help you determine how to invest your time. You can start by scheduling a specific time each day to meet with your heavenly Father.

Steps of Faith

Loving Father, help me make my time with You a priority. Please forgive me for the times when I get caught up in my own activities and forget the importance of spending time with You.

Deeper Walk: 1 Samuel 12:24

I Do

She brings him good, not harm, all the days of her life.

Proverbs 31:12

"I DO." TWO LITTLE WORDS packed with layers of meaning that you unwrap as the years go by. Two little words that can be your undoing if you remain stiff-necked.

I remember the excitement of my wedding day: The man I loved also loved me and wanted to spend his life with me! That day seems like it was yesterday, but it's been several years now.

Recently I was listening to my friend Denise speak at our women's ministry lunch. Her topic? "My husband is the only person on earth I have made a vow to. When we say 'I do,' we are making a solemn promise to our husband-to-be about our commitment to him and to the marriage," she said.

God whispered to me, *This means that after Me, he is second in your life. Not your children, not your job, not your parents. Me first, him second.*

I have always been very close to my parents, Lord, I answered. *You know that. And my children are young and needy. And I love my job, Lord; You gave it to me.*

God responded, *Yes, but he needs you too. He needs your faithfulness, your steadiness, and your nurture. The world is a harsh place full of traps and snares for him. You know this.*

Yes, Lord, but I'm tired, I argued. (Imagine, arguing with the Lord!) *And I get so tired of being the cheerleader.*

I know, but I can help you. I have called you to this. And this is My plan for marriage.

When you say "I do" at the altar, you are making a solemn promise to build a God-honoring life and home with the man you are marrying. There are so many distractions that call you to put him on the back burner: children, a job, family, the house. But after God, your husband is the only person you have made a vow to, promising to love, honor, and cherish him, in sickness and in health, until death parts you.

Steps of Faith

Father, help me honor my husband and build a life with him that honors You.

Deeper Walk: Genesis 2:18-24

Unexpected Mission

*Put into action the generosity that comes from your faith as you
understand and experience all the good things we have in Christ.*
Philemon 1:6

IN MY TEENAGE YEARS, I was 100 percent certain that I would go on the mission field. I read stories of Amy Carmichael, Lottie Moon, and Annie Armstrong, women of God who gave their lives to sharing the gospel. I knew that as soon as I graduated from college and got the proper training, I, too, would be one of these women.

But God had other plans. It wasn't that my desires were wrong or that I didn't hear God properly. He just revealed that He had another path for me. A few weeks after college graduation, I married my incredible husband, a man who loves Jesus and seeks Him with his whole heart. A year later, we welcomed our first child into our family, and three other precious children followed.

My life looks a little different from what I envisioned as a teen. Instead of living in a foreign land and sharing the gospel in another language, my home is my mission field every day. I am fulfilling the great commission as I share the truth of God's Word with my little ones and point them toward Jesus, relying on the Holy Spirit to work through me to touch their hearts. It's not the mission work I planned, but I still have the opportunity every day to lay down my life to share God's love.

Some Christians are called to mission work overseas or to a formal ministry position, but we are *all* called to the mission field—whether it's our city, a foreign country, or our own home. As disciples of the Lord, we share the Good News of Christ in response to what He has done for us. Because of His death and resurrection, we live and we live abundantly.

We can't keep such good news to ourselves. Wherever God has called you to be, in whatever role He has given you, be assured that He is at work and wants to make Himself known through your life. Trust in His Holy Spirit to work through you, and get ready to watch Him do amazing things.

Steps of Faith

Lord, help me make Your name known everywhere I go.

Deeper Walk: Matthew 28:19-20

The Long Wait

Hannah was in deep anguish, crying bitterly as she prayed to the LORD.
1 Samuel 1:10

LISA FORCED A SMILE and slipped the invitation into her Bible. "Thanks, Michelle. I'll check my calendar."

She hurried to the ladies' room, where she tossed the invitation into the trash and lost her fight against tears. The bathroom door opened, and Lisa grabbed a tissue.

"Lisa?" She recognized her friend Anne's voice. "I overheard Michelle inviting you to Jessie's shower. Are you okay?"

Lisa nodded. Then she shook her head, thankful that she didn't need to explain. Anne knew about her struggle to conceive. She had rushed over to Lisa's house several days earlier when Lisa discovered once again that she wasn't pregnant after all. Anne understood why a baby shower felt like too much. She'd waited eight years to conceive her daughter.

"How did Hannah and all those other women in the Bible do it?" Lisa wiped her eyes. "I can't even handle a party invitation."

"One thing that I'm thankful for is that the Bible lets us see how hard it was. If women threw showers back then, I bet Hannah would have fought back tears at every one."

"I want to be able to celebrate with Jessie. I just know that once I get there . . ."

"We can go together if you want," Anne said. "Then if it gets too difficult, we can slip out."

"Maybe I can try." Lisa hugged Anne and thanked her. *God, help me to trust You and to be happy for other new moms*, she prayed.

What is harder than waiting month after month, year after year, to get pregnant while other women have baby showers and show off beautiful newborns? Women in the Bible like Hannah, Sarah, and Elizabeth offer hope and encouragement to those battling infertility. Whether you can relate to their pain or not, consider how you can offer support and love to a woman who is still waiting to be a mom.

Steps of Faith

Heavenly Father, help me to be sensitive to women who are struggling to conceive. Prompt me to pray as they persistently wait on You.

Deeper Walk: 1 Samuel 1:1-20

Creating a Covenant Friendship

As iron sharpens iron, so a friend sharpens a friend.
Proverbs 27:17

MOST OF MY FRIENDSHIPS DEVELOPED without much attention to the direction they were taking. Honestly, I suppose that's why, until recently, some of those friendships were characterized by things like gossip, whining, and criticizing our kids' teachers or coaches. I never meant for my friendships to be built on such petty practices; it just happened. But then I made a new kind of friend at Bible study last year.

When Sherry and I first met for lunch, we immediately found common ground, the conversation flowed easily, and I knew I'd found an easygoing, enjoyable friendship worth investing in. Soon we began meeting twice a week at the park for a walk. On our second walk, Sherry surprised me by explaining that she would like to avoid common friendship traps like gossip, criticizing others, and husband bashing. She suggested that instead we focus on encouraging one another and sharing what the Lord was doing in our lives.

I was amazed. It had never occurred to me to intentionally build a solid friendship from the ground up. Plus, I had never met anyone who was willing to be so candid about relationship boundaries, and I found Sherry's directness refreshing. Her willingness to address these issues up front made me feel valuable and accountable. Now, not only do Sherry and I have a truly golden friendship, but I have also begun taking the same steps with my other friendships, and the results have been amazing!

In 1 Samuel 18 we learn that David and Jonathan's friendship began with a covenant of loyalty and love. Right from the beginning, these two men promised to build their relationship on certain godly commitments to each other. What are your relationships with believing friends built upon? Do you bring out the best in one another? How could you begin today to build or rebuild your friendships on biblical principles? Could you bravely initiate a covenant conversation with a friend today?

Steps of Faith

Father, show me if my friendships with other believers reflect the character of Christ. Give me discernment to rebuild wisely as You direct.

Deeper Walk: 1 Samuel 18

The Right Woman

You have heard me teach things that have been confirmed by many reliable witnesses. Now teach these truths to other trustworthy people who will be able to pass them on to others.

2 Timothy 2:2

MICHELLE DROPPED HER SON off in child care and walked to her women's Bible study. But instead of feeling eager for discussion time as usual, she felt butterflies swarming in her stomach. Today she intended to put herself out on a limb and ask Beverly if she would mentor her.

Michelle poured a cup of coffee. When she got back to her chair, Beverly was there.

"Good morning, sweetie," Beverly said as she wrapped her arms around Michelle's shoulders in a familiar embrace. "How are you doing?"

After returning her older friend's warm greeting and sharing a few anecdotes about her toddler, Michelle sat down beside Beverly and took a deep breath. In her nervousness, she blurted out her question. "Beverly, will you be my mentor?"

Beverly looked stunned, then pleased, then thoughtful. She took Michelle's hand and smiled.

"I love that idea. I can't think of a reason in the world why we couldn't meet regularly and talk about the Lord and about being a mom and a wife. I'm honored that you asked. But let me pray about it for a couple of days and get back to you, okay?"

Michelle smiled and nodded. She knew she had asked the right woman.

Initiating a mentoring relationship calls for vulnerability and courage.

Titus 2:3-5 teaches that older women in the faith should invest in the lives of younger women and model a life of wisdom and purity to them.

If you are seeking a mentor, look for a woman who fits the Titus 2 qualifications: one who behaves reverently, guards her words carefully, lives free of addictive substances or habits, and capably handles the Word of God. And if you are such a woman, ask God to direct you to a younger woman in whose life you might invest.

Steps of Faith

Lord, You have commanded us to live in community, pouring our lives into one another. Show me if there is a woman with whom I should seek out that kind of relationship.

Deeper Walk: Titus 2:3-5

The Transition

Direct your children onto the right path, and
when they are older, they will not leave it.
Proverbs 22:6

BITTERSWEET FEELINGS poured through Christa as she watched members of her high school small group walk across the stage and receive their diplomas. As the group leader, Christa knew she'd have to let go of these girls when they went away to college. But still, letting go was tough.

A few days after graduation, Christa coordinated a dinner for the small group to share, kicking off their transition into college life. While talking over dinner, one member, Hannah, spoke up. "Christa, we're going to miss you so much when we go off to college. You're the most thoughtful, kind, honest, and godly leader we could've ever asked for. And we're going to miss you so much that we decided that you can't stop being our small group leader."

All the girls nodded in agreement. "Well, I can't be at five colleges at once," Christa chuckled.

"Yes, we know that." Hannah smiled. "But we can Skype together every week." Hannah went on to explain how this transition was one of the most important they would ever face, and having someone meet with them, even remotely via the Internet, would keep them all connected to each other, to church, and to God.

Christa was glad that this special group of girls that God had brought together would still be able to meet, even if it wasn't in their traditional setting. She would be able to continue investing in their lives and point them toward Jesus in a season of new beginnings. *Thank You, God, for each of these girls*, she prayed. *May You grow them into beautiful women of faith.*

Steps of Faith

Father, guide and protect the students in our church as they transition into college. Help me and others to be intentional in staying connected to them.

Deeper Walk: 1 Peter 5:1-5

Little Things

You see me when I travel and when I rest at home. You know everything I do.
Psalm 139:3

WITH MY TRAY OF FOOD IN ONE HAND, I gathered my napkin, ketchup, and a straw in the other. Then I saw the little packets of mayonnaise. They were just the right size and low fat, too.

I'd been preparing for a six-day backpacking trip on the Appalachian Trail with some friends. In our efforts to pack as lightly as possible, we had decided small packs of tuna with English muffins would be a part of our trail diet. Light, full of protein, and healthy, these simple tuna sandwiches would probably be a daily staple. But I wondered how I could stomach the tuna without mayonnaise.

Standing at the condiments counter of the fast food restaurant, I realized I'd found my answer. I filled my tray with the tiny packets and headed to the booth my husband had chosen. But as we bowed our heads and my husband thanked God for His provisions, I knew I couldn't just take the handful of mayo packets out of the restaurant. Before I began eating, I returned to the counter and asked for the manager. When I told him my story and explained my request, he smiled and said, "No problem. Help yourself. But hey, thanks for asking first."

Integrity is a huge character trait that is made up of the little things we do. The world may tell us that a little lie here and a little indiscretion there don't really have any consequences. After all, we can get away with many little things that no one ever knows about. But Psalm 139 teaches us that God is intimately aware of our every move. First Chronicles 28:9 says He even sees beyond our private actions to our hearts and minds. And just as He chose Noah, David, and Daniel based on their integrity, He is looking for women of integrity so He might give them special tasks, divine understanding, and positions of honor. Are there any little things keeping you from walking in integrity?

Steps of Faith

Father, examine my life and show me any ways in which I am dishonoring You. I want to live with integrity.

Deeper Walk: 1 Kings 9:1-5

A Public Spectacle

How can they call on him to save them unless they believe in him?
And how can they believe in him if they have never heard about him?

Romans 10:14

CHURCH IN THE PARK sounded fun, but I hesitated. We would have a full church service, complete with music and a sermon, followed by baptisms, a picnic, and activities. Everyone was encouraged to bring an extra lunch to share. To share? Did that mean I had to approach a stranger and invite her to sit down? Would passersby mock the sermon and our music? But as I saw people getting excited over the event, I knew I wanted to be part of it.

When I got to the park, I was relieved to discover a collection table for the extra lunches, which would be distributed by the pastors and volunteers who had signed up to reach out. By the end of the day, over 150 lunches had gone out to the homeless. People who heard the music stopped and accepted our invitation to stay.

As I watched a homeless couple talk with a man from church, I prayed that this creative outreach event would give them and others an attractive picture of what it meant to belong to God's family. I hoped that as they received much-needed food, they also saw evidence of changed lives and felt how deeply our church family enjoyed each other, cared about our community, and adored the Savior who loved them, too.

"We need to do this more often," several friends said. I agreed, and I'm so glad God helped me overcome the fears that almost kept me away.

How do we reach those who need to hear about Christ? This often requires us to go where the needs are. When we are willing to step out of our comfort zones and show our communities through action, "We care about you," we not only connect with those who might not enter a church otherwise, but we also shine a positive light on what it means to be a Christian. Eventually we see that making our faith public does not always require a formal event; we can display God's work in our lives on a daily basis, simply by asking Him, "How can I draw someone to You today?"

Steps of Faith

God, help me take You into my community by showing love to those who need it.

Deeper Walk: Romans 10:13-15

JUNE 5

Vicarious or Victorious?

"I know the plans I have for you"—this is the LORD's declaration—
"plans for your welfare, not for disaster, to give you a future and a hope."
Jeremiah 29:11, HCSB

I HAVE ALWAYS LOVED this particular verse, but since my daughter turned seventeen, it has taken on new significance. She is smart, beautiful, and talented, and she makes excellent choices. Lately, I've noticed that I've been bordering on the more "vicarious" side of parenting: "Have you thought about majoring in accounting?" "You should learn to play the guitar." "Can I borrow your brown pumps?" "That new boy at your work is cute. Why don't you talk to him?"

For parents, it can be so tempting to try to live *through* our children. But we need to remember that their lives are just that—*theirs*. They are a reflection of their Creator, not of us. And He has plans for their lives, just as He has plans for ours.

The decisions my daughter makes for her life are every bit as much a part of God's plans for her as the decisions I have made for mine. Because the truth is that she has her own God-given talents, abilities, likes, and dislikes, and her own God-filled future to fulfill.

In parenting an older, about-to-leave-the-nest teenager, there's a fine line between giving advice and taking over. In matters that don't put them in danger or allow them to mess up too badly, we must guide, not pressure. We must give biblical counsel, and we must teach them to seek God for what He wants them to accomplish through the plans He has for their lives.

So whenever you find yourself struggling to "let go and let God" where your children are concerned, remember: He knows the plans He has for *them*, plans for *their* welfare, plans to give *them* a future, plans to give *them* a hope. And don't forget that He has plans for our lives too, so let's live victoriously, not vicariously.

Steps of Faith
Father, thank You for the loving, personal plans You have for each one of us. Help us teach our kids to seek You and to live victoriously in Your plans.

Deeper Walk: Jeremiah 29:11-13

Meanwhile . . .

He will end their pride and all their evil works.
Isaiah 25:11

KAITLIN AROSE FROM HER KNEES, where she had been praying beside her bed. She took a tissue from her nightstand and wiped away her tears. Taking a big breath and exhaling slowly, she picked up the telephone and dialed her mother's number.

When her mother answered, Kaitlyn cried, "Mom, I'm sorry. I was disrespectful and shouldn't have said the things I said. Will you forgive me?"

"Oh, Kaitlin," her mother said softly, "you know I do. At first I was so angry I couldn't see straight! But then the Lord drew me to Himself in prayer. I was just saying 'Amen' when you called."

"That's odd," said Kaitlin. "I just finished praying too. I'll admit, at first I was telling God how angry I was with you and Dad, but then I felt Him changing my heart. By the time I got up from my knees, my heart was broken over what I had done, and I wanted desperately to make things right again."

Kaitlin's mother chuckled. "That's not odd, dear; that's God! You know that Satan is on a mission to destroy everything God has established, including our testimonies, our marriages, and our families. But we can know that God always has the upper hand. In the end, Satan will be destroyed."

"Well, meanwhile, I don't want to give the enemy even one more victory!" Kaitlyn said. "I'm so glad he didn't win this time."

In John 10:10, Jesus likened Satan to a thief that comes into a home to steal, kill, and destroy. Even though Satan cannot rob us of our salvation once we have entrusted our lives to Christ, he is still bent on destroying our testimonies, families, and churches. And he attempts to steal our joy, along with every other gift God gives. But if you're vigilant in prayer and suited up in the armor of God (Ephesians 6:10-18), you can stand your ground until the day Jesus puts an end to the enemy's treachery.

Steps of Faith

Jesus, make me aware of the enemy's schemes, and help me not to lose heart in the battle. I know the victory is Yours.

Deeper Walk: Isaiah 25:6-12

God's Plans Are Better

*Go wash seven times in the Jordan and
your flesh will be restored and you will be clean.*
2 Kings 5:10, HCSB

ANGELA WAS EXCITED about her job as a summer intern with a mission organization. She dreamed of one day going into the jungles of Africa or the mountains of Nepal and doing big things to spread the gospel. But on her first day at the center, she was assigned to clean the offices and bathrooms each morning and spend the afternoons on the telephone raising support. That night she decided to pack her bags and go home. She felt that God couldn't possibly want her to do such an ordinary job when she was willing to do so much more.

In 2 Kings 5:1-14, we read about Naaman, an army commander who had carried out raids on Israel. When he contracted leprosy, his Israelite servant girl urged him to visit the prophet of Israel to be healed. When Naaman arrived, the prophet Elisha's messenger instructed him to wash seven times in the Jordan River. Rather than follow the simple directions, Naaman became angry. Because he considered himself so highly, the ordinary instructions Elisha gave offended him and hurt his pride. But Naaman's servants convinced him to follow through. Naaman swallowed his pride, did as he was told, and was healed of his leprosy.

Naaman's pride almost prevented him from being healed by God. In the same way, our pride keeps us from acknowledging that God's plans are always better than our own. We should be humbled and grateful for any opportunity He gives us to serve Him. Remember that it is a privilege to serve God at all, and be willing to do even the most basic and unappealing job for Him.

Steps of Faith

God, I'm amazed and humbled that You would choose me. Please help me to give You praise and glory for who You are and for what You have done in my life.

Deeper Walk: 2 Kings 5:1-14

Proactive Parenting

Prepare your minds for action and exercise self-control.
1 Peter 1:13

"What am I going to do with Trey all summer?" I asked my husband, Jake. "He's full of energy and testosterone, and he's hard for me to control. The other day he was watching YouTube videos of guys skateboarding through flames and into fountains. I'm afraid that if I don't keep him busy, he'll just look for crazy things to do."

"Well, he is a fourteen-year-old boy," Jake said. "I just read an article that said that in teenagers' brains, the back regions that control sensory and motor skills develop long before the prefrontal cortex that controls judgment and impulses. Trey needs to learn to make wise choices and know his own limits. But he also needs to be carefully supervised so he doesn't try stupid stunts. You know, the community center downtown runs a summer camp for younger kids. Maybe he could volunteer there and put some of that energy to good use."

After putting in a call to the director, I took Trey to the center. As soon as we walked in, he spotted the rock-climbing wall.

"Sweet! I want to help with that!" Trey announced.

The director said that Trey could attend training classes and then help out during the summer, assisting the instructors with the children.

I felt relieved that Trey could not only harness his energy and enthusiasm, but also channel it into something beneficial.

When children hit their teenage years, the challenges we face may tempt us to get discouraged or lax in our parenting. But teens need loving, caring, involved parenting more than ever, parenting that teaches them to rely on God in their struggles. It is especially important to be proactive in giving teens safe environments and opportunities to use their energy and resources in a positive way. Ultimately, we want our children to know that no matter what stage of life they're in or what they have to offer, God has a plan for them and can use them for His glory.

Steps of Faith

Lord, give me wisdom in parenting the children You have made, and help me to point them toward You.

Deeper Walk: 2 Peter 1:5-7

A Healthy Sacrifice

I plead with you to give your bodies to God because of all he has done for you.
Let them be a living and holy sacrifice—the kind he will find acceptable.
This is truly the way to worship him.

Romans 12:1

SARAH OBSERVED HER SISTER Tammy's journey to better health with interest and joy. She had long been concerned about Tammy's extra weight, stressful lifestyle, and minimal exercise. Even when Tammy's husband was diagnosed with diabetes, she hadn't altered her poor habits. And she hadn't responded well when Sarah expressed her worries about the consequences of neglecting her health. Sarah had finally determined to stop fretting and began praying for God to work in Tammy's heart.

It wasn't long before Tammy finally decided to pursue healthy changes. Over a two-year period, she began exercising regularly and eating a more balanced diet. As her size changed and her health improved, so did her temperament. She smiled more often and took a greater interest in her relationships. Sarah continued to pray and cheered her on.

One day Tammy confided to Sarah, "God finally got my attention by reminding me that the way I treated my body was one reflection of my commitment to Him. He expects me to be a living sacrifice, holy and pleasing. I wanted that too. It hasn't been easy to break my bad habits. But making that surrender has changed my life."

Sarah smiled and breathed a prayer of thanksgiving that God had answered her.

The Bible is full of verses regarding the need for self-control in our lives. Developing that discipline is one of the keys to presenting our bodies as a living sacrifice. God is our power source, and His strength truly can work best in our weaknesses (see 2 Corinthians 12:9), whether we struggle with poor eating habits, a lack of exercise, or working too much and resting too little. But we must be willing to give Him control when we struggle. If you have health issues that need to be addressed, offer yourself to him as a "living and holy sacrifice."

Steps of Faith

Father, thank You that You are able to help us overcome our weaknesses. Show us where we are weak, and give us Your strength to make choices that are right and acceptable. We want to be holy and pleasing to You.

Deeper Walk: 1 Corinthians 3:16-17

El Roi

Have I truly seen the One who sees me?
Genesis 16:13

HAGAR WAS AT THE END OF HER ROPE. Mistreated by Sarai, she had run away into the wilderness. She was alone, exhausted, and pregnant. She collapsed by a spring feeling isolated, distressed, and insignificant. And there she met God. After that divine encounter, she called God *El Roi*, which means "The God Who Sees." (Read Hagar's story in Genesis 16 and 21.)

I have often wondered whether God sees me, my circumstances, and my cares. *God, our financial ship is sinking, and no one knows or cares. God, it's 11:30 p.m., and I'm folding laundry while everyone else sleeps. God, I cannot get everything done, but no one notices. God, I am waiting for scary test results, and I'm afraid. God, my husband is depressed, but he won't ask for help. God. God. God.*

But El Roi sees, hears, and knows. He knows our scary test results before we even get them. He sees our small bank balances and our big stacks of bills. He hears when someone slanders us. This name means He is sovereign. He knows everything about us, and He still loves us. He sees when we sin or are sinned against, and He still searches us out. He hears when we complain about all the laundry and chores, and He still blesses us.

The next time I'm in need of God's help, I'm going to my spiritual spring in the wilderness to encounter El Roi. He will meet me there when I feel insignificant and lonely, afraid and worried, and when I've sinned and been sinned against. His eyes are always on me.

Hagar learned a great truth about God: We are constantly under His watchful eye. We never go anywhere, face any situation, or do anything that He does not see. This is a huge comfort—even when we have sinned—because absolutely nothing happens that He does not see and know about. We are never invisible, never unloved by El Roi.

Steps of Faith

El Roi, thank You that You see us: every tear, every joy, every failure. You see and You care.

Deeper Walk: Genesis 16

Mrs. Kwon

Stand up in the presence of the elderly, and show respect for the aged.
Fear your God. I am the LORD.
Leviticus 19:32

"CASSIE," WENDY SAID, "there's an older lady asking for your help in the fitting room. She said you're the one who usually helps her get dressed."

I nodded. "I know exactly who you're referring to. Would you please tell her I'll be right there?"

I quickly finished rearranging the clothing rack and headed toward the fitting room. It lifted my spirits to know I'd get a chance to show Mrs. Kwon the love of Jesus by serving her again. I didn't know if she was a Christian or not, but I certainly felt God's presence whenever I helped her.

"She's waiting for you in the community fitting room. I've already brought her clothes back," Wendy said, smiling.

"Thanks so much, Wendy. I appreciate you letting me know she's here." I went to the back room and called out, "Mrs. Kwon, it's Cassie."

"Come in," Mrs. Kwon replied. "I'm so glad you're here today, Cassie." She smiled at me as I walked through the curtain. God tugged at my heart when I saw her. I could tell she'd lost some weight recently. I wondered if she was sick again, but I didn't want to ask about it unless she mentioned it first. So instead I smiled and asked her which outfit she'd like to try on first.

She pointed to the slacks she'd picked out and reached for my hand. She remained seated as we began the slow process of getting her undressed and re-dressed. As I knelt there on the fitting room floor in front of Mrs. Kwon, I prayed silently for her. I was glad that God had given me the privilege of serving this sweet lady. I felt blessed to minister to her in such a simple way.

While our culture sometimes has a tendency to disregard the elderly and downplay their value, God's Word encourages us to respect them. Ask Him what you can do to minister to the elderly today.

Steps of Faith

Father God, thank You for giving me the opportunity to serve You through helping others. Please help me to see these encounters not as a burden but as a way to bless others in Your name.

Deeper Walk: 1 Peter 4:10-11

Filling a Need

Never be lazy, but work hard and serve the Lord enthusiastically.
Romans 12:11

ALLISON PUT HER PURSE and Bible on the kitchen counter. Her husband, Jeff, took the children to change out of their Sunday clothes. She would have a few minutes to look over the church bulletin before everyone arrived at the table for lunch.

Looking through the announcements, Allison paused at an ad for a volunteer to take photographs for the church's website and publications. She'd been looking for a way to serve in her new church home, but she had never imagined she would find something so suitable. In order to stay home with her children during their preschool years, she had resigned from her job as a commercial photographer.

Although she loved being a stay-at-home mom and she often took pictures of her own family, Allison missed using her talents to benefit others. Could she use her skills in photography to fill a need in her church?

When lunch was over and the children were settled, Allison told Jeff about the ad. They agreed that the volunteer position fit her skill set and the time commitment would be something she could handle. They sensed God at work. Allison decided to call the church office the next morning to volunteer.

Paul told the people in the church in Philippi to not only look out for their own interests, but to be constantly aware of the needs around them (see Philippians 2:4). He wanted them to look for opportunities to serve. What kind of church member are you? Do you focus on what your church has to offer you, how it ministers to your needs, and how it meets your expectations? Do you complain when things go undone or when something is not done well? Or do you see the needs, problems, and shortcomings and offer to be part of the solution? Ask God to help you see opportunities instead of problems.

Steps of Faith

Father, show me how I can serve in my church. Open my eyes to opportunities so I can be a part of the solution.

Deeper Walk: Philippians 2:1-11

JUNE 13

The TDY Dilemma

Let's not merely say that we love each other;
let us show the truth by our actions.
1 John 3:18

LAURA FELT NERVOUS ABOUT hosting Stephanie and her children for dinner. She had never had a friend whose husband was in the military, much less one whose spouse was deployed. But when she met Stephanie at church and learned her husband would be overseas for a year, her heart went out to her.

After dinner, Laura and Stephanie visited in the kitchen while the children played in the family room. They had shared easy and casual conversation during dinner, but Laura wanted to know more about Stephanie's life as a military wife. So now she let the questions fly.

"I wouldn't trade our lives for anything," Stephanie finally said, after answering questions about where they'd lived, how her children handled the frequent moves, and what her husband was doing overseas. "Some days I feel like a single parent, but God has been faithful to equip me for the task. In fact, we've witnessed some of God's greatest provisions while John has been on a tour of duty, or as we say in the military, TDY."

"Is there anything we can do to help you while John is . . . TDY?" asked Laura.

"Actually," Stephanie said with a laugh, "you're doing it right now. I consider friends like you to be part of God's way of caring for us. This evening has been such a blessing."

Military spouses have the unique dilemma of being married but functioning as single parents. While deployed spouses often communicate frequently with their families via Skype, telephone, or e-mails, the ones who are left behind must shoulder the majority of family and household responsibilities on their own. These parents must help their children adapt to numerous moves, adjust to the other parent's absence, and overcome the fears that come with having a parent on active duty.

You can serve those who are serving you by praying for the families they leave behind, befriending them, and reaching out with practical assistance and companionship.

Steps of Faith
Father, help me to be more sensitive to the plight of military families. Show me how I can lend a hand.

Deeper Walk: Galatians 5:13-14

Taking Church to a Friend

I was naked, and you gave me clothing. I was sick, and
you cared for me. I was in prison, and you visited me.
Matthew 25:36

KELLY HUGGED RACHEL one more time before leaving. "I wish I could stay longer, but it's my Sunday to greet."

Rachel wiped her cheeks. "I'm sorry for falling apart like this. I just miss attending church."

Kelly squeezed Rachel's hand. "Everyone misses you." Over the past year, Rachel's health problems had grown worse. As a single woman, she relied on friends for transportation and companionship. Until recently, church had provided Rachel with a break from the isolation of home. But after two bouts with pneumonia, the doctor had ordered her to avoid public places until the latest flu bugs stopped going around.

As she drove to church, Kelly's heart ached for Rachel. She prayed, *God, help me come up with something to fill the void on Sundays for Rachel.* During the service, as she updated a few friends on Rachel's health, a plan took shape. Maybe she could bring church to Rachel.

By the end of the second service, she had two elders committed to bringing Communion to Rachel, a small group of worship team members booked to sing for her, and several ladies who wanted to visit on a regular basis.

Kelly pulled into the parking lot of Rachel's favorite Mexican restaurant and took out her cell phone. "Hey, Rachel, how about if I bring over some lunch? I have a surprise for you."

For those suffering with ongoing health problems, isolation can be as debilitating as pain, fatigue, surgeries, and medications. A fragile immune system, long recoveries, or the inability to drive can keep them away from activities, services, and connections with friends. If they can't join the church body for a time, how can we bring the body to them?

"I was sick, and you cared for me," Jesus said. Consider how you can bring Christ to someone who is chronically ill, whether through a visit, a phone call, or a team that can take church to someone who longs to be there.

Steps of Faith

Father, help me to remember those who suffer daily, and show me creative ways to reach out to them.

Deeper Walk: Matthew 25:31-46

Needing Help

This same God who takes care of me will supply all your needs from his glorious riches, which have been given to us in Christ Jesus.
Philippians 4:19

"MOM, THE LAWN MOWER doesn't work," my son Tyler informed me.

I sighed. Becoming a single mom had forced me to try many new things, but this mechanically inept woman knew nothing about lawn mowers. "I'll call someone from church."

In the months since my husband had left, my church family had jumped on board to help with everything from transportation to child care to small repairs. While I appreciated the assistance more than I could express, I wanted to do as much as possible on my own and encourage my sons to be more self-reliant. One friend suggested that I make Tyler figure out what was wrong with the mower. But was it really wise to point him toward a tool filled with gas and blades and say, "Wing it"?

God, which friend will provide the help we really need?

I immediately thought of a close friend's husband, who was handy and also understood how desperately my boys needed to learn some manly skills. He and his wife dropped by that night. It turned out that the lawn mower was officially dead, but he helped Tyler come up with a solution for cutting the grass. Afterward, he took both boys out for ice cream. Asking for help doubled as a teaching moment for one son and provided both of my sons with much-needed "guy time," showing me God's faithfulness to send the exact help I had been praying for.

The apostle Paul wasn't a single mother, of course, but he understood being in need and relying on the kindness of others. One of the first lessons that a single mom learns is that she cannot do everything by herself. Once we have learned to set aside our pride and fear of burdening our friends and family, we often begin to see blessings in our dependency—for ourselves and our children as well as for those we call on for help. Along with the relief of scratching an item off our lists, we see the truth in Paul's words that God truly does supply all our needs.

Steps of Faith

Father, thank You for knowing exactly what I need. Give me the courage to seek not just help but the right kind of help.

Deeper Walk: Philippians 4:12-20

VBS? Yes!

Anyone who welcomes a little child like this on my behalf is welcoming me.
Matthew 18:5

As BETH LOOKED AT THE mound of supplies on her kitchen table, she wondered what she had gotten herself into. When she agreed to teach the kindergarten class in her church's Vacation Bible School, she hadn't realized all the work involved. But now Beth faced the most daunting task—preparing the Bible lessons outlined in the curriculum.

Beth sat down with the curriculum guide, her Bible, and a notebook and prayed, *Lord, I know You called me to this, but I feel very overwhelmed. I could really use some reassurance.*

Beth opened the curriculum and began reading the teaching plans. The more she read, the more excited she became. As she imagined herself engaging the children through songs, games, and Bible stories, her enthusiasm grew at the prospect of telling them about Jesus.

I guess I'd forgotten why I'm doing this, Lord, she prayed. *I have the privilege of telling children about my Savior, and some of them may have never heard about Him. Thank You for this opportunity.*

Whether you're working in your church's Vacation Bible School or not, you can support this important ministry by your prayers, by encouraging those involved, or by inviting children to participate. Many church leaders would say that VBS is one of their church's most important evangelistic events. It reaches hundreds of thousands of children nationwide, many of whom do not attend church any other time.

Chances are your church or one nearby is gearing up for this important ministry or is right in the middle of carrying it out. Pray for the workers who are telling children about Jesus, and consider how you can contribute to this life-changing program.

Steps of Faith

Father, so many children need to hear about Jesus. Please use Vacation Bible Schools this summer in a mighty way to accomplish that purpose.

Deeper Walk: Matthew 18:1-6

Thanks, Dad

A faithful man will have many blessings.
Proverbs 28:20, HCSB

MY FATHER IS A GREAT DAD.

On this Father's Day, I salute you, Dad. Thank you for all you've done for me, like making sure I was fed and clothed, teaching me how to drive, sending me to college, and always, always being on my side. Thank you for the fun times, like coaching my softball team and buying me my first puppy and learning how to roller-skate with me. And thank you, Dad, for standing by me, believing in me, and supporting me every day of my life.

As a child, I watched you walk the talk. I watched you hold on to your beliefs even when others around you were following the world. I watched you serve your church in any way you could. I watched you love and support Mama, showing me what a godly marriage looks like.

Thank you, Dad, most of all for leading me to Jesus. You and Mama took me to church from the time I was born, showing me the Way, the Truth, and the Life.

I remember that when I was nine years old, you showed me the plan of salvation and introduced me to the Savior. Then you taught me what it means to walk with Jesus, day by day, through good times and hard times.

So thank you, Dad, for all you've done—from protecting to providing—and for all you've taught me—from how to do calculus to how to drive a stick shift to how to love Jesus. I can never repay you for your selfless, sacrificial, unconditional love. You brought me closer to the Father heart of God, the ultimate Father, my heavenly Father.

You may not have had an earthly father like mine. Your dad may have been absent—emotionally or physically—or he may have never told you about God. But remember: You have a heavenly Father who is crazy about you. He longs to be a Father to you. And our earthly dads and their love, though imperfect, are just a tiny mirror of our heavenly Dad's love for us.

Steps of Faith

Abba Father, thank You for our earthly dads. Be the Father that some of us have never had.

Deeper Walk: Ephesians 6:2-3

Learning to Listen

Your own ears will hear him. Right behind you a voice will say,
"This is the way you should go," whether to the right or to the left.
Isaiah 30:21

A FEW MONTHS AGO, our family went on a six-mile bike ride at a local biking trail. Leah, our youngest daughter, is seven, and she isn't great with a bicycle yet. So I was a little worried about crashes and falls.

The entire trail was an anxious ride for me. My oldest daughter was leading our pack, with my husband and me bringing up the rear. "Turn left, Leah!" "Slow down, Leah!" "Leah, tree root!" Our warnings to our little one rang out through the woods as we tried to keep her from getting hurt.

Sometimes she didn't listen, and she received a jarring bump or had a collision. One time she didn't slow down and slid on some gravel into a hairpin curve. Near the end of our ride, I screamed, "Go left!" but she kept going straight, plowing into a sign. She fell off her bike and skinned her knee because she didn't listen. I picked her up, wiped her tears, dusted her off, and hugged her.

I realized that God warns me every day when I'm about to crash into a wall of sin. He tells me to slow down when I'm rushing headlong into a hairpin curve of gossip or busyness or jealousy. He calls out, "Turn right!" when I'm about to make a big mess.

When I don't listen and have skinned my knees on sin and life, I repent. Then He reaches down, picks me up, dusts me off, and gives me a hug. He wipes my tears, reminds me of His love, and encourages me to try again.

Just like I did for my Leah.

Let's learn to listen for the voice of our Abba Father, who always looks out for us. He goes before us and behind us to protect us from the potholes and bumps that the enemy uses to make us stumble. When we obey God's leading, we are on a path away from what will harm us and are headed toward His deep blessings.

Steps of Faith

Lord, thank You for Your leading and protection. Help us to listen to and obey Your voice.

Deeper Walk: Psalm 32:8-11

Option B

The instruction of the wise is like a life-giving fountain.
Proverbs 13:14

"JULIE, I KNOW THIS IS AWKWARD," said Pastor Scott as he looked across his desk at Julie. "But I couldn't, in good conscience, let you enter into this marriage without talking with you first."

"I was afraid that's why you called," said Julie, pools of tears collecting in her eyes. "No one seems to think I should marry Jim."

The pastor handed Julie a box of tissues. She dabbed at her eyes and tried to regain her composure.

"My friends and parents are concerned because Jim's been married twice, but I don't think it's fair to hold that against him. Both of his ex-wives had problems."

Pastor Scott sat back in his chair and looked at Julie with compassion. He had watched her grow into a beautiful, competent, and godly woman. But he'd also been aware of the pain she felt as the years passed and her friends married while she remained single in her midthirties. He had been bewildered by Julie's singleness, but he also believed God had a plan for her. He hated to see that plan shipwrecked by a foolish, hasty decision.

"I think the bigger issue is Jim's lack of commitment to the Lord," Pastor Scott offered. "Let's stop and pray for guidance before we continue this conversation."

When our dreams fail to materialize, we may be tempted to take shortcuts, settle for second best, or disregard our convictions. But such a misstep may prove to be a dangerous, ungodly, foolish path.

Whether we're hungry for companionship, longing for a better career, or aching to hold a baby in our arms, we're wise to allow the Bible to shine its light on our steps. God also provides wise and caring friends who can give us perspective and wisdom. Do you need to evaluate a current decision by the illumination of God's Word and the wise counsel of friends?

Steps of Faith

Father, help me resist the temptation to take matters into my own hands when I don't see You acting fast enough. I know You are working even when I can't see it.

Deeper Walk: Proverbs 3:5-18

Queen of Confrontation

Can two people walk together without agreeing on the direction?
Amos 3:3

MICHELLE PUT TWO BOWLS OF oatmeal on the table and sat down across from her husband. "Could you pray for me to have wisdom for handling the situation in Jessica's Sunday school class?" she asked. "After the occurrence yesterday, I can't stay silent any longer."

Pete prayed for Michelle to have wisdom and courage and then asked God to bless their breakfast and the day ahead.

"I know how much you dislike confrontation," he said. "I suppose we all do. If you'd like me to handle this, I will."

Michelle considered her husband's offer. "No," she finally said. "I've developed friendships with Jessica's Sunday school teachers, and I want to honor those relationships. I want to share my concerns and hopefully see some changes in the way they handle discipline in the class, but I also want to preserve my friendship with them. I hope they will hear me without getting upset with Jessica. I don't want to hurt them either."

Pete smiled and said, "Sounds like you want good for everyone involved. You know, Michelle, if you pray for God to go ahead of you and prepare your heart for unity, I don't think you can go wrong here."

No one enjoys confrontation. But there are times, even in the church, when we must gently confront a brother, a sister, or even a spiritual leader about an injustice or mistake. When we confront with respect and love, we stand the best chance of reaching a good outcome.

If you must confront someone over a conflict or difference of opinion, pledge your commitment to the relationship, pray before approaching the person, propose a time and place to meet face-to-face, prepare yourself spiritually before meeting, permit total forgiveness, and practice love.

Steps of Faith
Father, you made Queen Esther wise and courageous so she could confront an injustice. Give me wisdom and a pure heart when I must confront others.

Deeper Walk: Esther 4:4-17

Not-So-Clear Communication

*Accept each other just as Christ has accepted you so
that God will be given glory.*

Romans 15:7

"GOOD MORNING, KAYLA," my mother-in-law said as she walked into the kitchen. My in-laws were visiting us for the week.

"Morning, Sherry," I replied, reaching for the coffeepot.

"Did Mark tell you what we're doing on Sunday?" Sherry asked. "Dale and I want to take you and the kids to Callaway Gardens for the day."

I sighed before answering her. "No, he didn't. I was hoping we could all attend the church picnic after service on Sunday."

"Oh, Mark didn't mention the picnic. It sounds like he's still not communicating very well," Sherry said.

"I don't get why he doesn't tell me things. Is it a guy thing or just a Mark thing?"

"Men do communicate differently from women, but I think it's also a Mark thing. Dale is the same way." Sherry shook her head. "I'll keep praying for you two," she said empathetically. "I know how hard it can be to deal with the differences in personality and habits of a spouse."

"Thanks, Sherry," I said as I handed her a cup of coffee and joined her on the couch. I thanked the Lord for my godly mother-in-law, and I asked Him for help understanding my husband and accepting the way He made us both unique.

Learning how to handle differences between you and your spouse can be challenging at times, but you don't have to struggle alone. Colossians 2:2 says, "I want them to be encouraged and knit together by strong ties of love."

God created each of us to be one of a kind. With that uniqueness comes a special set of challenges for both you and your spouse to not only accept one another but also appreciate the differences.

Steps of Faith

Lord God, please help me to bridge the differences in my relationships with loved ones. Teach me to be a good listener, and help me to accept others the way You have accepted me.

Deeper Walk: Colossians 2:2-3

God's Grace in the Clouds

You live under the freedom of God's grace.
Romans 6:14

LATELY, I've taken a profound interest in clouds. Puffy, fluffy, billowy white clouds or cottony swishes splashed across the sky that reflect brilliant sunbeams behind and around them. And at dusk—oh my!—the colors are magnificent. Magentas, ambers, baby blues, burgundies, silvers. It's as if the angels grabbed a box of Crayolas and decorated the heavens. Almost every evening, I walk outside, and like a five-year-old, I identify flying dragons and dogs wearing party hats.

What's most wonderful about the clouds, though, is that every day they are brand-new. There are always new shapes and colors for me to enjoy and appreciate (even the gray, dull, dreary ones). Don't like today's clouds? No problem. Tomorrow will offer a plethora of new choices. No need even to wait for tomorrow. Just wait a few minutes, and the sky will change.

Looking at clouds reminds us that God isn't a God of second chances. Woe to us if He were. God is a God of *infinite* chances. Just as those clouds change and re-form over and over, God's grace toward us is new every day, every minute.

When we need grace, we don't have to wait minutes or days for it to materialize. We have grace available to us right then—when we humbly ask for it.

I'm not sure I'll ever look at clouds without a renewed sense of hope. They point to a God who loves to creatively pour out grace on us whenever we need it, whose faithfulness to us is as certain as the sky.

Steps of Faith

God, everywhere I look, I see Your creativity and the newness You offer. Even the sky shows that You bring renewed hope and grace to me. Help me look up as often as I can.

Deeper Walk: Psalm 36:5-10

How She Does It

I have learned the secret of living in every situation,
whether it is with a full stomach or empty, with plenty or little.
Philippians 4:12

LORD, SHOW ME HOW to minister to Gina today, Sandi prayed, hoping that lunch would be a welcome break for her friend. *I don't know how she does it with her husband's health problems and the financial stress attached to it all.* Gina couldn't afford luxuries like dinner out, treats at the grocery store, or new clothes.

Help her to feel free to open up or even rant. I'm sure she needs to. Sandi knew that if she were in Gina's position, she would be completely depressed.

An hour later, Sandi sat across the table from Gina. While she was concerned about a setback in her husband's health, she didn't seem to have a single complaint about living on next to nothing.

"Be honest," Sandi said as she offered Gina more salad. "Has it been difficult to work so hard and still scrimp?"

Gina shrugged. "It's hard when the kids need something that we can't afford. But God has been so faithful to provide that I can't even complain about that. When I started recognizing how He has taken care of us, I stopped asking God to improve our finances and started asking Him to help me be content no matter what. And He has."

Sandi swallowed her embarrassment. *God, help me to follow Gina's example and learn to be content.*

We have little control over our circumstances, but we do have some say in how we face them. We can either complain and beg God for a better hand of cards or do everything in our power to be content right where we are. Paul enjoyed seasons of plenty and endured times of extreme need. Through these ups and downs, he learned to be content in all circumstances. His writing reveals no sign of playing the martyr; instead it reflects a heart that chose joy and trust in his Provider.

Steps of Faith

Lord, help me to stop wishing for improved circumstances and to start enjoying the life that I have right now. Show me Your goodness in whatever today brings.

Deeper Walk: Philippians 4:10-13

Patience Is a Virtue

Do not owe anyone anything, except to love one another,
for the one who loves another has fulfilled the law.
Romans 13:8, HCSB

TAMARA HAD FIFTEEN MINUTES to get lunch for herself and her kids. She was already running late, and since Kristin needed to use the restroom, they had to go inside the restaurant instead of going through the drive-through. Now as she stood in line, one child whining about being hungry and the other walking in circles around her, Tamara felt her pulse racing.

"Mommy, I eat?" her little one begged.

"We're getting food, sweetie," Tamara assured her gently. "You can eat soon." Meanwhile, her older child had discovered the gum ball machines.

"Mom, can I get some candy out of the machine?"

"Just stay here in line with me. We'll be at the front soon."

Tamara gazed at the cashier's fingers, hovering indecisively over each button. *Good grief!* she thought. *Why is this taking so long?*

By the time Tamara made it to the front, they had been in line twenty minutes. As she looked up, she caught the cashier looking at her apologetically. "I'm so sorry, ma'am. This is my first day."

Tamara could see how nervous he was, and her heart instantly softened. Here was an opportunity to show Jesus' love to someone who needed some encouragement.

"Every new job has a learning curve," she said with a smile. "You'll get the hang of it soon."

One of the fruits of the Spirit is love. As followers of Christ, we should be marked by a loving attitude that considers others' needs as well as our own. How did you treat the last unhelpful customer rep you spoke to? How about the repairman who was running late and didn't call? Remember that, just like you, everyone you meet is loved by God and created in His image. So the next time you're tempted to be critical, ask yourself, *How can I show this person the love and care of Jesus?*

Steps of Faith

Lord, help me to care about the people I come into contact with each day. Help me to love them with Your love.

Deeper Walk: Romans 13:8-10

Power Internalized

I take joy in doing your will, my God,
for your instructions are written on my heart.
Psalm 40:8

"YOU'VE INVESTED A LOT IN this apartment ministry," Jill said to Amanda as they cleaned up. "Don't you get discouraged when only a few women show up for Bible study?"

Amanda smiled. "I would, except that Galatians 6:9 says, 'Let's not get tired of doing what is good. At just the right time we will reap a harvest of blessing if we don't give up.'"

Jill asked, "How do you know Scripture like that? You must have a great memory."

"No," Amanda said, chuckling, "but I do memorize Scriptures. I choose a verse that speaks to my current needs, write it on an index card, and say it several times a day until I have it memorized. I have to work at it, but storing Scriptures away in my heart has paid huge dividends. It's amazing how often God has brought just the right verse to mind when I've been discouraged, tempted, or confused. You should try it."

Jill didn't respond but appeared to be contemplating Amanda's challenge.

"If you want to give it a try, we could swing by the store on the way home and get some index cards," Amanda suggested. "Then we could both pick out some verses over coffee."

"Sounds like a good plan to me," Jill replied.

While many of us feel that we can't possibly memorize Scripture, we manage to learn personal identification numbers and passwords almost daily. Don't you suppose the enemy wants us to think Scripture memory is too hard because he knows the power of the internalized Word of God? Ephesians 6:17 makes it clear that the better the grasp we have on Scripture, the more we will be able to use it effectively in victorious living. Consider memorizing one or two Bible verses each month. Choose Scriptures that are meaningful to you right now, enlist an accountability partner, and do the necessary work to hide God's Word in your heart.

Steps of Faith

Father, I know memorizing Scripture is well worth the effort. Help me to successfully store Your powerful Word in my heart.

Deeper Walk: Psalm 119:97-104

Friends

Walk with the wise and become wise; associate with fools and get in trouble.
Proverbs 13:20

MOVING IS NEVER EASY, but my husband's employer offered him a promotion and a generous relocation package, so we moved—again. Jack and I knew it would be more difficult because the kids were getting older. We hoped they would easily adjust to their schools and make friends.

Our twelve-year-old son, Michael, was laid-back about the move, but Noelle was fourteen and more emotional. Much to our relief, she began to adapt without any major meltdowns.

After we'd been in our new home for a few weeks, Noelle invited a class-mate over after school. Initially, Paige seemed nice and polite, but later I became concerned when I overheard a conversation in Noelle's room. Paige was giving graphic details about a recent date she'd had with a senior on the football team. She was also using language that never came up in my teenage years.

After dinner I told Jack about Paige's foul language and descriptive account of her "date." We prayed and asked God for wisdom, knowing that if we came down too hard on Noelle, she might rebel. Yet we needed to stand our ground and make our point about being wise in choosing her friends.

That evening Jack and I asked Noelle about Paige. She said that Paige had said some things that made her really uncomfortable, and she was going to pursue friendships with other girls who seemed to share her values. We praised God that she was already thinking about the issues that concerned us.

When our children grow more independent, we may worry about the friends they choose, and with good reason. God's Word is very clear about how much our friends can influence us. Pray that your children will make wise choices in all areas of their lives, and ask God to give you wisdom as a parent.

Steps of Faith

Father, please help me to guide my children so they can have healthy and wholesome relationships. Protect them from harm, and help them choose their friends wisely.

Deeper Walk: Proverbs 10:23; 14:7

Serving Attitude

*Do everything without complaining and arguing, so that no one
can criticize you. Live clean, innocent lives as children of God.*

Philippians 2:14-15

DANA AND HER BIBLE STUDY GROUP WERE always encouraging one another, sharing each other's burdens, and finding new and fun ways to serve in their community.

One of their favorite serving opportunities was playing with children at a local recreation center. After a few months, someone suggested broadening their service opportunities to other demographics—namely, the homeless shelter in the inner city.

The shelter needed help with serving meals, cleaning up afterward, and sorting clothing for distribution. One of those opportunities didn't sound as appealing to Dana—serving meals. But she decided to go and participate, hoping she'd be placed in the sorting room.

When the group showed up for duty on their assigned day, the volunteer coordinator called out names, giving everyone a responsibility. When Dana was assigned to the food line in the dining hall, she groaned internally. As the night wore on, Dana complained and let her annoyance show.

At the end of the night, her friend Shelley confronted her. "What was with your attitude, Dana?"

"Nothing." Dana shrugged. "I was just doing my duty."

"Well, if that's the way you serve, then maybe you shouldn't," Shelley said. "Serving is more than just showing up and trudging through. It's giving out of a spirit of grace and joy."

Dana felt a flash of anger, but she knew Shelley was right.

Have you checked your attitude lately? Are you doing good things but grumbling the whole time? Make sure you're serving in areas that tap into your God-given giftedness, and carve out time from your schedule to regularly read the Bible and pray. As you seek to fill up your heart with God's Word, He will work to refresh your heart, enabling you to serve Him with gladness.

Steps of Faith

*Father, replace my grumbling with praise. Renew my mind with Your joy as I
rely upon Your strength.*

Deeper Walk: Philippians 2:1-18

Sight Unseen

We don't look at the troubles we can see now; rather, we fix our gaze on things that cannot be seen. For the things we see now will soon be gone, but the things we cannot see will last forever.

2 Corinthians 4:18

RECENTLY, it seemed that Angie's life was being thrown into chaos—her fiancé lost his accounting job, there were managerial shake-ups at her workplace, her parents were in a car accident, and now her "check engine" light had come on.

As the engine light glowed, Angie squelched her anxious thoughts of *What else could happen?* She knew all too well that more could happen—both good and bad.

So she did the only thing she could do in rush hour traffic—turn off the music and pray. *Lord, this morning, I asked for help and direction, and now my check engine light has come on. I feel really overwhelmed right now. Please be merciful as I place my trust in You. You are my strength.*

Angie continued her prayer as she drove into the car repair shop. The mechanic looked over the car and suggested that she leave it overnight. While waiting to be picked up, Angie was surprised to hear herself telling the mechanic about the storm that seemed to be swirling around her. He perked up and told her that the mechanic shop was looking for a bookkeeper and office manager. Hopeful, Angie asked for a job description and contact information. She knew that a job for her fiancé wouldn't tie up everything in a nice little bow, but she took it as a sign that God was working, even when she didn't clearly see all the details.

Sometimes when life gets overwhelming, we focus on fixing the problems. But what if we stopped in the middle of the storm and asked God to open our spiritual eyes? What if an engine light leads you to someone who has an answer to your problem or who needs a word of encouragement? We can ask God to show us how He's working in the midst of our circumstances. Then we can serve others better, respond more peacefully, and trust more deeply.

Steps of Faith

Father, attune my heart and spiritual eyes to the unseen things You are doing. Give me discernment, and open the eyes of my heart as I seek to serve You.

Deeper Walk: Ephesians 1:15-23

Do Not Fear

Can any of you add a single cubit to his height by worrying?
Matthew 6:27, HCSB

WHEN I WAS A KID, I would fall asleep within minutes, sleep through the night, and wake up refreshed. But now that I'm a grown-up, I deal with grown-up issues, which sometimes keep me up at night. Being the editor of a magazine means that as soon as I meet one deadline, there's another one looming just ahead, and I worry that I won't have enough time for all the work I have to complete. And while it never occurred to me years ago that I would worry about my grown children, I do. My three children are all married, with jobs and children of their own, but like any mother, I am always wondering, *Are their work situations stable? Can they meet all their financial obligations? Are the grandkids okay?*

I've been a Christian for a long time, and I know God tells us not to worry, but following through is another matter. So one night, I asked the Lord to help me to trust Him more and put a stop to all the worry. The next night, my husband and I came across a program on TV about outer space. We watched with amazement as they showed things like the Sombrero Galaxy and nebulae where stars are born. We listened as the narrator talked about black holes and distance that is measured in light-years (1 = 5.9 trillion miles).

That's when it clicked. The Creator of this amazing universe, who also created me, my husband, our kids, and our grandkids—created time, space, and matter. He has everything under control. I can trust Him with my deadlines, my loved ones, and everything else in my life.

If you have a tendency to worry, stop and think about who God is and some of the incredible wonders He created. He is the One who keeps the earth spinning on its axis and tilted at exactly the right angle toward the sun, and He can keep you safe. The next time you're tempted to worry, think about the amazing God who created you in His image. Isaiah 41:13 says, "For I, Yahweh your God, hold your right hand and say to you: Do not fear, I will help you" (HCSB).

Steps of Faith

Lord, You said that I shouldn't worry about anything, but in everything, through prayer and petition, with thanksgiving, I should make my requests known to You. Then Your peace, which surpasses every thought, will guard my heart and mind in Christ Jesus (Philippians 4:6-7, HCSB). Thank You for Your promise.

Deeper Walk: Matthew 6:25-34

Drawing Near All the Time

Commit yourselves wholeheartedly to these words of mine.
Deuteronomy 11:18

"IT'S BEEN A GREAT WEEKEND," my friend Susan said. We had gone for a long weekend away from our normal roles of mom, wife, mother, and career woman, to name a few. One aspect of my weekend getaway wasn't sitting well with me, though. I had neglected to spend much time with God. My relationship with God is very important to me—it affects all my life—so why didn't I bring Him on vacation with me? I hadn't studied His Word at all or even really prayed except for mealtimes. My heart felt cold, and the Holy Spirit prompted me to confess my laziness to my friend.

"It's been a great weekend, Susan, but I have really slacked in my desire to draw near to God. I miss Him, and I realize that because I chose to ignore His Word, I missed out."

"I know what you mean. Why don't we read some Scripture together now, and we can pray that our girls' weekend next year will be more Christ-centered instead of 'us'-centered."

When summer comes, we leave behind the routine of school and work to go on vacations, visit relatives and friends, and spend quality time as a family. Yet we are never meant to take a break from knowing and loving God more every day. Instead of leaving God's Word at home this summer, let's make it part of our daily life wherever we are and in whatever we do. Incorporate Bible reading and prayer into your vacations and use family devotionals to encourage your family members to do the same. Seek out a place to worship Him in spirit and in truth, even if you are away from your home church. Live in an attitude of godliness as you seek to glorify Him and make Him known to others in whatever travels or activities you pursue. The reality of what He has done for us through Christ should impact our lives every day, even on summer vacation!

Steps of Faith

God, help me make every day an offering to You, giving my life, time, and energy to serve You and make You known.

Deeper Walk: Psalm 73:25-28

Scared but Doing It Anyway

*Be strong and courageous. . . . For the LORD your God will
personally go ahead of you. He will neither fail you nor abandon you.*
Deuteronomy 31:6

NATHAN AND HIS COUSINS HAD been talking about Splash Mountain all day long, and we were finally in line. But the closer we got to the front, the more hesitant Nathan became. I couldn't blame him. The final drop went straight down. The distant sound of cartoon characters singing "Zip-a-Dee-Doo-Dah" as screaming people plummeted down a waterfall was creepy. The whining boy behind us didn't help matters.

Nathan grabbed my arm. "I don't want to go."

Neither do I, I thought and almost pulled him away to leave.

But I knew Nathan would regret it the minute his cousins exited the ride, chattering about how much fun they'd had. As nervous as I felt, I didn't want him to miss out. So I pointed to the giant log ahead of us. "Look, it doesn't even have seat belts. It can't be that bad."

God, give him courage.

His cousins boarded. A young boy climbed in without hesitation.

"Okay, I'll do it," Nathan said.

I put my hand over his as we took off, determined to model bravery. I sensed his terror through the entire ride. The final plunge felt like dropping off the earth. Nathan let out a loud scream, but I detected a hint of joy in it. As we floated toward the unloading point, he couldn't stop laughing. "That was so cool!"

I thanked God for helping Nathan step forward. Despite his fear, I prayed that he would save this memory as a reminder that whether it's a ride or a life challenge, true courage is the ability to say, "I'm scared, but I'm doing it anyway."

God's people were told to take courage through battles, persecution, and other horrors that made cowering over a thrill ride seem laughable. They would have been inhuman not to be afraid, yet they obeyed. We may not be required to face enemy armies, but God still calls us to be strong through things that we would rather run from. As we draw on His strength instead of avoiding challenges, we begin to recognize that "Do not fear" means refusing to let the fear win.

Steps of Faith

Lord, give me the courage to obey You, no matter what.

Deeper Walk: Deuteronomy 31:1-8

The Long Road

May integrity and honesty protect me, for I put my hope in you.
Psalm 25:21

JILLIAN WAVED ACROSS THE PARKING LOT, hoping Brenda would walk in her direction, give her a hug, and ask about her family. That would have happened just a few weeks ago. But now things were different. Instead, Brenda waved back with a faint smile and continued quickly toward her own car.

Brenda and Jillian had been good friends until recently. But as soon as Jillian had finished telling the ladies in their mutual Sunday school class about Brenda's marital problems and asking for their prayers, she knew she had crossed a dangerous line. When Brenda heard about Jillian's "prayer request," she had phoned her, angry and in tears.

Jillian had apologized sincerely and offered to ask their Sunday school class's forgiveness for her betrayal as well. But Brenda hung up the phone that day still angry and unrelenting.

Two days later Jillian went to Brenda's house and apologized again. Brenda listened and this time offered forgiveness. The friends even prayed together before hugging good-bye.

But when Jillian saw Brenda the next Sunday, she could tell that it would be a while before she earned her friend's trust back. Since that day she and Brenda had encountered each other at mutual gatherings and acted friendly, but not like close friends.

Lord, Jillian prayed, *show me the way back to Brenda's trust. And help me to be patient, regardless of how long the road may be.*

Trust, once broken, is not easily restored. Even when someone offers you wholehearted forgiveness, don't expect them to be able to trust you right away. Pray for the person you hurt so that your heart stays soft toward him or her. Chip away at the pain you caused by consistently being genuine, truthful, and protective of the damaged relationship under repair. Most importantly, draw near to God; He offers complete and unrestrained restoration.

Steps of Faith

Father, when I sincerely ask someone's forgiveness, I want immediate restoration. But help me have patience for the journey of rebuilding trust.

Deeper Walk: Psalm 15

Filling Hearts

God has given each of you a gift from his great variety of spiritual gifts.
Use them well to serve one another.

1 Peter 4:10

I SERVED AS A GREETER AT my small local church, and occasionally someone that I didn't recognize would walk through the door.

During one summer, after a textile factory on the outskirts of town shut its doors, I noticed a few new faces every other week—which also coincided with our church-wide fellowship lunches. Usually they trickled in late and sat in the back, then quietly made their way into the lunch line after the service.

After a few months of this, I began to hear the stories of their hardships—families struggling to make ends meet, fathers out of a job, mothers working double shifts.

I started thinking about the steadily growing number of guests every other week at church. As I looked in my pantry one afternoon, I realized I had more than enough food. I cleaned out my pantry, gathered the food in bags, and took it to the next fellowship lunch. There, I handed out a few canned, non-perishable items to the men and women gathering in line.

Over the next two weeks, I made some calls to a few of my friends and asked them to clean out their pantries. One friend, on her weekly family grocery trip, decided to save the free items from buy-one-get-one deals and give them away.

Word spread, and within eight months, a functioning food pantry was organized for the community.

Times are a little better now, but people still need food. I'm thankful that God showed me a need that I was able to fill.

Is there something you've been thinking about helping with at your church? Do you see a need for a service that doesn't exist yet? Do you know of a family who could use some financial help like a bag of groceries or a gas card? Is there a community food pantry you could assist? First, ask for God's guidance and discernment. Then begin by doing what you can for just one person.

Steps of Faith

Dear Lord, give me discernment that I might see the needs of others clearly. And Father, give me courage so that, when You call me, I will act and serve according to Your Spirit's guidance.

Deeper Walk: 1 Peter 4:8-11

"Are We There Yet?"

A day is like a thousand years to the Lord, and a thousand years is like a day.
2 Peter 3:8

WHEN OUR THREE CHILDREN WERE YOUNGER, we loved traveling, but Rob and I couldn't afford airline tickets for five people. So we drove—everywhere. From the Midwest, we took car trips to California, New England, Florida, Colorado, Texas, and many points in between.

Our car trips were before the days of handheld video games, DVD players, and MP3 players. So I made sure the kids had plenty of books, coloring books, crayons, and card games. All five of us played word games as we drove down the highway. We made frequent stops to stretch our legs. But the children's frequent cries were always the same: "Are we there yet?"

Their question reminded me of the times I've waited for God to act. Sometimes I feel like a kid sitting in the backseat of the car, waiting to get to my destination. When I'm in the midst of suffering, I impatiently ask God, "Are we there yet? Is it time for the pain to be over?" Or when I'm waiting on an answer to prayer, I want to know if He's heard me and when He's going to respond. However, God's timetable is vastly different from ours, and He may not answer in the way we expect or hope. But He will answer.

As we get older, our perspective on time changes. It seems to drag by in our youth, but when we become adults, it flies by, and we may wonder where it went. An entire lifetime is only a speck on God's timeline of eternity. While our suffering or waiting may seem to take an incredibly long time, God knows how much we can bear, and He is full of mercy. Paul reminds us, "We can rejoice, too, when we run into problems and trials, for we know that they help us develop endurance. And endurance develops strength of character, and character strengthens our confident hope of salvation" (Romans 5:3-4). So the next time you have to wait for God to answer a prayer, take heart. He will answer, but it will be according to His timetable.

Steps of Faith

Father, please forgive me for the times I've been impatient as I've waited on Your answers to prayer. Help me to trust in You and wait for Your perfect timing.

Deeper Walk: John 11:1-44

Open Service

Pure and genuine religion in the sight of God the Father means caring for orphans and widows in their distress and refusing to let the world corrupt you.
James 1:27

WHEN WE APPROACHED the shanties, we saw children running barefoot and half-naked through the alleyways. They jumped over open fire pits that were roasting food for dinner. Dried-up animal bones and flesh littered the ground and ditches. Flies were everywhere. At many shacks, several children were gathered outside an open window leaning in on each other toward a television. Despite all the necessities these children lacked, one thing they had an abundance of was television.

The purpose of our church group's mission trip was to refurbish a library by painting and building new shelves. As we worked, I wondered how these books would compete against the allure of television. When I and my team members talked with members of the community, we found that adequate clothing and school supplies—pens, paper, scissors, glue—were pressing needs.

Together, we pooled some money, went to a market, and bought supplies, including small Bibles. We bought resealable plastic bags and made about fifty supply kits. As we walked to the library to complete our work, we handed out the kits to the children.

When we returned home, some of the team members and I decided to send a large shipment of supplies to the community every year.

Before the mission trip, I wasn't involved in my local community, let alone one halfway across the world. Now I know that I can easily provide something that these children desperately need. This knowledge has colored how I spend my money and my time.

Open yourself up to the possibilities of serving on a mission trip. You'll become aware of needs beyond your own. You'll experience the power of prayer as you share the gospel. And your heart will become more tuned to compassion, doing unto others as you would want others to do to you.

Steps of Faith

Father, help me to be sensitive to the needs of others. Prick my heart to align with Yours. Show me where You want me to serve, and help me to obey.

Deeper Walk: James 1:19-27

The Blurter

Take control of what I say, O Lord, and guard my lips.
Psalm 141:3

SOMETIMES I JUST DON'T act as smart as I know myself to be. I'm a blurter—someone who just blurts out what I'm thinking, in rough-and-tumble ways, not realizing the offensiveness of my words.

One day in high school, I asked a girlfriend, "Is that a new outfit? Do you think you look good in it?" What I meant and what she heard were two different things, and my words damaged our friendship.

Even now, with my fiancé, I find that I sometimes speak rashly, excitedly, or carelessly and say things that I don't mean. I've spoken in hurtful ways when I didn't intend to, and I've expressed fears that weren't as serious as my words sounded. My ill-chosen words created distance between us and sometimes prompted him to respond in irritation.

I am prone to sin. I realize that by this lack of filter, I hurt others and misrepresent myself and my God. Sometimes, my carelessness draws others into sin toward me. When I read Psalm 141:3, I dared to hope that there was help for me. In this psalm, David is pleading with God to keep him from sin. He desires God's grace to guard him against saying something offensive or something that would give his enemies ammunition against his God. So I'm going to pray this prayer daily for the next week and watch to see what happens. God never leaves me unchanged when I ask Him to do something in me, so I'm expecting His grace to prevail!

How well do you guard the doors of your lips? How well do you watch the words that come out of your mouth? Likely, we've all had the experience of misspeaking at one time or another, of hurting someone, or of provoking them to act dishonorably. If you were to pay close attention to the words that you speak, would you find those words to be an honorable representation of God?

Steps of Faith

Dear God, thank You for guarding me in all ways, including what I say and how I say it. Help me to speak words of life and to resist mindless speech.

Deeper Walk: Psalm 19:7-14

Because They're Boys

I want women to be modest in their appearance.
They should wear decent and appropriate clothing.
1 Timothy 2:9

"Um, Mom . . ." My eight-year-old son said nothing more. Instead he pointed toward the strap of my tank top, which had slipped off my shoulder.

Embarrassed, I did a quick clothing check. "Thanks, Zach."

The sudden arrival of warm weather had sent me searching for anything sleeveless or lightweight. I'd failed to notice that this day's outfit was a bit revealing when not adjusted correctly. I must admit I was relieved that Zach pointed out the sagging strap instead of making a joke. It showed me that he was growing up and learning to value modesty. I took his correction as a healthy reminder that, as a mother of sons, I need to model modesty. I need to do it not only because one son is precocious and extremely aware of girls while the other is embarrassed by all things female, but also because they are young men living in a world where immodesty and impurity are presented as the norm. If they see me in outfits that are too revealing, I'd be sending the message that it's the norm for Christians, too.

I don't limit myself to ankle-length skirts and blouses buttoned up to my throat. I simply keep young male eyes in mind when I dress, knowing that I want my sons to grow into godly men who respect women and honor God's plan for purity.

Mothers of sons may deal with fewer debates than mothers of daughters over appropriate clothing, but stressing the value of modesty and purity to our sons is just as crucial. How are we equipping them in their fight against temptation? How do our clothing choices reflect the biblical teaching we are trying to instill in them? We can model purity that is tasteful and attractive and pray that our example will help our young men avoid images, movies, or relationships that are contrary to God's will.

Steps of Faith

Lord, keep me aware of how my choices impact the young men in my life. Give me the wisdom to guide them in ways that please You.

Deeper Walk: 1 Timothy 2:9-10

Moving Past Disappointment

But whenever they were in trouble and turned to the LORD,
the God of Israel, and sought him out, they found him.

2 Chronicles 15:4

JANNA LOWERED HER HEAD INTO her hand as she listened on the phone to the camp director explain her son's expulsion from the program due to drugs. Evan had been caught smoking pot behind the boathouse after curfew; no other children were involved.

As Janna and her husband, Stephen, drove the hour and a half to pick up Evan, they discussed consequences and treatment for his habit—this wasn't the first time Evan had been caught.

In the coming days and weeks, Evan was treated for his addiction and adhered to his restrictions at home. Yet even as he made progress, Janna continued to grieve and sink deeper into disappointment over his choices. Soon, she began to struggle with depression. Finally, Stephen asked Janna to seek counseling within their church community.

In counseling, Janna was able to unearth and identify her feelings of disappointment and move past them. As the counselor guided her through prayer and Scripture reading, Janna began to gain perspective and forgiveness for Evan. Stephen noticed Janna's mood lighten and her interaction with Evan soften. Because of God's work through the counselor, and through prayer and Scripture, Janna truly felt as though God were renewing her mind, as the Bible proclaimed.

It's natural to have certain expectations for our children. And when their decisions fall short of those expectations, it's natural to feel disappointment. Left to fester, disappointment may take root and lead to distance, unforgiveness, and even depression. Extend forgiveness and open communication, expressing yourself in the love and grace of the Lord Jesus. Bring to the Lord anything that may lead to roots of bitterness.

Steps of Faith

Father, while I have hopes, dreams, and expectations for my children, help me to remain connected to You through reading Your Word. Help me to manage my feelings through the guidance of Your Holy Spirit.

Deeper Walk: 2 Corinthians 4:7-18

"If You Love Me . . ."

If you love me, obey my commandments.
John 14:15

JOAN GROANED AS the obnoxious beeping jarred her out of a deep sleep. It could not be 6:30 already. After a day of river rafting with friends, a barbecue, and a long drive home last night, she dreaded the process of dragging the kids out of bed and out the door to church. Sunburned and achy, she dreaded dragging herself out of bed even more. Would it hurt to take one Sunday morning off to sleep in?

Her husband stretched and sat up slowly. He didn't have to usher this Sunday, so they had no obligations forcing them to go.

We can have our own family church service, she thought.

But would they? Really?

She watched Mark get out of bed without a word about possibly staying home. What would her parents have said if she'd asked to skip church on a morning like this as a child?

Would God "make her pay" for sleeping in? No, but what kind of a model did she want to be for her children? The answer came quickly. She wanted to be a mom who loved to worship God and study His Word with other believers.

"Kids," she called as she slowly got out of bed, vowing to take an afternoon nap, "time to get up for church."

As believers saved by grace, we are not bound by the law. We know that Christ's sacrifice released us from the burden of trying to maintain God's favor through our ability to obey. Yet Jesus said, "If you love me, obey my commandments." His Spirit lives within us, stirring a longing to obey God's commandments, not so that we can earn His love, but as an expression of how much we truly love Him. We show our commitment through our willingness to put God's desires above our own. How do we reflect commitment to our Savior through our daily choices and priorities?

Steps of Faith

God, forgive me for using grace as an excuse. Instead, may my gratitude for this gift trigger a desire to listen to the Holy Spirit's prompting to please You first.

Deeper Walk: John 14:15-21

A Different Person

The King will say, "I tell you the truth, when you did it to one of
the least of these my brothers and sisters, you were doing it to me!"
Matthew 25:40

"I'M READY TO GO," Katie said to Beth, replacing the lid on the salad she'd brought to the luncheon. Saturday was half-over, and she still needed to go grocery shopping and plant the rest of her summer veggies.

"You may be ready, but I don't think Ruth is." Beth gestured toward the older woman, who was laughing and talking with a group of women. "I've never seen her so chatty before."

Katie picked up her bowl. "I know. Today has been good for her. Ruth has become more isolated since she had to give up her driver's license. On our way over here, she told me she hasn't been out of her house all week."

"Does she live alone?"

"Yes, her husband passed away a couple of years ago. People take turns driving her to church, but other than that . . ."

"We should get her out for lunch or something once in a while," Beth said.

Katie couldn't take her eyes off Ruth. When Katie had called to offer her a ride to the luncheon, Ruth had sounded so down, but today she seemed like a different person.

God, prompt me to call her more often, Katie prayed. *I can't imagine how lonely she must be.*

Ruth turned to Katie and asked, "Are you in a hurry to get home?"

Katie shook her head. "Jeff took the kids to a movie. Take your time."

While rushing through our busy days of work, car pools, soccer practice, and errands, we may not think about those who have become isolated in their later years. As older men and women lose precious spouses, health, or their ability to drive, they also say good-bye to their independence, meaning a less active social life.

As we consider how we might minister to "the least of these" as Jesus taught, let's remember the elderly, knowing that one day we may be old and alone and praying for someone to remember us.

Steps of Faith

God, it's so easy for me to forget about those who are alone. Bring them to mind and show me ways to reach out to them.

Deeper Walk: Matthew 25:31-40

Got Prayer?

When you pray . . .
Matthew 6:5

LIKE MOST BELIEVERS, I have experienced several dry spiritual seasons in life. Just after college, I started teaching at a struggling rural school. I only had a writing degree, so I also took classes in the evenings to earn a teaching certificate. I had no idea what I was doing in that classroom, regularly felt in over my head, and often cried from stress and exhaustion on my way home. I couldn't spare a second to add a regular prayer time to my to-do list.

I also had dry times just after the births of my two children. Like all new moms, I was sleep deprived, hormonal, crying my way through painful nursing, and figuring out how to survive and keep my babies healthy and content. With my second child, I was also in a lot of pain from the birth and took months to fully heal, which limited me physically. Prayer time, once again, fell to the bottom of my priority list.

Looking back, I can see that my lack of a daily prayer time during those seasons was more a faith issue than a time-management problem. Yes, those were busy times, but they were also hard times. If ever in my life I needed help and strength, it was then. Instead of asking God, I tried to handle everything myself. A little time on my knees, humbling myself before God and casting all my anxieties on Him, would have made those trials more bearable by allowing the Lord to lead me through them.

However we may rationalize our prayerlessness, at the core it is always a matter of faith. Colossians 4:2 says, "Devote yourselves to prayer." Be honest with yourself about why you aren't opening up to the One who loves you most, and allow Him to work through that heart issue with you.

Steps of Faith

Lord, forgive me for the times I've neglected prayer. Reveal any faith issues I'm having and help me to make prayer a priority.

Deeper Walk: Matthew 6:5-13

Blended Blues

He heals the brokenhearted and bandages their wounds.

Psalm 147:3

ONE SATURDAY OUR church offered a seminar for blended families, and I was the first one there. The speaker, who was both a stepdaughter and a stepmom, had many helpful things to say about blended families. Afterward, I asked her advice about my relationship with my stepdaughter.

"Greg and I have been married for a year," I said, "and his daughter, Melissa, still doesn't like me."

"It takes a long time for children to heal," Julie said. "Think of it from her point of view. When her parents divorced, she lost a lot of things—most important of all, her mother and father living together. What children want most is for their parents to be together."

"But Greg and his first wife argued a lot. Their house was filled with tension."

"That doesn't matter to Melissa as much as her desire to have them together," she said.

"But I do things for her. I make sure she has alone time with her dad. I talk to her, but she only gives one-word answers. I've even taken her out for some girl time, but she doesn't enjoy it. I'm feeling discouraged and defeated."

"All these things are great, but she's probably still grieving," Julie said.

"What else can I do?"

"Be patient and loving with her as she processes the changes in her life. Talk about how Jesus understands her pain and can heal her heart. Give her time. She'll learn that she can count on you."

Oftentimes in second marriages, parents don't recognize the pain children feel from the loss of the other parent through divorce or death. Happy about the new marriage and new life, parents can't see the situation through their children's eyes. But God can give these parents wisdom, fill them with love for their kids, and help them make good decisions for their blended families.

Steps of Faith

God, please help our family to know You, love You, and follow You.

Deeper Walk: Colossians 3:12-13

Me Do!

Otherwise you are boasting about your own pretentious plans,
and all such boasting is evil.

James 4:16

AFTER STRUGGLING ALL DAY with her toddler's newfound independence, Trudy knew bath time might be problematic. In order to ward off any arguments about what Chesney would wear to bed on a hot summer evening, she laid her cotton gown out ahead of time. Then she ran the bathwater before getting her from the playroom where her father was entertaining her.

But the jockeying for control began the minute Trudy set Chesney down on the bath mat to undress her.

"No!" Chesney said, moving her mother's hands away from the buttons on her sundress. "Me do!"

Trudy waited patiently as Chesney fumbled with the buttons, knowing her small, chubby fingers couldn't possibly unfasten them. Praying for patience, Trudy sat on the floor until Chesney asked for help.

By the time Chesney had given up unbuttoning her dress on her own, she was no longer the good-natured little girl who had been stacking blocks with her daddy. And when Chesney finally got into the tub, the water had grown cold, resulting in more complaints.

Later, Trudy checked on Chesney as she slept peacefully in her crib. She sighed with relief and whispered a short prayer.

"Lord, now I see what my own arrogance must do to Your heart. Forgive me for all the times I insisted on doing things my way when all along You knew best."

The stubbornness of a child may be just a mild inconvenience that tries a mother's patience, but our own arrogance is met with even more resistance from our holy Father. James 4:6 says, "God opposes the proud." Picture God taking up full battle array against the person who defiantly insists on doing things his or her way. Why? Because God loves us too much to allow us to hurt ourselves or cause damage to His Kingdom with our arrogance.

Steps of Faith

Father, please reveal any arrogance in me and help me to honestly confess it and repent. I want to humbly submit to You.

Deeper Walk: Obadiah 1:1-4

Grounded

Teach us to realize the brevity of life, so that we may grow in wisdom.

Psalm 90:12

"HEY, JUDY," TRICIA CALLED as they exited the sanctuary. "How did Kyle's knee surgery go?"

"Great. Didn't you see my Facebook updates?"

"Actually, I grounded myself from Facebook for a while."

Judy let out an exaggerated gasp. "*You*, the social networking queen?"

Tricia laughed. "My daughter inspired me. She took herself off everything, calling it a time sucker. Apparently she flunked a test after spending more time doing online quizzes than she spent studying. If a college girl can be that wise . . ."

"Good for you," Judy replied.

"I got my own reality check too. I didn't finish my Bible study lesson because I'd been spending so much time on Facebook and Twitter. Suddenly I felt guilty about how much time I'd wasted."

Judy's stomach tightened. "You aren't alone. Yesterday I missed my son's double play because I was telling the world, 'I'm at Brad's baseball game.' Maybe I should ground myself too."

As much as she enjoyed reconnecting with long-lost cousins and classmates, Judy had to admit that she'd let it get out of hand. What might happen if she took a break for a week? Maybe she could have lunch with her sister instead of tweeting back and forth, or call one of her 238 Facebook friends.

Social networking sites have made it possible to catch up with high school friends, keep in touch with long-distance relatives, and share news with hundreds of people at once. It doesn't take long, however, before a fun social tool becomes a time-consuming addiction, drawing us away from responsibilities, time with God, and opportunities to cultivate deep, lasting relationships with true friends. As with any good thing that can be taken to the extreme, we must occasionally stop and ask, *Is this how God wants me to spend my time?* When we consider how quickly a day passes, how much of it do we really want to spend online?

Steps of Faith

God, You gave me one precious life with only so many days in it. Help me to see each one as a gift and to faithfully guard how I use it.

Deeper Walk: Ephesians 5:15-17

A Mom's Priority

*If you love your father or mother more than you love me,
you are not worthy of being mine.*
Matthew 10:37

STACY SETTLED HER TWO CHILDREN at the picnic table she shared with Maggie and Linda and their preschoolers. The young moms had gathered at the park with their kids for a playdate and picnic.

"I want to run something by you gals," Stacy said as she helped her two-year-old with his juice box. "Do you ever have a hard time finding significance in your role as a mother? I mean, I so desperately wanted to stay home with my children while they are young, but now that I'm doing that, I feel somewhat less important. Do you ever feel that way?"

"I know what you mean," said Linda. "At least we're doing something constructive with our kids today. So I'll feel pretty good about myself as a mom tonight. But other nights, after I've gotten the kids to bed and I'm straightening up the house, I struggle with feeling as though I'm failing at my most important role."

Maggie said, "Being a mom is important, but we all have to remember that we are Jesus followers first. Believe me, I'm talking to myself here too. If we remember that our significance is found in Him, the other roles we fill seem to fall into place. I find that when I concentrate on my relationship with Jesus and seek my significance from Him, He affirms my roles as wife, mother, and friend."

In Matthew 6:33, Jesus said to seek the Kingdom of God and His righteousness first, and the rest of life will fall into place. A prioritized relationship with Him will give proper significance to other roles. What's your most significant role?

Steps of Faith

Lord, help me seek You first. Then I will have something to bring to the roles I fill.

Deeper Walk: Philippians 3:7-21

Just Once

Wine produces mockers; alcohol leads to brawls.
Those led astray by drink cannot be wise.
Proverbs 20:1

IT STARTED WHEN MY HUSBAND and I took a cruise to celebrate our twentieth anniversary. It seemed natural to have a glass of champagne at the captain's reception, where the stewards were passing out glasses of bubbly left and right. Emboldened, the next night I decided to order a glass of wine with my meal. My husband looked a little surprised but said nothing.

I had never in my life bought a bottle of wine, but a week later, after an especially rough day at work, I decided at the last minute to put a bottle in my grocery cart. Just this once I'd enjoy a glass while I unwound from the day.

But it wasn't just once. Within a few months I had developed a habit of tossing a bottle or two into my grocery cart every time I shopped. And before long I was nursing a glass of wine every evening in an effort to relax. Then it became two glasses.

Just last week, as I drove home from work, I found myself looking forward to the wine—more than I looked forward to seeing my husband, resting my aching feet, or reading a book. Suddenly, I realized I had a problem, and it scared me. That's when I heard a still, small voice say, *Seek Me instead.*

I didn't expect to have a problem with drinking, especially since I had limited myself to wine. But the alcohol's hold has been difficult to loosen. Truly, only through the Lord will I break this bondage.

Proverbs 31:4-5 teaches that alcoholic beverages can impair one's ability to think wisely and relate properly to others. Not only does alcohol hinder a person at the time of consumption, but it is also a powerful substance that has a way of gaining control over one's life. If you struggle with an addictive substance or activity, recognize that this is not God's best for you. Ask Him for deliverance.

Steps of Faith

Father, show me if I have allowed anything to gain dominion over me. Help me to break free through Your grace and power.

Deeper Walk: Proverbs 23:29-35

Blessed

Feed the hungry, and help those in trouble. Then your light will shine out from the darkness, and the darkness around you will be as bright as noon.
Isaiah 58:10

THE YOUTH GROUP SHARED stories from their trip to Mexico. They showed pictures of an eight-year-old boy washing his only school outfit by hand, families who couldn't afford medical care, and thankful people receiving bags of dried beans, flour, and rice that the group handed out.

Several months later, a retired doctor spoke about his visit to Indonesia, where he sponsors several children. He had helped rescue a little girl found living alone.

"I'm just grateful to have the means to help," the man said when I thanked him for his talk. "I wish I could do more."

I'm not doing anything, I thought as I walked away. Then I thought about that boy in Mexico who couldn't go to school until he'd washed his only outfit, families celebrating over rice and beans, and a sad, frightened, abandoned girl.

Troubled by these needs, I asked God to increase my desire to help the poor, and to open up opportunities to serve in a practical way. My family may not have a lot, but we have prayerfully committed what we have to use as God directs.

Throughout Scripture, God implores His people to not only remember the poor, but also to provide for them. Too often we give in to the misconception that we barely have enough for ourselves, let alone extra. But when we compare our idea of "not enough" to what families struggle to survive on each day and thank God for, we see our abundance. It doesn't take a lot to make a difference. Churches and trusted Christian ministries can take a shoe box filled with toys to bring boundless hope and joy to needy children; a pocketful of change to provide a hot meal for a homeless person; and ten dollars to provide a lifesaving mosquito net. Prayerfully consider how you can contribute to those less fortunate today.

Steps of Faith

Father, thank You that You have always provided for me. Show me ways to help those who have so little.

Deeper Walk: Isaiah 58

Spending

The Holy Spirit produces this kind of fruit in our lives: love, joy, peace, patience, kindness, goodness, faithfulness, gentleness, and self-control.
Galatians 5:22-23

LATELY, OUR CHECKING ACCOUNT HAS gotten frighteningly low toward the end of each pay period. We have one income, and within the last year, we added three big expenses to our budget. The wide financial margin we had previously, with no debt payments, car payments, or school tuition, narrowed uncomfortably, but our spending habits did not change.

Even with our necessary added expenses, we can easily live on what we make if we get our spending under control. We cannot continue to eat out as often, impulse buy our way through stores, or continue our memberships at our gym.

As we work on tightening the budget belt, I recognize that there are wrong beliefs about money behind our lack of financial self-control. No matter how much financial margin we have, our habit of spending as we please, without asking God for His will and wisdom about our purchases, reflects a selfish, worldly view of our money that needs to change as well.

Now that money is tighter, we are relearning what God says about money and how He wants us to handle it. We are also trying to trust God more to meet our physical and emotional needs (instead of relying on retail therapy). It isn't easy, and we do mess up, but I'm confident that as we seek God's wisdom and strength concerning our financial changes, we can do it.

Do you live paycheck to paycheck, or worse, beyond your means, racking up debt? If so, you may have some worldly views about money that have led to a lack of self-control in this area. Self-control comes from knowing God's truth and basing your decisions on it. Continuously renew your mind through the Word to combat any wrong thinking, and adopt sound financial practices so that you may be a good steward of all God has entrusted to you.

Steps of Faith

Father, I don't want my spending habits to be out of control. Please help me to change my thinking about money. I surrender financial control to You.

Deeper Walk: Galatians 5:16-26

Moments

My heart has heard you say, "Come and talk with me."
And my heart responds, "Lord, I am coming."
Psalm 27:8

MY TEN-YEAR-OLD DAUGHTER was engrossed in a video game.

"Kara," I called from the kitchen, "will you please come here and help me set the table?"

She didn't answer, so I went into the family room and repeated my request.

This time Kara answered, but without looking up at me. She sighed, and her shoulders slumped. "Just a minute. I'm almost done."

I knew Kara would have preferred to continue playing her game instead of spending time helping me in the kitchen. But sometimes we had really good discussions while we worked together. During those times, she frequently opened up about her day at school or what was going on with her friends—the good and the bad. I longed for her company.

Soon Kara put down her video game and joined me in the kitchen, but the moment was lost. She was disappointed that she had to put her game away, and I was disappointed that she hadn't come when I first called.

Later, I thought about how I do the same thing with God. I feel a stirring in my spirit and know that He's calling me to come and meet with Him. But sometimes, I put Him off. I continue reading my book, or I think, *I can tackle one more chore. I'll be there in just a minute.* Then when I finally obey, the momentum is gone. I want to connect with my heavenly Father better, but many times I've lingered over less important things.

Before I went to bed that evening, I asked God to help me obey immediately when He calls. His purposes are always good for me, and He longs to spend time with me.

When God calls you, do you sometimes delay answering? Do you continue on in your momentary distraction and ask the King of the Universe to wait? Next time, be aware that He longs to spend time with you. When He calls, say, "I'm coming" and run to His waiting arms.

Steps of Faith

Lord, when I feel a stirring in my spirit, help me to obey the prompting quickly.

Deeper Walk: 1 Samuel 3

Time to Start Over

We know that God causes everything to work together for the good of those who love God and are called according to his purpose for them.

Romans 8:28

I FOUGHT THE POSSIBILITY OF bankruptcy from the moment I was told I would probably need to file. I paid debts long after being told, "You can't afford it anymore" and refused to see the process as a fresh start.

To this day, I know I did the right thing by honoring those bills. But when it came time for the inevitable consultation with an attorney, I stopped fighting. I sensed God assuring me that I had been as responsible as possible for as long as I could, that bankruptcy was not something I wanted or caused, and that He would turn the process around for my benefit, as wrong and unfair as it seemed.

One Saturday, I sat at my computer taking the second half of a required credit counseling course. Unlike the first half, which only stood as a reminder of the financial mess I was in, this section covered budgeting and other habits to avoid a repeat spiral. God used the material to help me see the new beginning ahead. For the first time in years, I had control over my financial future. Those debts—many of which I had not participated in accumulating—were a thing of the past. I could now keep up with bills, save, and give back to His Kingdom based on what He provided. It was officially time to start over.

Life includes mistakes, unforeseen tragedy, and suffering in the fallout of someone else's poor choices. Thankfully, we also get opportunities to put those bad times behind us and start again. Sometimes it takes a while to see the do-over for what it is because it comes in an unwanted form. But when we make up our minds to move forward with God, we are better equipped to see His grace in the muck of our circumstances and thank Him that it truly isn't the end of the world. Instead, new and better things await us.

Steps of Faith

Lord, You turn experiences that I did not sign up for into new beginnings that I can gratefully embrace. Thank You that I can trust fully in You no matter how my circumstances may look.

Deeper Walk: Isaiah 43:18-19

Treasures in Trials

What we suffer now is nothing compared to the glory he will reveal to us later.
Romans 8:18

AMANDA SHUFFLED TO the kitchen to start coffee and get out cereal before she woke the children. She had recently learned that the unsettling physical symptoms she was experiencing were early signs of multiple sclerosis (MS). She was fearful that the future loomed dark before her.

Amanda glanced through a newsletter she'd received at the doctor's office. She began reading the story of a woman diagnosed with MS on her fortieth birthday. The woman shared that she had experienced a new appreciation for the gift of life and the value of each new day. She had even come to benefit from the forced slowing-down process as it drew her closer to God. This trial had strengthened her faith and given validity to her testimony, and she considered it "great joy" (James 1:2). While she had not chosen this disease, she had found in it benefits and worth.

Amanda's heart was comforted as she, too, was assured that God would faithfully provide His grace and power sufficient for her weakness (2 Corinthians 12:9).

There is probably no better poster person for victorious suffering than Joni Eareckson Tada. Paralyzed for more than forty years, she now battles chronic pain and, more recently, breast cancer. Yet in the grip of trials that make us horror-struck, she still declares her trust, her joy, and her great expectation of a future glory. She also continues to serve in Kingdom work far more productively than many physically healthy believers. If we need a courageous role model, she's it.

When suffering comes, the only place to run is to God, the all-sufficient One who brings light out of darkness. Hold fast and keep your eyes on Jesus, the source and perfecter of your faith (Hebrews 12:2).

Steps of Faith

Father, help us turn to You when life hurts. Reveal Yourself, giving comfort, peace, and strength.

Deeper Walk: James 1:2-3

Learning to Lean

Share each other's burdens, and in this way obey the law of Christ.
Galatians 6:2

TIFFANY TURNED ON THE computer and found Julie's recent e-mail. Weary from tossing and turning all night, she took a gulp of her steaming black coffee and read the message one more time. But this time she was ready to respond to her friend's offer of help.

In recent weeks, Julie had asked Tiffany repeatedly to tell her if she needed anything at all.

"You have a Sunday school class that loves you and your family. We want to support and help you during this time," Julie had said. "Please don't be afraid to take us up on it."

But ever since the car accident, Tiffany had insisted she could hold her family and her home together on her own. Never mind that her husband, Brad, would be in the rehabilitation center for at least another week, and she was hobbling around with a cast on her foot. She'd stubbornly tried to keep her house clean, take care of her children, and visit Brad daily, but she was beginning to feel frazzled.

Tiffany clicked on "reply" and began to type her response.

"God showed me in my quiet time that I've been prideful," she wrote. "It's time to lean on my church family instead of trying to live independently. The meals the small group offered would be greatly appreciated. And yes, I'll even let someone clean my bathrooms! Thank you."

For some, it is especially hard to lean on another's shoulder, even in times of crisis. But it's often nothing less than pride that keeps us from accepting help from others.

Paul wrote, "I can do everything through Christ, who gives me strength" (Philippians 4:13), but he followed that bold statement by admitting to the church in Philippi that they had lightened his burden by coming alongside him in difficult times.

Do you practice biblical give-and-take in a local church family? Do you lend a hand to those who struggle? And do you willingly let others help you as well?

Steps of Faith

Father, thank You for my church family. Show me how I can contribute to those in need, and help me to be more willing to receive help when I need it.

Deeper Walk: Romans 12:9-15

In It for the Long Haul

Let's not get tired of doing what is good. At just the right time
we will reap a harvest of blessing if we don't give up.
Galatians 6:9

My TEN-MONTH-OLD DUMPED cereal all over the floor. Then my three-year-old came waltzing in to breakfast with Magic Marker all over her face and hands. All before 7:00 a.m.

I wanted to respond with tears. After all, the day had just begun. There would be diapers to change, food to prepare, games to play, books to read, and laundry to be done all day long. I worked so hard every day just to keep us afloat, and there seemed to be no end in sight. I shot up a prayer to the Lord for grace and perspective and resolved to plug away until naptime. I sent a text to a good friend who is also a mother of little ones: "SOS! Tough day today already! Need some words of wisdom to get me through!"

Julia sent a message right back: "Gal. 6:9. Don't give up!"

After I put my little ones down for naps, I made a cup of tea and sat down with my Bible. I read the verse Julia sent me, and it brought tears to my eyes. God is a big-picture God, and He is calling me to be faithful step-by-step, day by day so that I can point these little ones toward Him. I may not see fruit today, and I may not ever receive praise or thanks for the hard work of every-day life, but He sees and He promises a harvest one day. What a blessing to know that my work is eternal and significant to Him.

Parenting is a calling to give your life away, to serve your children every day in ways that often mean dying to self and putting their needs before your own. What a beautiful picture of the gospel, mirroring the sacrifice that Jesus made for us by laying down His own life. The Lord is honored and glorified when we serve with humility and joy in any capacity, and those who press on will obtain the prize (see Philippians 3:14).

Steps of Faith

God, help me to set my eyes on You and value Your promises above any earthly praise or reward.

Deeper Walk: Hebrews 12:1-2

Lost and Found

The LORD is the One who will go before you. He will be with you;
He will not leave you or forsake you. Do not be afraid or discouraged.
Deuteronomy 31:8, HCSB

WHEN KEVIN WAS about four years old, he went to the grocery store with his mother. He walked through the aisles with her as she checked her list and put items in her cart. When he saw the toy aisle, Kevin became distracted and wandered away. He stayed there for a minute or so, but when he looked around for his mother, he didn't see her. Panicked, Kevin ran from one aisle to the next. Of course, his mother was looking for him as well.

Finally, he decided that she must have finished her shopping and gone out to the car. So little Kevin ran out into the parking lot. He looked around where he thought she had parked the car, but he didn't see it. Then Kevin burst into tears, thinking she had driven home without him. He stood there in the parking lot, wailing, devastated to think that he had been left at the grocery store all by himself.

Then a man walking into the store stopped and asked him what was wrong. Kevin told him that his mom had gone home and left him there. So the kind stranger took him by the hand and led him back into the store. The manager made an announcement over the loudspeaker that a young boy was waiting for his mother at the customer service counter.

Minutes later, Kevin's mother came rushing over, relieved to find her son. "Kevin," she said, "you are my son. I love you, and I would never leave you."

Sometimes we may feel alone or even abandoned, but God loves us so much that He gave His only Son to die for us. He has promised that He will never leave us or forsake us (see Hebrews 13:5). Memorize a few key verses so that even when you don't feel His presence, His Word will remind you that He's still there.

Steps of Faith

God, thank You for being with me when I feel lost or abandoned. You are my refuge and strength in times of trouble (Psalm 46:1).

Deeper Walk: Isaiah 41:10

Joy in My Soul

The hope of the righteous is joy.
Proverbs 10:28, HCSB

As a brand-new Christian in college, I was a member of an a cappella group. One of my favorite songs was a southern gospel–style quartet called "Feeling Mighty Fine." The opening lyrics, toe-tappingly upbeat, are "I woke up this morning feeling fine. I woke up with heaven on my mind. I woke up with joy in my soul, 'cause I knew my Lord had control."

Though I loved that song, for most of my life I struggled with the joy concept. After becoming a Christian, I thought maybe something was wrong with my faith. I thought I was supposed to be so visibly joyful that non-Christians couldn't help but notice and ask the reason for my joy. Then I would share Jesus on the spot, bringing another precious lamb into the fold.

After walking many years with Jesus, I still love that song, and I have learned two things about joy. One, it isn't something I can force. As a fruit of the Spirit, it is a natural result of remaining connected to the Vine. And two, joy is more about where I put my hope than about feelings. Just as the song says, when I remember and meditate on what I have to look forward to after this life—God restoring me and all of creation to perfection, no more tears, and no death to fear—that's joy.

You are not letting Jesus down if you're not the type of Christian who always has a smile on her face and a bounce in her step. Joy is about living in the truth that "the sufferings of this present time are not worth comparing with the glory that is going to be revealed to us" (Romans 8:18, HCSB). Believers can be joyful even through difficult seasons. We can have hopeful anticipation in the future because of the righteous standing God has given us, and He is faithful to His promises.

Steps of Faith

Lord, help me to remember the imperishable, uncorrupted, and unfading inheritance I have in Christ, and let that hope fill me with Your joy.

Deeper Walk: Galatians 5:16-25

Just Listen

The wisdom from above is first of all pure. It is also peace loving, gentle at all times, and willing to yield to others. It is full of mercy and the fruit of good deeds. It shows no favoritism and is always sincere.

James 3:17

"ABBY REALLY APPRECIATED your support last week," Kate said as we walked into church.

I recalled my last conversation with Abby. Several of us had been having lunch when she shared about the conflict with her ex-husband that was taking the fun out of her daughter's wedding plans.

"I don't remember saying anything profound." All I had done was listen and assure Abby that I would be upset in her situation too.

"Nobody else but you noticed how upset she was. Abby told me that having you there, so sweet and sympathetic, kept her from bursting into tears."

At the time I was new in town and too shy to do anything but listen. This was one of my most powerful lessons in the impact of listening without judging, making light of the situation, or giving unsolicited advice. More than a decade later, I found myself listening to another friend as she unloaded an overwhelming difficulty in her life. Instead of wishing I had more to offer, I thanked God for the privilege of quietly sharing her burden.

"Thank you for being a safe friend," she said as we hugged good-bye.

I prayed that I would continue to be, both for her and for others.

Whom do you call when you need to talk? Do you run to the friend who responded to your last crisis by telling you to toughen up and trust God, or the gentle sister who sat at your side as you poured out your heart? Friends who reflect Christ's spirit of gentleness provide a safe haven for honesty and raw emotion, reminding us why Scripture calls us to be kind rather than harsh or cold. Memories of friends who took our late-night phone calls, shared our tears, and set their opinions aside and let us unload show us how to respond when someone else needs support.

Steps of Faith

Lord, I want to be a friend that others know they can call on in a crisis or share their hearts with. Show me what I need to change in order to be a safe friend.

Deeper Walk: Galatians 5:22-23

Pet Perks

God said, "Let the earth bring forth living creatures after their kind:
cattle and creeping things and beasts of the earth after their kind";
and it was so. God made the beasts of the earth after their kind,
and the cattle after their kind, and everything that creeps on
the ground after its kind; and God saw that it was good.
Genesis 1:24-25, NASB

ALTHOUGH I DON'T consider myself political, I recently discovered that my family and I have something in common with a number of US presidents. Like Teddy Roosevelt, we once shared our home with guinea pigs. Like Lyndon Johnson, we learned to love the baying of our beagle. And like the Clintons, we've cozied up to a cat (or, in our case, four cats over twenty-five years), as well as a Labrador retriever. In addition to these family pets, my kids have been the caretakers of assorted fish and turtles, as well as a hamster and gerbil.

Without a doubt, pets require a commitment of time and energy—even if it's mostly Mom and Dad getting after the kids to take care of the pets they begged for! Yet these animals are also an unending source of joy and fun. Whether I'm holding the oversized paw of a tiny Lab puppy in my hand, watching the cat taunt the dog from the top of a bookshelf, or gazing at turtles as they glide through an aquarium, pets remind me daily of the diversity and creativity found in God's handiwork.

Of course, you don't have to own a pet to enjoy the animal kingdom. Whether you stop to watch a bee hovering between the flowers in your garden, follow a squirrel's path as it hops from limb to limb in the tree in your backyard, or step around the pigeon pecking at the city sidewalk in search of crumbs, you are acknowledging the wonder of God's design. Today when you notice an animal, bird, or insect, won't you take a moment to agree with God that it is good?

Steps of Faith

Gracious Creator, thank You for displaying Your power, majesty, and beauty through Your extraordinary creation. Enable me to notice the wonder all around me today!

Deeper Walk: Psalm 145:10-16

Running on Empty?

Anyone who believes in me may come and drink! For the Scriptures declare,
"Rivers of living water will flow from his heart."
John 7:38

SHARON SAT ON THE park bench looking out at the water. She had packed a sack lunch to avoid her coworkers' usual invitations to join them in the cafeteria. At the pace her life had recently taken, Sharon needed time alone with God to reflect and refuel.

Unwrapping her sandwich and breathing in the mild summer breeze, Sharon thanked God for giving her strength to handle the extra responsibilities she had recently acquired due to her mother's surgery. Not only did she have to care for her family, balance work, and get her mother settled in an assisted living center, but she would also need to tend to her mother's plants, pets, and bills while she recuperated.

Father, Sharon prayed, *I read in Psalm 1 that if I meditate on Your truths, You will make me like the trees planted by this river. Even in the stressful times, I can flourish.* Sharon paused to look at the tall, strong trees lining the bank of the river. She listened to their leaves rustling in the wind and to the sounds of the birds perched in their limbs.

A lot of people seem to need me right now, Sharon continued, *and that's a little daunting. But I know I can serve them well if You strengthen me. I'm really counting on You.*

While it's true that seasons come and go, some seasons of life are decidedly more stressful than others. When we encounter especially daunting circumstances, we may be tempted to dig a hole and hide or at least whine in self-pity. But the Bible teaches that we can accomplish all God calls us to do if we depend on Him to supply the nourishment our souls need for the task.

Psalm 42:5 reminds us to hope in the Lord when we are distressed; His presence will restore our praises. If you are going through a stressful season, make time to seek God. Allow Him to fill your soul so you can pour yourself out without resentment or reservation.

Steps of Faith
Father, fill my soul with living water so I can pour freely into those around me.

Deeper Walk: Isaiah 55:10-11

Serving through Giving

*You must each decide in your heart how much to give. And don't
give reluctantly. . . . "For God loves a person who gives cheerfully."*
2 Corinthians 9:7

LORI SAT BESIDE HER FIANCÉ, TIM. This week's premarital counseling homework involved working out a budget. Tim listed the obvious things like rent,
utilities, car payments, and insurance.

"How much do you think we'll spend on food each week?"

"Wait," Lori said. "We need to budget for tithing first."

"Let's work out the most important items first," Tim said.

"But I've learned that if I don't budget for it immediately, I give God my
leftovers."

Growing up, Lori had resented the pressure to drop 10 percent of everything from paychecks to birthday money into the collection plate. But a few
years ago, she'd started noticing a young mom, whom she knew struggled
financially, slipping dollar bills into an envelope each week without hesitation.

"I'm sure God will understand if you don't give," Lori had said to her one
Sunday. "I mean, if it's between groceries and tithing . . ."

"I've never gone without groceries," the young mom said. "God has taken good
care of me and my daughter. I give out of gratitude and to help others in need."

That woman's attitude changed Lori's heart, stirring her to see tithing as a
thank-you to God and a way to serve others through the ministries of her church.

Lori saw the concern on Tim's face when she suggested they list tithing
before rent. "Don't worry. God will provide everything we need," she said.

Why is it that tithing doesn't excite us as much as serving God through our
talents or sharing our faith? In the apostle Paul's letter to the Corinthians, it's
interesting that he felt the need to remind Christians that God loves a cheerful giver, even after he praised their eager generosity. It's as if he understood
that handing over hard-earned cash does not come easily.

Seeing tithing as an act of service, both to our Lord and to our church
family, can stir us to give generously and joyfully, not with our spare cash,
but out of the first of whatever He provides.

Steps of Faith

*Father, forgive me for the many times I've held out on You financially. Help me
to find joy in giving You the best of everything I have.*

Deeper Walk: 2 Corinthians 9:6-15

Appreciate Every Season

We know that all things work together for the good of those who love God:
those who are called according to His purpose.
Romans 8:28, HCSB

"ALL MY FRIENDS ARE GETTING MARRIED," said Chloe. "When will it be my turn?"

"God has a plan, sweetie," her mother, Karen, encouraged her. Then she had an idea.

"How is your volunteer work going at the senior center?"

"It's fun. I got into a serious chess match with Mr. Parker last week," Chloe said, her tone brightening. "I still can't beat him. I'm taking an apple pie to him and Mrs. Hall this week."

"It sounds like you're happy helping out there."

"Yeah," Chloe admitted cheerfully. "I really am."

"Chloe, you're making a difference in the lives of the people there," Karen said. "If you had a family to manage right now, the senior citizens would be missing out on the blessings you bring by ministering to them."

"I hadn't thought about it that way," Chloe reflected.

"God has a purpose for you in the present, Chloe," her mother replied gently. "You're smart and talented. I know you love Jesus and have a heart for serving others. But do you trust God with your future?"

"Yes, I do, Mom."

"Then don't waste this season by wishing it away. I see God doing a beautiful work in you, Chloe, for your good and for His glory. Keep your heart focused on what brings Him joy, because that's where your joy lies as well."

God has a unique purpose for each of our lives. Being single can be a time to plant yourself firmly in the Word without the distractions of marriage and raising a family. Ask the Lord to show you His plan for you, and pray that He will help you to find joy in serving others and growing deeper in Him.

Steps of Faith

Father, thank You for the many blessings You generously give. Reveal to me the opportunities You have for me, and use me for Your glory.

Deeper Walk: 1 Corinthians 7:32-39

Tempted

Since he himself has gone through suffering and testing,
he is able to help us when we are being tested.
Hebrews 2:18

EVER SINCE I'D BEEN LAID OFF, we'd struggled to make ends meet on my husband's salary. My kids needed school supplies, but we could only purchase the bare necessities. And we would be eating the cheapest meals possible for the rest of the month.

On a recent trip to the grocery store, I walked across the parking lot toward the entrance and spied some money on the sidewalk. On closer inspection, I discovered it was a fifty-dollar bill. *Did the woman in front of me drop it when she was fumbling through her purse?* I wondered. *Maybe it's been there longer than that. And who knows where it came from? Anyone could have dropped it.*

I reached over to pick it up. *Fifty dollars! That could help us with the groceries we can't afford.*

As I grabbed a cart and walked in the door, the Holy Spirit pricked my conscience. *What if the fifty dollars belong to the woman who walked into the store before me?*

I caught up with the woman and asked her, "Did you drop some money outside?"

The woman began rummaging through her purse and got a panicked expression on her face. "It was right here. I had a fifty-dollar bill I was going to use for groceries . . ."

I smiled and handed her the money. "I was behind you when you dropped it."

"Oh, thank you so much!" she said.

Thank You, Lord, for helping me to resist temptation.

Jesus was tempted, just as we are, and yet He did not sin. He understands our struggle, though, and can help us if we go to Him. Pray that He will reveal your weak areas and help you prepare ahead of time to resist temptation. Memorize Scripture verses that apply to your weakness, and the Holy Spirit will bring them to mind when you're tempted. Above all, fix your gaze—and your heart—on Jesus.

Steps of Faith

Father, thank You that Jesus understands what it's like to be tempted. Help me flee from sin. Thank You for forgiving me when I fall.

Deeper Walk: Proverbs 4:20-27

Read

Your word is a lamp to guide my feet and a light for my path.
Psalm 119:105

MY DAUGHTER CARRIE SIGNED up to be a reading tutor to help struggling students at her son's school. She works with kids one-on-one and patiently listens as they read. When they struggle with pronunciation, she helps them sound out the words. She's always encouraging and lavish with her praise.

Carrie told me that by the end of one semester, the students had made progress and were more confident about their ability to read.

While I know that some children may have difficulty with reading, public education is available to every child in the United States.

But recently while attending a program at the library, I became more aware of the issue of illiteracy in other countries. Oftentimes this affects women most. They are not given opportunities for education and therefore don't have a chance for higher-paying jobs and a better quality of life.

After prayerful consideration, I felt that this was an area where I could help. I decided to contribute to a women's literacy program.

Illiteracy is a big problem in some parts of the world. When people learn to read, they can understand contracts well enough to avoid bonded labor. They won't get cheated at the marketplace because they will be able to read numbers and know how to add. And they can read the Bible for themselves and teach it to their children.

Steps of Faith
Father, show me what I can do to help others read, study, and understand Your Word so they can know You and experience Your love and forgiveness.

Deeper Walk: Psalm 119:33-40

A Day Off

For everything there is a season, a time for every activity under heaven.
Ecclesiastes 3:1

I PASSED A SANDWICH TO each of my sons as my husband opened a soda. For the first time in several weeks, we all had a day off together. We seized the opportunity to get out of the house.

Summer was almost over, and we would soon be too consumed with school, church activities, and raking fall leaves to spend a whole day together as a family. With Lake Tahoe less than an hour away, we had no excuse to stay at home, where the kids would most likely get sucked into a video game.

As I watched my oldest son playfully tease my youngest, it was hard to believe that we'd had to practically force him into the car to join us. Even he was enjoying our simple picnic at the lake, which would soon be followed by playing in the water, a walk to our favorite bookstore, and finally ice cream before heading home.

Today, a framed picture of my smiling sons sits in the dining room as a reminder of that spontaneous outing and how important it is to snatch spare days for fun and relaxation with family. We spent less than fifteen dollars between used books and ice cream, but the free hours spent together talking, joking, and playing was worth ten times that much.

Life has a way of eating away our spare time before we have a chance to enjoy it. And oftentimes budgets are tight, making weeklong summer vacations out of reach for many families. How can we work in family time with so few free days and minimal funds? And does family time really matter to God? Solomon saw the benefits in enjoying both work and play. Even Jesus took His disciples away from the crowds occasionally. Why not take advantage of summer's warmth, longer days, and academic breaks by enjoying small getaways? When we appreciate how quickly the time passes, days become treasures, especially days spent with those we love.

Steps of Faith

God, prompt me to set aside time to just enjoy my family. Thank You for surrounding me with so much to enjoy with those I love.

Deeper Walk: Ecclesiastes 3:1-13

Cheese

*His brothers hated Joseph because their father loved
him more than the rest of them.*
Genesis 37:4

"ARE WE OUT OF CHEESE?" I asked as I searched the small refrigerator at our family's vacation cabin.

"We'll pick some up on the way back from the lake," Dad said.

My sister Sherry wrestled her two-year-old into his swim trunks. "Cheese isn't worth stopping for."

"You mean it's not worth it for you," I said as I sprinkled grated cheddar on my sandwich.

"Are we really that desperate for cheese?" Sherry asked.

Deep down I knew it was silly to use grated cheese on a sandwich. Still, I sprinkled it on. Why? I didn't want my sister deciding whether I could have cheese on my sandwich. (I'm the oldest and obviously oozing with maturity.)

My sisters and I get along amazingly well compared to some. We are all Christians raising our children to follow Christ, and we truly love being together. Yet, like preteens, we have our moments of sibling rivalry. We're still learning to nurture and treasure our relationship as sisters rather than letting silly differences put a damper on our precious time together.

Cain and Abel, Jacob and Esau, Joseph and his brothers. These familiar siblings are remembered for their battles as young adults. They stand as reminders that sibling rivalry does not end with childhood—it is a part of our sin nature that lurks in our hearts long after we have children of our own. While as Christian women, we are more likely to argue over cheese than push our sisters into a cistern, even little fights tear down family bonds, offer our kids a poor example, and keep us from enjoying pleasant events.

Whether we have good relationships with our siblings or not, we should look for ways to avoid childish arguments, show love, and shine Christ's light into the lives of those God gave us as family.

Steps of Faith

Father, while my family isn't perfect, it's precious to me. Help me to treasure each moment that we have together and to seize opportunities to let Your love flow through me.

Deeper Walk: Genesis 37:1-11

Here and There

Therefore, go and make disciples of all the nations, baptizing them in the name of the Father and the Son and the Holy Spirit.
Matthew 28:19

WHILE GROWING UP, I listened with fascination to stories of my grandparents and other family members traveling domestically and abroad, building churches and spreading the gospel to indigenous people groups.

Strangely, I never thought participating in missions was for me until I stepped out in faith and traveled to Africa with a group of coworkers to help renovate an orphanage. After that, I understood why people had told me that I would "leave a little of my heart behind."

After I returned home, I began planning my next international trip, and the next and the next. I'd caught the mission trip bug.

Fast-forward a year or two, and a group of friends approached me about joining a service-focused small group that would meet each week, serving various shelters and nonprofits. I hesitated, unsure if I would be able to split my energy between local serving and international missions. Seeing my hesitation, a dear friend suggested I spend some time in prayer before making a decision.

After praying about it, I decided to join the group. I was amazed at the great need for help in my community. People I recognized from my local grocery store were now in line at the clothing ministry, getting better shoes and jackets for the upcoming winter. I've grown to love serving in this local ministry while looking forward to my next mission trip.

Jesus clearly instructs us in Scripture that we are to spread the gospel to all nations. Sometimes, we may forget that we live in a nation that needs the gospel as much as a nation across the globe does. But spreading God's love doesn't start on the plane ride to a foreign country. It starts inside our homes, on our doorsteps, and down the street.

Steps of Faith

Father, thank You for the life-giving message of Jesus. Provide opportunities for me to spread Your message to my community by serving and giving. Please bless the work of my hands, in Jesus' name.

Deeper Walk: Mark 16:14-20

A Young Exodus

Whenever we have the opportunity, we should do good to everyone—especially to those in the family of faith.
Galatians 6:10

JILLIAN AND CASEY HAD become fast friends working together at an ad agency in a big city, but Jillian felt a huge wall come up when she began to talk about her personal relationship with God. Casey made a reference to growing up in church, but she didn't seem interested in spiritual matters now.

"Hey, Casey! Do you want to grab dinner tonight with me and some of my girlfriends from Bible study? We're going to that new place on Ninth."

"Ummm, I have something going on tonight," Casey mumbled.

"Casey, I get the feeling that you don't really want anything to do with anything related to God. Didn't you grow up going to church?"

"Yeah, I did. But it didn't do anything for me . . . I mean, I don't have it all together, and I'm not going to pretend that I do."

"I know what you mean," Jillian said, "but I think if you find a real, authentic community of people who love God and are honest about how much they need Him in their lives every moment of every day, you would see people who do mess up and don't have it all together, yet they trust in Him through it all. It's about a relationship with God through Jesus, and the church is the means that God uses to help us walk with Him," Jillian said.

"Well, I have my reservations, but I know it's important to you, so I'll go along. Maybe I should see for myself," Casey admitted.

Do you know any young people who aren't plugged into the church? Engage them, pray for them, and invite them along to be a part of your life and your church. You might be the means God uses to draw them into deeper fellowship.

Steps of Faith
God, show me ways to invite others to share in Your good gift of the church.

Deeper Walk: Ephesians 4:15-16

Ever Present

Give all your worries and cares to God, for he cares about you.
1 Peter 5:7

AFTER THE WORSHIP SERVICE, I glanced over at Charlotte. I hadn't seen her at Bible study in a while, so I caught up with her and gave her a hug.

"How's your mother?" I asked.

Charlotte sighed. "Her health issues are getting more complex, but Bill and I are committed to keep her with us as long as we can."

"And how are you?"

"I'm okay. It's just . . ."

Her eyes filled with tears. "It's just that I'm so lonely. I can't leave her by herself for very long, so I can't go to Bible study or meet a friend for coffee or lunch. Even running quick errands is difficult. And Mama doesn't want anyone but me. It was hard this morning when we told her Bill was staying with her so I could come to church."

Handing her a tissue, I said, "I'm sorry, Charlotte. I didn't know."

"I'm okay. I know God is with me, but sometimes I feel so isolated."

"I know how hard loneliness can be. Is there anything I can do for you?"

"No, but thank you. Talking about it helps. Please keep us in your prayers."

"I will. Why don't I pray for you right now?"

She nodded. Afterward, I hugged her again and made a mental note to call her regularly.

When dealing with family needs, it's easy to feel alone. God's Word is full of promises about His continuing presence with us. Thank goodness His promises don't depend on how we feel! Ask Him to remind you that He's always with you and to send a friend along to help.

Is someone in your church or community experiencing family problems? Pray for her, call her, invite her out, or take her a meal and some flowers. If possible, help with her family member. We all deal with loneliness at times. Reaching out in Jesus' name helps others—and us.

Steps of Faith

Father, thank You for Your presence. Remind me that You're all I need. Help me reach out because others need You too.

Deeper Walk: Psalm 46

Committing to Serve

Since you are so eager to have the special abilities the Spirit gives,
seek those that will strengthen the whole church.
1 Corinthians 14:12

WHEN I SAW THE ANNOUNCEMENT in the church bulletin, something tweaked my heart: "Small group discussion leaders needed for middle school girls' Bible study." I had been a member of the church for a few months but hadn't really gotten involved. I was thinking about getting plugged in, with the emphasis on "thinking about."

But I didn't know a thing about working with middle school girls, except that I'd been one long ago. I liked discussion, especially about the Bible, but I had never led a discussion before. I wasn't sure that I was cut out for this particular service opportunity, so I shelved it in my brain for a while. Yet the Holy Spirit kept bringing it to the forefront of my mind.

I might not have been an expert in communicating with middle school girls, but that wasn't the point. They simply needed someone to point them toward Jesus, to help them understand the Bible, and to explain how God's love had made a difference in my life. I knew God would equip me—I just needed to step up and help. That school year, I got to love on and invest in eight middle school girls. What I didn't count on was how much God would enrich and encourage me in my faith through my time with them.

It's easy and comfortable to show up at church on Sundays and have a great worship experience, but that's not the sum total of the church's role in the life of a believer. As members of the body of Christ, we are to be His hands and feet, serving and loving one another faithfully, while also serving the world that they might know Him too. If you find that your role in church is that of a pew-sitter, pray that God would use you and your gifts, resources, and relationship with Him to build up the body and share the glory of His name with the world.

Steps of Faith
God, thank You for the amazing gift of the church. Thank You for dying for us so that we might live in You.

Deeper Walk: 1 Corinthians 12

Seeing God

For the LORD is a great God, a great King above all gods. He holds in his hands the depths of the earth and the mightiest mountains.

Psalm 95:3-4

I WIPED MY HANDS ON my pants and waited as my hiking partners scrambled up the stretch of loose rock below. Hikes like these make the central Alaska Range one of my favorite places on earth—no trails, no other people, just endless summer sunlight and rugged mountains for miles. But what had started out as a hike quickly turned into a scramble once we'd cleared the timberline.

Up to that point, we'd stuck close to a small stream that fed into the Delta River, following its path up the mountainside. If we'd kept following the stream, we would have had to navigate lots of loose rock, so we'd turned to go up a different route. Now, a few hours later, we were switchbacking up the exposed mountainside, the incline far too steep to take a straight path.

With the clouds sitting low and the moss underfoot increasingly slippery, we realized the conditions were becoming too treacherous to keep going. The last time my friends had gone up this route, a member of the hiking party had twisted an ankle, requiring a self-rescue nobody was eager to repeat.

So we slung off our backpacks and settled ourselves on an outcropping to enjoy the view. We perched there, alternately talking and sitting in quiet.

"I don't know how people can't see God," one of my friends commented at length.

"What?"

"All this," she said, gesturing to the magnificent range surrounding us. "It shows you that you're so small and makes you see something . . . *Someone* bigger. You can't see this or drive through it or hike it and walk away without seeing God."

I nodded, and silence settled on us again as we listened to the wind and the cries of birds soaring below us. I tried to absorb the incomprehensible scale of it all and the God so clearly evident in it. I've seen many beautiful things in the Alaska Range, but the most incredible, by far, was God.

Steps of Faith

Lord, You show Your strength and creativity in the world around us. Thank You for the beauty of nature and for friends to share it with.

Deeper Walk: Psalm 89

Coming Home

I prayed to the Lord, and he answered me. He freed me from all my fears.
Psalm 34:4

Megan watched her friend Teresa's pinched face as she dumped laundry detergent into the washer and closed the lid.

"You must be thrilled to have Ryan home." The whole church had been praying for Teresa's son during his year of deployment in the Middle East.

Teresa forced a smile. "I've been making him all his favorite foods. I don't even mind doing his stinky laundry."

"Then why do you look so sad?"

Teresa took a deep breath. "Did I tell you about the rare, deadly spider that stowed away in Ryan's duffel?"

"No."

"It crawled out when Ryan was unpacking. I screamed and sprayed the thing with bug spray, watching it flail about as it died, like something out of a horror movie. It's as if that spider represented all the ugliness that Ryan has experienced." Teresa's voice cracked. "He says his faith kept him sane, but he's not the same person."

"I'm so sorry." Megan gave Teresa a hug.

"Please pray that God will heal his mind and heart," Teresa pleaded as she fought back tears.

"I will." As she left Teresa's house, Megan prayed, *Lord, please remind me to pray just as hard for Ryan now as I did when he was away.*

Each day, military families celebrate the safe return of their sons, daughters, husbands, and wives only to discover that the person they said good-bye to, worried about, and prayed for has experienced horrors that have changed him or her forever. When we hear news stories of attacks on our troops, we can pray for God to mend their emotional scars as only He can, and to send them the necessary help and support. Pray that He will strengthen their loved ones for the healing process that awaits at home.

Steps of Faith

Father, I don't know what horrors our military men and women experience while serving our country or the impact that their experiences have on their families. Prompt me to pray as these precious families recover while also celebrating long-awaited homecomings.

Deeper Walk: Lamentations 3:21-24

Standing Strong

Children, obey your parents because you belong to the Lord,
for this is the right thing to do.
Ephesians 6:1

AMY WAS ENTERING HER senior year of high school, and although she had much to be thankful for—a great youth group, awesome school friends, good grades, and a loving family—she longed for something more. She wanted a boyfriend, a guy who would make her feel special and provide attention and security.

Thankfully, Amy's parents were clued in to her desires and had placed some safeguards on dating relationships. Amy could go out only with a group of guys and girls. She enjoyed doing that, but she saw other guys and girls in relationships at school, and it seemed like such a wonderful thing.

Amy's mom took her out for frozen yogurt after back-to-school shopping, and she brought up Amy's desire for a boyfriend. "I know how you'd like a boyfriend, but I hope you understand that you don't need to rush that. You have plenty of time in the future to develop those relationships."

"I get it, Mom, but it's still hard. It feels like everybody has a boyfriend except me. And homecoming will be in a couple of months, and it's all everybody will talk about."

"Yes, I can see how that would be hard. Why don't you get a group of friends together to go to the homecoming dance? Your dad and I will be happy to host a party at home afterward and make it a special night for you and your friends."

"Really? That would be awesome!"

It is easy for teenagers to get sidetracked by what they feel like everyone else is doing, but by encouraging them to make wise choices and by equipping them to stand by those choices, parents can help release the grip of peer pressure. God's Word tells us that His people are set apart. When we make choices out of respect for His authority and the authorities He has put in our lives, we can stand strong in His mighty power.

Steps of Faith

Lord, thank You that You are always with us. Give us the strength and courage to make good choices and stand by them.

Deeper Walk: 1 Corinthians 10:12-13

Relating Jesus

Your love for one another will prove to the world that you are my disciples.
John 13:35

"LET ME HELP YOU," Elana said.

Josie gratefully handed over her suitcases to a girl with a sweet smile.

"I'm Elana, and I'm your RA."

"Oh, hi! What's an RA?"

"Residence assistant. If you need anything, you just come see me. I'm in room 12. Do you have anyone to eat lunch with today? If not, get your stuff unpacked and meet me in the lobby at noon. We'll go eat in the cafeteria."

Josie ate lunch with Elana that day and every day that semester. There was something different about Elana. She was genuine, and she cared about other people. She was always doing something for someone else. Soon Josie started attending a Bible study Elana taught for girls on their hall. After a few months of hanging out together, Elana asked Josie if she felt that God was real. Josie realized she did feel that way. She had never thought much about God one way or the other, but over the semester she saw that God was real and personal in Elana's life, and she wanted the same kind of relationship with Him. Josie and Elana talked about how our sin keeps us from God, but Jesus died for our sins so we could know and be forgiven by God.

That night, Josie prayed for the first time, and her relationship with God through Jesus came to life. Josie's time in college brought her many valuable relationships, but her most precious relationship—with God—grew out of her friendship with Elana.

We often think that sharing Jesus with someone means having a formal conversation about the gospel. That's important and has its place in evangelism, but there are also incredible opportunities to witness to others through our relationships. As we invest time, energy, and love in other people, we gain their trust, respect, and companionship. They can see that Christianity isn't just something we do on Sundays; it's a real relationship that impacts every part of our lives. It's who we are and what we live for.

Steps of Faith

Jesus, please use me and my relationships to draw people to a saving knowledge of You.

Deeper Walk: Acts 10:39-43

I'm So Tired

He gives power to the weak and strength to the powerless.
Isaiah 40:29

I COULD BARELY CONCENTRATE during choir practice, usually a highlight of my week. Instead of bringing me joy, singing felt like a chore. Summer had introduced me to the ugly world of divorce. In addition to juggling that heart-breaking process and the responsibilities of being both Mom and Dad, I was dealing with two confused sons, lost relationships, and life-altering decisions.

I had known this new phase of life would be hard, but I completely under-estimated how exhausting it would be. As the music played and the friends around me sang, I fought to keep my mind from spinning and my head from drooping. *God, how will I get through this year if I'm already worn out?*

After practice, my friend Jill gave me a hug. "Hey you, how are you doing?"

All I could get out was "I'm so tired."

Two other friends gathered around me to pray, strengthening me with their love and willingness to listen. Over the next week, each of them followed up in some way, checking in on me, finding little ways to encourage me and my sons, and referring me to helpful resources. More overwhelming weeks would come, but that evening at choir practice reminded me that I had friends to call on for help.

The nonstop demands of solo parenting can quickly lead to exhaustion, especially when a mom is also dealing with the divorce process, ongoing custody or child support battles, or other extra challenges. The emotional upheaval of grieving the loss of a marriage, explaining changes to children, and accepting that life will never be quite the same adds pain to an already energy-sapping situation. If you are a newly single mom and are feeling over-loaded, remember to ask for assistance, seek balance, and call on God for added strength. If you have a friend in this situation, ask God to keep you sensitive to her needs and look for opportunities to lighten her load.

Steps of Faith

Father, give me the strength to face the challenges You have allowed and the heart to recognize when another woman is depleted and needs help.

Deeper Walk: Isaiah 40:28-31

Follow That Dream

You know what I long for, Lord; you hear my every sigh.
Psalm 38:9

CHERYL HAD JUST FINISHED sharing at a women's event about her successful midlife pursuit of writing—a dream she had held on to since her youth. Afterward, a slightly older woman approached her. She expressed appreciation for Cheryl's story and began to share her own.

"As my children were growing up, I began to think about what I would do when my nest was empty. I decided that would be the perfect time to pursue my love for poetry and short stories by writing and attempting to publish my work."

The lady continued with sadness in her voice. "My oldest daughter married and had a little girl. Then she died in a car accident, and I've spent the last fifteen years raising my granddaughter. She's about to head to college, and I'm wondering if it's too late to follow my dream of writing."

Cheryl said, "It's never too late to pursue a dream God has placed on your heart. Let's ask Him to give you wisdom and open doors for your dream."

Women are wired to pour themselves out for the needs of others. God is honored by those sacrifices, and a servant heart is pleasing to Him. But He often plants within us a longing to bless lives in a wider circle. He accompanies that longing with giftedness to pursue that dream. For many of us, those dreams are put on hold to bring us fresh purpose in our later years. One of my friends opened a catering business. Another is pursuing a nursing career in her fifties. The excitement of new challenges can bring great joy and energy to our lives.

Don't put your longings and dreams on a shelf because the years are passing. Take them to God, who is your Dream-Giver. Ask Him to open doors, make provision, and bring Himself honor as you touch lives in a new way.

Steps of Faith

Father, thank You for Your work in us and through us. Help us to recognize Your plans and dreams for us. Give us courage to follow those dreams.

Deeper Walk: Psalm 20:4-6

Speak a New Language

Many waters cannot quench love, nor can rivers drown it.
Song of Songs 8:7

MY HUSBAND SEEMED DISTANT LATELY. We weren't arguing, really, but we weren't talking much either—just the superficial "How was your day?" and "How are the kids?" We were out the door in the mornings with a peck on the cheek and a hurried good-bye. At night, we would collapse without much relationship building going on.

I prayed about it. *Is it me, Lord? His job? The economy?*

I thought back to when we were first married, before kids, a cat, a house, a long commute, and other grown-up responsibilities. We used to do things together: hug, laugh, and spend time talking with each other. We were so connected then, but not now.

My mentor advised me to check out the book *The Five Love Languages*, written by Dr. Gary Chapman. Dr. Chapman says that we all have a love language, and husbands and wives should learn each other's love language.

After reading the book together, we discovered that my husband's primary love language is physical touch, while mine is quality time together. We realized we had been trying to meet each other's needs through our own love languages, rather than each other's. He would reach for a hug or rub my back, and I would try to get him to run errands with me or go for coffee. It just wasn't working.

So I am learning a new language, his love language. I hold his hand, massage his back, or touch his arm. And now I've noticed he's willing to walk the aisles with me at the grocery store!

Learn to speak your husband's love language, and encourage him to learn yours. Does he thrive on encouraging words or a back rub or a trip to the coffee shop with you? Speaking another's love language will probably not feel natural to us, and we do have to invest some time to discover the best way to express love. But it will be so worth it!

Steps of Faith

Father, You created marriage as a way to express and receive love and intimacy. Help us to love our dear ones well.

Deeper Walk: 1 Corinthians 13

Betrayed Confidence

A gossip goes around telling secrets, but those who are
trustworthy can keep a confidence.
Proverbs 11:13

THE TWO NURSES SAT AT the nurse's station talking during a quiet moment. Anita set her coffee cup down and lowered her voice as she whispered to Jill.

Jill's eyebrows went up. "Are you serious?"

"Trust me," Anita said flatly.

Jill began to feel uncomfortable with the discussion. She knew she was crossing a line from sharing information to gossiping, and the Lord was pricking her conscience. But she chose to ignore the inner warning and plunged ahead. "Maria told me she's really been upset lately because her son was arrested for drunk driving."

Immediately Jill regretted repeating information that had been shared in confidence. She remembered the pain in Maria's dark eyes when she had confided in Jill. "I shouldn't have said anything," she told Anita. "Please don't repeat that. Maria begged me not to tell anyone."

Anita shrugged. "Whatever."

As Jill swiveled around in her chair, her eyes met Maria's. There was an uncomfortable silence, then Jill said, "Oh, hi. I didn't think you were working tonight."

"Obviously," Maria said. Tears appeared in her eyes. "I thought you were supposed to be a Christian, and I thought you were my friend," she said.

Jill rushed over to Maria. "I'm so sorry. Please forgive me. I never should have said anything."

Jill's heart felt as if it was sinking. *Oh, Father, please forgive me for gossiping, and help Maria to forgive me too.*

The Bible warns us not to gossip, and for good reason. Malicious talk contains a poison that can ruin another's reputation and the witness of the person who shares it. A betrayed confidence can damage or even destroy a friendship. Heed the Word of God and don't gossip or pass along information you know isn't edifying.

Steps of Faith

Dear Lord, thank You for Your words of wisdom. Please forgive me for the times I have betrayed someone's trust or gossiped. Help me to speak only those words that will glorify You.

Deeper Walk: Proverbs 16:28; 18:8

Joy over the Smallest Gifts

*You have given me greater joy than those who have
abundant harvests of grain and new wine.*

Psalm 4:7

IT WAS ONE OF THOSE DAYS. I awoke—on time—to see the sun shining brightly and hear the birds singing a happy tune. I made it to work on time with no rude or crazy drivers annoying me. Throughout the day, everything seemed to align itself in my favor. My bank account actually had money in it, my friend was available for a spontaneous lunch, my kids didn't whine when I asked them to pick up their stuff, and my mother gave me a compliment when she called.

What bliss!

I know these days don't come every day (how I wish they did), but when they do, I'm grateful for them. The thing is, though, they really *do* come more often than I realize. When I consider all the good things that cooperated to make my day so joyful, none of them is huge. Each thing is a small bit of the day—such as arriving to a meeting on time—but they all add up to make one whole day wonderful. How many times do I overlook or take for granted those small things? When I pay attention to the little gifts and rejoice over them, my entire perspective shifts and I feel a deep sense of joy.

What if you determined every day to focus on the good things—no matter how trivial? Caught a green light? Excellent! The server brought your lunch order correctly? Way to go! You arrived home after work safely? Thank You, God. Every bit counts. You don't have to have "abundant harvests of grain and new wine"—in other words, you don't have to be the most successful or have the greatest and best things—before you can rejoice and be grateful for the life you have. And with each moment of gratitude you offer God, you can build more moments and see opportunities for joy everywhere!

Steps of Faith

God, thank You for blessing my life with things that for too long I've overlooked and neglected to appreciate. Make me aware of every good gift that comes into my life—no matter how seemingly insignificant—so that I may praise You more and experience more of Your joy.

Deeper Walk: Psalm 65

Hall of Faith

Faith shows the reality of what we hope for;
it is the evidence of things we cannot see.
Hebrews 11:1

Do you ever read passages of Scripture and imagine a real or maybe a not-so-real setting?

Recently I was reading through Hebrews 11, which has been called the "Hall of Faith." I imagined a hall of portraits, with God walking down the middle of it, pointing out faithful people who pleased Him. "There's My son Noah, who obeyed Me and built the ark. Here's My son Abraham, who offered up his beloved son. And My son Moses, who led My people out of Egypt." All these people had great faith and obeyed God without the benefit of study Bibles, small groups, or weekly prayer meetings.

As I imagined this scene, I was ashamed. I wasn't sure my portrait would be there. After all, God had provided for us throughout my husband's start-up business, but I still worried about the future. He had kept me safe in a bad car accident, yet I continued to remember that dark time with fear. He had used me in ways I could never have imagined, but I was still tempted to try to accomplish things for Him on my own.

God is pleased and honored when we believe and hope, even though we can't see. In fact, Scripture says, "It is impossible to please God without faith" (Hebrews 11:6).

I want my portrait to hang in the Hall of Faith. I want to share wall space with Gideon, Samuel, Jacob, and Rahab. And most of all, I want Him to point out my portrait, held up by nails of grace.

When a father brought his son to Jesus to be healed, Jesus told him that "anything is possible if a person believes" (Mark 9:23). The man said, "I do believe, but help me overcome my unbelief!" (verse 24). Then Jesus healed the man's son. When we have faith, we allow Jesus to work in our circumstances. When we believe, we begin to act like Him. And when we remember His faithfulness, we free Him up to free us. Lord, help our unbelief!

Steps of Faith

Thank You, Father, for the examples in Scripture of faithful men and women.
We want to please You, Lord.

Deeper Walk: Hebrews 11

On a Rock

He lifted me out of the pit of despair, out of the mud and the mire.
He set my feet on solid ground and steadied me as I walked along.
Psalm 40:2

JESSICA SHIVERED AS she thought back to the night that she learned of her husband's affair. Devastated, she had withdrawn and spiraled down into a crisis of faith.

Cade and Jessica had met in the college ministry at their local church. They dated for a year before getting married and served together in their church and community. During their engagement, they often shared that God had brought them together, and they were expectant about the witness they could be as a married couple.

Now Jessica's thoughts and prayers were consumed with fear, doubt, and bewilderment. *How could I have been so wrong?* she wondered. *God, were You in this at all? Why did You allow this to happen?*

At first, Jessica's crisis of faith drove a wedge between her and Jesus. She stopped going to church, took a leave from service at the homeless ministry, and slept through her morning devotional time. However, over time and through the encouragement and care of her family and friends, she recognized God's provision and comfort even amid such pain.

As she moved back into a closer relationship with Christ—through serving, Bible study, and daily devotions—Jessica found a new, stronger faith to stand on. In the troubled, murky, entrapping mud of betrayal, Jessica sought and found a sure foundation—the rock-solid foundation of Christ alone.

Sometimes we are painfully affected by the sin of others. Devastating situations can cause a crisis of faith for some believers. During those times, we may doubt or question or even distance ourselves from the One who can comfort and heal us. Be frank with the Lord about your doubts, fears, and questions. He is a big, loving God who wants to walk with you through life's trials.

Steps of Faith

Father, thank You for being able to handle my questions and doubts. Thank You for patiently teaching me Your ways as I learn to stand on faith.

Deeper Walk: Psalm 34

Treasured Inheritance

*Now we live with great expectation, and we have a priceless
inheritance—an inheritance that is kept in heaven for you,
pure and undefiled, beyond the reach of change and decay.*
1 Peter 1:3-4

WHEN I TURNED SIXTEEN, my grandmother handed me a small jewelry box. "I'd like you to have this," she told me. When I opened the lid, I got my first glimpse of a simple yet exquisite silver ring, which featured a light-green peridot nestled between two diamond chips.

I looked up at my grandma in surprise as she explained: "You are the only granddaughter with an August birthday like mine, so I want you to have my engagement ring." I'd never seen her wear anything other than a diamond-studded eternity ring my grandfather had given her for their fortieth wedding anniversary.

Thirty-five years after my grandmother gave me her ring—and more than fifteen years after she died—I still wear it every day. I like to think back to 1928, when my grandfather, a lumber salesman, took some of his earnings and bought an engagement ring featuring his beloved's birthstone. I like to remember my grandmother, a bright, loving, and gentle woman who encouraged my love of reading and taught me to bake and (less successfully) to knit.

Sometimes when I look at the sparkling peridot, I reflect on another inheritance—one even more precious. Scripture reminds us that our salvation guarantees God's presence and peace with us now and indescribable joy in the life to come. That is a treasure worth reflecting on every day!

Steps of Faith
Jesus, thank You for the priceless gift You have given me. May I treasure it always and freely share it with others today.

Deeper Walk: Ephesians 1:14-18

Free Time

Teach us to realize the brevity of life, so that we may grow in wisdom.
Psalm 90:12

ROXANNE FOUGHT BACK tears as she gave Emily one last hug and left the kindergarten room. Her friend Anne met her outside.

"You okay, Mama?"

"Yeah, I just can't believe my baby is in kindergarten." Tears welled up.

"Some of the moms are going out for coffee. Would you like to join us?"

"That would be wonderful." Roxanne wiped her eyes. "I don't know what I'm going to do with these free mornings." She had plenty to do at home, but the idea of doing it all in a quiet house felt depressing.

"Before you know it, you'll be looking forward to those moments when you can just have some alone time. But I know the adjustment is hard. There's a new ladies' Bible study that starts next week. You should sign up."

Roxanne gave her eyes one last dab before opening her van door. She had wanted to join a Bible study for a long time. As she followed Anne to the coffee shop, the idea of having some free time started to sound appealing. What else could she do besides Bible study? Start playing piano again, perhaps? And then there was a plea in the most recent church bulletin for help with the food pantry.

God, help me to make the most of this time now that all my kids are in school. Let this be an opportunity to grow, especially in my relationship with You.

For some mothers, the new school year means an empty house for the first time in ages. We are on the threshold of a different season of life with new opportunities and possibilities to prayerfully explore. A milestone for our little ones can also be a milestone for us as we use the gift of a few quiet hours for prayer, Bible study, fellowship, and exercising our God-given talents.

As difficult as it is to send our children into the world, God can use every season for our growth and good, and for His glory.

Steps of Faith

Lord, help me to see changes as new opportunities to grow. May I make the most of every moment as I seek Your will.

Deeper Walk: Ecclesiastes 3:1-8

Economic Envy

A peaceful heart leads to a healthy body; jealousy is like cancer in the bones.
Proverbs 14:30

FIVE YEARS AGO THIS PAST SPRING, we met with our real estate agent to discuss putting our house on the market. Our home was older and was too far from our work, church, and friends.

After showing us prices of comparable houses, our agent shocked us with the decline of the home values in our neighborhood. We owed more than our home was worth, and therefore, we couldn't afford to sell it.

I had really been looking forward to living in a nicer house in a better neighborhood. For a while, I struggled with being envious of friends who were in the type of house and neighborhood I wanted. It didn't seem fair that they had what I'd been dreaming of. For several months, I traded my joy and peace for discontent.

Then one day I read a story about families in developing countries who were barely able to meet basic needs like food and water. I was deeply convicted. Despite being upside down on our mortgage, we had many financial blessings. Blessings that I was in danger of taking for granted. Blessings that aren't a guarantee in many places.

Though others may have fared better in the tough economy than we had, we had never wondered whether we would be able to feed our children. I had never lacked clean drinking water. We had clothes and a safe, dry home (even if the kitchen needed updating). We had working cars and no debts beside our mortgage. I knew I needed to take a moment to repent and ask God's forgiveness for my attitude.

Envy is a symptom of ungratefulness. Thankfulness for all that God has done for us is the cure for it. God wants us to be content with what we have and trust His providence. If you've been envious of others who are financially better off than you, ask Him to remind you of what you have to be thankful for and to redirect your heart toward gratitude.

Steps of Faith

Lord, forgive me for being envious of what others have. Help me to be grateful and focus on all You've done for me.

Deeper Walk: Romans 13:11-14

Missing Out

Clothe yourselves with tenderhearted mercy, kindness,
humility, gentleness, and patience.
Colossians 3:12

"I DIDN'T SEE YOU AT soccer sign-ups," Nancy said when she ran into Diana at church. "Remember, today is the last day."

"I decided not to start Cody in soccer this year. I can't work it in. The practices are either right after I get off work or on Saturdays when I catch up on chores. I know Cody is disappointed."

Nancy noticed how tired Diana's eyes looked. How did single moms like her do it? As long as she'd known Diana, it had just been her and Cody with no dad in the picture. Nancy couldn't blame her for letting something go with all she juggled. But how sad that Cody had to miss out.

"I have an idea," Nancy said. "We can ask to have our sons on the same team, and I'll take Cody to and from practice."

Diana shook her head. "No, that's too much."

Nancy thought about it. It did mean going out of her way. But for some reason she didn't mind. "It's no problem, really. I even have an extra pair of cleats that will probably fit Cody."

Tears welled up in Diana's eyes. "You don't know what an answer to prayer this is. Cody will be so happy."

Nancy hugged Diana. "It makes me happy to be able to do it."

Along with loneliness and extra financial stress, single parents face the exhausting responsibility of juggling work, children, household tasks, and transportation without the help of a spouse. It's easy for those of us who aren't in this situation to underestimate the daily burden of having to do literally everything. When we respond to God's nudges to help with simple things like rides to school or activities, babysitting, small repairs, or just companionship, we can get a glimpse of how much single parents carry and what gifts our offers really are.

Steps of Faith

Father, I get so caught up in my daily routine that I forget about the burdens others may be struggling with. Show me how to help with little things that so quickly add up.

Deeper Walk: Ecclesiastes 4:9-12

Find Us Faithful

A faithful [woman] will have many blessings.
Proverbs 28:20, HCSB

SEVERAL YEARS AGO, I became interested in using dogs for therapy work, so I contacted a therapy group in my area and took the necessary steps to train my Doberman pinscher. After he passed his tests, Diesel and I were ready to go.

I made a commitment to visit a local nursing home twice a month. Every other week, I bathed and groomed Diesel. Then I tied a bandanna around his neck and loaded him into my SUV for the trip to the nursing home. The residents looked forward to our visits, and Diesel loved the extra attention.

Sometimes I was tempted to sleep in on Saturday mornings. As a busy working woman, I didn't always feel like getting up early and going through the routine of bathing and grooming Diesel. But I had made a commitment, and I thought it was important to keep it.

We developed a special relationship with an eighty-five-year-old widow. Mrs. Tate stroked Diesel's sleek black coat while she told stories about her husband, who had served in World War II, and her children and grandchildren, who lived in other states.

One Saturday as Diesel rested his head in Mrs. Tate's lap, I began to tell her about the love of Jesus. While she had always had a basic belief in God, she didn't have a personal relationship with Him. During each visit, I told her how God was working in my life and that He wanted a special relationship with her, too.

After several weeks of my witnessing to Mrs. Tate, she embraced Jesus as her Savior. Two weeks later when Diesel and I visited the nursing home, her bed was empty. She had gone home to be with the Lord. I'm thankful that God helped me to be faithful to my commitment.

If you feel the Lord is leading you to make a commitment to something or someone, ask Him to provide you with the grace and strength you'll need to follow through. Don't let schedules or the little details of your life derail God's plan for you. If He has called you to do something, He will bless you for being obedient.

Steps of Faith

Father, thank You for being interested in the details of my life. Please help me to be faithful to the commitments You have called me to make so that others will give glory to You.

Deeper Walk: Psalm 18:24-27

Building Endurance

We can rejoice, too, when we run into problems and trials,
for we know that they help us develop endurance.

Romans 5:3

EVERYTHING WAS FALLING APART. So why wasn't I?

A few years earlier I had been drowning in depression and anxiety, reduced to tears by the smallest thing. How would I ever deal with a major life crisis if I couldn't even hold myself together through everyday misunderstandings or disappointments? As I grew stronger, however, I sensed God challenging me to trust Him. If He allowed a crisis, it would be because He knew I was strong enough for it. And amazingly, I experienced many and survived! Trials increased in intensity, gradually strengthening my faith, including my faith in His ability to keep me strong no matter what came my way.

But in this current situation, peace seemed almost unnatural considering the hugeness of what was going on. Was I in denial or experiencing a peace that could come only from God and several years of seeing Him at work? Suddenly I understood what Philippians 4:7 says when it mentions how the peace of God surpasses all understanding (ESV). Yes, life was falling apart in ways that seemed beyond repair. I needed to prepare for the worst-case scenario, but I didn't need to give in to despair. As I'd seen firsthand so many times, God wouldn't allow anything unless He was prepared to ride it out with me, provide for me, and keep me strong through it.

It doesn't require much faith when every prayer is answered immediately, bills are paid ahead of schedule, and everyone we love is in perfect health and making the right choices. We experience growth spurts of faith not when life is going smoothly, but when it's so out of control that only God can fix it.

God's Word provides answers not for *if* we face trials, but for *when* we face them. He also promises to use each trial, from daily disappointments to heart-shattering losses, to increase our faith as we seek and obey Him. Reflect on how past tests have prepared you for any current crises.

Steps of Faith

Thank You, Father, for never wasting a crisis, but for using each one to deepen my relationship with You and strengthen my ability to trust Your plan.

Deeper Walk: Romans 5:1-5

Never an Unkind Word

*Don't use foul or abusive language. Let everything you say be good and helpful,
so that your words will be an encouragement to those who hear them.*

Ephesians 4:29

"WHERE IS MY CHECKBOOK?" Brenda said aloud as she searched her purse again. "Mike probably took it to pay bills. Why didn't he put it back? He knew I was attending this kitchen supply party."

"You can pay with a credit or debit card," Sandy, the kitchen supply rep, said.

"Thanks, but it still makes me mad."

"Face it," her friend Louise piped in. "Men don't think."

Brenda nodded. "I know what you mean."

Louise nudged Sandy. "So what are your complaints about Allan?"

Sandy smiled. "Allan painted the kitchen cabinets. How can I complain about that?"

Brenda noticed that Sandy never had a negative word to say about Allan. All Brenda ever heard about was Allan's projects and how great he was with the kids.

Suddenly it hit her how refreshing Sandy's attitude was. While Louise encouraged Brenda's rants, Sandy's respect and appreciation for Allan made her want to stop criticizing and say more nice things about Mike.

How often do we focus so intently on frustrating traits or annoying habits (as if we don't have any) that we are blinded to what we love about our husbands? And how often do we vocalize such complaints in public, presenting the man we love as thoughtless, brainless, or insensitive?

"Don't use foul or abusive language," Paul wrote in Ephesians 4:29. Surely this applies to discussions about our husbands. How can we replace our tendency to criticize with a desire to set an example of respect, admiration, and praise for the man we promised to honor and cherish?

Steps of Faith

Father, sometimes I can't believe what comes out of my mouth. Replace my critical spirit with a desire to sing my husband's praises.

Deeper Walk: Ephesians 4:29-32

AUGUST 26

Interfering In-Laws

You must all be quick to listen, slow to speak, and slow to get angry.
Human anger does not produce the righteousness God desires.
James 1:19-20

WHEN MY MOTHER-IN-LAW, LINDA, moved in with us two years ago, I naively thought we'd agree about almost everything. But having another family member in the house proved to be a challenge, especially when it came to how I disciplined the children.

"Mom," Chandler called one morning, "Maggie is breaking my model airplanes again."

"Am not!" Maggie hollered back.

"Maggie," I called from the kitchen, "are you ruining your brother's things?"

"No," she replied.

I sighed and walked into the living room, where the argument was becoming louder. "Both of you, listen to me. Dad and I have talked with you about respecting each other's things, right?"

Chandler and Maggie nodded.

"But I didn't break anything, Mom," Maggie insisted. "I was just playing with it."

"That is not true," Chandler shouted. "Quit lying, Maggie!"

Just as I was about to split the two of them up, Linda walked into the room.

"They're just being kids, Charlotte." She looked at me disapprovingly and clicked the TV remote to the cartoon channel. "Now, why don't you kids just watch some TV? You know all the yelling around here gives me headaches."

As she turned to walk out of the room, I felt my anger rising. *Lord, help me to deal with Linda's constant interference.*

Interfering parents are nothing new. Some of us have had to endure the painful reality that no matter how hard we try to raise our own families, it won't ever be up to our own parents' standards. That can leave us feeling that we can't do anything without being criticized. But God doesn't want us to harbor anger toward anyone. Pray for patience with the offending person and for the wisdom to work through the situation.

Steps of Faith
Father, please help me learn to focus on the positive qualities in others instead of dwelling on our differences. Help me to leave my anger at the foot of the cross.

Deeper Walk: Proverbs 19:11, NIV

238

Living Outside the Box

Trust in the LORD with all your heart;
do not depend on your own understanding.
Proverbs 3:5

MY HUSBAND WAS LAID OFF six years ago and has still not found a full-time job. He's had some contract work and some part-time work, but oh, how he wants to work full time!

We've had to make plenty of adjustments. I've returned to work full time. We haven't taken any large vacations, we don't eat out, and we had to take our daughters out of the private Christian school they were attending.

My husband homeschools them, and they are excelling. Among other things, they are each learning to play a musical instrument, they are good at math (because he's good at math), he's teaching them martial arts, and he has shown them household tasks like woodworking and how to change the oil in the car.

As a family, we've been learning to live in an outside-the-box situation. It's difficult because my husband wants to be working full time, and just like any stay-at-home parent, he misses the daily adult interaction.

But it's also been beautiful because our daughters get to spend time with their dad that they never would have gotten to if he was working sixty hours a week. They're learning things from him that I'm not good at. And they're seeing firsthand that they don't have to do things the world's way.

The best thing about this nontraditional situation is that we are all learning on a real-life, real-time basis what it means to trust God. We absolutely do not understand why my husband can't find a job—it's certainly not for lack of trying.

We don't understand why he's the one homeschooling them when it's what I originally wanted to do. And though we'll probably never know the answers on this side of eternity, we're trusting the Lord. His ways are best. Always.

Are you living in an outside-the-box situation? Where are you learning to trust the Lord? He will never let you down.

Steps of Faith

Father, sometimes it's so hard to trust You when things are upside down. Yet You have a plan for our lives and know what is best. Thank You.

Deeper Walk: Proverbs 3:5-8

Crisis

You must be holy in everything you do, just as God who chose you is holy.
1 Peter 1:15

I FOUND OUT ABOUT "the birds and the bees" quite accidently. My older sister and two of her friends were discussing a teenage girl in the neighborhood who was pregnant. I knew this girl wasn't married, and I didn't understand how she could be having a baby. So later, after Pat's friends left, I nagged her until she caved in and told me.

It was 1959, and Nancy, the pregnant girl, just disappeared for a while and reappeared a few months later—not pregnant. That's the way it was done in the fifties. Everything was very secretive.

Today, it's not so scandalous or even unusual when an unmarried girl or woman becomes pregnant. Unwed mothers in Hollywood proudly flaunt their baby bumps, and many have no intentions of marrying the father of their child.

A couple of years ago, my neighbor Helen sat in my kitchen in tears. Her seventeen-year-old daughter was pregnant, and Helen was crushed. The family attended church every week. Emma was an honor student, active in the church youth group, and had scholarship offers from several universities.

But Emma and her boyfriend gave in to temptation, and now she was pregnant. And while no one in Hollywood blinks an eye at single motherhood, Emma's family was in crisis mode.

Emma turned down the scholarships because she didn't want to give her baby up for adoption. She finished high school and works at a grocery store while taking one or two college classes at a time. Emma has learned the importance of waiting. Her life is very different from what she dreamed it would be, but the love and support of her family and the church are providing a nurturing place for her faith—and her baby—to grow.

God's rules are rooted in His knowledge of what's best for us. Ask the Holy Spirit to give you the strength to follow in Jesus' footsteps each day.

Steps of Faith

Lord, please help me to be obedient to Your laws and to walk in Your ways.
I want to honor You.

Deeper Walk: 1 Thessalonians 4:1-8

Emergency Love

Don't look out only for your own interests, but take an interest in others, too.
Philippians 2:4

VICKI SAT IN THE EMERGENCY ROOM cubicle that her husband had left minutes earlier. When they wheeled Charles off to run some tests, she had remained behind as instructed. Vicki sighed loudly. This was not how her vacation was supposed to go.

I guess I should stop whining and start praying, Vicki thought to herself. But the simple act of closing her eyes prompted tears to form. And instead of praying for Charles, Vicki caught herself complaining to the Lord about how her husband's chronic health problems seemed to frequently interrupt their plans. She also feared the added cost of a hospital visit would make Charles cut back on their vacation budget.

Vicki purged her heart of all the bitterness she had accumulated over recent months about Charles's health problems and the inconvenience they had become to her. But after several minutes of woeful complaining, she felt a gentle voice interrupting her negative thoughts.

To her surprise, she seemed to hear her mother's sweet voice echoing the gentle warning she'd given Vicki on her wedding day several years earlier.

"Vicki, marriage isn't about you; it's always about two," her mom had stated plainly.

"You're right, Mom," Vicki said aloud now, "and it's time I learned that once and for all." Vicki wiped her tears away, closed her eyes, and began praying for the ability to love selflessly on this difficult day.

Some say that marriage is a fifty-fifty arrangement, but 1 Corinthians 13 describes a 100 percent variety of love. How can you better show love to those closest to you today?

Steps of Faith

Lord, true love often demands a sacrifice. You have shown me how to love that way. Help me follow Your example.

Deeper Walk: Philippians 2:1-11

241

Childlike Faith

"I assure you," He said, "unless you are converted and become like children, you will never enter the kingdom of heaven."
Matthew 18:3, HCSB

MY SISTER AND I HAVE probably watched the movie *Enchanted* with our kids ten times. We never tire of displaced princess Giselle, lost in modern-day Manhattan, where she meets cynical divorce attorney/single dad Robert.

While heartbreak has given Robert plenty of reasons not to raise his daughter on fairy tales or believe in happily ever after, Giselle holds on to her cartoony "faith" that dreams come true and that true love's kiss is the most powerful thing in the world.

The more I watch the movie, the more I appreciate how Robert is changed by Giselle, who breaks into song in public, weeps when she hears that a couple is getting divorced, and never gives up on the arrival of her prince. Her innocence, uninhibited joy, and ability to see the best in everything and everyone slowly softens Robert, and she never wavers even as she gets a few tastes of real life.

Recently, I began to see their relationship as a reflection of the power of childlike faith. I found myself thinking of women I've known whose faith in God remained as pure and firm as Giselle's belief in happily ever after, even in the midst of trauma. The more I felt my own circumstances threatening to toughen me, the more I looked to them as examples of how I wanted to live, and I prayed that I would never lose the peace and joy of childlike faith.

Jesus pointed to children as examples of the faith required to enter His Kingdom. Unlike sometimes-jaded adults who have experienced too much of life to simply believe someone who says "I am the way, the truth, and the life" (John 14:6), children embrace His truths without question. Once we have accepted Christ with this unspoiled faith, our challenge is holding on to it through the pain, uncertainty, and loss of living in an ungodly world. Often, we need to see a believer with faith that seems too idealistic to be true before we can recognize the benefit of childlike faith. In what area is God asking you to believe like a child?

Steps of Faith

Lord, life can be so complicated, but You remain trustworthy. Help me to believe this even when my head tells me not to.

Deeper Walk: Mark 10:13-16

Close to Home

Be happy with those who are happy, and weep with those who weep.
Romans 12:15

As CATHERINE WALKED INTO CHURCH, she spotted flowers from yesterday's memorial for an older woman who had died suddenly.

"I didn't see you at Betty's service." Sandy's voice startled Catherine.

"I know. I can't go to funerals anymore. They bring back too many memories of when my mom passed away."

"I understand. But I guess because I know what it's like to lose someone I love, I try not to miss funerals. I want to be there to offer support."

Catherine felt a twinge of guilt. She slipped into the back row of the sanctuary, where she spotted Melanie, a young woman who had been like a daughter to Betty. Tears dripped down Melanie's face as the music played. How many times had Catherine wept her way through worship after losing her mom? Sandy's comment about funerals came back to her. Two years had passed since her mother's death. Although Catherine still missed her and probably always would, she recalled how others had comforted her throughout that first year. If only she had been willing to push past her own issues and be there for women like Melanie yesterday.

But she was here now.

Catherine edged close to Melanie, feeling her grief through her sniffles and silent tears. She took Melanie's hand. *Help me to be more like Sandy, God, and to look for opportunities to offer comfort instead of avoiding what hits close to home.*

Paul's words in 2 Corinthians 1:3-7 remind us that suffering equips us to comfort others. How sad it is when we realize that the only thing holding us back from offering comfort to a grieving sister in Christ is an inability to set our personal pain aside for hers. While sharing someone's sadness might stir up heart-wrenching memories, recalling God's faithfulness to send us solace can stir us to be present to others in need.

Steps of Faith

Lord, forgive me for the times when I hid from the pain that equipped me to help someone through a storm. Give me the courage to comfort even when it's painful.

Deeper Walk: 2 Corinthians 1:3-7

Standing Up and Sticking Out

If someone asks about your hope as a believer, always be ready to explain it.

1 Peter 3:15

GRACE ANN WAS A FRESHMAN in college when she took Philosophy 101, a huge lecture class. When the professor taught on relativism—the belief that truth is relative to each individual and cannot be fully known—Grace Ann felt compelled to point out the holes in that argument. She asked the professor if he believed that relativism was true. When he said he did, she mentioned that if relativism says there is no absolute truth, its proponents can't even say that *it* is true.

The professor smirked and said he had heard that argument before. He told Grace Ann that she should start thinking for herself now that she was in college and not fall back on the beliefs she was raised on.

He then said he would be happy to put any other naive freshmen in their place. Grace Ann shrank down in her seat, embarrassed and a little angry.

After class, several students thanked her for taking a stand. Even students who didn't agree with her said they admired the fact that she stood up for what she believed. The rest of the semester, Grace Ann continued to feel like the professor singled her out, so she always tried to be prepared for class and make comments that were respectful yet pointed toward a godly worldview. She stuck with the class and got a decent grade despite her professor's obvious dislike of her. But the greater reward was that she was faithful to the Lord and His Word.

God uses even the smallest daily acts of courage to build up His people, share His glory, and grow His Kingdom. Defending the weak, befriending the lonely, healing the broken, sharing the gospel, proclaiming the truth—those are the things Jesus spent His earthly ministry doing. And those things require great courage from us as we live in a way that shows what we truly believe.

Steps of Faith

Lord, give me courage and confidence to speak the truth in Your mighty name and to trust You with the results.

Deeper Walk: 2 Corinthians 4:16-18

Giving to Get

When you give to someone in need,
don't let your left hand know what your right hand is doing.
Matthew 6:3

CRYSTAL WATCHED THE CONGREGATION trickle toward the platform and drop their contributions into the basket to help a family whose daughter was fighting cancer.

Mark handed Crystal a check to take up front. She remembered the ten dollars in her purse, set aside for coffee with friends and other treats. She would give that, too. After hearing stories of how God rewarded acts of generosity, she had felt challenged to give more freely. Finances were a constant struggle for her and Mark. Maybe if she gave more, that would change.

A month later, Crystal balanced the checkbook. She had hoped to cover all the bills and have enough left over to splurge on dinner out or to save for their summer vacation. Instead, the remainder would only cover groceries, and even there, she needed to tighten the budget a little.

"God, I don't get it," she said out loud. "I thought You promised to bless generosity, but it looks like we're still just barely making it."

As Crystal heard her own words, the selfishness of her motives hit her heart. What had gotten into her? Did she regret sacrificing her coffee money? No. But she did regret giving in hopes of getting something from God in return.

God, I'm so sorry. You sacrificed Your Son, Jesus, on a cross to pay for my sin. I want to give out of obedience and my love for You. Please teach me how.

When we read verses about God blessing generosity and hear testimonies that suggest charity will always be followed by earthly blessings, it's easy to start giving with strings attached. Sometimes we don't recognize our conditional giving until God makes us aware of it; other times, we know exactly what we're doing. In Matthew 6, Jesus encourages giving that is so secret that one hand doesn't even know what the other hand is doing. When we're tempted to give in hopes of receiving a windfall, perhaps we can apply this verse by giving cheerfully in secret without strings attached.

Steps of Faith

God, forgive the hidden motives behind my giving. Show me how to be a cheerful and unconditional giver.

Deeper Walk: Matthew 6:1-4

All the Friendly People

Live wisely among those who are not believers, and
make the most of every opportunity.
Colossians 4:5

WHILE OUR FAMILY VACATIONED in an RV this summer, we visited six churches. My husband and I felt it was important to continue worshiping alongside other believers, and we wanted our children to experience the diversity of the body of Christ. Not only did we hear God's Word proclaimed, we were warmly welcomed by church members as we joined them in worship. However, there was one exception.

I know there were warm and welcoming people at this church; we just didn't meet them. During the "welcome time" a few people shook our hands, but then they quickly moved on to others they knew already.

Our experience visiting these churches reminded me of when we moved to a new area and were looking for a new church family. We found one church where the preaching was outstanding and the worship was amazing. But when it came to developing relationships, we felt like we just didn't fit in.

Week after week, we tried to get to know the people, but it seemed as if they were so busy with the people they already knew that they didn't take the time to reach out to visitors. We ended up finding another church where the people welcomed us with open arms.

The lesson I took from those experiences was that I need to make an effort to be friendly to the visitors who attend my church.

The apostle Paul ends many of his epistles by expressing numerous greetings, both personally and on behalf of others. We can learn something from Paul's friendly habit: Greetings are important. When we welcome others into our church warmly, we help create an atmosphere in which they can hear the Holy Spirit and respond to Him. Consider how you can be more welcoming to visitors at your church. How might you help create a warm atmosphere so others can feel God's love?

Steps of Faith

Lord, help me be more aware of others' needs. Show me how to help others feel welcome so they can hear from You.

Deeper Walk: Colossians 4

Dealing with Disappointment

*Work willingly at whatever you do, as though you were working for the Lord
rather than for people. Remember . . . that the Master you are serving is Christ.*
Colossians 3:23-24

I WAS AN IDEAL EMPLOYEE AT the university's communications office. I came
in early, stayed late, and produced some successful pieces that drew lots of
attention to the university within my first few months on the job. But when a
management position opened up and I applied, I was overlooked.

The day I found out about not getting the promotion, I was hurt and angry.
My emotions fluctuated between disappointment and resentment. One minute
I felt I should just quit my job and go to another workplace entirely, and the
next I was vowing to work harder and better so that someone would notice.

Lying in bed that night, I prayed about my situation for what seemed like
the millionth time that day. And suddenly a thought popped into my head.
Someone had noticed my hard work—Someone who mattered much more
than my boss or my coworkers. God noticed every time I used the gifts He had
given me for His glory and every time I did my best work for His name's sake.

I was still disappointed that I hadn't received the promotion, but I clung
to the promise that God had a plan for me—something better than I could ask
or imagine. I knew He'd be with me and recounted all the ways He'd blessed
me already. I couldn't be disappointed for long if I considered all the goodness
that He showed me every day.

Disappointment is a part of life because heartbreak was introduced at
the Fall, but we serve a Savior who has overcome the world (see John 16:33).
Will we allow disappointment to drive us away from God and His promises,
or will we consider how God might be working through our disappointments
to make us more like His Son and to accomplish His big-picture plan in our
lives? How awesome that we serve a God who uses all things—even things we
see as negative—for our good and His glory.

Steps of Faith
*Lord Jesus, thank You for never disappointing us, and thank You for the honor
and love that You bestow on us by calling us Your own.*

Deeper Walk: Hebrews 10:19-23

Count Your Blessings

O LORD my God . . . if I tried to recite all your wonderful deeds,
I would never come to the end of them.

Psalm 40:5

MANY YEARS AGO a friend gave me what was to become one of my most trea-sured possessions. On the outside, the book appeared to be a simple journal with a lovely cover. When I opened it, however, I discovered that for each date listed, there were five blank lines, with the encouragement to "be sure to remember five things to be grateful for every day."

"It's a blessings journal," my friend told me. "I started using one, and I've been amazed by how keeping track of the things I have to be grateful for has revolutionized my life. I love it—and thought you might want one too."

I was touched and promised that I'd start using it.

My first blessing I listed was my friend who thought of me. Friends are great blessings! From there, my brain exploded with things to be thankful for—from the big items, such as the fact that my father's cancer surgery went well, to the small items, such as how ducks make me laugh and how wonderful soft blankets feel on a chilly day.

Soon I found myself going through each day thinking, *I'll have to write that in my blessings journal.* My friend was right; keeping a list of daily bless-ings revolutionized my outlook and attitude. And as I looked back over the blessings, I saw God's sense of humor, His protection, His joy, His healing, His creativity, His love, and most important, His faithfulness to me.

Have you ever tried to list all of God's wonderful deeds? They're endless! You don't have to invest in a blessings journal to practice gratitude, but writ-ing down ways that God has been active and present in your life every day will remind you of how very blessed you are, and it will revolutionize your outlook and attitude, too.

Steps of Faith

God, Thank You for being so good to me. It's easy to overlook Your continual work in the world and in my life. Let me see blessings everywhere I look. Grow my sense of gratitude each day.

Deeper Walk: 1 Chronicles 16:7-36

A New Journey

I am certain that God, who began the good work within you, will continue his work until it is finally finished on the day when Christ Jesus returns.
Philippians 1:6

I SAT IN THE CROWDED AUDITORIUM. Somewhere in the students' section sat my eighteen-year-old son. In just a few days he would begin classes as a university student. Friends who had warned me, "Enjoy the high school years because they go fast," weren't exaggerating. Here we were at freshman orientation.

As I listened to the speeches, school song, and advice about the importance of getting involved, I tried to predict Christian's response to the program. Knowing him, he was probably listening politely to the speakers but did not praise his college through those sentimental lyrics. Would he actually play Frisbee in the quad and join a club as suggested? Would he make friends and become involved in a campus ministry? Would he graduate in four years, change his major repeatedly, or decide that college wasn't for him after all?

Bottom line, my son was now an adult, moving on to a new stage of life. He would face pressures, frustrations, and disillusionment. His freedom to make decisions without asking Mom and Dad's permission meant the consequences were also his. Was he ready? According to the calendar, he was. All I could do was pray and hope that the love and faith he'd been raised on would make the difference when he needed it.

When we hold our newborns, it's hard to fathom ever sending them out into the world. Eventually parents must say good-bye as a precious son or daughter starts college, joins the military, gets married, or moves into a new apartment. That's when our ability to trust God with our children is truly tested. While we are not being asked to lay our child of promise on the altar, letting go is a painful moment. But it is also full of hope. While we wait on what God has in store for them, we can pray that they hold on to Him, trust His Word, and live as His beloved children.

Steps of Faith
Heavenly Father, when we are raising and enjoying our children, it's easy to forget that we received them on loan. Help us as we let go and let them embrace adulthood.

Deeper Walk: Philippians 1:3-11

Talking Away the Stress

You will keep in perfect peace all who trust in you,
all whose thoughts are fixed on you!
Isaiah 26:3

I HAD PLENTY TO DO and a lot on my mind. I felt convinced that I wouldn't be able to focus until I got some peace. I called a friend whom I often prayed with, but we spent more time discussing problems than bringing all that was on our hearts to God. I poured out my frustrations in an e-mail to a Christian friend from work, and then when the phone rang, I seized the opportunity to rehash everything again. I set the phone down at almost 9:00 p.m. Instead of feeling more relaxed about my circumstances, I felt guilty for wasting so much time.

How often had I criticized other family members for turning to television, the computer, or sleep when life felt out of control? Like them, I was searching for a false source of peace. Instead of turning to a screen or a pillow, I turned to the phone and e-mail, chattering away hours and walking away just as discontent.

Now, with regret piled on top of what was already going on, I felt even worse than when I started the day. *God, help me to make up the time*, I prayed silently. I began praying through everything that had driven me to the phone. The calm I longed for came, finally.

Lord, help me start here next time, and never let me forget the consequences of seeking comfort in the wrong places.

As believers, we know where true peace comes from, so why do we run so quickly to time wasters like the television, the computer, gadgets, or gossip? Isaiah's words remind us that God promises peace not to those who zone out in front of the television or who run around in a blur, but to those whose minds are steadfast. The assurance that comes after times of prayer can serve as a reminder of what we gain when we seek Him above all else.

Steps of Faith

Lord, why do I expect to find peace in anything but You? Help me to run to You first, before anyone or anything else.

Deeper Walk: Isaiah 26:3-7

Exercising the Sanctuary

Don't you realize that your body is the temple
of the Holy Spirit, who lives in you?
1 Corinthians 6:19

COURTNEY WAS DISAPPOINTED to learn at her checkup that her cholesterol was slightly elevated. She wasn't really overweight, but the doctor told her it would be harder for her body to manage cholesterol levels as she got older. He advised her to cut certain fatty foods out of her diet and to exercise three or four times a week. He assured her that if she just made those lifestyle changes, she could avoid taking medication.

Courtney made a mental list of her daily routine: up before dawn for time with Jesus, at work by 8:30, often working through lunch, making it home by 6:30, fixing and eating dinner, spending time with family, getting the kids ready for bed, watching a TV show or two, and collapsing into bed. Every Tuesday she had her women's Bible study, and every Thursday was book club. Weekends were spent trying to do household chores for which there was no time during the week. *Oh, Lord, help me figure out when I could possibly work exercise into my busy life*, she prayed.

Paul tells Timothy, "Physical training is of some value" (1 Timothy 4:8, NIV). Exercise is one way to take care of the bodies God has given us and prepare ourselves to be more effective in the Kingdom. Studies have shown that exercise not only keeps us healthier but also elevates our energy levels and has a positive impact on our moods. If you're struggling to find the time to work out, here are a few tips that might work: Try several smaller workouts throughout the day, even ten minutes at a time. Find free exercise routines online, and work out during TV time. Take a walk during lunch, maybe even a prayer walk. Find a workout partner or someone to hold you accountable to your goals. And don't forget to pray about it. God will help you find time you didn't know you had so you can feel better and be healthier!

Steps of Faith

Dear Lord, I know You want me to take care of my body and have energy to serve You. Please help me to find time and the discipline to exercise.

Deeper Walk: 1 Corinthians 9:24-27

Don't Give In

Those who love money will never have enough.
How meaningless to think that wealth brings true happiness!
Ecclesiastes 5:10

AFTER I PICKED MALLORY UP from Shelby's party, we walked past several Mercedes, Acuras, and Audis to get to our trusty Honda. Mallory described the mountain of birthday gifts Shelby had received. "She got an iPhone for her birthday, Mom. When can I get a cell phone?"

"We talked about this, remember? You can have a basic one next year."

"Everybody but me already has one."

"I doubt it, but it doesn't change anything. You don't need one." Mallory and I live in an affluent suburb of a big city, though we are anything but affluent. Mallory's friends' houses are big enough to swallow ours. Their rooms are stuffed with the latest in fashion, decor, and technology. Blessed though we are, we can't keep up. And I don't want to.

"Mom, can't we get things because we *want* them and not because we *need* them?"

"We do, sometimes. But the problem comes when we give in to what we want all the time. We buy more stuff, but that doesn't make us happy, so we buy even more. Do you know what that's called?"

"Shopping?"

"Sort of. When we keep wanting more money or things, that's greed. God wants us to be content with what He has given us. He wants us to focus on Him rather than on money or stuff. It's for our good. He knows those things won't fill us up inside. Only He can do that."

"But it's hard not to be greedy."

"I know. Let's pray right now for Him to help us."

Our culture feeds our greed. We don't really need to be taught "the gimmes"—our human nature takes care of that. The toddler's fingers grasp for more and keep grasping until those fingers are wrinkled with age. But Scripture tells us that we came into the world with nothing and we'll leave it with nothing. We should hold our God-given resources with open hands. When we turn our hearts toward Him, there won't be room for greed.

Steps of Faith

Father, forgive me for grasping for more. Help me to find my fulfillment in You.

Deeper Walk: 1 Timothy 6:6-10

Faithful

My grace is sufficient for you, for power is perfected in weakness.
2 Corinthians 12:9, HCSB

MY HUSBAND, BRIAN, has been blessed with a job that provides a generous salary, good benefits, and a company car. Unfortunately, it also requires him to travel three or four nights a week, and I miss him terribly when he is gone.

When our children were growing up, I got to see the first toothless smiles and the first wobbly steps, while Brian missed a lot of those precious "firsts." And yet he always worked "enthusiastically, as something done for the Lord and not for men" (Colossians 3:23, HCSB). He worked hard without complaining, because he put his family's needs above his own.

I was so moved by his wonderful attitude that I decided to do the same. In his absence, I learned how to swing a hammer, use a drill, and call a repairman when I couldn't fix the broken item myself. Looking back, I see how the Lord used Brian's job to teach me to be more patient and capable than I might have been otherwise. I also learned how to be grateful for a husband who knew the value of hard work and rarely missed a day.

While he might not have been there to see every "first," he did model for our children the virtues of faithfulness, hard work, determination, and a job well done. By watching him, they learned how to become responsible adults who are now valued by their own families, friends, and employers.

Women whose husbands travel regularly begin to appreciate the challenges single moms face on a daily basis. If your husband travels frequently, enlist the help of family members and friends. Know whom you can call in case of emergency. And if you happen to know others who are struggling to make it on their own, be the friend they can turn to in a pinch! Above all, saturate yourself in God's Word and spend time in His presence every day. His grace is sufficient for you.

Steps of Faith

Father, please give me an extra dose of Your grace to follow the path You have set before me. Help me be diligent in fulfilling Your will for me.

Deeper Walk: 2 Corinthians 12:1-10

Fear No Evil

For God has not given us a spirit of fear and timidity, but
of power, love, and self-discipline.
2 Timothy 1:7

SOME YEARS AGO while in New York City on a business trip, I walked to Ground Zero. I watched quietly alongside others as construction crews busily worked on the memorial and museum to take the place of the Twin Towers demolished on 9/11. I was glad to see that at least some of what had been destroyed that terrible day was being made new. I felt a little hope inch its way into my cynical heart. But in my mind the scene below me still held the scent of evil. And as I turned to walk away, the all-too-familiar fear of evil pushed out any sense of hope the construction scene had given me.

As I walked back to my hotel that afternoon, I thought about how I had changed since 9/11. It occurred to me that I had begun to live in a sort of pervasive fear. My husband had recently surprised me with arrangements for a long-anticipated trip to the Holy Land but later canceled it based on nothing more than my irrational fear. How long would I continue to live this way?

Climbing into bed that night, I told God I didn't want to make any more decisions based on fear. Instead I wanted to be guided by His love and wisdom. It wouldn't be easy to live fearlessly in our unstable world. But I realized that God is still in control, even if it doesn't look like it at times.

Evil rears its ugly head in our world on a regular basis, and we see graphic portrayals of it on the news most days. With such fresh glimpses of potential tragedy at every turn, it's no wonder we sometimes fear the worst.

But the only thing we are to fear is our good and sovereign God. When we believe that He is who He says He is and trust Him to do what He says He will do, all other fears fade.

Steps of Faith

Sovereign God, I do not want to fear evil. Instead I will trust You and seek Your guidance. I am comforted because You are still on Your throne.

Deeper Walk: Psalm 103:15-22

Called to Comfort

He comforts us in all our troubles so that we can comfort others. When they are troubled, we will be able to give them the same comfort God has given us.

2 Corinthians 1:4

THE TABLES AT THE LADIES' DINNER were beautifully prepared. As Amy walked to her assigned table, she realized she didn't know the other women sitting there. She took her seat beside a friendly woman with red hair and kind eyes. Her name was Diane.

While the women enjoyed the special music and their meal, Amy discovered Diane had recently moved to the area from another state. Diane also mentioned that her husband had health problems.

When Amy shared that she had been widowed several years earlier, Diane became attentive and inquired about her husband's death. Amy responded, "He had cancer. It was non-Hodgkin's lymphoma."

With a trembling voice, Diane confided, "My husband has colon cancer. We don't know what the outcome will be."

Amy knew then why God had brought her to a table full of strangers. She shared with Diane about God's comfort and goodness even as her family had dealt with the disease and treatment. She hoped Diane would leave the dinner with new hope and encouragement.

All of us know someone affected by cancer. Some of us know the journey up close and personal, while others observe its raging from a distance. Sometimes the cure seems to be more devastating than the disease. The emotions that accompany the ordeal can also be very draining. Financial considerations add to the burden, as well as the agony of tough decisions. And there is always the waiting for test results and remission.

Faith in God is a stronghold and refuge for cancer victims and their families. Knowing Him can mean the difference between going under and overcoming. Whether God chooses healing or heaven (the final healing), He can always bring abundant good out of painful circumstances.

As in any trial, the body of Christ must take the opportunity to pray and serve. If you know a family facing cancer, rally the church. Let God use His people to share their burdens.

Steps of Faith

There is so much, Lord, that we don't understand about suffering and loss. Give us faith to walk in confidence with our Good Shepherd.

Deeper Walk: 2 Corinthians 1:3-7

Giving Grace

From his abundance we have all received one gracious blessing after another.
John 1:16

As I WAS GROWING UP, my parents seemed happy. They provided a loving and protective environment for me and my siblings. But just after my youngest brother graduated from high school, my parents divorced.

I was devastated. Had their marriage been a sham all those years? Had they stayed together only for the children, but never really loved each other? Somehow their divorce tainted the memories of my childhood, even though I had been out of their home for some time and had always looked back on those years with fondness before.

Talking with my parents separately about their decision to divorce shed some light on the situation. Over time my confidence in them, my respect for them, and my security in our life as a family began to be restored. But it was only after I had spent some time seeking God's wisdom and healing that I was able to give them grace. And that was what they needed—grace.

I still don't understand why my parents divorced, but by the grace of God I have continued to love and respect them.

Have you ever been surprised when someone close to you ended their marriage? A loved one's divorce can leave you with a mixture of confusion, anger, sadness, and great loss. God hates divorce because it damages the people He loves.

When someone close to you divorces, refrain from casting stones. Instead offer the abundant grace you have received from God, who freely gives to the brokenhearted. What does grace look like in such a situation? Maybe it's a continued friendship, a listening ear, a prayer for healing, a loving attitude, or acts of service to wounded single parents. Your gift of grace could have an even bigger ripple effect than the devastation of their divorce.

Steps of Faith

Father, help me not to throw stones when others make decisions I don't understand. Help me give grace instead.

Deeper Walk: John 8:1-11

The God of Second Chances

*He has not dealt with us as our sins deserve or
repaid us according to our offenses.*
Psalm 103:10, HCSB

"Okay, what's going on?" I had waited until his brother and dad were in bed, and now it was time to find out why tension was oozing from my eighteen-year-old. Without looking up, my son confessed, "I have a test in precalculus tomorrow. I know I'm going to fail."

"How do you know that?"

"I didn't really study."

In a way I had seen it coming. Like many other college freshmen, he was learning the importance of self-discipline. A friend's daughter had already discovered the hard way that it did matter if she attended class, studied, and read the syllabus. And now it was my son's turn. I forced myself to remain calm.

"Well, it's not tomorrow yet," I reminded him.

"There's no way I can study enough to make a difference," he said.

"It's better than nothing," I suggested.

"I guess." As he pulled out his textbook, I prayed that the material he crammed in would stick.

And it did. Over the weekend, he checked online to see if his grade was posted. "Wow. God really looked out for me. I got a B on that test!"

"Thank You, Lord," I prayed aloud. Then I turned to my son. "Please say you won't test God's willingness to be merciful by doing that again."

"Trust me," he assured me, "I learned."

How incredible it is that while God will discipline us when necessary, He also exercises mercy. Even in His holiness, He understands our humanness. The author of Lamentations vividly describes the consequences of Israel's sin and rebellion. Yet even in the midst of deserved but devastating discipline, he recognizes God's mercy. "Because of the Lord's faithful love we do not perish, for His mercies . . . are new every morning; great is Your faithfulness" (Lamentations 3:22-23, HCSB).

Steps of Faith

Lord, thank You for the countless times when You held back what I deserved. May Your mercy drive me to please You more and to seek You daily and obey. For You are my portion, and I put my hope in You (see Lamentations 3:24, HCSB).

Deeper Walk: Psalm 103

The Apron of Service

He . . . poured water into a basin. Then he began to wash the disciples' feet,
drying them with the towel he had around him.

John 13:4-5

MARY UNFASTENED HER NEW BRACELET. She would have her hands in soapy dishwater later in the evening, after all. She put the bracelet in her jewelry box and reached for a short necklace.

In the past, Mary had served as a greeter at the annual women's conference her church hosted. She loved welcoming the women, finding out where they were from, giving them their registration packets, and pointing them toward the refreshments. Not only did she enjoy being on the front lines, but she also felt like it was a good use of her gifts and outgoing personality.

But Mary had been out of town for a couple of weeks during the summer helping her mother after surgery. Those just happened to be the weeks when women in the church signed up for their conference duties. So when Mary returned to church, the only responsibility remaining was cleanup crew—something for which Mary felt no enthusiasm or calling. Still, the women's ministry director had convinced Mary she was needed, so she had taken the less glamorous job.

Mary looked in the mirror to see if the necklace complemented her bright pink sweater, which would later be covered with an apron. When she caught a glimpse of her downcast expression, she gasped. Normally bright-eyed and exuberant, Mary knew her feelings about the evening were showing on her face.

"Lord," Mary prayed aloud, "I'm so sorry for my pathetic attitude about my duties tonight. Please forgive me. I may be in the kitchen, but I can spread some enthusiasm and joy there, too. Help me serve with gladness . . . even while wearing an apron."

The Son of God willingly put on the apron of service and washed His disciples' dirty feet. Have you limited your service to only the areas you feel gifted for or attracted to? Ask the Lord where He wants you to serve in your church, your community, and beyond.

Steps of Faith

Lord, You have demonstrated true service. Help me step outside my comfort zone to serve where I am needed.

Deeper Walk: John 13:1-11

God Loves Obedience

What is more pleasing to the LORD: your burnt offerings and sacrifices or your obedience to his voice? Listen! Obedience is better than sacrifice.

1 Samuel 15:22

TEN MINUTES AFTER asking my preschooler to get dressed, I found her building a block tower instead. When I asked her why, she informed me she didn't want to get dressed. The morning got worse. Instead of cooperating, she fussed and wiggled while I tried to brush the tangles out of her hair, squirted toothpaste all over the sink despite my warning to squeeze the tube gently, and couldn't find her shoes because she had not put them away the night before.

My husband and I were frustrated with her lack of cooperation, and our discipline was met with tears and pouting. By the time we left the house, our whole family was stressed, irritable, and running late.

Later, when peace had been restored in our family, I reflected on how my daughter's disobedience had affected all of us. Out of selfishness, she chose to do what she wanted instead of what we asked, causing tension and discord in our home. As a preschooler, she had a bent toward disobedience. But she knew it displeased us and finally said she was sorry.

As a parent, I understand God's view of sin on a whole new level. He loves us and wants unbroken intimacy with us, and our sin gets in the way of that. He knows we will fail sometimes, but our heavenly Father is pleased when we consistently choose to obey.

The Lord loves our obedience because He knows what is best for us and knows our sin causes distance between us and Him. This is why He sent His Son to die on the cross for us. Jesus is our model for obedience. "For God in all his fullness was pleased to live in Christ, and through him God reconciled everything to himself. He made peace with everything in heaven and on earth by means of Christ's blood on the cross" (Colossians 1:19-20).

Steps of Faith

Father, help me to better understand Your heart for relationship and obedience. Grow in me a stronger desire for consistent obedience in all areas of my life.

Deeper Walk: Jeremiah 7:21-23

A Difficult Past

*You made all the delicate, inner parts of my body and
knit me together in my mother's womb.*

Psalm 139:13

ANGIE HAD BEEN ASKED TO share her testimony at a weekend women's retreat. She was scared to death—partly because she didn't like speaking in front of people but mostly because her story wasn't easy to share.

Angie had been a rebellious, indifferent teenager. She had made many sinful choices that she deeply regretted, none so much as her decision to have an abortion. But when Angie went to college, she learned about Jesus. God called her into a relationship with Himself, forgave her sins, and gave her a new heart. Yet how would these women react to her story? Would they look down on her because of her past? Angie wasn't sure, but she knew that telling her complete story would give God the most glory for the change He had made in her heart.

After Angie shared, many women came up to her and personally thanked her for her transparency in sharing what God had done for her. One woman, teary-eyed, shared that she, too, had had an abortion in her teen years and that it took a long time to really believe she was forgiven. She wanted to get together with Angie and talk more about how to reconcile her current faith with her past choices. Angie was overwhelmed by God's faithfulness. She couldn't change the decision she'd made years ago, but she could choose to share how God had healed her and set her free, thereby encouraging others to accept God's forgiveness and experience freedom from shame.

Abortion does not conform to God's ways—that's clear from the teaching of Scripture. However, the reality is that there are many women who have had abortions and many who are considering it. We are called to share God's Word and His truth, as well as His love and compassion. Equip yourself with the knowledge of the truth regarding the sanctity of life, and then seek to love and serve those who've had abortions.

Steps of Faith

God, You are the Author and Giver of life. Help me to see others as Your image bearers and to show them the love and care You have shown me.

Deeper Walk: Job 10:11-12

Own Up to It

You desire honesty from the womb, teaching me wisdom even there.

Psalm 51:6

I HAD JUST STARTED A new job and wanted to make a good impression, but on my very first day of work I found myself in an uncomfortable predicament. While I was parking my car in the parking garage, I accidentally scraped the car next to mine. I was nervous about making a good impression at work and didn't want to report what I had done. On the first day? Really?

I was tempted to back up and find another parking place. But would I want someone to damage my car and not admit it? I could make an easy decision and pretend it didn't happen, or I could make the Christlike choice and leave my name and cell number in a note on the other car. I knew in my heart what I would want someone else to do. And I knew in my heart what the Lord wanted me to do.

I sighed as I pulled out a piece of paper. I wasn't going to make a great impression on my first day, but I knew that leaving the note was the right thing to do.

Sometimes we can find ourselves in situations where we have to make a choice. We can deny our wrongdoing and act like everything is fine, or we can admit it and be willing to accept the consequences. God calls us to be Christlike in everything we do. He wants us to take personal responsibility for our actions, regardless of what the cost may be. If you've said or done something that has hurt someone, don't take the easy way out. Go ahead and do the right thing. Following in Jesus' footsteps is always the right choice.

Steps of Faith

Gracious Father, please help me to do the right thing in all situations even if I have to pay a price. Help me to own up to my mistakes and wrongdoing and to do right by others.

Deeper Walk: Ezekiel 18

Crème de la Crème

Teach us to realize the brevity of life, so that we may grow in wisdom.
Psalm 90:12

As I strolled through the mall, I stopped at the cosmetics counter in a department store. The woman behind the display case didn't waste any time swooping in to tell me about the latest wrinkle solutions for my slightly-past-middle-age face. She began rubbing creams onto the back of my hand, saying, "This one is only $100, but if you want the crème de la crème, you should try this one."

Well, "this one" turned out to be "only" $150, but if I wanted the "best value," I could purchase the two-ounce jumbo size for $250. What a deal! Then my wrinkles would be history—not to mention that my entire face would be as smooth and soft as a baby's bottom. It sounded appealing.

I have to admit that since I have been well grounded in the "You deserve a break today" culture, I was tempted to cave in and fork over my favorite plastic card to pay for the cream that promised to be a fountain of youth. After all, I worked hard at my job, so didn't I deserve it? But I wondered if purchasing the miracle cream would put a bit of a strain on my budget that month.

I left the cosmetics counter empty-handed, knowing that I had done the right thing. Not that the Lord doesn't want me to take care of myself (including my aging skin), but to stay within my budget, I would purchase a perfectly good brand of wrinkle cream at the drugstore.

Everywhere we turn, we are bombarded by messages devised by marketing teams that appeal to our selfish nature. These messages tell us that we deserve it, that their products will make us more beautiful, youthful, and socially acceptable. But instead of falling for the next sales pitch you hear, ask the Lord for wisdom in handling the resources He has so generously given you.

Steps of Faith

Father, help me to be wise in the way I spend the resources You have given me. Let me bring You glory in everything I do.

Deeper Walk: Proverbs 2:1-5

Never Stop Learning

An intelligent heart acquires knowledge, and
the ear of the wise seeks knowledge.
Proverbs 18:15, ESV

I SPEAK AT WOMEN'S RETREATS around the country. Especially during the fall and spring, my calendar is full of opportunities to share truth and hope with women. And while I am pleased when these women affirm my ministry by telling me that God used me to challenge, convict, and instruct them, I am still very humbled by the calling God has given me.

Once, after a busy season of speaking at women's events each weekend for a month and a half, I had the opportunity to attend my own church's one-day women's retreat. To be honest, I was not looking forward to it. Only a handful of women had registered, it was to be held at a rustic encampment, and the speaker, while well qualified, was a local woman I had heard several times before. In the end, I attended only out of obligation and with low expectations. But ten minutes into the first session, I realized that while I may have been there out of duty, God had me there to learn.

As our speaker presented biblical truth, I felt it wash over me like a refreshing, cleansing rain. Oh, how I needed to be taught!

As the day went on, I received many words of wisdom, and I hadn't even been aware of how desperately I needed them. At the end of the day, I drove home pleasantly spent and spiritually refreshed.

It's easy to become so overwhelmed with our busy schedules that we forget to take time for ourselves. But in order to be a blessing to others, we need to make sure our own spiritual cups are full as well. Always be on the lookout for opportunities to refill your emotional and spiritual tank. And remember, sometimes God uses unexpected people and events to accomplish His goals. So don't judge a book by its cover. You never know what pearls of wisdom are waiting inside.

Steps of Faith

Father, show me if I have become proud, preventing You from blessing me as You desire. Help me to be careful to give You all the glory for the good You do in my life.

Deeper Walk: Proverbs 9:9

Thrill at the Soup Kitchen

*Go and make disciples of all the nations, baptizing them in the
name of the Father and the Son and the Holy Spirit.*
Matthew 28:19

"LET'S GO TO THE soup kitchen downtown," I said to Carl.

"Are times that lean, Hannah? You gotta go to the soup kitchen?" he teased.

Carl knew what I was getting at. A couple of times a month, I'd get a few people together to show up at the soup kitchen and serve the homeless. Every time, I asked Carl. And every time, he teased me and declined.

"The people are going to get fed whether you show up or not," he argued.

"But Carl, what they won't hear and what they won't see is the love of Jesus. I know you're not comfortable sharing your faith with strangers, but I've found that talking to someone who doesn't know Jesus is a thrill!" I explained.

"A thrill? How so?" Carl asked skeptically.

"Well, the more I talk about Jesus, the more I realize just how amazing He is. And then sometimes, I might get into a discussion with someone that really challenges me to communicate about Him effectively. I guess I just see it as putting my faith into action in an atmosphere that isn't exactly my comfort zone."

Carl still declined. And he probably will next time. But eventually, he'll say yes, and he'll see that telling his Jesus experiences to others will deepen and enrich his relationship with God.

Not everyone is called to serve as a long-term or short-term missionary to a country overseas. However, we are called to be missionaries right where we are—in our cul-de-sacs, in our towns, in our counties, in our states. Right down the road from you, someone needs to hear the life-giving news of Jesus Christ. Someone on your street, in your child's school, or at work is waiting to hear your story and how you came to know the Lord. Look for appropriate ways to not only serve your community but also speak about what the Lord has done in your life.

Steps of Faith

Father, give me the courage to talk about You with those in need. Give me an increased measure of discernment as I open myself up to have conversations about You.

Deeper Walk: Romans 10:10-17

Righteous Anger?

Don't sin by letting anger control you. Don't let the sun go down while you are still angry, for anger gives a foothold to the devil.
Ephesians 4:26-27

AFTER CHURCH, I caught Jean in the hall. "How are you? We haven't talked lately."

"I'm okay. But my son called to tell me my granddaughter Katie got married. She didn't let any of us know."

"Really? To Brayden?" A supposed Christian turned atheist, Brayden had wooed Katie in college. Jean nodded, her eyes filling with tears.

"Oh, I'm sorry," I said, putting my arm around her. "Have you talked to her?"

She shook her head. "I've called, e-mailed, written. Katie has cut herself off from us. All her life I've loved her and pointed her to Jesus. I didn't speak ill of Brayden, but I did point out the truth to her in a loving way. I've prayed and prayed . . ."

I handed her a tissue.

"And I've been filled with anger toward Brayden for taking Katie away. I thought my anger was righteous, but it's eaten away at my heart, affecting my relationship with God and others. I've been asking God to help me let it go. It's been hard, but I've started praying for Brayden. And you know what?"

Shaking my head, I reached for my own tissue.

"God has helped me to see Brayden for who he is: a lost soul in desperate need of Jesus. The Lord has softened my heart, and the pain is fading."

Marveling at how God had righted Jean's anger, I asked myself, *Would I have responded to Him so well?*

Anger is an emotion; it's not wrong in itself. But Scripture tells us not to sin in how we deal with it. Righteous anger for the Lord's reputation or His people or the oppressed can lead to good things, but anger can also lead to sin. Ask God to teach you how to express anger in a way that honors Him.

Steps of Faith

God, as Psalm 145:8 says, help me to be slow to anger and filled with Your love.

Deeper Walk: Psalm 145:8-13

The Buck Stops Here

The man replied, "It was the woman you gave me who gave me the fruit, and I ate it."

Genesis 3:12

DENISE WAS THE ONLY child of a couple in our church. They doted on her and gave her everything her heart desired. She expected the world to revolve around her, and nothing was ever her fault. Every speeding ticket she received was because a traffic sign wasn't posted properly or a police officer was picking on her.

There were numerous car accidents: Denise rear-ended another car because "the brakes didn't work." (They were fine when checked later.) One morning on her way to school, Denise brushed the snow off her windshield so she had a viewing area about the size of a basketball. Snow completely covered the other side of the windshield, as well as the windows. Pulling out of their cul-de-sac, she sideswiped a neighbor's car, then blamed it on him, claiming he was driving too fast.

Denise's parents prayed and sought advice from our pastor, who counseled them to make Denise pay the $500 deductible. They also took the car keys away from her until she demonstrated more responsible behavior and was able to pay for her own insurance.

The brand-new car that Denise's parents gave her on her eighteenth birthday remained parked in the garage while she rode off to college with friends. As her parents started implementing meaningful consequences, Denise began learning to accept responsibility for her actions.

Ever since the Garden of Eden, people have been blaming others for their own sins and mistakes (see Genesis 3:12). It's part of human nature to want to avoid punishment by pushing the blame onto someone else. But one sign of maturity is accepting responsibility for our actions. Even though our sin is repugnant to God, our honesty is pleasing to Him. Next time you mess up, be willing to admit it. Then accept His forgiveness.

Steps of Faith

"Search me, O God, and know my heart; test me and know my anxious thoughts. Point out anything in me that offends you, and lead me along the path of everlasting life" (Psalm 139:23-24).

Deeper Walk: Psalm 51

The Art of Play

See the ships sailing along, and Leviathan, which you made to play in the sea.
Psalm 104:26

SEVERAL YEARS AGO I visited Chicago's Shedd Aquarium and watched the beluga whales. A baby was swimming around with its mama. As I stood at the glass, Baby Beluga blew out a series of bubbles from his blowhole and then swam quickly around to grab as many as he could in his mouth. Even the adult whales got in on the fun. I could sense that they were all playing and enjoying themselves.

Look at any babies in the animal kingdom or watch any children at a playground and you'll see them doing exactly what God created them to do: play. Play can produce contentment, reduce stress, and allow us to live in the present moment. At some point, though, as we grow older, we lose the art of play. We get too busy, too "grown up," too important to indulge in letting go and having fun. And stress and unhappiness are the results. What if we intentionally pursued playing and became more playful? What if we did this not just because it's healthy and fun and brings contentment, but because the simple act of playing makes God happy with us?

Just as we love to watch others play, God loves to watch His creation play. Why else would He have created Leviathan "to play in the sea"?

God is a happy God—a God of joy (see Psalm 45:7), so of course it stands to reason that He delights when His creation rejoices in life. Today, let go and have a little fun. As you do, think about God's smile shining down on you.

Steps of Faith

God, how often do I let the responsibilities and struggles of life keep me from doing something You created me to do—play? Too often I need help loosening up and having fun, so help me become more playful and experience the kind of life that You desire me to have.

Deeper Walk: Psalm 104:24-26, 31

We're All Missionaries

Proclaim the message; persist in it whether convenient or not; rebuke,
correct, and encourage with great patience and teaching.
2 Timothy 4:2, HCSB

RECENTLY, my friend Eleanor and I were talking about our high school selves and how much we had changed. Eleanor said, "I became a Christian my junior year in high school, and I felt God calling me to the mission field. Little did I know what kind of mission field He had in mind!"

"What do you mean?" I asked.

"I planned to be a medical missionary in a developing country. Then I met Scott in college, we got married, and I got pregnant right away. I was happy to let go of my own plans because I knew God's plans were best, and I initially thought I left those missionary dreams on my college campus. But then God showed me that in reality, I am very much a missionary right here."

"How so?"

"I'm living out the great commission by making disciples of my children. Together, we're being salt and light to our neighbors and the families at their school, sharing our faith and telling them what Jesus has done in our lives."

"Wow," I said. "I hadn't thought about it like that before. It kind of changes the way you look at your life when you see it that way—we are ambassadors for God's Kingdom, missionaries right here where He has put us."

That day, Eleanor and I promised to pray for more opportunities to share God's Good News to the world around us, right where we live every day.

We often think of missions in a global context—taking the gospel to every nation—and that's a huge component in expanding God's Kingdom. But we are missionaries right where we are in whatever roles God has given us. How can we advance the gospel here and now? First, pray for opportunities and for guidance from God. Second, plug in. Get to know people, love on them, and build relationships with them. Third, share what God has done in your own life and share the truth of the Bible. We need both local and global missions to reach people with Christ's love.

Steps of Faith

Lord, would You provide opportunities for me to share about Jesus today?
Help me to live boldly and speak in Your power.

Deeper Walk: Matthew 5:13-16

Not Just Anyone

A friend is always loyal, and a brother is born to help in time of need.
Proverbs 17:17

I KNEW THE PROBLEM WAS too big to handle alone. But whom could I talk to? It was one of those things that I didn't want to share at Bible study or my recovery group. Even as I considered close friends who'd helped me through bouts with depression, struggles with my kids, a stressful time at work, and a year when I couldn't seem to stay out of the hospital, I kept sensing God saying no to each one. *You need a special kind of friend for this one.*

Who, God?

I needed biblical wisdom, not emotionally charged suggestions for action. I needed someone who would listen, pray, and keep the issue confidential, but also recognize when it was time to involve someone else, like a pastor. I needed someone who had not only experienced a similar problem, but had also seen a good outcome.

None of my close friends qualified. But one lady at church did. For two weeks, I hesitated. How would she respond to my sharing something so huge with her? It wasn't like we knew each other very well. But God kept nudging me.

Finally, I made the call. As we prayed together after our first talk, I knew God had sent me to the right person.

Chances are you've learned the hard way how important it is to use discretion when sharing sensitive prayer needs and problems. Often the burdens that we need the most help carrying are those that only a certain type of friend can handle. As we seek God for direction and see His perfect connections make a difference, we will experience growth and healing. If you are struggling with an issue that can't be shared with just any friend, ask God to lead you to the sister in Christ that He has chosen for you.

Steps of Faith

Father, I've been hurt before by impulsively entrusting my burdens to the wrong friend. Help me to look to You for guidance when I need the encouragement of a trustworthy believer.

Deeper Walk: Proverbs 2:6-11

When a Dream Dies

My hopes have disappeared. My heart's desires are broken.
Job 17:11

HAVE YOU EVER WATCHED a dream die? You prayed, you hoped, you planned, you prayed some more, and still the job fell through, the doctor's report was grim, the engagement was broken, your daughter turned her back, the open door slammed shut.

Every bit of hope died with the dream, and you were left asking, "What now?"

I've been there. I laid that dream, along with my heart, before the Lord and asked Him to handle it gently. I thought it was the dream He had for my life. I was sure it was the direction He wanted me to take.

But as I watched my dream die, I wondered if God was mad at me. If it was my own selfishness that dreamed this dream. If He was out to get me. If I didn't believe enough or dream enough or pray enough.

And it hurt.

I learned a few things in the aftermath, though. First, don't try to sidestep the grief; it's an important part of healing. Ask your Abba Father to hold you and comfort you. Second, though other people may mean well, try not to listen to things like "It wasn't God's will," or "You didn't have enough [fill in the blank]," or "He's trying to grow you." When you're deeply disappointed, these things can sound so hollow and empty. And third, dig into the Word. Pray. Worship. Give of yourself to others.

Finally, even though your dream wasn't fulfilled, it may be that He has something better in mind, or He's going to fulfill it in a different way. For example, do you remember the story of King David's dream to build a temple for God? God's plan was for David's son Solomon to build it instead.

An unfulfilled dream doesn't mean that God doesn't care. Instead, place your life and your plans into His hands, then watch what He does. His plans for you are always loving and good.

Steps of Faith

Father, please comfort us when our dreams die. In the right timing, let us know the plans You have for us.

Deeper Walk: 1 Chronicles 22:6-19

Growing Pains

We know that the law is spiritual, but
I am made out of flesh, sold into sin's power.
Romans 7:14, HCSB

"I'M JUST SO FRUSTRATED," I told Olivia, a sweet Christian friend who had taken me under her wing when I started college. I was a relatively new Christian, and Olivia had been challenging and encouraging me in my walk with the Lord. But I was getting irritated with myself. I just kept on seeing more and more sin in my life.

"I mean, I've definitely changed," I began. "I'm not the same person I was a year ago. But the more I read God's Word and study and pray, the more I see all this filth in my life. For example, I never realized how selfish I am. Just the other day, I got upset when one of my professors praised another student instead of me. Then I got angry at one of my sorority sisters for using my nail polish without asking. I mean, it's nail polish! Who cares?"

Olivia smiled. "You're right. But how *awesome* that God lets you see that those attitudes are sinful. A year ago, you wouldn't have given those feelings a second thought. But now the Holy Spirit is living inside you, working to make you more like Jesus!"

"Wow. Is that what's happening?" I asked.

"Yep," Olivia said. "You're not a terrible person. We *all* have that same sinful nature. But moment by moment, day by day, God is sanctifying us. As our awareness of our sin gets bigger, so does our understanding of Jesus and His saving Cross. He means more and more to us as we see what He has saved us from!"

As God continues to conform us to the image of His Son, our sins become even more apparent, as does our gratitude for all that He has done for us. Ask God to reveal weak spots in your life. Pay attention to the counsel of close Christian friends, and depend on God's Word and Spirit to do their sanctifying work in your heart.

Steps of Faith

Lord, thank You for Your Spirit, who reveals sin and changes my heart. Help me to be sensitive to Him today.

Deeper Walk: Romans 7:14-25

Running Over

If you help the poor, you are lending to the LORD—and he will repay you!
Proverbs 19:17

LIKE MANY COLLEGE STUDENTS, Sarah lived paycheck to paycheck. During her sophomore year, a friend introduced her to Jesus. As Sarah grew in her faith, she began giving offerings from her wages and tips as a waitress. Sometimes it was hard to give when she knew tuition bills and other expenses were piling up, but she stretched her dollars and worked extra shifts.

When Sarah received an unexpected scholarship, she was excited about having a bit more wiggle room in her budget. But she soon experienced a financial roadblock—the transmission in her thirteen-year-old car went kaput. If she used all her savings, she'd be able to pay for the car repair in full. But she had already planned to give two hundred dollars to the homeless shelter in her community.

Sarah thought about how she could postpone giving the money, but the idea bothered her. So she resolved to find another way: she explained to the mechanic shop owner why she was two hundred dollars short. Moved by her faith and generosity to those less fortunate, he allowed her to pay him back over her next two paychecks.

A month later, Sarah was still recovering from her financial pitfall and times were tight. When checking her e-mail, she received a reply to a writing job inquiry she had made months ago to a well-known blog. They had accepted her submissions and were sending her a check for five hundred dollars.

Sarah knew it wasn't coincidence. It was God's faithfulness and provision.

Since the beginning, God has given generously, and He promises to continue this generosity throughout eternity. Make giving to others a regular part of your family's activities. Choose to allow the generosity of Christ, now living within you, to change not only your community but also the world.

Steps of Faith

Lord, thank You for blessing me. Help me to reflect Your generous heart by sharing my time and resources with those in need.

Deeper Walk: Deuteronomy 15:7-11

Guilty

I listen carefully to what God the LORD is saying.
Psalm 85:8

MY HUSBAND, KEVIN, LOVES SPORTS. When he's watching a game, whether it's baseball, basketball, football, hockey, or golf, he frequently interrupts whatever I'm doing to tell me what's going on in the game. Sometimes I give him my full attention, but if I'm listening to a podcast or reading a book, I glance in his direction, nod, or give a few uh-huhs to make him think I'm listening— but I'm not.

If I give Kevin a quizzical look when he wants to discuss the game again later, he asks, "You weren't listening, were you?"

I give him a weak smile, and he knows my mind was elsewhere. Guilty as charged.

Sometimes I do the same thing to God. My life as a busy working mom seems to take over, and I don't always listen well.

Recently, I began to see how the constant noise I allowed in my life was impacting my ability to hear from the Holy Spirit.

I spend a lot of time in the car toting noisy kids to their sports practices, music lessons, and youth group. But even when I'm by myself in the car, I turn on the radio. The first thing I do when I roll out of bed in the morning is to turn on the TV, and the last thing I do at night is to turn it off. Sometimes God interrupts what I'm doing, but the constant noise makes it more difficult for me to hear His still, small voice.

When God brought my lackluster listening skills to my attention, I was ashamed. I asked Him to help me to be still so I could hear Him clearly and without distraction.

We're so accustomed to being wired 24-7. We live in an age where we can listen nonstop to news, sports, and every genre of entertainment available on TV. But if we don't unplug long enough to be still, how will we be able to hear the voice of God?

Ask the Lord to help you hear His voice and to be obedient. God is speaking. Are you listening?

Steps of Faith

Father, Your Word says that You will answer when I call to You (Psalm 4:3). Let me be attentive to Your voice when You call to me.

Deeper Walk: Matthew 17:1-6

2:00 a.m.

Can all your worries add a single moment to your life?
Luke 12:25

AFTER A FULL DAY AT WORK, I raced home, paid the sitter, and herded Kevin and Riley into the car. Since their dad was away on business for the week, I had to chauffeur the boys to and from baseball practice and decided to pick up dinner at a drive-through on the way home.

I tried to unwind after the boys were in bed, but my mind was racing about everything from issues at work to mounds of dirty laundry. Collapsing in bed, I didn't even take time to pray. A quick *Thanks, Lord, for keeping us all safe today* was all I could manage before I began to get sleepy.

But instead of falling asleep, I started thinking about everything I had to do at work the following day. *Oh no!* I thought. *I forgot to send Rita the proposal. It was due to her last week!*

Once I began to worry, I became more and more agitated. Why couldn't I just let go of things and let God handle my burdens? There was nothing I could do about it at midnight. But I was awake, watching the clock. I fretted about work until I finally drifted off, which was sometime after 2:00 a.m.

The next morning, I checked my e-mail and discovered that I had sent the documents to Rita after all. I had just forgotten about it. I had spent much of the night tossing and turning because of something that wasn't even an issue.

The Lord gently reminded me that when I'm worrying about something, I'm not trusting Him.

Many of us seem naturally inclined to worry. We fret about everything from getting to church on time to how we're going to pay our bills. We know that God created the universe, but do we actually trust Him to keep all things under control? God tells us throughout His Word that we are not to worry. Philippians 4:6 says, "Don't worry about anything; instead, pray about everything. Tell God what you need, and thank him for all he has done."

Steps of Faith

Heavenly Father, please forgive me for worrying. Help me to release all my burdens to You and to leave them in Your hands.

Deeper Walk: Luke 12:22-34

He Forgets

*I—yes, I alone—will blot out your sins for my own sake and
will never think of them again.*

Isaiah 43:25

MY FRIEND AND COWORKER AMY became a Christian a few months ago. It's been my privilege to see her grow and to be her mentor.

Recently, she seemed preoccupied. So one morning I stopped by her office and asked if everything was okay.

Amy started to tear up. She asked me to close the door of her office.

"A couple of years ago, Justin and I weren't getting along very well. We didn't talk much about what was going on in our marriage, and I started to feel neglected. A friend of Justin's was only too happy to step in and pile on lots of sympathy for what I was going through."

I had a pretty good idea where the conversation was headed, but I let Amy continue.

"We had an affair that lasted a few months, and when Justin found out, he left for a while. I thought our marriage was over, but we started seeing a pastor for counseling. Things are better, but we're still working on some issues."

"What's bothering you now?"

"Well, I know God has forgiven me, and Justin even forgave me, but . . ."

"Are you having a hard time letting go of it?"

Amy nodded and grabbed a tissue.

I said, "When you confess your sins, God forgives you. He says He won't even remember them, and He doesn't want you to dredge them up again either. I know it's hard to forget, but when you feel condemnation, remember it's not from God; it's from the enemy."

Have you ever had a scab that you couldn't stop picking? Just about the time it starts to heal, you're tempted to dig at it and start the process all over again. Sometimes it's the same with our sins. We know that God has forgiven us, but we keep dredging them up over and over again. The next time you're plagued by a past sin that you've confessed, remember Jeremiah 31:34: "I will forgive their wickedness, and I will never again remember their sins." And let that wound heal.

Steps of Faith

Lord, You are so merciful. Thank You for not only forgiving my sins but also forgetting them.

Deeper Walk: Jeremiah 31:31-37

True Delight

He will take delight in you with gladness. With his love, he will
calm all your fears. He will rejoice over you with joyful songs.
Zephaniah 3:17

MY DAUGHTER HANNAH CAME bouncing through the front door. "Hey, Mom! I'm grabbing my tennis bag and going to practice!"

"Hang on, hon. Just a reminder: You need to finish your last couple of college applications by this weekend. Also, don't forget you have an orchestra concert tomorrow night and the Habitat for Humanity build on Saturday."

"Mom, I know. I've got it all in my calendar on my phone!" she yelled as she ran upstairs.

Sometimes the push toward college seemed overwhelming. It dawned on me that as hard as I was working to help Hannah build up her college applications, this time with her at home was fleeting. I was forgetting where she was right now and how precious this time with her really was. I realized I was what one of the college reps referred to as a "helicopter parent."

I prayed, *God, instead of thinking of Hannah's life as a project, help me to enjoy her and to spend this time preparing her heart and soul for life as an adult, trusting that Your plan for her is best.*

When Hannah came downstairs, I asked her to meet me for dinner after practice, just the two of us. I said we wouldn't talk college or schedules; we would just talk. Hannah was excited, and so was I.

The Bible says that God delights in us. We are His children, and He not only cares for us, but He also knows us deeply. We can model God's love to our children by spending time listening to them, entering into their interests, and sharing their joys and sorrows. Spend a few minutes today with your children and don't have any sort of agenda. Just do what they enjoy doing or talk about what's on their minds. Quality time will build your relationships and give your children a sense of your love and interest in who they are.

Steps of Faith

God, thank You for intimately knowing and caring for me as Your child. Help me to freely show that love and care to others.

Deeper Walk: 1 John 3:1-3

Look What I Did!

Pride leads to disgrace, but with humility comes wisdom.
Proverbs 11:2

WE LOVE TO SHOW OFF our skills and get recognition for it, but God knows that this kind of setup can feed our pride. Too often, as a result of focusing on ourselves, we forget about Him.

Honor, recognition, and fame are some of our society's most coveted values. However, Christians are warned against taking pride in ourselves. God is very clear about His opinion of pride—He hates it (see Isaiah 13:11). Pride tells us we can do everything on our own rather than depending on God.

Paul's accomplishments included successfully starting churches all over the Mediterranean, bringing countless people to Christ, and writing more than one-third of the New Testament, but his words in Romans 15:18 give us his humble perspective: "I dare not boast about anything except what Christ has done through me."

As long as we're prideful, we haven't truly grasped that we are nothing without Christ. We are unable to earn anything from God, so we can't brag about anything except what Christ has done for us and through us. When we seek honor for ourselves, we fail to recognize that it is Christ who truly deserves the recognition for anything we accomplish.

Make an honest examination of the motives behind your actions. For example, if you lead worship, is it because you love to praise God by using the musical gifts He gave you, or do you love being in the spotlight? Are you eager to serve others behind the scenes, or are you more likely to help when others will notice your good deeds?

Take your prideful thoughts and give them to the Lord. Ask Him to help you transform your motives so that you act out of a desire to serve and love Him. This week, do something for another person secretly so that you don't receive any recognition except from God.

Steps of Faith

Lord, help me to let go of pride and to recognize that You are the Author of everything good.

Deeper Walk: Matthew 6:1-18

Come Alongside

This is my commandment: Love each other in the same way I have loved you.
John 15:12

ON A SUNNY SATURDAY MORNING, my husband, two little boys, and I started off on a mile-long bike ride through a local forest preserve. As we fell into an easy rhythm, I breathed in the smell of pine and delighted in the chirping of birds. Occasionally one of the boys excitedly pointed out a scampering squirrel or a hawk hovering overhead.

I followed my younger son, Luke, as he pedaled hard up another hill. We stopped at the top and looked back. My husband was partway up the incline, coaxing our older son, Nate, who appeared to be pedaling very slowly.

"This is just so hard!" Nate said, stopping for a moment to catch his breath.

We kept urging him forward, and I had to bite my tongue to keep from pointing out that his little brother could have ridden circles around him. Even after making it up that hill, Nate continued to struggle. I finally pedaled back to him. Just before launching into more motivational mumbo jumbo, I glanced down at his back tire. Almost flat! Here I'd been coaxing my son to keep up when clearly he didn't have the means to do so.

I was reminded of something important that morning: I should never assume that someone falling behind or failing to meet my expectations is just not trying hard enough. The apostle Paul offered a better way when he said, "Share each other's burdens, and in this way obey the law of Christ" (Galatians 6:2). That morning, my husband and I took turns helping Nate guide his bike back to the van—and we made a mental note to bring the air pump on our next outing.

Our family and friends don't need our judgment; they may, however, need us to come alongside them. Together we can determine what is slowing them down and figure out a way to move forward. After all, isn't that what Christ has done for us?

Steps of Faith

Lord, please give me the patience today to walk alongside, rather than run ahead of, someone who is struggling.

Deeper Walk: John 15:12-17

Healing for the Broken

The Lord is my inheritance; therefore, I will hope in him!
Lamentations 3:24

As Christy and six-year-old Annie pulled into the church parking lot, Christy looked around hesitantly. *Lord, I can only do this with Your help,* she prayed silently.

The young mother had moved her daughter to a new town following a difficult divorce. Her ex-husband's violent behavior hadn't stopped just because the divorce was finalized, so Christy had moved closer to her parents. But the shame and pain of her failed marriage accompanied her.

Christy got out of the car that Sunday and found classes for herself and her daughter. She also managed to return each week. Gradually Christy met some women in the church and began to enjoy Sunday mornings again. But still, she dreaded the day when someone would ask about her husband.

So Christy surprised even herself when she voluntarily shared some details about her divorce in Bible study one Sunday. But she also felt relieved when no one looked at her with scorn. In fact, after class the teacher casually mentioned that Christy might be interested in a new DivorceCare program that was starting the next month. Christy agreed to attend, but she knew her healing had already begun that day.

Most people who have been through a divorce will tell you that their broken marriage is a source of not only frustration and hurt, but also shame. Many believers who promised faithfulness until death never dreamed they would end up divorced. But God's grace does not fall short at the threshold of a broken marriage. He offers forgiveness, mercy, restoration, and healing for every broken heart. If you or someone you love is struggling to rebuild after a divorce, pray for God to bring healing to that which has been broken.

Steps of Faith

Father, our lives don't always turn out as we hoped. But thanks to Your loving grace, we don't have to live with shame or regret.

Deeper Walk: Lamentations 3:19-22

Death by Chocolate?

Come and show me your mercy, as you do for all who love your name.
Guide my steps by your word, so I will not be overcome by evil.
Psalm 119:132-133

EVEN THOUGH HE GREETED me with a wagging tail and an eager look in his big brown eyes, I knew my puppy, Wrigley, was in trouble.

The evidence was all over his doggy bed—smears of chocolate and torn-up pieces of foil and wrapper. Somehow our four-month-old black Lab had retrieved a large bar of chocolate from our pantry and devoured it.

Fortunately, I'd been away from our house for only an hour; still, I knew chocolate and dogs don't mix. I called our vet.

"How much did Wrigley eat?" the receptionist asked.

"It was a big bar," I said as I looked frantically for a shred of wrapper that would tell me the number of ounces. *Strike one.*

"Was it dark or milk chocolate?" she asked.

"Eighty-five percent cocoa," I said. *Strike two.*

"How much does Wrigley weigh?"

"About thirty pounds." *Strike three.*

I wasn't surprised when she told me, "The vet would like you to bring him right in."

Let's just say the next hour was pleasant for neither me nor Wrigley. Fortunately, the vet was able to take the necessary steps to prevent Wrigley's body from absorbing the chocolate, and I brought him home soon after.

Just as Wrigley was oblivious to the grave threat posed by downing a chocolate bar, I am prone to thoughtlessly dabble in sins like gossip, bitterness, or even eating too much chocolate. Often I never consider just how toxic those deeds can be to my soul. I may feel and act fine, but God sees the evidence of my sins and won't let me remain mired in them. In fact, Christ took the consequences of my misdeeds on Himself.

Thankfully, Wrigley showed no bad effects from gorging on chocolate. For now, however, I store our dark chocolate on the top shelf in the highest cupboard!

Steps of Faith
Jesus, how grateful I am that You sacrificed all so that I no longer need to fear death but can anticipate eternal life with You.

Deeper Walk: Hebrews 9:27-28

Counting On Accountability

The heartfelt counsel of a friend is as sweet as perfume and incense. . . .
As iron sharpens iron, so a friend sharpens a friend.
Proverbs 27:9, 17

WHILE CLEANING MY BASEMENT RECENTLY, I came across an old scrapbook into which I'd taped the first contract I ever signed. Just before our freshman year ended, my friend Cindy and I had agreed that we'd join the cross country team that fall. Other than the mile run in gym class, we had never run before. Because we wouldn't be able to train together, we created a contract to hold each other accountable. It read:

I agree to run three miles a day or four miles for five days each week.

A calendar is made for me to sign each day of the week. I must record my miles!

I will work with my full ability to do the best I can.

Signed _____

P.S. If I miss a day, I will run six miles the next day.

I am sure I didn't run three miles my first time out, and I think we were a wee bit harsh when assigning a consequence for missing a day. Still, it worked. I ran faithfully that summer and couldn't wait for the season to begin.

God created friendships in part to provide the support and incentive we need to better ourselves and reach our goals. He never meant for us to go it alone. Today Cindy and I live five hundred miles apart, and I'd be surprised if she even remembered that old contract. Yet she was a big reason that I'd been ready to join the team and that I still enjoy running today. How has a friend shaped your life?

Steps of Faith

God, today I thank You for my friend _____, through whom You've enriched my life. Shower her today with Your love, joy, and peace.

Deeper Walk: Romans 1:8-12

A Work of Art

The LORD is like a father to his children, tender and compassionate to those who fear him. For he knows how weak we are; he remembers we are only dust.
Psalm 103:13-14

AFTER HE RETIRED, my grandfather took up painting. He was naturally talented, and a few of his pieces—a giant sunflower in oil, a watercolor rabbit—now hang in my home. When my brother and I were little, Grandpa took us out to his studio so we could create our own watercolors. We each held the paintbrush, but he guided our hands.

My brother's piece is quite good. It's a forest scene of rich greens and browns. My painting features a flower-dotted hill set against a bright blue sky with some high-floating clouds. But at some point when Grandpa wasn't watching, I took some white paint and dabbed it on the hill to make a river or stream. It looks all wrong—no stream starts and stops in the middle of a hill! What might have been a fairly polished watercolor was ruined (though my parents framed and displayed it anyway).

Have you ever tried to follow the Lord's will, only to sense that you have moved too far from His plan? Perhaps you wonder whether God can use you after your divorce, your betrayal, or your relapse into addiction. Just as I messed up a simple painting when I didn't let my grandpa guide me, perhaps you feel as if you've made such a mess of things that God can't redeem your situation.

We can take comfort in the way our heavenly Father continually woos His straying people throughout Scripture. King David killed a man to cover up his adultery; later he failed to act when one of his sons assaulted his own half sister. Yes, David paid a steep price in both cases, yet God never abandoned the one He called "a man after my own heart" (Acts 13:22).

Your Father hasn't given up on you either. Just ask, and He will take your hand in His and begin to restore your life.

Steps of Faith
Father God, I confess that I blow it often. Remind me today that You are the ultimate Redeemer—and You are not finished with me yet.

Deeper Walk: Hosea 14

Welcome Words

Kind words are like honey—sweet to the soul and healthy for the body.
Proverbs 16:24

"No, Sam, you can't finish level eight on your video game. The bus will be here in five minutes, and you aren't dressed! What are you thinking?"

April scrubbed the kitchen table harder. It wasn't simply to loosen caked-on syrup, either—she was frustrated. Why was Sam so obsessed with that game?

"Sam!" she called again. "If you miss the bus, you'd better get your running shoes on because I am *not* driving you today."

"All right! I'm going," her son said, stomping up the stairs.

Minutes later, April handed Sam his backpack and pushed him out the front door. "Don't forget to bring in the trash cans after school!" she called. She watched as he sprinted toward the bus.

She had barely shut the front door when the phone rang.

"April?" she heard. "It's Aunt Linda."

April was surprised. Her aunt lived three states away, and they saw each other only on the holidays. Sam, though, had stayed with Aunt Linda overnight the month before when their church youth choir was touring her city.

Sam, April thought. *I hope Sam didn't do something bad.*

"How good to hear from you!" April said. "Everything okay?"

"Oh, honey, I've been meaning to call you all month," her aunt said. "I just wanted to tell you how much I enjoyed visiting with Sam. He is such a polite young man! Did you know he filled the dishwasher after supper and made his bed without my asking? Anyway, I just want you to know that you and Bob are doing a wonderful job. Oops—got to go. My ride to the hair salon is here. Love you! Bye!"

April held the phone, sobered. In just a few words that morning, she had shut Sam down. In just a few words, Aunt Linda had built her up.

Why was I so hard on Sam? . . . Nope, I'm not going there. Aunt Linda said we're doing a good job. I'm going to remember that. And I can't wait to tell Sam how proud I am of him!

With that, April went back to polishing the kitchen table—with a lighter hand *and* a lighter heart.

Steps of Faith
Lord Jesus, may my words be like honey today to all those I meet.

Deeper Walk: 2 Timothy 2:24

OCTOBER 11

The Old Book

The word of God is alive and powerful.
Hebrews 4:12

MY PATH THROUGH the used bookstore took me past the locked case for special books. That's where I spied an employee outfitting a customer with oversized latex gloves—and the old book they were about to carefully handle. My book-loving heart plummeted.

"Wait!" I said, racing over. "I have cotton gloves. Use these instead. They won't harm the pages."

The potential customer's eyebrows shot up to his hairline, but he took the clean cotton gloves I offered. After a minute or two of looking, he decided not to purchase the book. Now that I was thoroughly intrigued, I took some time to examine it.

What I found exceeded all my expectations: I was handling a 1683 Greek Old Testament. I already had several older books in my personal library, but this was in a class of its own. The vellum binding had faded over the centuries of use, and the binding was a little on the stiff side, but it was nothing proper storage and a good book cradle wouldn't accommodate. The aged paper was in remarkably good condition and free from many afflictions that can damage old books.

While the bookstore recognized the book's value and was sad to part with it, I was thrilled to add it to my collection. Since then I've taken great care in its preservation. I've made sure it's padded in unbuffered tissue paper, packaged in a special archival box, and stored in a proper environment. It's my hope that this book, which predates the Declaration of Independence by nearly a century, will last for many years to come.

This year, my special Old Testament turns 335. Each time I handle it, I'm reminded that this book is unlike all other books. It's crossed oceans and endured the centuries, yes, but it's more than that. This book contains the very words of God. Unlike other books, which may become laughably outdated, this one is just as true today as it was centuries ago.

Steps of Faith

Lord, thank You for giving Your Word to guide and encourage me, just as You have for countless generations. Help me to understand and apply it.

Deeper Walk: 2 Timothy 3:16-17

284

New Life, Old Guilt

The accuser of our brothers and sisters has been thrown down to earth—
the one who accuses them before our God day and night.
Revelation 12:10

WHEN SHE MOVED AWAY TO COLLEGE, Haley was excited about starting a new life and finding a church home to plug into. She quickly found a wonderful inner-city church where she could volunteer and teach kids.

When she joined a college singles small group, she was amazed at the purity and graciousness that poured out from her sisters in Christ. As they talked one day about God's provision, blessings, and forgiveness, Haley grew uncomfortable.

They all seem so righteous, as if they have it all together, she thought. Some of her new friends from the city seemed to be much more "spiritual" than she was. *I'm not sure I can open up to these girls*, she thought. *I'm so ashamed of the bad choices I made in the past.*

Just then, Haley realized everyone was staring at her, waiting for a response. "I'm sorry," Haley stammered. "What was the question?"

"The question was 'What are you struggling with lately?'" replied the small group leader.

Haley was quiet for a moment before thoughtfully replying, "False guilt." From there, Haley told them briefly and discreetly about some of her past struggles.

"I know I'm forgiven," Haley said. "Now the struggle is turning away Satan's accusations."

God doesn't bring up our past sin and rub our noses in it. But Satan tries to. He weasels his way into our thinking and tells us that our sins are too big, too bad, and too deeply ingrained in us for God to use us. He blames, he accuses, and he stalls our good works with false guilt. He silences our testimonies with fear and doubt. And if he can get us to believe him for even a second, he may actually alter our godly influence on the lives of others. What has Satan accused you of that has stopped you from proclaiming Christ's salvation?

Steps of Faith

Lord God, I confess my sins and ask Your forgiveness. Thank You for dying on the cross to save me. I pray that Your protection would surround me as I resist Satan's accusations.

Deeper Walk: Romans 3:9-26

The Real Thing

Faith shows the reality of what we hope for;
it is the evidence of things we cannot see.

Hebrews 11:1

"HEY, YOU FORGOT THIS," called my coworker, leaning out the third-floor office window with what looked like an expensive camera lens. I was standing in the quad below with students who would be studying photography in the upcoming semester.

I shifted the camera bag I was carrying and held out my hands. "Thanks! Go ahead and drop it."

Wide-eyed, the students watched as my coworker let go. The object plummeted down to where I was waiting. Catching it, I turned back to see the horrified looks on the students' faces.

"Oh," I said, suddenly understanding their reaction, "it looks like a lens, but it's just my travel mug."

To clarify, I popped off the "lens cap" and turned it to reveal the empty mug. They laughed in relief that a several-thousand-dollar lens hadn't just been thrown out a window. My real lens was safely stowed in my camera bag.

From a distance, the real thing and its look-alike can be hard to tell apart. But up close, it's easier to tell: The subtle differences in shape, weight, quality, and feel become more pronounced. In the same way, casual faith can look a lot like real faith—until we get a little closer. Real faith naturally mimics the faith that Jesus Himself modeled and taught in doing good to the people that God puts in our lives. These "good works," as James calls them, are the vital signs of genuine faith. And such acts aren't cheap or careless; they are precious and prized in the Lord's sight.

Do your words and actions reflect Jesus and His ministry? Today, consider how you can model Jesus' love and teaching in your life.

Steps of Faith

Father, help me to have genuine faith. May I grow to be more like You each day.

Deeper Walk: James 2:14-26

From the Mountains to the Prairies

The LORD is a great God, a great King above all gods. He holds in his
hands the depths of the earth and the mightiest mountains. The sea
belongs to him, for he made it. His hands formed the dry land, too.

Psalm 95:3-5

WHEN I WAS LITTLE, my family once made an overnight stop in Gatlinburg, Tennessee, on the way to visit my grandparents in Florida. We were all smitten—my parents by a scenic trail in the Great Smoky Mountains, and my brother and I by the hotel pool and the taffy-making candy kitchen we passed on the way to the miniature golf course built on the side of a steep hill.

From then on we made annual trips to Gatlinburg. My dad always planned several hikes. At first, I hated those excursions. All I wanted was to get back to town so we could go to the arcade or ice cream shop.

Gradually, though, I came to treasure those walks. We'd hike for long stretches under ancient trees, by babbling brooks, and past huge rock formations. Occasionally we would spot a black bear or a lightning-quick salamander on the bank of a stream. Often we'd walk for miles to the background music of rushing water, only to turn a bend and see a thundering waterfall.

My favorite moments came after we'd hiked past thick clusters of trees and came to a vista overlooking the mountain range. Sometimes the sky would be bright blue and the deep-green peaks would seem to go on and on. At other times, a thick haze shrouded the mountains or shadows from the clouds danced along the summit.

"The world is charged with the grandeur of God," observed Gerard Manley Hopkins in his famous poem "God's Grandeur." I couldn't have expressed the sight from those clearings any better.

I haven't visited the Smoky Mountains in years, but even today I look for glimpses of God's grandeur when walking along the path near my home or along the river that cuts through a nearby town. All I have to do is spend some time outside to remember God's power and love. The works of our Creator's hands always "proclaim the glory of God" and "display his craftsmanship" (Psalm 19:1).

Steps of Faith
Lord, I praise You for the wonderful works of Your hands!

Deeper Walk: Psalm 19:1-6

Never Too Busy

The eyes of the LORD search the whole earth in order to
strengthen those whose hearts are fully committed to him.
2 Chronicles 16:9

MY DAD WAS A high school English teacher. Most weeknights, after dinner was over and the dishes were done, he would grade papers in his "home office"—a metal desk and a filing cabinet at the bottom of the stairs of our unfinished basement. I would often head down the stairs myself in the evenings to sharpen a pencil, to search for my cat, Cricket—or simply to talk to my dad.

I can't remember a single conversation we had, but I do remember this: No matter how high the stack of essays he needed to grade, Dad would always stop what he was doing when he heard me clomping down those stairs. I can still picture him, wrapped in an afghan or wearing his jacket to ward off the basement chill, putting down his pen and turning toward me when he saw me hit that bottom step. He was never too busy for me.

Without preaching and without my knowing it, my dad was showing me what our heavenly Father is like—always searching for the one who seeks Him out. He longs to spend time with His children, and He is never preoccupied or too busy with more important stuff to listen to us.

I have a wonderful dad, but he is not infallible. God the Father, however, is perfect—perfectly loving, perfectly powerful, and perfectly wise. Do you need direction? Ask Him for guidance. Do you wonder if you matter? Seek Him out. Do you struggle with fear? Cry out to Him.

Your heavenly Father is near you, and He is just waiting to hear your voice and respond to your need.

Steps of Faith

Abba Father, how thankful I am to know that I can come to You anytime. No matter how unworthy or lost I feel, You are waiting to fill me with Your presence, peace, and love.

Deeper Walk: Isaiah 30:15-21

Road Construction That Brings . . . Soul Repair?

Be thankful in all circumstances.
1 Thessalonians 5:18

HERE I SAT AGAIN—stalled in traffic. Running late. Orange cones and yield signs to my right. A guy in a neon jacket waving cars to slow down. I kept my foot on the brake pedal and waited for my turn to wind through the obstacle course.

I hate construction. Worse, it seems as though every road in my area has some type of construction going on—*year-round*! This day was no exception.

As I felt my blood pressure rise, I glanced at the other drivers—fingers tapping steering wheels in frustration, jaws clenched. One guy's face was as red hot as his sweet cherry-red Corvette.

Then I noticed a young woman singing along with what I assumed was a tune on the radio. She appeared as though she didn't care if she never inched from that spot. She looked . . . *happy*.

As I merged in front of her, I waved my thanks, and she smiled and waved back—still singing and shimmying her shoulders as though she were dancing. I couldn't help but laugh.

How could I remain frustrated over something beyond my control when I'd just received a wave, a smile, and a noiseless song-and-dance routine?

She'd broken up the frustration of the moment. It hit me that I, too, could enjoy my time stuck there. I could actually be grateful that the construction was forcing me to slow down! I didn't have to like the delay, but I could be content. I had a car, after all. It ran and was warm—or cool!—inside, whichever I needed to combat that day's temperature. I decided to spend my time trapped on this constricted road thanking God that I was . . . trapped on this constricted road.

In a world that jumps so quickly to frustration and anger when things don't go perfectly, we can choose to find something to be grateful for—even when our circumstances aren't the best.

The next time I was stuck in construction, I sat back and listed every good thing I could think of. And the strangest thing happened: I, too, felt happy.

Steps of Faith

Lord, in every circumstance, let me focus on those things that I can be grateful for.

Deeper Walk: Psalm 77:11-14

Preach On, Pastor!

Preach the word of God. Be prepared, whether the time is favorable or not.
Patiently correct, rebuke, and encourage your people with good teaching.
2 Timothy 4:2

CHRISTINE SAT DOWN across from her husband and placed the tray of food between them. Todd took his wife's hands in his, and they bowed their heads.

"Lord, bless this food and help us to be a blessing to those we encounter today. We love You and want to serve You wholeheartedly. In Jesus' name, amen." But Todd quickly closed his eyes again, bowed his head once more, and gently squeezed Christine's hands.

"And thank You for Pastor Dave," Todd added. "He's been such a blessing to us. Amen."

Christine smiled across the table at her husband, tilted her head, and said good-naturedly, "And just how has Pastor Dave been a blessing to you? I thought you two weren't seeing eye to eye these days."

Todd nodded and grinned at his wife's teasing. "Well, we did disagree about a couple of small things in the last deacons' meeting," he admitted. "But there's one thing we can always count on with Dave."

Christine lifted her eyebrows and waited for Todd to continue. But before Todd explained, he put down the burger he had been unwrapping and glanced away. For a moment Christine thought he was going to cry; he seemed so touched by something.

"Christine, we are so blessed to have a man who preaches God's Word to us with authority and love each week."

October is Pastor Appreciation Month. Your pastor may or may not have a charismatic personality, be a dynamic leader, or provide a compassionate shoulder to lean on in times of distress. But if your church's leader is faithful to the Word of God in preaching, attitudes, and deeds, then you have a gem. Thank God for the blessing of godly leadership and express your appreciation to your pastor as well.

Steps of Faith

Father, help me not to hold my pastor to a standard of perfection or to my ideals. Help me support my pastor's efforts to preach Your Word boldly and with conviction.

Deeper Walk: 2 Timothy 4:1-8

Sharing the Plenty

Love each other. Just as I have loved you, you should love each other.
John 13:34

IN THE GENTLY ROLLING HILLS OF southwestern Wisconsin is a piece of heaven on earth, a farm run by a kind family who welcomed me into their lives and onto their property. Nestled among two-lane country roads and deep river valleys, the land itself is beautiful, and never more so than at harvesttime.

The changing trees provide a colorful backdrop for nonstop activity. From before dawn until after dark, the combine and tractors methodically move through the fields, and the harvested crops are quickly stored away. Dusty pickup trucks line the gravel driveway leading up to the farmhouse, and inside, fresh vegetables and fruits overwhelm every kitchen surface. The earthy smell of harvest wafts in through open windows, and the sun sets earlier each day, giving way to bonfires, hoodies, and clear starry skies.

But as much as the harvest itself is something to witness, it's the people living here who make the farm a haven. Hardworking but unhurried, they've always made it a point to share what they have—and not just physical things like fresh milk or produce. Intangible things like time and energy are often the most valuable and sometimes the hardest to give. But in that sharing, I clearly see Christ's love shown to me.

Having experienced the love of Christ lived out in quiet and unassuming ways, I'm challenged to model it too. So while I may not have a farm, I'm trying to share the two things I often hold on to: my time and attention. With life's frenetic pace, giving these things is sometimes inconvenient but always worth it. When we show love to each other, "his love is brought to full expression in us" (1 John 4:12).

Steps of Faith
Thank You, Father, for the people You've put in my life. Help me to show Your love by sharing my time and energy.

Deeper Walk: 1 John 3:16-19

Passing Along Good Deeds

Let us think of ways to motivate one another to acts of love and good works.
Hebrews 10:24

I COULDN'T BELIEVE IT. I'd gotten home from a weeklong conference and was exhausted. As soon as I walked through the door, my nose caught the most wonderful aroma. There on the kitchen counter sat a pizza from my favorite pizza joint, along with a bottle of my favorite grape soda.

"Wow!" I exclaimed and smooched my husband.

But he wasn't finished with the surprises. After eating and discussing my conference, he pulled me out of my chair. "Come with me," he said, as he grabbed my hand and winked.

He ushered me into my office and stood back so I could easily see my desk. My eyes locked onto a beautiful new computer with speakers and the works. I had a big project I was working on, and he knew I needed something more substantial than my old, cranky laptop. Not only had he seen a need; he'd done something about it. He took the time to make my life easier. I was overjoyed and grateful for his kind and loving act, but I also felt convicted. How often do I look beyond my own needs and the "have to" responsibilities and pay attention to the "above and beyond" stuff, as my husband had?

I thought about how good it felt to experience this surprise and determined that I wanted to offer that same kindness or, as Hebrews says, "acts of love and good works." When we pay attention to others and go beyond the call of duty to meet those wants and needs, we show the kind of joyous love that God lavishes on us—and we motivate others to do the same. It feels great for everybody involved—the one who receives *and* the one who gives.

Steps of Faith

I love to receive surprises, Father. Let me remember how good that feels and help me give that same wonderful feeling to those around me. Remind me to pay attention to the "above and beyond" needs of others and work to make their lives easier.

Deeper Walk: Philippians 4:5-17

Living beyond Myself

Wake up and look around. The fields are already ripe for harvest.
John 4:35

I'VE DECIDED THAT READING too many headlines and listening to the news nonstop is not good for me.

Why? Because I've become inward-focused and fearful. Economic disasters and natural disasters. Terrorism and corruption. Persecution and epidemics. Wars and rumors of war. And fewer people than ever who want anything to do with Jesus (or so it seems). All of this has combined to make me feel unsettled and afraid.

The truth is that we live in an unsettled world. I can't rely on false securities, like having enough money, enough food stored, enough professional contacts—enough of anything, really, but Jesus.

Our world is crying out for answers, but I have the Answer. People are preoccupied with the storm, but I know the Storm Calmer. They are worried about the future, but I know the One who makes every day possible. They look to worldly sources for their protection, but I know the Protector.

Since God is for me, how can I be afraid? Since He holds my life in His hands, why do I worry? Since He is the Creator and Sustainer of all, why do I feel that every decision is up to me?

I believe He is calling me to live beyond myself. To cast all my cares upon Him so that I can care for others freely. To shed my fear, focus on Him, and get to work for His Kingdom. To understand that every day that passes is one day closer to His coming.

I think that living beyond myself is going to be freeing.

Our world is facing many challenges today. As Jesus followers, we must not be fearful; instead we must be preoccupied with Him. Yes, the battles we face can be damaging. And yes, we are frail and vulnerable. But He is on our side. What do we have to fear? Let's live beyond ourselves.

Steps of Faith

Father, You are our Protector in these times of trouble. Help us to keep our eyes on You and live beyond ourselves.

Deeper Walk: Psalm 46:1-7

What They Really Need

Share each other's burdens, and in this way obey the law of Christ.
Galatians 6:2

BARBARA SET A PLATE OF cookies on the table. "Our small group wants to help military families in the congregation," she explained. "I felt God nudging me to get some ideas from those of you who are actually living it."

Kendra spoke up first. "I can think of one thing that would help. I'd love to have a few women I can call for child care on days when I need to grocery shop in peace, clean my house, or just have some alone time."

"My biggest struggle is keeping up on repairs while my husband is deployed," one of the other women said.

Another woman needed an oil change but feared a repeat of last time, when the mechanic talked her into unnecessary repairs. Could she hire someone from church to do it?

The one dad in the group had a daughter who clearly needed a woman to do girl stuff with.

These everyday things had never occurred to Barbara. She realized that they were essentially functioning as single parents. As she listened, she jotted down ideas and prayed that God would move many people in the church to reach out to these families.

"Thank you for thinking of this," Kendra said with tears in her eyes. "Sometimes I feel so alone. This meeting is an answer to my prayers."

As unrest rages in the world, families are left behind as mothers or fathers are deployed. While some military spouses have families to lean on, many have no one beyond their church families. What can we do besides pray, include them in activities, and offer emotional support? Consider the daily tasks and frustrations that can be overwhelming even when your spouse is not half a world away. As we strive to "do good to everyone" (Galatians 6:10), may we make a special effort to be mindful of those left behind as their spouses serve.

Steps of Faith

Father, help me to remember the many families represented by the men and women serving in the military. Show me how I can help.

Deeper Walk: Luke 6:31

Wide-Eyed Wonder

*I will praise you, LORD, with all my heart; I will tell of
all the marvelous things you have done.*

Psalm 9:1

"MOMMY, WOULD YOU COME with my class on our field trip? Ple-e-e-ease?" my little boy asked, grabbing my hand as we walked out the front doors of the church that housed his preschool.

That's all it took for me to put a big check mark on the permission slip next to the line asking for chaperones.

On the appointed day in early October, five parents stayed after drop-off. We were each assigned a small group of kids before we all hopped on the bus for the short ride to a nearby forest preserve.

Once there, the lead teacher, Mrs. Morgan, quickly got everyone's attention. "Children, do you remember that the Bible tells us that God created every living thing, like plants and animals? Look around. This forest is full of living things." Then she announced we were going on a treasure hunt. She held up a laminated sign illustrating several items we were to look for: a milkweed pod, a red maple leaf, a bird feather, and more.

The kids were raring to go; there was much shrieking and jumping as we started down a well-marked trail that circled a small lake. Soon I was caught up in the preschoolers' excitement, looking under trees for a pinecone. I was thrilled for my son when he scooped up a perfectly intact acorn—one of the other items on our list—and held it aloft like a trophy.

For about forty minutes, I lost myself in the joy of a crisp but sunny autumn day and the elation of small children for whom so much of God's creation is still brand-new. The highlight came when one of the children spotted a deer swimming on the other side of the lake. That wasn't even on the list!

In the book of Genesis, we read that God once walked in the Garden with Adam and Eve in the cool of the day (3:8, NIV). I sensed that, in some way, our heavenly Father was walking among the children in the forest during their treasure hunt, delighting in their wonder on a nearly perfect October day. I'm glad I was right there with them—and with Him.

Steps of Faith

Father, even at this time of the year—as the days get shorter and the air gets colder—the world is filled with wonder. Open my eyes that I might see the glory of Your creation, and stir my heart that it might overflow with thanksgiving.

Deeper Walk: Genesis 2

The Rewards of the Risk

Now do as I tell you. . . . Be sure to notice where [Boaz] lies down;
then go and uncover his feet and lie down there.
Ruth 3:3-4

I'VE ALWAYS LOVED THE biblical character Ruth. She risked going to a foreign land to live, where the only person she knew was Naomi, her *mother-in-law*. She risked finding work in a stranger's field. She risked obeying her mother-in-law's request to lie down at the feet of a man and ask him to marry her and care for her. That's seriously scandalous!

I would have balked if my mother-in-law—or anyone!—told me to make such a request. I'd feel as if I were reliving my freshman year, in which I told a senior that I had a crush on him—to which he replied awkwardly, "Uh, thanks," and then avoided me like the plague for the rest of his high school career.

Never again. Better to play it safe, and no one will think you're crazy.

But Ruth trusted Naomi and took the risk. And did it ever pay off! God used her willingness to step outside her comfort zone to accomplish His will—not only in her life but in the life of an entire nation.

Imagine, had she not trusted God and Naomi, she might not have married Boaz or had a baby (Obed), who would never have married and had a baby (Jesse), who would have never had a son, David—the David who became the famous king of Jewish history and acclaim, and who was the ancestor of our Savior, Jesus. So much history set in place—all because Ruth took a risk.

Is there something you feel God calling you to do, but fear keeps you from pursuing it? Perhaps today is the day to say yes to the risk—and the potential reward.

Steps of Faith

Jesus, You came to earth through the lineage of a woman who moved beyond her fears and said yes to scary and crazy things—things well out of her comfort zone. I want to have that kind of willingness and faith to trust You even when I don't know the outcome that You have planned.

Deeper Walk: Ruth 3:1-13

Going beyond First Impressions

The seeds of good deeds become a tree of life; a wise person wins friends.
Proverbs 11:30

MANY YEARS AGO, on my first day at a new job, I had the simple task of typing out envelopes. Envelope after envelope went through the printer and came out fully addressed. I was whizzing through and feeling good about it all.

And then Patricia walked into my work space.

She hovered over my shoulder and announced loudly, "You're doing those wrong. The addresses are supposed to be *all capitalized*. You'll have to do them all again."

I was crushed. This woman wasn't my boss. And anyway, I thought, who cared? It wasn't as if the post office would refuse to deliver an envelope addressed to "John Doe" versus "JOHN DOE." And I seriously doubted that the envelope's recipient would see the address and think, *What's that company's problem? Don't they know the address is supposed to be capitalized?*

This was going to be my new job? Enduring this woman who was loud, bossy, and inserted her busybodyness into my work?

That night I went home and cried. I wasn't sure I now wanted the job I'd been so excited to get.

I stuck it out, though, determined to give Patricia a wide berth. But since she was in my department, I couldn't completely ignore her, and soon, to my shock, I found I *liked* her. She was fun, funny, caring, boisterous, and generous. She never met a stranger. And five years later, she was a bridesmaid at my wedding.

I'm grateful I stuck it out. If I'd allowed that first impression to rule over me, I'd never have been blessed to have such a sweet friend.

Sometimes we just have to dig down a little beneath the surface with people to discover why they irritate us so much. Sometimes we simply need to give them the benefit of the doubt and another shot. Many times, when we do those things, we'll discover that God put them in our lives to offer us greater blessings than we'd realized.

Steps of Faith

Lord, some people in my life annoy me. To be honest, I haven't given them the benefit of the doubt. Help me see them as You do—and perhaps I'll make a friend in the process.

Deeper Walk: Proverbs 27:17

Fix Your Thoughts

Fix your thoughts on what is true, and honorable, and
right, and pure, and lovely, and admirable. Think about
things that are excellent and worthy of praise.
Philippians 4:8

I SMILED AS I WATCHED my three-year-old granddaughter sleeping peacefully. Madison didn't have a care in the world. Happy, healthy, and well loved, her biggest concern was whether she would receive the new doll she had been asking for. I wished I could experience the peace she had.

Instead I was filled with so much worry and anxiety that it was disrupting my sleep. My son-in-law was battling metastatic melanoma, and we didn't know what the outcome would be. As a result, our oldest daughter was shouldering a huge burden of stress. Our youngest daughter faced severe financial problems, and her husband's company had just announced layoffs. My mother had married a man who was isolating her from the rest of the family, which made maintaining a relationship with her difficult. And my own mental health was deteriorating.

Night after night, I could feel the anxiety churning inside. I tried not to get up too often so I wouldn't disturb my husband, but he wasn't sleeping very well either.

One night we were both awake about 2:00 a.m., so I turned on the light and picked up my Bible. It fell open to the verse in Philippians that says, "Fix your thoughts on what is . . . pure, and lovely" (4:8). We prayed that the Lord would give us peace while we went through life's storms and that He would help us to focus on Him and His faithfulness.

When we're overwhelmed with our circumstances, it's hard to focus on the pure and lovely things in our lives. The Lord wants us to face our concerns and give them to Him. Because of Jesus, we no longer have to let our burdens consume us. The next time you're tempted to fret, pause, take a deep breath, and picture giving your burdens to the Lord. He is more than able to carry you through.

Steps of Faith

Lord, You are good, and Your love is eternal. Your faithfulness continues to all generations (see Psalm 100:5).

Deeper Walk: Philippians 4:4-9

If They Only Knew

Just as the rich rule the poor, so the borrower is servant to the lender.
Proverbs 22:7

LOIS FOUGHT BACK TEARS AS she arranged the stack of bills according to their due dates. How would she ever cover them all? Her husband finally had full-time work after almost a year, but in the meantime they had piled up debt that could no longer be ignored.

Lois thought of Michelle, whom she'd met at a ladies' tea. Michelle's husband, Kent, was a financial counselor who offered services free of charge to anyone at church who expressed a need. Maybe he could help. But then Kent would see their mess.

Most of it wasn't their fault. Bills didn't stop for reduced work hours. The kids still needed shoes, lunches, and school supplies. But as Lois looked over the credit card statements, she recognized purchases from days when, tired of feeling poor, she'd justified a splurge. *God, show me what to do*, she prayed.

Michelle and Kent kept coming to mind, along with the thought that perhaps God had placed her beside Michelle at the tea for a reason. Maybe she needed to set aside her pride and call.

It doesn't take long for reduced employment, medical emergencies, or even occasional impulsive spending to turn tight finances into overwhelming debt. With debt comes stress and often shame. *Why wasn't I more careful? I should have planned ahead. If I ask for help, I'll have to admit that I wasn't a good steward of my finances.*

Proverbs 22:7 says, "The borrower is servant to the lender." But we don't need to stay servants. Sometimes freedom requires sharing our burdens with someone who can provide wise counsel. In the process we learn that we are not alone—those who have learned financial lessons the hard way often have tools to help us avoid getting buried again.

Steps of Faith

God, debt is hard enough on its own without the embarrassment that goes along with it. Give me the humility to seek help when I need it before my financial stress gets out of control.

Deeper Walk: Proverbs 3:13-15

Praying for Your Husband

Pray for each other so that you may be healed. The earnest prayer of a righteous person has great power and produces wonderful results.
James 5:16

OVER A YEAR AGO, I began praying regularly for my husband. I was frustrated with his lack of spiritual leadership in our family and tired of trying to coax him into stepping up. Not long after I began praying, I made a series of discoveries that culminated in a confession from him that nearly tore our family apart.

In the wake of his confession, I turned to God. I spent hours simply sitting with Him, letting Him hold me. I read the Bible, looking for comfort and wisdom. I began to journal. And out of that place, though my anger and hurt were still raw, I began to pray more desperately for my husband and my family.

I was deeply convicted about how little I had prayed for my husband during our marriage. For many years I had thought we had a nearly perfect Christian marriage and life. I frequently prayed for people with cancer, the poor, and the oppressed. But I had no idea how much my husband needed my prayers, no idea that he was battling temptation and falling prey to the enemy.

I don't take responsibility for my husband's sin, but I know that when I began taking my concerns about his spiritual state to God, he was rescued from a dark and destructive path. Not only has our marriage survived a crisis, but I have also seen more evidence of spiritual growth and maturity in him in this past year than I ever had before. God has answered specific prayers for my husband many times, and I now understand how much he needs my prayers daily.

Maybe your family or marriage isn't in crisis. Maybe you just feel that your husband needs to fold a little more laundry or help with the kids more. Perhaps he's struggling with anger, anxiety, or depression, and you don't know how to help. Prayer is more powerful and effective than nagging or complaining. Whatever the case may be, bring him to the Lord in prayer.

Steps of Faith

Lord, teach me how to pray for my loved ones. Help me to develop the habit of praying for them regularly.

Deeper Walk: Ephesians 1:16-17

Unfamiliar Territory

We who are strong must be considerate of those who are sensitive about things like this. We must not just please ourselves.

Romans 15:1

JACKIE PUT THE TELEPHONE BACK ON the desk and sighed as she sat down. Her friend Mary's husband had called to say that Mary's mother had died during the night.

Mrs. Arnold had been only fifty-six and had seemed healthy, but now her thirty-year-old daughter was grieving her death.

Lord, Jackie prayed, *I don't know what I'm supposed to do. This is unfamiliar territory. Do I go see Mary? Or do I just call her later? Should I fix her family a meal? I don't mean to make this all about me, but I honestly don't know how to help my friend with something I've never experienced.*

As Jackie sat in silence and waited for the Lord to speak, she wept for her friend. She knew Mary must be hurting terribly or she would have called Jackie herself.

Father, please be gracious to Mary. Comfort her with Your presence. As she continued to pray for Mary, God began to impress upon Jackie's heart how she might help her friend. More importantly, He caused her heart to swell with love for Mary so that, by the time she finished praying, she no longer feared not knowing what to do, but she was ready to help.

When someone we love encounters a tragedy unfamiliar to us, we can feel ill equipped to help. We may even miss opportunities to express our concern and love because we fear doing something wrong in the process. But 1 John 4:18 says God's "perfect love expels all fear." When we allow His love to motivate and direct us, we'll be freed up to move out of our comfort zones and into unknown territory so we can express compassion.

Are you allowing the fear of saying or doing the wrong thing to keep you from ministering to someone who is hurting? Pray for your grieving friend and ask God to give you His love for him or her. Then follow His lead.

Steps of Faith

Father, may Your love motivate me to go beyond myself and minister with compassion to those who hurt.

Deeper Walk: 1 John 4:11-13

Critical Damage

Why do you condemn another believer?
Why do you look down on another believer?
Romans 14:10

THE TUPPERWARE PARTY WAS in full swing, and the ladies were passing around products when someone joked about her husband carrying leftovers to work.

Jessica laughed. "My husband thinks he's too good for leftovers. Heaven forbid I suggest he take a serving of last night's dinner for his lunch. It's really annoying that he's so wasteful."

Jessica continued to criticize her husband—to the group and in side conversations. Stories of his bad habits launched her into berating his integrity, which led to a diatribe about how he was a bad example to their children.

During a conversation with Brenda, an older lady, Jessica bashed her husband once more and was met with rebuke. "Stop criticizing your husband, Jessica," Brenda said. "You're diminishing his reputation in front of everyone. I've always known the two of you to be happy. What's going on?"

Jessica felt the heat of embarrassment and defensiveness rise to her cheeks, but she knew Brenda was right. After a pause, Jessica's eyes welled up. She apologized and went on to express some of her recent stress. Brenda gently encouraged Jessica and prayed for her. Before leaving the party, Brenda slipped Jessica a note. On it were written Scripture verses and a couple of books about marriage that specifically addressed communication and criticism.

Are you eager to build up your husband or to tear him down? When you speak poorly of your husband to others, not only are you damaging him; you're also damaging yourself. Others may find you to be negative or critical. When you're tempted to disparage your husband, examine your thought process and confess your sin to the Lord. Ask Him for a renewed mind and a heart that is set on Him. Be a good example of a Christlike wife for those who don't know what that looks like.

Steps of Faith

Father, renew my heart and mind to focus on You. Replace my critical heart with one of joy and gratitude. May words of praise be on my lips.

Deeper Walk: Romans 14:1-12

Worship through Eating

He satisfies the thirsty and fills the hungry with good things.
Psalm 107:9

I LOVE TO EAT. I can think of nothing better than sitting down to a table over-flowing with the best home-cooked foods and taking my time enjoying every morsel. This tends to be easily done when I'm noshing on a holiday meal. I ooh and aah over the delicious offerings, stuff myself, and then consider how rude it would be to undo the top button of my pants because I'm so full!

God has provided us with wonderful food. Our cabinets and refrigerators are overflowing, and our choices are endless. Food and drink are so readily handy that too often I've failed to practice true gratitude over what sits on a plate before me. Too often I've become guilty of saying a quick prayer of blessing, "Thank You for this food. Amen," before I dive in. Then while eating I distract myself watching TV, checking my phone, or counting calories. Been there?

What if our eating became a time of worship and communion with God? What if when we sat down to eat, we considered God's character and His gifts to us through food? The beauty of the different colors; the tastes; the aromas; the textures of the meat, vegetables, fruits, and grains; the nutrients He placed in each and how they work together to bring us health and energy; and how food brings us together with our friends and family.

Today when you get something to eat, use that time to worship the Creator who loves you so much that He created amazing food for your nourishment *and* enjoyment.

Steps of Faith

How creative You are, God! You designed me to need food to keep my body healthy and strong, but You also made eating it so wonderful for all my senses. Thank You for the tangible ways that You show You love me, soul and body.

Deeper Walk: Psalm 107:1-9

Best Face Forward

The man and his wife heard the LORD God walking about in the garden.
So they hid from the LORD God among the trees. Then the LORD God called
to the man, "Where are you?" He replied, "I heard you walking in the garden,
so I hid. I was afraid because I was naked."

Genesis 3:8-10

MY FAMILY'S FAVORITE pumpkin farm features hay bales for jumping, a corn maze for exploring, and a sandbox filled with seed corn for digging. It's only after my kids have worn themselves out from all those activities that we get to what is, for me, the high point of our visit: picking our pumpkin.

As we pull our wagon toward the field, my eyes begin scanning the rows for that perfect pumpkin—one with a rich orange hue, a deep green stem, and a symmetrical shape. Normally it doesn't take us long to spot a prime candidate. But too often when we turn a pumpkin over to examine it more closely, we are disappointed. Although it appeared healthy and shapely from afar, we discover that the back has a flat or discolored section. Sometimes it has a crack or spots, or it doesn't sit up straight. The search continues.

It's not only pumpkins that tend to show their good sides: I do the same thing. I'm well aware of my flaws, but if I can hide them, I generally will. After all, if people see my weaknesses, will they reject me? And if they see where I struggle, will I be forced to give up a habit or attitude I've become comfortable with? Life feels much more manageable when I show only my good side and hide my fears, vulnerabilities, and weaknesses.

Perhaps you feel misshapen or broken today. Feelings of shame may make you want to hide from God, just as Adam and Eve hid from Him in the Garden. If so, I have good news. When we turn our lives over to Him, our heavenly Father uses even our weaknesses and failures to shape us until we are "conformed to the image of his Son" (Romans 8:29, ESV).

Take heart: The pumpkin in late October has finished developing, but God is still at work molding you, His beautiful and beloved daughter.

Steps of Faith

Merciful Father, thank You for loving me just as I am and yet desiring to shape me into all that You created me to be. I invite You to continue Your refining work in me today.

Deeper Walk: 1 Corinthians 1:26-29

False Sense of Security

*Don't count on your warhorse to give you victory—for all its
strength, it cannot save you. But the LORD watches over those
who fear him, those who rely on his unfailing love.*

Psalm 33:17-18

YEARS AGO, our family took a trip to Yellowstone. One day as we were driving through the park, we noticed that several vehicles had pulled off along the side of the road. When we spotted a small herd of buffalo grazing in a nearby field, we decided to stop as well.

While my husband and I were content to watch them through the windshield, our twelve-year-old son, David, decided he wanted a closer look. He got out of the car and took a few steps toward the pasture. His movement must have startled the animals because they looked up and a few began ambling toward him. Though they were moving slowly, they looked bigger and stronger than David had expected.

In a panic, he sprinted back toward the van. We watched helplessly as he jumped into a vehicle that looked exactly like ours—same color, make, and model. The only problem: It wasn't ours. Within five seconds he jumped back out, red faced. The vehicle he'd counted on to provide refuge from the approaching buffalo wasn't the safe place he expected after all.

Though we all (even David) get a good laugh from that memory, some of the other places we turn to for security aren't so funny. I've been tempted to look to money, connections, and experience to shield me from trouble or hardship. Ultimately, however, anything apart from God, our Creator and Sustainer, will fail us, just as surely as a stranger's van wasn't the sanctuary David had been looking for.

The good news is this: Our heavenly Father always welcomes us with open arms. Though He may not remove the difficulty we long to escape, He is our Refuge in any storm.

Steps of Faith

Heavenly Father, help me to find my security in You and You alone.

Deeper Walk: Jeremiah 17:5-8

The Long Road

Be strong and courageous, all you who put your hope in the LORD!
Psalm 31:24

ALISA TUCKED THE appointment reminder card into her purse and left the dentist's office. As she walked to her car, she thought about the significance of the date on that card. It marked two years since she finally took the advice of her Christian counselor to seek shelter and protection for herself and her children from her brutally abusive husband.

Driving toward the office where she worked, Alisa thought about the differences in her small family since that anxious day. She had wondered then if she and her two preschoolers would ever be safe, happy, and able to live normal lives.

Alisa had left her home on foot with her children and three small bags early in the morning, just after her husband had left for work. She knew they would need that much time to ride the bus to the safe house in the next state before her husband returned home that evening. That day she and her children had nothing but each other—no car, no job, no hope. The only thing Alisa had plenty of was despair.

But now Alisa and her children had their own apartment, her ex-husband was in prison for other crimes he had committed, and she slept peacefully through the night. More importantly, thanks in part to a small group of women who had visited the shelter from a nearby church one Saturday, she had a relationship with Jesus Christ. And He gave her hope every day.

"Lord, it's amazing how far You've brought us," Alisa prayed aloud as she pulled into the parking lot. "Thank You for changing the course of our lives."

Some situations seem too desperate for hope. But whether we encounter loss, physical suffering, danger, or financial ruin, we can still have hope if we know Jesus Christ. Do you know someone in crisis today? Consider how you can encourage or assist him or her. But most importantly, remember to share the hope of Christ.

Steps of Faith

Father, crisis situations can seem daunting and rob people of hope. Show me how to bring hope to someone who is fearful or hurting today.

Deeper Walk: Psalm 71:12-16

Minutes, Coins, and Promises

You have been faithful in handling this small amount, so now I will give you many more responsibilities.
Matthew 25:23

HAVE YOU EVER ASKED your children to clean up their rooms, and they didn't do it? Have you asked your husband to take out the garbage, and he forgot? Have you ever had an employee who could not make it to work on time, no matter how often you brought it up?

And when you asked your child, or your husband, or your employee, "Why didn't you do what I asked? Why didn't you honor your commitment?" have you heard something like this? "No, Mom, I didn't clean my room, but can I have a cookie?" "I forgot to take out the trash. I'll get to it after the game." "I'm late because I'm tired and traffic was terrible."

Sure, these moments can be frustrating. But haven't we done the same thing with God? "Yes, Lord, I know I'm supposed to tithe, but money is so tight." "Lord, I know they need help in the nursery, but I just don't have time. Besides, I need a break." Or, "I'm sorry I fell asleep while I was trying to read my Bible. I'm just so tired because of all I have to do."

I'm finding out that because I follow Jesus, every aspect of my life is stewardship to Him. He owns my whole life. Money. Time. Talents. Family. Job. House. Car. Everything.

What it really comes down to is minutes and coins and promises. Or rather, faithfulness in the small things. He asks me to serve because in serving, I'm giving Him and His Kingdom my most precious commodity: time. He asks me to tithe because when I give, I'm obeying His Word and showing His love to a dying world. He asks me to honor my commitments because when I say I'm going to do something and I keep my word, I'm more like Him.

Our minutes, coins, and promises are small things that make a big impact for the Kingdom of God. Let's make them count! When we are faithful with the little things, He can trust us with many greater things.

Steps of Faith

Father, help me to be faithful in the little things that You have called me to do. I know this is evidence of my love for You.

Deeper Walk: Luke 16:10-13

The Words We Say

The tongue can bring death or life;
those who love to talk will reap the consequences.
Proverbs 18:21

"I DON'T KNOW WHY we can't sit down to one dinner without someone making a complete mess of the table," I yelled as I sopped up the milk my oldest had spilled.

"It was an accident, dear," my husband, Jared, said.

After dinner, my youngest trampled my feet while rushing to put her dishes in the sink. "Ow!" I shouted. "Watch where you're going!"

As I hopped on one foot, Jared excused our children to the living room. Then he turned to me and asked me what was going on and if anything was wrong.

"Why does anything have to be wrong?" I questioned.

"It just seems you've been . . . a bit critical of things lately," he replied. "What's bothering you?"

I resisted the temptation of a snappy retort, and instead I shared with him how busy life had been lately and how out of control I felt.

"It sounds like we need to pray about how to lighten your load," Jared said. "We also need to focus on God more so we don't get impatient with each other and say hurtful things."

"Like what?" I asked.

"You seemed harsh with the children earlier," he replied. "Sometimes words we think are harmless get imprinted in our kids' hearts—they internalize stuff that would bounce off you or me."

Now that was something I'd lost sight of. Focusing on Jesus as Jared encouraged would help me to choose my words more carefully.

Words are powerful. We know this because we've all been hurt by what someone has said to us or about us. The Bible says that the tongue has the power of life or death. Are the words you speak to your husband, your children, your coworkers, and others life-giving? Are they fruitful, positive, and God-honoring? Listen to yourself. Ask the Holy Spirit to put a check in your heart when you're speaking inappropriately. And when you feel that check, obey it.

Steps of Faith

Father, convict me when I'm speaking in a way that doesn't honor You. Help me to be an example to others of how words hold Your light.

Deeper Walk: Proverbs 12:18; 15:4

Looking Up

It is the Lord who created the stars, the Pleiades and Orion.

Amos 5:8

WITH THE SEASONS CHANGING, brisk days give way to cold, long nights, and the winter stars rise up from under the earth to sweep across the sky. For thousands of years, people have watched the night sky turn above them, imagining patterns among the stars and telling stories about them.

Among the most recognizable is a constellation commonly called Orion, a large hourglass-shaped figure. It's a prominent feature of the winter sky and rises in the east a few hours after sunset. And since Orion can be seen from every inhabited place on earth, it's no wonder that this constellation appears in legends and literature all around the world.

I first learned about Orion, both its shape and its significance, from my mom. To her, the night sky was good to observe alone but far better when shared with another person. And so she shared it with me.

Together we've spent countless hours observing the stars and the planets, marveling at the beauty above us. Sometimes we can get away from the sky glow that plagues our urban area, find a spot where we can actually see the horizon, and regain the perspective of just how *big* the sky is. The longer we look, the more stars we see, until it's hard to pick out even the most familiar constellations, like Orion, from the myriad stars.

It's easy to feel small in those moments and let the stillness of a clear, moonless night speak to the soul. It's easy to enjoy the company of a loved one and be in awe of the God who "made all the stars—the Bear and Orion, the Pleiades and the constellations of the southern sky" (Job 9:9).

Steps of Faith

Thank You, Lord, for the beauty You've placed in the heavens and for loved ones to share it with.

Deeper Walk: Psalm 8:3-5

Grateful?

*Be thankful in all circumstances, for this is God's will for
you who belong to Christ Jesus.*
1 Thessalonians 5:18

"Mom," my son asked me, "whose car is that pulling into our driveway?"

I craned my head around toward the family room window to get a better view. "It looks like Tom's car—Dad's friend from work," I said.

I heard the garage door go up, and in walked my husband. "Hey, honey," Mike said with a grin. "Guess what I got for you today?" He held up a set of keys and excitedly pushed them into my hand.

"You bought me a car?" I asked, dumbfounded. "Without seeing what kind of car I might like?" I looked out the window at the used sedan in a color of green I absolutely hated. "I know you meant well, but seriously?"

The excitement drained from my husband's face, and he looked dejected. "Since your old car died, I thought surprising you was a great idea. That way you wouldn't have to get stressed over the actual purchase. I'm sorry we couldn't afford a new one. Tom gave me a really good deal on it. It runs great and gets good mileage."

I felt the Holy Spirit prompting me to stop and think before I said another word. I paused, then said, "Mike, I'm sorry I'm upset right now. I'd hoped you and I were going to look for a car together." I hugged my husband and continued my silent prayers asking God to help me see the positive in this situation. I glanced over at my son, who was now distracted with a television show. I hoped he hadn't seen me behaving like a spoiled child.

God gives us many opportunities to be grateful for the things He provides for us. At times we might not feel thankful at all. But instead of giving in to the flesh and complaining about what we don't like, let's ask God to help us to set a good example for our children by being grateful in all circumstances. "I give you thanks, O Lord, with all my heart; I will sing your praises" (Psalm 138:1).

Steps of Faith

God, please help me to remember to show gratitude for the things You provide for me. Please forgive me for the times when I have acted childish and ungrateful.

Deeper Walk: Ephesians 5:15-21

The Knowing

The LORD is good to everyone. He showers compassion on all his creation.

Psalm 145:9

I WAS RAISED IN THE CHURCH and became a Christian at a young age. I remember learning in Sunday school that God is good and that He has a plan for my life. On some level, I'd always known this but never owned it for myself.

It wasn't until I was forty-one that God's goodness went from being something I knew in my brain to something I knew in my heart.

Our second daughter was born with a seizure disorder. We suspected there was something going on the moment we left the hospital to bring her home after she was born. At fourteen months of age, she had a grand mal seizure that lasted for five long minutes as I waited for the ambulance to arrive.

Over the next several months, we went through numerous doctor visits and lots of tests. When she was only eighteen months old, she was put on a powerful seizure medication.

Not long after, she had another seizure that landed us in the emergency room again. We were absolutely devastated because no one had any answers for us. It was so hard to see our blue-eyed, blonde-haired angel in a hospital bed hooked up to machines. But as we stood in the ER, grieving and afraid, we were surrounded by people who loved us. My parents, my sister, my sister's pastor, and other friends held hands and prayed for our baby. It was then that God intersected my life, changed my thinking, and grew my faith in a huge way. I looked around at all those people, I looked at that baby, and I knew: God is good, He is good all the time, and He is good to me. Even though my circumstances looked dark, He was good. Even though we didn't know what our baby's life was going to look like, He was good. Even though we were scared and grieving, He was good. And He is good. All the time. To us.

That knowledge has been in my heart ever since.

If you are facing hard, scary circumstances, know that God is good. Know it not just in your head, but in your heart.

Steps of Faith

Father, thank You for being so good to us. Help us to know that You are good in every situation and every circumstance.

Deeper Walk: Psalm 145

A Giveaway Vacation

Don't just listen to God's word. You must do what it says.
Otherwise, you are only fooling yourselves.
James 1:22

A TRIP TO NEW YORK HAD become an annual family tradition for Megan and Alex.

After making plans for their vacation, Megan, Alex, and their ten-year-old twins were dismayed when they tracked the devastation of Hurricane Sandy that fall. They decided to pray before making a decision on canceling their plans.

Days went by, and no family member felt any direction from God. Then Alex came home from work with an idea. One of his coworkers had been collecting money to send to a local church near the New Jersey shore, and had raised nearly $2,500. A lightbulb went off in Alex's mind. Why not join in Christian relief efforts and work a few days of their vacation to help others? Alex and Megan sensed this as God's direction to continue with their trip and use their time and resources to help others.

Of the four days their family was in New York, they gave two days to serving with members of local churches. During their time of service, they made new friends and experienced God's leading in deeper and more personal ways.

Family vacations are an important time for resting and bonding together. If your schedule allows, consider using some of your vacation days to serve others in a different place. Research ways that you can serve while you're visiting another city. God directs us to care for others and to serve those in need. Why not set aside some vacation days for this purpose?

Steps of Faith

Father, I want to serve You. Show me how and where You would like me to serve, whether locally or in another place.

Deeper Walk: Luke 10:25-37

Broccoli and Prayers

Remain in Me.
John 15:4, HCSB

LAST YEAR I planted a winter garden of broccoli, cauliflower, and spinach in my backyard. I lovingly watered, fertilized, and hoed. My husband covered the plants at night if the temperature was going to drop below freezing.

Much to my youngest daughter's dismay, the broccoli and cauliflower began to grow, and they looked beautiful (the key word here is *looked*). One day I went to get a closer view of the plants, and much to *my* dismay, there were no flowering heads. The plants were tall and proud and the leaves were very green, but inside those leaves where the baby broccoli or cauliflower should have been, there was just an empty space. Their growing season was almost over, so I knew they were not going to produce.

Disappointed by their fruitlessness, I stomped inside. As I swung the door behind me, Jesus reminded me of my own inner lack of fruitfulness for Him lately.

My "leafy" exterior concealed the fact that I was fruitless and not abiding in Him, just like the cauliflower leaves concealed the plant's barrenness.

I was so overscheduled that I was not remaining on my Vine. Working full-time, managing a family and a home, volunteering at church, and tending this vegetable garden that wasn't producing anything—I was so busy that my prayer life had suffered.

That day, I resolved to make time for real prayer instead of giving God a quick list of demands before falling asleep at night. Instead of trying to pray while driving, I committed to sitting with Him in the morning and to keeping the lines of communication open all day long. Instead of always talking, I promised to listen for His voice.

Jesus said that apart from Him we can do nothing, that without Him we will be fruitless in our walk. But by remaining in Him—praying, sitting with Him, reading His Word—we can bear much fruit. Make prayer a part of your day, every day, and live in Him. Your fruit glorifies your heavenly Father.

Steps of Faith

Father, thank You for the gift and privilege of prayer. May we never take it for granted.

Deeper Walk: John 15:1-8

Sacrifice Worth Making

The one who has two shirts must share with someone who has none,
and the one who has food must do the same.

Luke 3:11, HCSB

TEN-YEAR-OLD REAGAN LAID A magazine on the table. "I decided what I want to do with the birthday money Grandma gave me."

Molly stirred the spaghetti sauce and set the spoon down. "What do you have in mind?"

"I want to buy some chickens."

Molly laughed. "No way. I don't care how trendy it is to eat eggs from your own chickens. We're not farmers."

"I mean for someone else." Reagan pushed the magazine across the table. "Remember when our Sunday school class collected money at Christmas last year to buy a cow for a family in the Philippines so they could have milk? Well, I thought it would be nice to do something like that."

"You would be willing to spend your birthday money on a family you don't even know?"

"It's not like I need anything after the big party I had. These people don't even have enough food. Can I do it?"

Molly looked at her daughter's eager face, then at the magazine filled with photos of impoverished children. As the baby of the family, Reagan often needed to be reminded to think of others, and now she wanted to sacrifice a gift for strangers in another country.

"Of course you can. In fact, I think I'll cut out buying coffee this month so I can buy some chickens too."

Although many of us are experiencing tough economic times, we are still prosperous compared to families in other places who lack suitable shelter, food, and clothing. It doesn't take much to change their lives for the better. Remember that God has a heart for the poor. Psalm 140:12 says, "I know that the LORD secures justice for the poor and upholds the cause of the needy" (NIV). And we read in Proverbs 22:9, "The generous will themselves be blessed, for they share their food with the poor" (NIV).

Steps of Faith

Lord, stir my generosity. Show me how I can meet the need of one who is crying out to You for relief.

Deeper Walk: Isaiah 58:6-12

Lights in a Dark World

Live clean, innocent lives as children of God, shining like
bright lights in a world full of crooked and perverse people.
Philippians 2:15

THEY'RE IMPOSSIBLE TO MISS. Every year, thousands of small candles dot a field in a park, shining in the dark to commemorate Veterans Day. With the time change, darkness falls earlier, and the evenly spaced tea lights are lit just before the evening rush hour. I like to get there just after sunset, joining the other photographers taking long exposures along the perimeter of the field.

There, on the fringe of the shadows, it's quiet despite the field's proximity to a major thoroughfare. The seemingly endless rows of light are a spectacle to behold and attract a great deal of attention.

Many passersby stop—some lingering at the outskirts, others congregating to converse in hushed tones, and still others joining silhouetted figures wandering the park. From where I usually sit on the cold grass, the people are as interesting to watch as the lights.

The people themselves are varied, but their reason for stopping is universal. "I wasn't planning to stop," they say, usually while waving a hand toward the field, "but then I saw the lights."

Lights have a way of drawing us in. We can see them a long way off, where they often serve as a guide or marker. They're just as comforting up close: They chase back the darkness and allow us to see unimpeded. Lights catch our attention and irresistibly hold it, inviting us to come closer and see.

"Now you have light from the Lord," wrote the apostle Paul, describing the Christian lifestyle. "So live as people of light!" (Ephesians 5:8).

When we live in a way that honors God, we stand out from a society that seeks to honor itself. We stand out like lights in a field of darkness, inviting people closer so that they, too, can see.

Steps of Faith

Thank You, Father, for the opportunity I have to shine Your light in a dark world. Help me to live in a way that draws people to You.

Deeper Walk: Ephesians 5:1-14

A Delighted Giver

The LORD . . . delights in every detail of their lives.
Psalm 37:23

I'D BARELY LET THE THOUGHT hover in my mind after lunch. *A small piece of chocolate sure would be nice.* No big dessert, just a little something sweet to end the meal.

My husband and I left the table with our bill and walked to the front of the restaurant to pay. Gloria, the hostess and cashier, whom we knew well, was standing by the register, chewing on something.

"What are you eating?" my husband said. They loved giving each other a hard time, so I knew he was ready to spring into some crazy remark about her eating on the job.

"Chocolate," she said and looked at me. "Want a piece?" She reached under the counter to her stash, pulled out a mini Dove chocolate piece, and handed it to me.

My jaw dropped as I took it. "Thank you," I said, amazed by what had just happened.

My husband's hand shot out, palm open. "Where's mine?"

"You don't get any!" Gloria said and laughed. "Just your sweet wife, since she has to put up with you."

We all laughed, but I laughed for another reason. I hadn't prayed for a piece of chocolate, but I'd thought about how good it would taste. And God, in His delightful way, provided.

Too often we don't want to bother God with the trivial details of our lives because He has so many more pressing issues to handle: war, famine, disease, abuses. But the psalmist David tells us that the Lord delights in *every* detail of our lives—even when we have a taste for an after-dinner chocolate. God wants to be involved with us. He wants us to know that He is present and listening to our every thought, that He cares about us, and that He loves to surprise us with His loving-kindness.

The next time you find yourself surprised by something trivial and good, consider it a gift from a loving Father who finds pleasure in providing even the smallest joys to His children.

Steps of Faith

Father, I'm so grateful that there is nothing too small or insignificant in my life for You to be interested in. Thank You that You delight in all of me.

Deeper Walk: Psalm 37:4

What I Learned

Can all your worries add a single moment to your life?
Luke 12:25

I'D BEEN AWAKE FOR at least two hours, worrying about bills, an overdue paycheck, the groceries we needed, a struggle that my son was having, and a series of poorly worded e-mails that I'd written long after my brain shut down for the night. Having a lot of experience with these toss-and-turn sessions, I knew deep down that I wasn't accomplishing anything. As usual, the dark and silence magnified everything times one hundred.

God, I need sleep. But my mind refused to let go, creating worst-case scenarios and potential solutions.

Just as I dozed off, my alarm clock jolted me awake again. I dragged through my morning. Why hadn't I given those problems over to God or gotten up to pray and spend time with Him?

That paycheck arrived. An hour later, God provided money for a big "stock-up" grocery trip. Not a word was said about those e-mails. My son's problem was still there, but I had made up my mind to trust that God was working. I decided for the future that I wanted to look back on times when I prayed and chose to trust Him rather than on sleepless nights when I worried, oblivious to what God was about to do.

What do we gain by worrying? Lack of sleep; headaches, stomach problems, and tense shoulders; an inability to focus or enjoy those around us; opportunities to regret all that wasted time when we discover that we worried over nothing or the issue was about to be solved. Jesus made it clear that we can't add one moment to our lives by worrying. We can, however, gain peace, reassurance, and confidence when we entrust our worries to the One who is able to resolve them.

Steps of Faith

God, I waste so much time worrying. Help me to remember how fruitless worrying has been in the past and to run to You instead and lay my concerns at Your feet.

Deeper Walk: Luke 12:22-31

A Good, Old-Fashioned Life

Remember the days of long ago; think about the generations past.
Deuteronomy 32:7

WHEN I WAS IN FOURTH GRADE, my teacher asked the class about the future and what would happen if we ran out of energy, oil, and electricity. She was looking for us to be creative about the ways we could survive.

I knew the answer and was thrilled to share it: "We could go back to the way things were in the 1800s. With horses and buggies and stuff." I thought my idea was brilliant; my teacher did not.

Looking back these many moons later, I am no longer thrilled with the prospect of returning to the days when there was no air-conditioning, cars, or DVRs that can record endless episodes of the latest television offerings. But while I may not want to travel on horseback, I still agree with my younger self about the value in the way things used to be. I yearn for the days of good old-fashioned relationships. When folks sat on front porches to greet neighbors passing by. When a handshake meant the same as a contract signed, witnessed, and notarized. When saying "I do" meant "until I die."

Obviously the "good old days" weren't always so good. But we can harness what was good about yesteryear and use those mores to become people who overflow with the beauty of Jesus in all our relationships.

That's what I consider when I think of being old-fashioned: I want to be a person who is respectful, who genuinely listens, who takes time to laugh and cry with others, who honors others, who forgives, and who focuses on the other person without having to check text and e-mail messages every few minutes. Someone who lets a yes be yes and a no, no. Someone who lives by the Golden Rule: "Do to others whatever you would like them to do to you" (Matthew 7:12). Those are pretty good traits to have whether you're riding a mustang with a tail or one that has a Ford emblem on its front grille.

Steps of Faith

Father, thank You that You never change—no matter how much our culture does. Help me to remember the good of the past and strive to live the kind of "old-fashioned" life that pleases You.

Deeper Walk: Deuteronomy 4:1-10

The Rake and Run

Whenever we have the opportunity, we should do good to everyone.
Galatians 6:10

ONE FALL SEMESTER IN COLLEGE, Lily had an idea. Together with some class-mates and friends from church, she wanted to do something for the commu-nity, no strings attached. They weren't looking for an official "outreach" or ministry event: They just wanted to show love.

At first they weren't sure the best way to go about it. They were in a col-lege town, after all, and most of them weren't even from the area. Then one gusty day as Lily was jogging to class and dodging the leaves in the wind, it clicked, and the Rake and Run was born.

The idea was fairly simple: Pick a Saturday, borrow a bunch of rakes, go rake people's lawns, and hurry off before they could be recognized and thanked. So Lily and her friends put out feelers to see who in the church and the community could really use the free yard work.

The response was overwhelming. Ministries to senior citizens, shut-ins, and widows responded quickly, and it wasn't long before someone put forward fami-lies with loved ones in the hospital. Then someone else suggested families of deployed service members. By the time first responders and teachers made the list, Lily knew they couldn't get all the houses done in one Saturday.

So they put the word out, and as their numbers increased, Lily divided them into groups and assigned houses to each group. Suddenly it was doable again.

When the day arrived, Lily and her friends put on the matching T-shirts they'd made for the Rake and Run. They piled into cars, borrowed rakes protruding awkwardly from trunks, and sped from house to house. It wasn't long before the secret was out. Residents came outside to watch and laugh good-naturedly as a group of college kids peeled up to houses, feverishly raked lawns, and dashed off, stopping only when asked what had prompted this act of kindness.

At the end of the day, there were sore backs and blisters. But there were also families whose days had been brightened and hearts touched by a group of college friends who saw the opportunity to do good and took it.

Steps of Faith
Father, help me to find ways of showing Your love and doing good where You've placed me.

Deeper Walk: Ephesians 2:8-10

Speak Up

Pure and genuine religion in the sight of God the Father means caring for orphans and widows in their distress and refusing to let the world corrupt you.
James 1:27

AMY AND WALT SAT separated by their two young children on their familiar pew. They'd come to church this Sunday night for the usual soup-and-sandwich fellowship followed by a time of worship and preaching. But instead they were greeted in the foyer by a captivating display about international orphans. And now they both sat spellbound by the couple standing at the front of the church testifying to the blessings of adopting an orphan from Ethiopia.

When the service ended and an opportunity for prayer and counsel was provided for couples interested in international adoptions, Amy gripped the pew in front of her. Just months earlier, she and Walt had decided their family was complete. How could she possibly tell him about the ache in her heart?

Later that night, when Amy returned to the living room after putting the children to bed, she was surprised to find Walt kneeling in front of the sofa praying. Gently, she eased onto the floor beside him. She didn't quite know what to expect, but Walt looked up at her, a huge grin on his face, and announced, "Amy, God has another child for us. We need to find her."

Over the following months, as the couple proceeded with adoption procedures, Amy looked back on the events, emotions, and conversations of that remarkable night as the birth of a calling. She had been hesitant to express the burden God had put on her heart during that service. But because Walt had been courageous enough to voice what was on his heart, a little girl in China would soon have a mom and dad.

Nehemiah is best known as the man who took charge of rebuilding Jerusalem's walls after the exile. But this man's passion for rebuilding began with a broken heart for a broken people. It wasn't until Nehemiah voiced his growing burden and the plan that had formed in his heart that God opened doors for his new calling (see Nehemiah 2:3-5). Does your heart hurt for someone? Is it time to voice your passion to someone you trust? To God?

Steps of Faith

Father, just as You broke Nehemiah's heart for the suffering Jews, You continue to break our hearts and propel us to action. Give me a heart that can break for others.

Deeper Walk: 2 Samuel 9:1-11

Living in Freedom

If the Son sets you free, you are truly free.
John 8:36

THE INVITATION CAUGHT me by surprise, although if I'd thought much about it, it shouldn't have. I ran my fingers over the embossed letters announcing my high school reunion.

Faces flashed across the yearbook pages of my mind. The cliques. The druggies. The football players. The nerds. The band geeks (that was me). Had time really changed anything? Did I want to go back and display all my inadequacies and flab? Did I want their potential judgments?

I delayed responding to the invitation. Maybe if I avoided it, it would go away. But then a high school friend contacted me. "Are you going? I think we should go. It'll be fun!"

I finally acquiesced and immediately went on a diet.

The reunion night came, and I shoved myself into the tightest body binder I could find to fit into a cute little green dress. I curled my hair and actually put on makeup. A bundle of nerves, I drove to the party.

I had the best time! Sure, I enjoyed the fact that many of the clique folks were chunkier and balding, but more so, I realized that they were all in the same boat as I was. They, too, were nervous and feeling insecure. Wanting to impress, to be somebody important, to be someone who mattered. But what really hit me was this: I could go and enjoy my high school reunion because *I'm not who I was.* I'm different. And I bet you are too. Older, obviously. Wiser, hopefully. But more important: I'm a new creation in Christ. And that new creation frees me from living under the fear, regrets, and mistakes of the past.

Thank God that what we used to be isn't what we always have to be. Thank God that because of Christ, we are truly free.

Steps of Faith

Jesus, thank You that You set me free. Thank You that I'm not who I used to be—and that I don't have to live under that weight any longer. Let me always remember, embrace, and live fully in the freedom of You.

Deeper Walk: 2 Corinthians 12:9-10

Watch Your Words

When there are many words, sin is unavoidable, but
the one who controls his lips is wise.

Proverbs 10:19, HCSB

MORGAN?" I called to my seven-year-old daughter. "Do you know where Grandma's ring is? I'd like to wear it tonight, but I can't seem to find it."

When I didn't get a response, I knocked on her door and then tried to open it. "Morgan? Please open the door so we can talk." I heard the door unlock and footsteps run away from it.

"Morgan?" I glanced around her room until I noticed two little feet poking out from behind the bunk beds. "Did you take Grandma's ring out of my jewelry box?" When she didn't respond, I started to get upset. Then I felt the Holy Spirit telling me that if I didn't keep myself calm, my words were going to end up hurting Morgan. *Help me to be patient and careful with my words, Lord*, I prayed silently.

"Listen, honey, I know something has happened to Grandma's ring. Would you please come out of there and talk with me?"

Morgan slowly came out of her hiding place and extended her hand toward me. I immediately recognized the ring as the one I'd been looking for, but the center stone had fallen out.

"I didn't mean to break it," she whispered as tears began forming in her eyes. "I just wanted to see if I was big enough to wear it."

I hugged her tightly to let her know I forgave her. "Thank you for telling me the truth. I know mistakes can be hard to admit." I ran my hand over her hair and silently thanked God for helping me to refrain from saying harsh words I would later regret. "Let's look through your room to see if we can find the missing stone."

When you find yourself in a situation that is stressful or upsetting, ask God to help you see things the way He sees them. Words can destroy someone's spirit if not used with care.

Steps of Faith

Forgiving Father, please help me to remember in the heat of my anger that the words I use carelessly can have long-lasting consequences. Please give me wisdom to choose words of life.

Deeper Walk: James 1:19-25

Rejecting Rejection

*See how very much our Father loves us, for he calls
us his children, and that is what we are!*

1 John 3:1

WALKING THROUGH the door was the hardest time for Karen. Getting home from a long day at work and coming into an empty, quiet house was more than she could handle. It had been six months since Jeff left her, and it wasn't really getting easier with time. His affair had broken her heart, leaving her abandoned and feeling rejected.

With the support of loving family members and great friends, she was getting through the darkest period. Yet it was the unwavering, faithful love of the Savior that held her close and gave her hope for the future. Through this difficult season, she was learning about God's deep love for her in a way she had never known.

Karen changed into some comfy clothes and fixed a hot cup of tea. As she sat down on the back porch, she was tempted to indulge her dangerous thoughts: that she would always be alone, that she wasn't worth anyone's time or attention, that there was something wrong with her. But she deliberately chose to break the pattern by speaking truth to herself: "God says I am His child and dearly loved. God says I am fearfully and wonderfully made. God says I am the apple of His eye." She prayed, *Lord, help me to remember that my value and worth are found in Christ in me, and that people may fail and forsake me, but You never will.*

God's Word promises that "He heals the brokenhearted and bandages their wounds" (Psalm 147:3). He alone is able to meet our deepest needs and give us an identity that is most precious, that never spoils or fades: His beloved child. And if we believe in Him through His Son, that is what we are! If you have been rejected or abandoned, look to the One who can meet all your needs according to His glorious riches in Christ (see Philippians 4:19). Pray for Him to use your pain to draw you closer to Him, and pray for healing from His hand.

Steps of Faith

God, You are the only One who can heal me, body and soul. Give me peace in my identity in You.

Deeper Walk: Isaiah 26:3

Embracing Who God Made You to Be

Whatever you give is acceptable if you give it eagerly.
And give according to what you have, not what you don't have.
2 Corinthians 8:12

SEVERAL YEARS AGO I met an interior decorator who told me she didn't feel as if she were really doing anything for God by decorating rich people's houses. I asked her about her clients, and among them she mentioned one whom she'd started to talk with about Jesus.

"That's your gift!" I told her. "You're reaching and influencing someone a pastor can't reach. Do you think maybe God gave you a designer's eye so you can connect and relate to people outside the church?"

Her face lit up. "I've never thought about it that way!"

How often do we overlook the amazing gifts God has placed within us because we think they aren't all that useful? But God can use *all* of us to further His Kingdom—even the things we don't think are useful.

When I think about the skills and gifts God has put within me to use for Him, I think, *God chose to give me these blessings for His glory. He trusts me with them. What a strange way to build His Kingdom.* It's sobering and amazing and thrilling!

God formed you. He gave you a personality and special abilities. He assigned those things purposefully just to you.

You may not be the best at something, but it doesn't matter—because as the apostle Paul reminds us: It's our *willingness* to use what we have been given that makes all the difference. Even though Paul was talking about giving money offerings, the same applies to giving our talents and abilities. Everything we have we can give to God as an offering that He will find acceptable if we give it eagerly. Embrace the gifts God has given you. They are special. And He has special plans for you to use them.

Steps of Faith

Father, when I become discouraged because I believe I have nothing to offer You, remind me of today's Scripture verse. The level of my skills isn't what impresses You as much as my willingness to use them.

Deeper Walk: 1 Corinthians 12

Home Sweet Home

My God will supply all your needs according to
His riches in glory in Christ Jesus.
Philippians 4:19, HCSB

MY DEAR FRIEND MALLORY RECENTLY MOVED TO A BIG CITY. Mallory's husband took a new job there, and though she was sad to leave her friends and community behind, she was really excited to move because they found the "perfect" house. Mallory described it to me over the phone, sent me pictures via text, and raved about what a great fit it was for her family.

A couple of months after their move, we went to visit Mallory and her family. And I totally underestimated how much I would envy her new house. It was huge, for one thing. And it was a new construction, so it was clean and beautiful. It had the most modern appliances, fixtures, and finishing touches. The laundry room made me swoon.

I began to think, *If only I had this, my life would be so much easier. My kids wouldn't fight so much because they would have more space. I wouldn't have to scrub old countertops or deal with a noisy dishwasher.*

When we drove back home the next day, I confessed my thoughts to my husband and he reminded me of the truth: God has met our every need—physical and spiritual. He gives us exactly what we need when we need it, and we can trust Him. He doesn't hold out on us.

As we pulled into our driveway, I looked at our sweet little house full of memories and love, and I thanked God for His gracious provision of our home. I prayed that He would be magnified in every part of it.

The Bible says that envy—wanting what somebody else has instead of what you have—is sin. When we struggle with envy, we can remember that Jesus humbled Himself and bore our sin on the cross so that we would lack for nothing. True contentment comes in knowing that we are found in Him.

Steps of Faith

God, thank You that You are my Provider and that You have met all my needs. Help me to be content with what I have.

Deeper Walk: Galatians 5:19-26

Pray without Ceasing

Be still in the presence of the LORD and wait patiently for Him to act.
Psalm 37:7

LATELY, JENNY NOTICED that her prayer times had gone on much longer than usual, but with much more repetition. When she got together to pray with her mentor, Miriam, Jenny repeated her prayer for her: "God, bless my neighbors. Bless Aunt Sue, Uncle Jim, and all of their children. And Lord, please bless Grandma Lucille; please heal all of her pain and disease. Bless our pastor and his wife, and their children. And bless my family."

When she finished, she looked at Miriam.

"Jenny, God wants to hear everything that's on our hearts, but He also wants to hear how much we love Him. If you can begin your time with the Lord by praising Him and thanking Him for everything He's done, I think you'll see a change in your prayer life.

"When our prayers are merely lists," she continued, "we miss out on the fellowship God wants to have with us. When Jesus prayed in John 17, He prayed for Himself and that He would glorify the Father. He prayed for His disciples, revealing more of Himself to them and asking God for their protection. He also interceded for those of us living today, so we may be one as He and the Father are one."

Jenny nodded. "Thank you. You've got a point."

Even Jesus took time to listen to God. When we pray and do all the talking, we don't allow enough time to listen to what He wants to reveal to us. It is in the quiet moments, when we're listening, that we hear His voice. Instead of laundry lists, our prayers should be more like Jesus' prayers—specific and motivated by our love for God and empathy for others. After praying, sit quietly before the Lord. He just might have a word for you.

Steps of Faith

Father in heaven, let me remember to express my gratitude to You. Teach me to pray specifically and listen to Your voice. You gave me one mouth to speak, but two ears to hear. May I use them wisely and for Your glory.

Deeper Walk: John 17

Sweet Service

In his grace, God has given us different gifts for doing certain things well.
Romans 12:6

As LATE FALL SETS IN, Alexa's kitchen is always abuzz with activity. Even with a full-time job and her family responsibilities, she still tries to make time for baking, not out of obligation but simply because she enjoys it and she's good at it. Come the first gust of cold air, cookies, truffles, pies, and cakes all begin making regular appearances at mealtimes and sometimes the break room at work.

Most of Alexa's treats, though, show up at her church. From holiday activities to weekly Bible studies, she combines her love of people and baking to provide treats when she can.

After helping with church dinners, she noticed that people with food allergies would peruse the food table but not find anything they could safely eat. So Alexa set about to find recipes she could alter for the most prevalent food allergies without losing the taste or texture. It took a while, but she finally figured it out.

When she first started serving in hospitality ministries, Alexa wasn't aware of the impact her behind-the-scenes service had. But as the years passed, she began to hear the stories of people who had been greatly encouraged by the seemingly simple act of having a hot meal ready.

Sometimes it's easy to fall into the trap of comparing the way we're equipped to serve with the ways other believers serve. Some Christians have been equipped to serve more publicly, with gifts like preaching and teaching. But others, whose gifts are no less valid or necessary, serve more privately.

"There are different kinds of service," wrote the apostle Paul, referring to the different abilities given to believers, "but we serve the same Lord" (1 Corinthians 12:5).

When it comes to the church itself, everyone is uniquely equipped to serve the Lord and each other. Each believer brings something special to the table, and for some like Alexa, that includes bringing something sweet to a literal table.

Steps of Faith

Thank You, Father, for how You've equipped us differently. Help me to respect and celebrate the different gifts You've given other believers.

Deeper Walk: Ephesians 4:7-8

Fine China

Now you must be holy in everything you do, just as God who chose you is holy.
1 Peter 1:15

"Mom, how come we only use these fancy dishes at the holidays?" my eight-year-old daughter Charis asked. She was setting the table for the big Thanksgiving meal we would host at our house the next day. Christmas was always at my sister's house, and birthdays were usually out at restaurants, but Thanksgiving was a meal I'd cherished making and serving for our family since my own mother had passed away when Charis was two.

"They're special dishes, Charis. They belonged to my mom. She got them when she and your grandpa got married. She always used them for holidays, so I do too. I think it makes our meal more special to use dishes that are set aside for special occasions."

Our conversation made me think about my own life as I walk with the Lord before my children and others. Is my life different? Does it make a difference that I know the Lord, or is my life just like everyone else's—looking for temporary pleasure or gain instead of living in light of eternity, valuing the Lord above all else? I belong to God; I am His prized creation, and He has set me apart to be holy, different, and special for Him. Yet sometimes I live my life as if it's a cheap paper plate instead of a beautiful piece of fine china. As I handed Charis the last of the beautiful plates, I prayed silently, *Lord, thank You for setting me apart to be holy as You are holy. Set my eyes on You as my Treasure.*

We read in God's Word the command to be holy, and we think it sounds impossible—and it is because we still sin. The good news is, God has provided One who was perfectly holy in our place—Jesus Christ, the Righteous One. He lived a sinless life and died a sinner's death so that we could be set apart for a relationship with the holy God. And out of love and gratitude we can obey Him, trusting the Holy Spirit to make us more like the Savior we serve.

Steps of Faith

Holy God, thank You for sending Jesus so that we could have a relationship with You. Set me apart as one who trusts in You in all things.

Deeper Walk: Leviticus 20:7-8

The Happiest Thanksgiving

I will exalt you, Lord, for you rescued me.
Psalm 30:1

THANKSGIVING DINNER THAT year was an affair to remember. Extra leaves had been fitted into the table to accommodate everyone, and nearly every inch of the tablecloth was covered with dishes and food. Lively music played, and the delicious smell of dinner filled the air. The holidays were a happy time for Sam's family, but this year was extra special.

As everyone sat at the table, Sam paused to say, "Do you remember where we were a year ago today?"

The unspoken answers to that question were as varied as the people sitting around the table. In the emergency room after being injured at work. Surrounded by unexpected bills. In need of a reliable car. Stuck in a dead-end job. Trapped in unhealthy relationships. On the verge of completely losing hope.

After months of seeming silence, God had swooped in and either rescued or strengthened each person from the impossible situation he or she had been facing. He had provided physical healing and given comfort in the midst of emotional turmoil. He had brought about the means for each bill to be taken care of. He had provided a used car at a price that was manageable. He had given strength and creativity to carry on in the dead-end job. He had created a way out of the damaging relationships and replaced them with healthy ones. He had provided a brighter future than could ever have been imagined. But most importantly, He had taught joy and peace and grace in the midst of hard circumstances.

With those dramatic memories so fresh, it was one of the happiest Thanksgivings on record. As they rejoiced that day, Sam knew they were celebrating not just the blessings themselves but, more importantly, the God who turns sorrow into joy, despair into hope, and misery into thanksgiving.

Steps of Faith

Father, "you have turned my mourning into joyful dancing. You have taken away my clothes of mourning and clothed me with joy, that I might sing praises to you and not be silent. O Lord my God, I will give you thanks forever!" (Psalm 30:11-12).

Deeper Walk: Psalm 40:1-10

Gracious Gatherings

Wise words bring approval, but fools are destroyed by their own words.
Ecclesiastes 10:12

I NEVER LOOKED FORWARD TO holiday gatherings with Dave's family. While I knew it was important to my husband that we spend time with his family, I found it difficult to fit in.

Jane and Jennifer, my two sisters-in-law, are very different from me. They both have demanding careers, employ nannies for their children, and live a jet-set lifestyle. At family gatherings the women often congregate in the kitchen, while the men watch sports on television. I struggled with the time I had to spend in the women's company without Dave. The competitive conversations made me feel trapped in a comparison game, and I kept coming out on the short end of the stick.

Then one Thanksgiving weekend, as I rode home, I silently poured out my wounded heart to God. That's when He gently showed me that I'd been missing His plans for those gatherings because I'd been indulging in a pity party for one. He began to change my heart toward Dave's siblings and their spouses. Finally I saw the opportunity to share God's grace with them instead of pouting about our differences.

Now when a conversation with the women in Dave's family takes a competitive turn, I know God's assignment for me is to speak words of grace into the mix. And I've been amazed at how much sweeter our time together has become, just because I finally let God's grace flow through me.

Do your extended family gatherings include challenging conversations? Gossip, competition, criticism, old resentments, and foul language can do more than leave a bad taste in your mouth. They can steal your joy, create tensions, and quench God's Spirit. Pray for wisdom and consider how you can graciously steer the talk in a different direction.

Steps of Faith

Father, You have spoken graciously to me through Your Word and Your Son. Help me speak only words that encourage and give grace to the hearer.

Deeper Walk: Ephesians 4:17-32

God's Currency

What is the price of two sparrows—one copper coin? But not a single sparrow can fall to the ground without your Father knowing it. . . . So don't be afraid; you are more valuable to God than a whole flock of sparrows.

Matthew 10:29, 31

WHEN I WAS A CHILD, finding a penny on the ground made my day. With it, I could buy a gum ball at the grocery store, or if I collected ten, I could afford one of the bouncy rubber balls from the dispenser next to the gum ball machine.

Not long ago, however, I walked right by a penny in a parking lot. In a nanosecond, I decided that stooping to pick it up wasn't worth the effort. After all, about the only time I use pennies now is when trying to give exact change to a cashier so I can avoid getting more of them!

Interestingly, Jesus found great value in pennies (okay, the copper coins of His day) as a teaching tool. When talking with His disciples about the troubles to come, He urged them not to worry. After all, God was aware of every sparrow, each of which was worth less than one copper coin. He added, "The very hairs on your head are all numbered. So don't be afraid" (Matthew 10:30-31). Only our awesome almighty God, who controls world events and establishes leaders (see Daniel 2:21), is big and powerful enough to track the tiniest details in our lives.

Later, Jesus watched wealthy worshipers dropping gifts in the Temple collection box. Along came a poor widow, who dropped in two small copper coins. Why did He commend this woman? "They have given a tiny part of their surplus, but she, poor as she is, has given everything she has" (Luke 21:4). Only our compassionate Creator, who loves us and longs for our love in return, prizes the smallest sacrifices offered with the greatest love.

In God's economy, the seemingly small and insignificant never go unnoticed. If you feel forgotten today, remember that Christ sees you and will provide all that you need. If you wonder whether your contribution—of time, talents, or treasure—is too small to make a difference, remember that God evaluates each offering, not on its size, but on the heart from which it is given.

Steps of Faith

Lord, thank You for assigning worth even to those things that the wider world views as insignificant. Help me to rest in Your watchful care and to give generously from a grateful heart.

Deeper Walk: 2 Corinthians 8:1-5

The New Purse

Give your burdens to the LORD, and he will take care of you.
He will not permit the godly to slip and fall.
Psalm 55:22

I WAS DELIGHTED WHEN the fashion industry started telling us that big purses were back in style. I found the perfect purse on sale for half off, and with my 30 percent customer loyalty coupon, the designer bag was a steal. I could fit everything I needed in it—makeup, a mirror, a brush, my overstuffed wallet, the hard case for my glasses, business cards, plenty of pens, a bottle of ibuprofen, a coupon organizer, hand sanitizer, lotion, my cell phone, even a water bottle—and there was still room left over.

Sometimes I joked to my friends that my new purse was so big, it was like hauling a small toddler around on my shoulder. But soon the humor gave way to some serious shoulder pain.

When I visited my chiropractor, he glanced at my purse on the chair and asked, "Do you carry that thing on your shoulder every day?"

Looking at him like he had no clue about fashion or women's necessities, I said, "Of course."

My beloved purse turned out to be the cause of my shoulder pain, and I realized I would have to take out some of the junk if I wanted to be healed. Either that, or I'd have to settle for a smaller purse.

Then the Holy Spirit quietly asked me, *What burdens are you carrying that you should let Me handle?* I stopped and thought about the question. There were worries that I had chosen to carry all by myself. When the Lord prompted me to let them go, sometimes I released them temporarily only to snatch them back again.

There were also sins I needed to confess. That day, I had a serious talk with the Lord. I asked Him to help me release sins, worries, or anything that would hinder my relationship with Him.

We're fragile humans, full of flaws and weaknesses. But, thankfully, Jesus came to save us from our sins and free us from our burdens. Sometimes we're reluctant to let go of our sins and worries, but God wants us to stop struggling with these things. Turn them over to Him.

Steps of Faith

I praise You, Lord, for you are my Savior who daily carries me and my burdens.
You are a God who saves (see Psalm 68:19-20).

Deeper Walk: Matthew 11:28-30

Lonely but Not Alone

The LORD is close to the brokenhearted;
he rescues those whose spirits are crushed.
Psalm 34:18

"DO YOU KNOW ANY SINGLE GUYS, JEN?"

Anna's abrupt question caught me off guard. Anna is a young widow with two small children. Her husband, Will, died two years ago in a car accident.

"So you're ready to start dating?" I asked gently.

"I think I am. I miss Will every day, but I feel ready to have someone in my life. You know, the financial aspect is hard, the solo parenting is difficult, but the worst part is that I'm so lonely. I want someone to share life with, to grow with, to laugh with. Will you pray with me that God will provide the right guy at the right time?" I agreed and began praying earnestly for Anna's loneliness to subside and for a second godly husband if that was God's will.

A couple of months later, Anna came up to me at church with a big smile.

"Has God heard my prayers?" I asked.

Anna knew just what I was talking about. "In more than one way!" she answered. "I've started seeing someone, and he's great. But God has drawn me so close. He is so faithful, and I feel that even if I don't marry again, I'm not alone. God is all I need. He's my best friend and my guide, and He promises to meet all my needs. I'd love to be married, but through this lonely time I'm learning that God is for me, and He's always with me."

Living as a single mom is difficult on so many levels. But perhaps the hardest part is the relational component—it's a lonely role. If you are living as a single mom, know that you are not alone. God is there to bear your burdens, carry your sorrows, and bring you deep joy that no human relationship can provide. Lean hard on His promises and seek godly fellowship with other believers who can encourage you and point you to Him.

Steps of Faith

Father God, thank You for Your constancy, Your compassion, and Your loving-kindness to me. Guide me and teach me as I walk the road before me.

Deeper Walk: Psalm 25:16-21

Standing Firm

Here on earth you will have many trials and sorrows. But take heart,
because I have overcome the world.

John 16:33

MARYANNE CLOSED HER Bible study booklet and turned to Holly. "I'm off to see what horrors await me at home."

Holly shook her head. "What do you mean?"

"In the past couple of months, my family has had two trips to the ER, a flood in the garage that we're still cleaning up, and a bout of the stomach flu, and now Erica's grades might keep her from playing basketball. Basketball is her ticket to college." Maryanne took a breath. "Sorry, I know you know all of this. I'm just tired of life being so stressful."

"This is going to sound insensitive—and believe me, I don't deny that you've been hit with a lot—but as long as we live in the world, life will be stressful."

Maryanne traced the design on her Bible. Holly was the only friend who could get away with saying such a thing to her. If anyone understood suffering, it was Holly. "Okay, then, what's your secret?"

"To be honest, I handle difficulties best when I remember that Jesus promised we would suffer but reminded us to be courageous."

Maryanne thought about Holly's words on the drive home. *God, I don't want to be a person who whines when life is hard. Help me to be strong no matter what happens next, knowing You are at my side.*

Before going to the Cross, Jesus made His disciples a promise: "You will have many trials and sorrows." But He also equipped them with a good reason to stand strong: "I have overcome the world."

Today, we may not suffer anything close to what the disciples withstood, but our experience continues to drive home the truth of Jesus' assurance that life includes suffering. Our ability to endure so often depends on our attitude. Will we complain our way through it, or call on God for the strength to follow our Savior's instruction?

Steps of Faith

You know, Lord, what I have endured and what I will face in the future. Help me to stand firm through all of it, knowing that You have already overcome this imperfect world.

Deeper Walk: John 16:25-33

"Knit One, Purl Two"

I am the one who made the earth and created people to live on it.
Isaiah 45:12

MY FOURTEEN-YEAR-OLD DAUGHTER IS trying to teach me how to knit. I am almost hopeless with the needles, but what I love is her patience and willingness to work with me.

I didn't know anything at all about knitting before. I once saw a woman knitting on TV, and I remember that she said, "Knit one, purl two." When I was growing up, my mom would say, "Tend to your knitting," which meant, "Mind your own business." That was the extent of my knitting knowledge.

But now I'm familiar with dropped stitches (which I do a lot), circular needles, and DK yarn, and I finally know what it means to purl.

One of the things I love most about knitting is taking my daughter to the yarn store. She is transported to knitting wonderland as she fingers the different yarns and stares at all the different colors, smiling as she imagines what it will all become. She lovingly chooses yarn and a pattern and spends a lot of time with her creation. When she finishes her piece, it is a work of art.

I imagine God smiling as He handcrafts each of us individually and uniquely with love and imagination. *Green eyes, curly brown hair, five feet two, a reader with a love of words and a dislike of rutabagas . . .*

On days when I wish I could do things like someone else, or when I lament my curly hair, or wish I were taller, or get discouraged because I can't knit, I remember the love that He put into designing me. He has said that we are His creation, His masterpiece (see Ephesians 2:10), and that He has formed us and called us by name (see Isaiah 43:1).

So I'm going to pick up the needles again and tend to my knitting. And I'm going to let God tend to His.

You are a magnificent creation, handcrafted with love and care. Remember that as a one-of-a-kind work, you have great potential for growth, as do all the one-of-a-kinds around you.

Steps of Faith

Lord, thank You for being mindful of me. You who formed the universe know my every detail. You knitted me together in my mother's womb.

Deeper Walk: Psalm 139:13-16

In the Gap

I urge you, first of all, to pray for all people. Ask God to help them; intercede on their behalf, and give thanks for them.
1 Timothy 2:1

AFTER MY MOM PASSED AWAY, I had the task of sorting through her belongings. Among the keepsakes, I found a pocket calendar in which she'd written summaries of prayers on each day. As I read them, I realized they were about my brother and me.

It's true that during different times of my life I made very poor choices that caused heartache for my family. Yet each time, I somehow was able to turn back toward the Lord and rekindle my relationship with Him. As I read my mom's entries, I realized why I had been able to turn back. She'd prayed for me to return to Him.

During one particularly depressing time, my mom suggested that I get involved in a local outreach ministry. Not one for reaching out, I was hesitant. Now, having read her prayers, I understand that she earnestly prayed for my guidance to "just the right community service program." The program I came to love was the women's shelter in the inner city. Though I'm grown and have long since moved away from my childhood home and that shelter, I continue to work at women's shelters today and have gained many rich relationships from my time there.

My involvement in the women's shelter was divinely guided, I believe, by my mother's intercession. She stood in the gap for me, when I didn't even know there was one. And she raised me up to the Father, where I was healed. Thanks, Mom.

We raise our children the best we know how. Then one day, they venture out on their own. But does our job end when they are "on their own"? Be challenged to pray for your children daily, interceding on their behalf, asking God for His presence, His grace, His healing, and His blessings. Your faithfulness in doing so will make a difference in their lives and in the lives of others whom they touch.

Steps of Faith

Father, I lift up my children to You. I pray that You will guide and protect them. Send Your Holy Spirit to grow their hearts in compassion and grace, that they may honor You.

Deeper Walk: James 5:13-20

Don't Be Afraid

*Do not be afraid or discouraged, for the LORD will personally go ahead of you.
He will be with you; he will neither fail you nor abandon you.*
Deuteronomy 31:8

AFTER I PUT THE casserole in the oven, I called my sister. "You won't believe this," I said. "The women's ministry committee asked me to be director next year."

"I'm not surprised," Sandra said. "What did you say?"

"I told them I'd pray about it. I feel as though I'm supposed to do it, but that's crazy. I don't know what I'm doing!"

"You're good at planning events."

"Spiritually, though, I'm not ready. I've been a Christian for only a few years."

"But you've grown so much these past few years! I've been amazed, actually."

"But I'm not equipped to lead myself, much less all those women!"

"That's where you're wrong. If the Lord is calling you to this, He will equip you. He's not going to send you out without giving you the tools you need to do it. His Word says that He will be with you. He'll never leave you."

"What if someone asks me a question about Scripture that I don't know how to answer?"

"You don't have to know everything. Tell them you'll find the answer for them or direct them to one of the women with more Bible knowledge."

I sighed and Sandra continued. "Keep praying for clear direction from the Lord, but I know that with His help you can do this. Don't be afraid."

Moses wasn't always a great leader. At first he was timid and tongue-tied. But the hand of the Lord was on him, and God equipped Moses to lead His people out of Egypt and into the Promised Land. If you're facing what seems as overwhelming as a meeting with Pharaoh, be encouraged by Moses' words to God's people at the end of his life. He told them—and us—what he learned from experience: that God would be with them and go before them. Trust in the Lord to help you, and do not be afraid or discouraged.

Steps of Faith

Father, You are the great I Am. Help me do the work You have called me to undertake. And help me do it well, for Your glory.

Deeper Walk: Joshua 1

Not on My Radar

Fear of the LORD is the foundation of true wisdom.
All who obey his commandments will grow in wisdom.
Psalm 111:10

I ALWAYS WANTED TO BE A MOM. Even when I was a kid, I imagined myself holding a baby in my arms or snuggling with a toddler in my lap. But parenting adult children was never on my radar. I guess I believed that something magical would happen when they turned eighteen. They would grow up, marry, and live happily ever after. It didn't occur to me that my husband, Bill, and I might have concerns about our children when they grew up.

While I do miss having young kids, there are advantages to having adult children. No more diapers, no more stepping on LEGOs when I'm barefoot, no more mounds of grass-stained laundry, no more repairing the trim on the garage door because it was scraped off in a novice attempt to park the car, and no more estrogen-fueled drama and youthful angst. My once less-than-perfect teenagers have become my best friends. Sometimes they actually ask for my advice instead of scoffing at it.

But there's a downside, too. I have to remember that these now grown-up people have minds and lives of their own. Bill and I try very hard not to offer unsolicited advice, but occasionally we have to bite our tongues. And although we're commanded by Scripture not to worry, sometimes we lie awake at night talking about what our grown-up kids are doing that we think they shouldn't be doing, or what they're not doing that we think they should be doing. Now that we're grandparents, we have a whole new generation to worry about. (Sorry, Lord.) But God is good, and we trust that He will keep all of us—His children—in His care and safe from harm.

Parenting adult children is a whole different ball game. We have to respect their opinions, desires, and boundaries in a new way. Sometimes it's difficult to let go. But we're learning, as they are, how to navigate this new kind of relationship. Pray for wisdom, and pray that you will be a blessing to them and a good example of what it looks like to be a Christ follower.

Steps of Faith

Father, please give me wisdom and help me to be a better daughter, wife, mother, sister, and friend.

Deeper Walk: Proverbs 3:13-18

The Blessing of Obedience

"Bring all the tithes into the storehouse. . . . If you do," says
the LORD of Heaven's Armies, "I will . . . pour out a blessing so
great you won't have enough room to take it in!"
Malachi 3:10

RECENTLY I ATTENDED a friend's church, and as the time came for the offering, I sat back. Since I'd already tithed online to my church, I figured this part of the service was not for me.

Then a whisper came to my mind: *Put twenty dollars in.*

I had only forty dollars in cash. No way was I going to give half of it! As the ushers started passing the offering plates, I wriggled uncomfortably in my seat. *No, God, remember?* I prayed. *I already gave my tithe.*

But the whisper came again: *Put twenty dollars in.*

I knew that if I didn't obey, I would feel awful. I didn't want to give this money—even though it was only twenty dollars—but I knew God was asking me to trust Him. So I reached into my purse, grabbed the crisp bill, and dropped it into the plate. Though I didn't feel excited over my obedience, I was at peace knowing I'd done what God had asked me to do.

After church, my friend and her family invited me out to eat. When the check arrived, the whisper came again. *Pay for lunch.*

But, God! I silently protested. *I have only twenty dollars—and I don't want to use my credit card.*

Pay for lunch.

With an inward sigh, I announced, "The meal is on me." I pulled out my credit card and handed it to our server.

After a while, he came back and handed me the card. "Our system is down, so the manager is taking care of your bill."

The bill's total was thirty-eight dollars.

God honors and rewards our submission. He simply asks us to trust Him. So the next time we hear Him whisper for us to do something, we can know that He is already preparing a blessing for our obedience.

Steps of Faith

I want to be obedient in all things, Lord. Sometimes I struggle, though, so strengthen me to trust You with everything I own—knowing that I can never outgive You.

Deeper Walk: 2 Corinthians 9:1-15

A Time for Giving

The LORD grants wisdom! From his mouth come knowledge and understanding.
Proverbs 2:6

MARGO TOUCHED THE paper angel hanging from the tree, reading the list of toys and personal items under the heading "Boy—age 5." But once she had removed the angel, she hesitated. There were needy angels in their own family this year.

Margo's husband, Dan, wanted to contribute significantly to his nephews' Christmas presents this year since his unemployed brother and sister-in-law were struggling financially. The previous week Margo and Dan had talked about the need to stick to their Christmas budget. They had three children of their own to buy for. Plus, several years earlier, Margo and Dan had begun giving to their church's Lottie Moon Christmas Offering for international missions each December. Because that offering goes toward spreading the gospel around the world, the couple had agreed it would be their primary charitable Christmas gift.

Still toying with the paper angel, Margo felt torn. It was difficult for her to resist worthy causes at Christmas. In fact, Dan and Margo's discussion of their Christmas budget had begun the day she came home from work telling him about the family for whom she and others in her office were going to "buy Christmas."

"Christmas is a time for giving," Dan had agreed, "but we still have to be wise stewards."

Placing the angel back on the tree, Margo whispered, "Lord, give us wisdom about where and how much to give this Christmas. And please provide for each of the precious children represented by ornaments on this tree."

God's Word is filled with verses about helping the poor and being generous. But it also contains many verses about wisdom. As you encounter opportunities to give and minister during the Christmas season, seek God's direction so you can serve in a way that is wise.

Steps of Faith
Father, give me a tender heart toward the needy, and help me to be wise in how I give.

Deeper Walk: Proverbs 3:5-6

Checking In to Check Out

Her sister, Mary, sat at the Lord's feet, listening to what he taught.
Luke 10:39

IT WAS A WEIRD CALL TO MAKE, but someone had to nip it in the bud.

At the last two family dinners, my sister and her new husband had been so engrossed in their phones that they barely conversed with any of us after the meal was served.

I dialed my sister's number. After our usual pleasantries, I jumped into it. "Jillsy, I gotta talk to you about something that's going to be uncomfortable," I said.

"Uh-oh," she said.

I briefly paused, then just said it. "You and Nick need to stop playing games on your phones at our family dinners. Neither of you spoke to any of us after lunch at the last two family meals. It's disrespectful."

Silence. "Ouch, Becca," Jill responded. "I can't believe you just told me to put away my phone as if I were a child."

The more I explained that the family wanted to spend time together, the more Jill took offense. She finally hung up.

Days later, Jill called, and we talked as if nothing had happened. As we neared the end of the conversation, Jill brought up our previous conversation. "My feelings were hurt, but ever since you said something, I feel like God has shown me how much I use my phone to check out from conversations. I didn't realize how addicted I was to playing games, checking Facebook, and reading Twitter. I'm putting my phone down a lot more these days, and so is Nick. We'll see you *and* talk with you this weekend at our family dinner."

Exercising self-control in things we find pleasurable is often difficult. With Facebook, games, or Twitter, the need for self-control may seem insignificant. But social media can be disrupting, disrespectful, and even destructive to relationships. Do you check in to social media more than you check in with your family? Social media is a tool for connection, but it's not connection. Face-to-face relationships are real connection.

Steps of Faith

Dear Lord, You made us for relationships. As I navigate social media and technology, I pray that You would give me strength as I exercise self-control.

Deeper Walk: Luke 10:38-42

How God Views Us

The LORD doesn't see things the way you see them.
People judge by outward appearance, but the LORD looks at the heart.
1 Samuel 16:7

THE DOG WAS THE ugliest thing I'd ever seen. Sometimes "ugly" is so ugly it's actually cute. Not in this case. This dog had matted, thinning hair over most of his back. The rest of him was bald. He had milky-white eyes, giving away his blindness. His lower jaw had a large underbite, revealing three discolored teeth. His breath could have taken out enemy forces.

When I first saw him, all I could utter was "Oh my. Bless his heart."

His owner chuckled at my shock as she picked up her dog and cuddled against him. "They were going to put him down at the shelter because nobody wanted to give him a chance. Everyone thought he wasn't valuable because of the way he looks. But this dog saved my life when I was going through depression. He accepted and loved me unconditionally. To me, he's priceless and beautiful."

As I watched this owner lavish affection on her pet, I stood amazed by how God often hides special gifts in plain wrapping paper. Too often we view the outward appearance and judge a person's—and our own!—abilities based on looks. God doesn't necessarily choose the most beautiful and perfectly urbane, refined, chic people to have the greatest gifts.

What freedom! When I look in the mirror and see someone "less than," I have the assurance that God sees the inner self and says, *To Me, she has value and purpose. She's priceless and beautiful.*

Thank God that He uses us no matter how we look! He doesn't expect us to be "prettied up" before He puts us to work in His Kingdom. We don't have to lose those thirty pounds first, or get the nose job, or have the right hairstyle, or clean ourselves up on the inside. God bless that ugly dog for using the gifts His Creator placed within him—it's a good dose of real beauty and humility.

Steps of Faith

Father, sometimes I can get so caught up in falsely feeling "less than" in my appearance that I think You would never use me. Forgive me for believing that lie. Use me today—just as I am. Thank You.

Deeper Walk: 1 Peter 3:3-4; 1 Samuel 16:1-13

Don't Melt

God blessed the seventh day and declared it holy, because
it was the day when he rested from all his work of creation.
Genesis 2:3

THE SNOW FELL IN THICK, silent flakes one Friday night as I returned home from dinner with friends. As I left to run errands the next morning, I watched two neighbor kids rolling snowballs nearly as big as they were.

When I arrived home a few hours later, I couldn't miss the finished snowman, glistening in the sunlight near the edge of our yards. He was a stocky fellow with rocks for eyes, a carrot for a nose, and a curved stick for a mouth. A purple scarf was tied jauntily around his neck.

After cleaning the kitchen, I left for the grocery store. Pulling out of the driveway, I noticed that the snowman was leaning and shrinking a bit. Uh-oh. Sure enough, by the time I returned home after attending church and sneaking in a few hours of work Sunday afternoon, all that was left of Frosty were some piles of snow and the purple scarf. By Monday morning, the scarf was gone and just a few small mounds of snow remained on the lawn.

Frankly, I felt a bit like that snowman: totally spent. Its short life span— Saturday morning to early Monday morning—reminded me of the state of my soul just then. The hours and minutes that seemed to stretch out on Friday began to melt away as the weekend wore on. I may have checked off the boxes on my to-do list, but I was exhausted by the time a new workweek rolled around.

My tendency is to cram in as many errands, outings, and chores as I can on a weekend. After all, how else will I get everything done? I'm old enough to know, however, that my body simply can't take that pace. When I ignore reality, I pay on Monday. On the other hand, when I obey God by observing the Sabbath—by "keeping it holy" (Exodus 20:8)—I am filled up rather than depleted. God knew that we needed the Sabbath as a time to connect deeply with Him and other believers, as well as a time to rest.

Just as that snowman wasn't made for sun, we weren't built for nonstop activity. We may not be able to do much about the weather, but we can choose to slow our pace.

Steps of Faith

Lord God, thank You for loving me enough to create the Sabbath. May I take that time this week to rest my body and allow You to restore my soul.

Deeper Walk: Isaiah 58:13-14

Christmas Mourning

What we suffer now is nothing compared to the glory he will reveal to us later.
Romans 8:18

CHRISTMAS IS THE "most wonderful time of the year," right? As Jesus followers, we celebrate the birth of the Messiah, the Long-Promised One. We honor the Savior who put on flesh and came to this earth to die for our sins. It's a joyous time. It's a family time. It's a time for making memories. We cook and shop and plan and decorate. We go to special church programs and Christmas musicals and office parties. But for some people, Christmas can be a time of sadness, even depression.

Each year, people face life-changing events that leave them devastated, broken, traumatized, afraid. These life-changing events can be close to home: Someone you love has been given a hopeless medical diagnosis. Someone you know is still dealing with unemployment. Someone you know is now a widow. Someone you love has had everything taken from her.

"Firsts" can be very difficult. The first wedding anniversary since he's been gone. The first year you've been unemployed. The first month he's been deployed. The first Christmas since he passed away.

Amid the celebrations of the birth of Jesus, let's remember those who are hurting. Is there a single mom you can help? Is there an unemployed family you could sponsor, maybe with toys for their children or a gift card for groceries? Is there a widow you could invite to your home for dinner or a gathering, or to your church's special music program? Is there someone you know who may be in Christmas mourning?

The Christmas season is not off-limits for suffering. Remembering and sharing with someone who is suffering is a beautiful gift.

At this time of year, remember those who are facing Christmas mourning. Be prayerful and creative about how you might help.

Steps of Faith

Jesus, thank You for all that You have done for us. Help us to help those who are hurting this Christmas.

Deeper Walk: Romans 8:17-23

Loving the Orphan

Pure and genuine religion in the sight of God the Father means caring for orphans and widows in their distress and refusing to let the world corrupt you.
James 1:27

LAST YEAR, my son and his wife participated in an orphan-hosting program. The program's purpose is to bring orphans from Eastern Europe and Asia to the United States so they can experience the love of a Christian family. The children learn about our culture and are immersed in the English language. Some of the orphans are eventually adopted, either by the host family or by someone who meets them during their four-to-six-week visit.

Our story began on December 16 when seven-year-old Janis (pronounced Yah´-nis) arrived from Latvia with a backpack and one change of clothes. Not only was there the usual language barrier, but Janis was also severely hearing impaired. But my son and his wife were equipped to help him because their ten-year-old son, Thomas, is profoundly deaf. They all know American Sign Language (ASL) and began teaching Janis how to communicate using ASL.

We took Janis to a hockey game, to the bowling alley, out for pizza, and to a Christmas service at our church. We took him to Build-A-Bear Workshop, where he chose a camouflage bear and a Batman costume.

I never dreamed that in the space of four weeks I would fall in love with a little boy who couldn't even speak the same language as me. When it was time for him to return to Latvia, we had a hard time telling Janis good-bye. I pray for him daily and hope that somehow I'll be able to see him again, whether that happens through adoption or another hosting opportunity.

There are millions of orphans worldwide. Some of these orphans have lost one parent, some both, and some are "virtual" orphans who have been turned out onto the streets by their families. God has a tender heart toward orphans. Ask Him what you can do to help these vulnerable children.

Steps of Faith

Father, Your Word tells us to care for the fatherless. Please give me a compassionate heart and show me what I can do to help.

Deeper Walk: Psalm 82:3-4

The Empty Cabinet

The LORD will give justice to his people and have compassion on his servants.
Psalm 135:14

IT WASN'T LONG AGO that my opinion about poor people was rather misguided. I felt that if they helped themselves, they probably wouldn't be poor. After all, hard work pays off, doesn't it?

But then the Great Recession hit and I lost my job. I was brought so low that I seriously wondered if God was punishing me for thinking ill of other people. I repented and asked Him what I should do. It wasn't long before I felt His answer: *Help others.*

How ironic, I thought. *I can hardly help myself right now.*

Soon I found myself volunteering in the area where I felt I had my greatest weakness. It was my turn to help others as God had called me to do. My church had a program called The Empty Cabinet, which collected food from local grocers and individuals. When people called the church asking for assistance in feeding their families, we would either bring them groceries or invite them to our collection center.

The first few days I volunteered, I was surprised to see that most of the people coming in looked completely average, although there were a few who definitely needed a shower and some clean clothes. I was struck with a sense of compassion that I didn't have before. Could it be that these people were doing whatever they could and, like me, had just suffered the loss of a job? I never realized the humility it took for people to ask for help.

God calls us to have the heart of Christ. We are to help the needy, have compassion on others, and not think of ourselves more highly than we should. He loves each one of us. "LORD, don't hold back your tender mercies from me. Let your unfailing love and faithfulness always protect me" (Psalm 40:11).

Steps of Faith

Lord, give me a heart of compassion. Help me to see others as You see them, and give me wisdom about how, when, and where You want me to serve.

Deeper Walk: Deuteronomy 15:7-11

Prayer Priority

Jesus often withdrew to the wilderness for prayer.
Luke 5:16

"GRACE, LET ME HELP you with dessert," Sonya said. The ladies from my weekly Bible study group were enjoying a Christmas luncheon at my house, but I had spent more time working in the kitchen than visiting with my guests.

"Thanks, Sonya. Since I've gone back to work full-time, I haven't had a chance to prepare as much beforehand as I would have liked. This time of year is just so busy!" I explained.

"I agree," Sonya said. "It's so easy to get caught up in all the doing and not enjoy the purpose behind what you're doing. For example, it would be a shame for you to have us all over here for fellowship and not get to enjoy any fellowship yourself. Let's go!" Sonya teased.

I thought about Sonya's words as I washed dishes after the ladies left. My busy lifestyle was affecting more than just my fellowship with friends; it was affecting my fellowship with the Lord. I had been on autopilot in my prayer life lately, believing that God was with me and that He would meet my needs, but not spending time in His presence confessing my sins, praising Him for who He is, and interceding for others. Prayer is also an opportunity for me to remember God's authority in my life and to submit myself and my desires to Him. I decided that I couldn't afford not to pray, so I put down the dishes and focused my heart and mind fully on the Father.

Some seasons of life are busier than others, but every season needs to be covered in prayer as we seek to live lives that glorify the Father. We need a balance—serving the Lord wholeheartedly like Martha, but realizing that being with Jesus is the most important thing, as Mary did (see Luke 10:38-42). As you fill your calendar this December, purposefully make time for prayer and fellowship with the Lord. Give Him the best of your day, for He is worthy.

Steps of Faith

Lord, sharpen my focus to see what is truly important. Draw me near to You in prayer, that I may know You better.

Deeper Walk: Luke 10:38-42

Jesus' Christmas List

The King will say, "I tell you the truth, when you did it to one of the least of these my brothers and sisters, you were doing it to me!"
Matthew 25:40

WHEN MY KIDS WERE LITTLE, they wanted lots of relatively inexpensive toys, dolls, and trucks. But as they grew older, their lists became pricier. Instead of toys, dolls, and trucks, they began asking for cell phones, golf clubs, and expensive video game systems.

Last year, my husband, Matt, and I wanted to remind our kids that Christmas wasn't just about how many presents they received. It was about the birth of our Lord and Savior. So Matt asked them, "What do you think Jesus would like for Christmas?" That question got them thinking in a different way about a holiday that has become highly commercialized.

My sixteen-year-old daughter, Megan, started looking through a Christmas gift catalog we'd received in the mail. But this catalog wasn't from the local department store; it was from a Christian organization that helps to alleviate poverty around the globe.

Megan and fourteen-year-old Adam decided that they would take money they had earned from babysitting and household chores to buy gifts for the poor. They talked about purchasing goats or sheep. They could also buy water filters, sewing machines, blankets, Bibles, and gospel tracts.

When they realized they could do only so much on their own, they enlisted the help of their youth group from church. Most of the kids participated. It was rewarding to see all of them get excited about helping the poor and how much they could accomplish together.

It's easy to get caught up in the excitement of parties, baking, and buying and receiving presents. This Christmas, ask the Lord to help you to keep your focus on Him. Ask Him what He would like you to give Him for Christmas. Consider doing something to help the poorest of the poor. Your generosity honors Him.

Steps of Faith

Heavenly Father, thank You for sending Your Son, Jesus, to be our Savior. Please help me to keep my eyes on You, and give me a generous heart to help those who are less fortunate.

Deeper Walk: Matthew 25:31-46

Personal Best

Whatever you do, in word or in deed, do everything in the name of the Lord Jesus, giving thanks to God the Father through Him.
Colossians 3:17, HCSB

As soon as my son Bryan got in the car, I could tell something was wrong. "How was your day?" I asked.

"Not good," he replied as he thrust a paper in front of my face, "because of this." I spotted the -2 at the top of his weekly spelling list.

"Honey, minus two is okay."

"No, it isn't," he replied.

I didn't even need to look over the seat to know tears were welling up. "Did you study?"

"Yes."

"Then you did your best," I said. "I bet you'll never misspell those words again." Then it dawned on me. "Bryan, this was only a pretest." It took an hour to convince my second grader that missing two words on a trial spelling test wasn't the end of the world. A few weeks later, a parent-teacher conference confirmed my concern: I had an academic perfectionist on my hands. I thanked God constantly for Bryan's intelligence and desire to do well in school, but I didn't want him to grow into a kid who sank into despair if he didn't get straight As. It was time to start helping him understand the difference between doing his best (making the most of the brain God gave him, doing all his work completely and neatly, and studying hard) and perfectionism (considering himself a failure if he didn't get 100 percent every time). It took a while to find the balance, but the next time he faced a -2, he did it without tears.

In our competitive society, it's easy to fall into the trap of perfectionism. For parents, the key to maintaining a healthy balance lies in our responses to both our children's mistakes and our own. As we model grace and present mistakes as opportunities to grow, we can show our kids that doing "everything in the name of the Lord Jesus" (Colossians 3:17, HCSB) does not mean being perfect, but using our talents and intellect to embrace learning about His world and His ways.

Steps of Faith

Heavenly Father, help me to raise children who love to learn and who know they are loved regardless of their performance.

Deeper Walk: Colossians 3:23-24

He Knows My Name

I have called you by name; you are mine.

Isaiah 43:1

DID YOU KNOW THAT scientists believe that at the center of every galaxy is a supermassive black hole, which holds the galaxy in place? I learned that on the Science Channel when they ran a program on what we know about the universe. At one point the TV screen swirled with all these multicolored, multishaped, multigaseous galaxies. When my eyes took them all in, I felt as if my brain exploded with the wonder of how awesomely vast and ordered our universe is—and how awesomely vast and ordered our *God* is.

Just looking at the photos from space of other planets—and even our own!—shows us the creativity and power of the Creator God. Whenever I drive through the mountains or stand on the beach and watch the force of the waves crashing against the sand, I find myself in awe of how immense God is. And I worship Him.

I worship the Creator God for His creativity and power, but I also worship Him because this great big, omnipotent, invincible God who created supermassive black holes to hold together galaxies knows my name. And He knows your name.

In the midst of a busy schedule—creating new worlds, overseeing the earth's entire population, handling the universe—He knows *your* name. Not only that, the God of the universe cares enough about you to number each hair that you have (see Luke 12:7). He knows every detail of your life. He calls you His.

So the next time you stand in awe at something in creation and are overwhelmed by how enormous and ordered and creative God is, you can rest in the knowledge that He's sovereign. He has everything under control, He knows you and what you need, and He's powerful enough to take care of those needs.

Steps of Faith

Creator God, You know my name! You know who I am—my strengths, my vulnerabilities, my joys, my sorrows, my fears, my successes. And You care about them all. Thank You that every day through creation You show me that You're powerful enough to handle everything in my life.

Deeper Walk: Psalm 8:3-4; Isaiah 51:12-13, 15-16

Christmas without Him

And this same God who takes care of me will supply all your needs from his glorious riches, which have been given to us in Christ Jesus.
Philippians 4:19

MELANIE SWALLOWED HER sadness as she looked for a place to sit at the Christmas banquet. Her husband had just been deployed, and this would be her first Christmas without him. As she listened to the recorded carols and smelled the cinnamon and ham, she dreaded the rapidly approaching holiday. She forced a smile and told herself that Mark would want her to enjoy the party.

"Melanie." A woman that she knew only by her first name—Sandra—touched her arm. "What are your plans for Christmas?"

"I'm going to my parents' house on Christmas Day." Melanie bit her lip to keep it from quivering. *God, what's wrong with me? Women all over America are facing Christmas without their husbands.*

"What about Christmas Eve?"

That was always their special night when they went to church, had a nice dinner, watched *It's a Wonderful Life*, and read the story of Jesus' birth before going to bed. "I have to work until noon, but I don't have any plans for the rest of the day."

"Would you like to come to our house? We can have dinner and drive over to church together."

Tears welled up in Melanie's eyes. "I'd love that." She knew she'd miss spending that evening with Mark, but she thanked God for providing a way out of the loneliness before she had a chance to pray for it.

The apostle Paul was not a military wife facing Christmas alone, but he certainly understood loneliness and need. A wife whose husband is overseas faces a unique aloneness during the holidays as she worries about her spouse's safety, fights the desire to be with someone she won't see for months, and wonders how she will spend a day usually enjoyed as a family. Whether we understand this kind of life or not, perhaps memories of times when we longed for someone to remember us will stir a desire to meet others' needs before they are expressed.

Steps of Faith

Lord, thank You for caring about our loneliness. Let memories of times when I felt alone keep me aware of those who are without their loved ones this Christmas.

Deeper Walk: Hebrews 13:1-2

The Reason for Our Joy

Yes, the LORD has done amazing things for us! What joy!
Psalm 126:3

I TOOK MY FAVORITE PICTURE OF my son when he was about four. He'd been spinning in circles as he ran around my parents' big backyard. In the photo, he is laughing and his arms are raised high. Both his body and his face express one emotion: pure joy.

No wonder I think of this picture when I read the opening verses of Psalm 126, which celebrate the Israelites' return from Babylonian exile. God had fulfilled His promise to bring His people home, and they couldn't stop singing, laughing, and telling others about His goodness. I even imagine them pinching themselves when the psalmist says their return was "like a dream!" (verse 1). Exuberance was on full display—just as it's written all over my son's face in that photo.

God pours His grace on us every day, giving us many reasons to rejoice. Of course, we still live in a broken world, and the psalmist acknowledges that, too. My son has faced many difficulties since that sunny day when he was four, and it's clear from the later books of the Old Testament that the Israelites faced challenges when they returned to their land. Perhaps that is why the psalmist also talks of weeping and planting "in tears" (verse 5) as he calls on the Lord to "restore our fortunes" (verse 4).

In this life, we treasure moments of pure joy in part because they are so fleeting. Yet embracing and capturing those glimpses of God's goodness—whether in our minds' eye or in our photo albums—leaves imprints of hope in our hearts. God's loving-kindness has become real to us, so even when difficulty creeps back into our lives, we know we can "harvest with shouts of joy" (verse 5).

So if you see the Lord working in an amazing way today, celebrate! And if the day brings trouble instead, remember that God will bless you as you faithfully follow His leading. He is at work redeeming and restoring your life, even as you wait for the day when He guides you all the way home.

Steps of Faith

Heavenly Father, thank You that joy is a hallmark of Your Kingdom. Whether or not my circumstances give me reason to be joyful today, help me to celebrate Your goodness and to wait with hope.

Deeper Walk: Romans 15:13

Grace for Gabe

Do everything with love.
1 Corinthians 16:14

"**Will Gabe be with your family** when you come for the Christmas Eve service and dinner?" Joanne asked her daughter Emily. Emily sighed in response.

"Actually," Emily said, "it seems that not only will Gabe not be with us that evening, but Jack won't be either."

"Why not?" Joanne asked.

Emily had prayed about this conversation before she picked up the phone to call her mother. Still, she understood her mother's reaction. Having the entire family gather for the church worship service, the traditional dinner, and the reading of the Christmas story from the Bible was a highly anticipated annual event for her parents.

"Gabe's mother decided they would take an earlier flight to Chicago. That's where her parents live, you know," Emily told Joanne. "Jack will have to take Gabe to the airport at five o'clock now, instead of nine as planned. I'm so sorry, Mom."

Joanne paused, then said, "Emily, we all knew when you married Jack that you would have a special set of circumstances at times like this. We love Gabe, and I'm sad he and Jack won't be there that night, but we understand. Hey! Maybe you all could come over the night before for hot chocolate. How would that be?"

Blended families face unique challenges during the holidays. Sometimes those special circumstances affect more than the immediate family. They affect grandparents, aunts and uncles, cousins, and close friends as well. If you're trying to make holiday plans with a blended family who needs some flexibility, consider ways you can give a little grace. Instead of pouting over changed plans, using guilt to manipulate, or insisting on your way, show the love of God through patience, kindness, compassion, and helpfulness.

Steps of Faith

Lord, show me if I have been intolerant and impatient when others have needed to change plans or make special arrangements that affected me. Help me instead to be gracious and flexible.

Deeper Walk: Romans 12:9-18

In Their Footsteps

Direct your children onto the right path, and
when they are older, they will not leave it.
Proverbs 22:6

THREE THOUSAND MILES AWAY from where I grew up is a small town that I've heard about since childhood. In their midtwenties my parents had passed through it, and for as long as I can remember, I heard about their adventures in the national park it borders.

Years later, when I was in my midtwenties, I visited the same area to spend time in the national park. I knew my parents had stayed nearby, but it wasn't until I got back that we realized I'd been to the same town. Looking through my pictures, we compared the few buildings and spectacular scenery to their thirty-year-old photos.

Wondering what had happened to the hotel where they had stayed, we pulled up Google Maps to look at the area. After sifting through memories and pictures, we realized that I had unknowingly stayed in the same hotel, albeit renovated and renamed. I had even stopped to take a picture in the very same parking lot, though now paved, nearly thirty years to the day after they had.

To be where a loved one has been years earlier can be a moving experience, even if you discover it after the fact. When I stood where they had stood, I saw the same scenery they had seen and probably felt a lot of the same feelings of awe and happiness. In those moments, we were separated only by time.

But as meaningful as it is that I could follow in their literal footsteps, they inspired me to follow in their spiritual footsteps too. I had the incredible privilege of seeing them model a relationship with God, and watching them honor Him with their time and resources encouraged me as I grew in my own belief. My parents have given me much, and of all the things they've imparted to me, I'm so grateful they passed to me the most important one of all—their faith.

Steps of Faith

Father, thank You for the blessing of family. Help me to live out my faith in a way that encourages my children to follow You.

Deeper Walk: Psalm 78:1-8

You're Forgiven

If we confess our sins to him, he is faithful and
just to forgive us our sins and to cleanse us from all wickedness.

1 John 1:9

MY HEART ACHED AS I saw Jamie from across the room. At one time, we had been close friends. Then I had an emotional spiral that escalated into depression, and my friendship with Jamie grew into dependency. Now that the crisis was over, I understood why she had pulled away.

Months earlier, I had sent her a card, apologizing for my clinginess, but our relationship had never fully recovered, and I continued to hammer myself for sabotaging it. *I need to ask her forgiveness again, God.*

I pulled Jamie aside and poured out a heartfelt apology.

"It's okay. We settled that," she said. "Our friendship is fine."

Then why didn't it feel fine?

You need to stop torturing yourself and accept the fact that she has forgiven you, a Voice urged.

But when would God heal our friendship? I poured my remorse out to Him for the hundredth time, begging His forgiveness for running to friends instead of to Him and seeing the loss of Jamie's companionship as divine punishment.

It took a long time for me to realize that I was rehashing the same routine with God that I'd repeated with Jamie—apologizing endlessly for an offense that He no longer held against me. Accepting that I was forgiven and could let go of the past brought the relief I'd ached for, in my relationships both with God and with Jamie.

Asking forgiveness is a difficult step, but accepting forgiveness can be even harder. When broken relationships and lasting consequences bring regret, we may be tempted to beat ourselves up, even though we've asked God and the person we offended for forgiveness. The familiar words of 1 John 1:9 assure us that we are forgiven the moment we confess: "If we confess our sins, He is faithful and righteous to forgive us our sins and to cleanse us from all unrighteousness" (NASB). May this truth stir us to accept that release from sins that God erased.

Steps of Faith

Lord, forgive my refusal to accept Your permanent pardon for my sins. Help me to embrace Your forgiveness as the gift that it is.

Deeper Walk: Psalm 103

Jesus' Family Tree

This is a record of the ancestors of Jesus the Messiah, a descendant of
David and of Abraham: Abraham was the father of Isaac . . .
Matthew 1:1-2

LONG BEFORE Ancestry.com was established, my grandfather was painstakingly building our family tree. He visited elderly relatives, listening to their stories and reviewing family Bibles, old letters, and newspaper articles; he uncovered privately published family histories; and he traveled out of state to scour dusty records in county courthouses.

Thanks to his years of work, I know I am descended from a Revolutionary War general—a close friend of Daniel Boone's—and several Civil War veterans, homesteaders, shopkeepers, and teachers.

Aside from the general, the people profiled in my family history were simple folk. They may have made a mark on their communities, but they would be forgotten if not for my grandfather. Ours is a pretty ordinary family—one that reflects the spirit, grit, and hard work we associate with America.

One thing I noticed: If my grandfather uncovered any bad apples among his forefathers and foremothers, they didn't make it into his record. How different that is from the genealogy of Jesus! Among the illustrious kings and fathers of nations are a few names we might have expected God to prune out of Jesus' family tree. Alongside obedient Abraham is the scheming Judah, who helped sell his brother into slavery; a few names after kind and gallant Boaz, we find Rehoboam, the foolish son of Solomon who lost half his kingdom. Just before the godly king Hezekiah, we find the name of his evil father, King Ahaz, who sacrificed many of his sons to idols.

Not only that: Along with the saints and scoundrels in Jesus' genealogy are several women—Tamar, Rahab, Ruth, and Bathsheba—some of whom were foreigners and some of whose children were conceived in scandalous ways. (Of course, Mary's first pregnancy must have shocked her community too.)

More than critical evidence that Jesus descended from the line of Judah, the first chapter of the first Gospel proves that nothing—not even the foolish or damaging choices of our parents or grandparents—will thwart God's plan to redeem His children.

Steps of Faith

Father, thank You for using the imperfect people who make up Your Son's
family line to remind me that Your plans and purposes can never be stopped!

Deeper Walk: Luke 3:23-38

They Remind Us

I recall all you have done, O LORD; I remember
your wonderful deeds of long ago.
Psalm 77:11

OF ALL THE CHRISTMAS TRADITIONS my parents passed down to me, our Christmas ornament tradition is something I appreciate more with every passing year. Each year, we would purchase an ornament that in some way symbolized the past year or a major event from it, and by the time I was an adult, I had quite a collection.

Some ornaments clearly commemorate life events, like the porcelain baby's-first-Christmas angel or the tiny college diploma. Others dangle as pleasant reminders of my travels, such as the copper-coated sequoia pinecone or the miniature Capitol building. Others are less obvious and more indicative of my interests and personality, like the castle from my favorite book series or the Chicago-style hot dog.

Each year as my family gathers together again, setting up the Christmas tree turns into a walk down memory lane. "Remember when . . . ," we say, holding up ornaments and pausing to remember. The memories and stories flow freely, often punctuated by laughter as we reminisce. Not all years have funny memories attached to them, and as we handle the ornaments from those more difficult years, the "Remember when we . . ." becomes "Remember when God . . ."

In a way, my parents' ornament tradition reminds me of the memorial Joshua had built. When the Jewish people needed to cross the flooding Jordan River, God miraculously held back the river so they could cross. To commemorate what God had done, Joshua told twelve men to pick out a large stone from the riverbed, which they piled up as a memorial.

Joshua explained, "In the future your children will ask you, 'What do these stones mean?' Then you can tell them, 'They remind us that the Jordan River stopped flowing when the Ark of the LORD's Covenant went across'" (Joshua 4:6-7).

My Christmas ornaments may not be as prominent as a stone memorial from the Jordan River, but they remind us what God has done throughout the years.

Steps of Faith

Thank You, Father, for the way You show Yourself strong through the years. Help me to remember what You've done in my life.

Deeper Walk: Joshua 4:1-8

Light of the World

The people who walk in darkness will see a great light.
For those who live in a land of deep darkness, a light will shine.

Isaiah 9:2

CANDLELIGHT CHRISTMAS EVE SERVICES hold a special place in my heart. Families and friends gather together, usually in the evening hours, and head off to church. It's a time to pause, celebrate, and take the focus off ourselves and shift it back to Jesus.

Tonight many churches will light the fifth candle of their Advent wreaths. The other four candles, representing the four weeks of Advent, are already lit. Not all wreaths have a fifth, but for those that do, it's usually a white candle sitting in the center of the wreath. This final candle, usually called the Christ candle, is lit on Christmas Eve or Christmas Day to symbolize Jesus' birth.

For churches that end their service with a candlelight hymn, the flame from this Christ candle is often used to light the congregation's candles too. As everyone carefully lights their candles from the people beside them, the flame of the Christ candle passes from relative to relative, from friend to friend, and even from stranger to stranger. It's a powerful moment, watching the light spread from one single candle to the rest of the congregation. And in the warm candlelight glow, we join voices with those we hold most dear.

So whether or not you physically light a candle tonight, take a moment to reflect on its symbolism. Tonight we share in the anticipation of Jesus' coming. Like those who waited thousands of years before, we take heart in the arrival of One who was promised to dispel darkness, bringing much-needed hope and peace to the world.

On this night—one of the darkest nights of the year—we remember the waiting and we celebrate the Light of the World.

Steps of Faith

Thank You, Father, for sending Your Son to live among us and carry out Your amazing plan to rescue us.

Deeper Walk: Luke 2:1-5

Forever Changed

Where is the newborn king of the Jews? We saw his
star as it rose, and we have come to worship him.
Matthew 2:2

MY DAUGHTER PLAYED Mary in the children's Christmas play at church recently. The children ranged in age from four to ten. There were lots of cute little angels running around, more interested in their glittery wings and shiny trumpets than the baby in the manger. The wise men came bearing their aluminum-foil-wrapped "gifts," which had gotten a bit tattered on the long journey from backstage. And while kneeling in worship, some of the tiny shepherds were playing with their paper-and-cotton-ball sheep, and some even wandered away. Amid all the clamor, one of the older boys recited Luke 2, telling us the Christmas story.

The production was so adorable and so touching that when Mary and Joseph sang the closing duet, I cried.

As we were driving home, I reflected on how spiritually accurate the play was. I get distracted by the glitter and shiny things of this world, while the One who truly deserves my devotion waits in the cold. I casually bring my hastily wrapped, tattered offerings to the King, when He really wants the gold of my love and obedience. And when I bow in worship, at times I mentally wander off to play with my to-do lists.

In that moment of truth, I realized that I had not yet celebrated Jesus this season, the real reason for Christmas. I prayed for my Savior's help to never take for granted His awesome gift of love.

This Christmas, let's give Jesus our very best. Let's slow down from busyness to bring Him presents of thankfulness, gifts of love and obedience, and stockings stuffed full of worship. Like the wise men and the shepherds, let us kneel and pay homage to the King. And when we walk away from the manger, let us be forever changed by our time in His presence.

Steps of Faith

Dear Lord, forgive me for all the times I've given You second best. Help me not to be distracted by what this world offers, but instead to be enraptured with You. Thank You for the love that compelled You to take on flesh and rescue us. Oh, and happy birthday, Jesus!

Deeper Walk: Matthew 2:1-12

Help Is Coming

Your God is coming. . . . He is coming to save you.
Isaiah 35:4

BLACK SMOKE BILLOWED FROM the burning car as April helped the driver to a safe distance. "Help is coming," she promised as the driver coughed and struggled to breathe. With the car now engulfed in flames, there was nothing to do but keep giving first aid and wait for the first responders to arrive.

In a lull in her conversation with the 911 dispatcher, April repeated her assurance to the driver in distress: "Help is coming."

Those three simple words, April would later contemplate, can make all the difference in the world. They offer the promise that we are not alone, that our predicament is seen and recognized, and that someone qualified to rescue us has taken notice of our plight and is on the way to do something about it.

The promise of help and rescue has inspired hope through the centuries, but it was never more needed than for the Jewish people over 2,500 years ago. The country had split into two separate kingdoms; one of them was on the verge of being destroyed, and the other didn't have a much brighter future. Things were looking grim, and God's prophets, the men and women He spoke through, were foretelling destruction and death.

But help was coming. Speaking on behalf of the Lord, the prophet Isaiah said, "That time of darkness and despair will not go on forever" (Isaiah 9:1). God was promising help in the form of a Messiah who would come on His behalf, saving Israel and the world. A child would be born, a Son given, and the Spirit of the Lord would rest on Him. God Himself would come down to earth and personally do the rescuing.

There was nothing to do but wait and hold on to the promise that the Messiah was coming. Over the next seven hundred years, the people of Israel anticipated His arrival. And then one night in the tiny village specified by the prophet Micah, the child was born. Now God was among humans, putting into motion His plan of hope and salvation.

Help had come.

Steps of Faith

Thank You, God, for the hope this Christmas season brings. Help us not take for granted the incredible gift we've been given.

Deeper Walk: Isaiah 9:1-7

The Perfect Planner

I trust in you, LORD; I say, "You are my God." My times are in your hands.
Psalm 31:14-15, NIV

IN THE WEEK BETWEEN Christmas and New Year's, my favorite aisle in the bookstore is the one stacked high with planners, which are always placed just below the racks of wall calendars. There is an organizer for everyone: students, moms, professionals, and athletes. Some feature weekly or daily spreads; others show a month at a time. I'm always drawn first to the ones with the artsy colorful covers. When I pick up one of those, I imagine how inspired I'd be by its beautiful design.

In the end, though, I always end up buying the newest edition of the same spiral-bound weekly planner because I like its layout best. I can block out meetings in a way that gives me a visual overview of how much uninterrupted work time I have each day. There is also plenty of room to take notes.

Still, every year I search for that perfect planner that will help me not only organize my schedule but perfect it. Maybe, I think, someone has invented a tool that will help me overcome all my bad habits while faithfully working in the good ones. Maybe I'll stumble across a planner that will magically reveal time in my day that I never knew I had—or at least help me organize my days so well that I'll be able to fit even more into my schedule.

Deep inside, I know that ideal planner doesn't exist. And I'm okay with that. God didn't create you and me to be automatons who never stop working or never relax and enjoy our families. He created stars to mark the passage of seasons and years, and He made a world that operates within the limits of time.

Planners, digital or paper, are wonderful tools that can help us steward the coming year well. They can remind us of our obligations and our priorities. However, they will never enable us to run the universe. Thankfully, that job is already taken: Our Lord Jesus "existed before anything else, and he holds all creation together" (Colossians 1:17).

That's good news we can plan on and rest in every day in the year ahead!

Steps of Faith

Lord Jesus, I commit this coming year to You, knowing that You go ahead of me and will cover me with Your mercy and grace.

Deeper Walk: Proverbs 16:1-9

Setting Goals—Together

Two people are better off than one, for they can help each other succeed.
Ecclesiastes 4:9

MY HUSBAND AND I SPENT THE week leading up to New Year's hidden away, strategizing our goals for the coming year. We listed the typical ones: pay off our debt, lose weight, invest more in our relationships. One of the most important goals we set was to actively pursue growing together spiritually—reading through the Bible together; praying together; doing service work as a team. We talked specifically about ways we could schedule each of those things to make sure they happened, and then we discussed setting mini goals and checking in regularly to determine our progress.

Whether or not you're married, setting goals with another person is a great way to make sure you stay accountable—especially with spiritual goals, since it is often more difficult to see tangible results in those areas. Friends or family members working with you can see differences in your life that many times you can't. They can share how they see God at work within you, which can boost your confidence to stick with those objectives.

If you've ever tried to set a goal by yourself—without anyone to encourage you along the way—you know it can be easy to give up. But if you've set a goal and had people challenge and cheer you on, you know you're more likely to make it. The Bible tells us that when people work together, "they can help each other succeed."

This year, set your goals and find someone who will come alongside you for success.

Steps of Faith

Holy Spirit, every year I make resolutions, and every year I fail at them! I don't want to repeat those mistakes this year. Help me find someone with whom I can set goals so we can encourage each other and reach our goals together.

Deeper Walk: Ecclesiastes 4:9-10; Hebrews 10:24-25

Take Time for You

Whatever you do, do it enthusiastically,
as something done for the Lord and not for men.
Colossians 3:23, HCSB

"SEE YOU TOMORROW!" I called as my coworker walked into the elevator. Once again, I was the last one to leave the office. The hours I stayed late or came in early were quiet and calm, so I could actually get work done without being overtaken with meetings. I pulled out a bag of chips from my desk and settled in for another two or three hours of work. On my drive home at 10:00 p.m., I called my best friend, Kim, to catch up.

"Hey," she answered, flatly.

"Hey," I said. "You okay?"

"Tonight was Kristi's going-away party; she leaves for Kenya tomorrow."

My heart dropped. I'd forgotten about the party for my cousin who'd answered God's call to serve in Kenya for a year.

For the remainder of the drive home, Kim spoke boldly to me about the dangers of letting my career consume me. "Overworking is taking a toll on your health and on your relationships," she said.

It was true. Lately, it felt like I practically lived at the office. So I asked Kim for help. We set up a daily phone call at 6:30 p.m. so that we could read a passage from the Bible and pray together. The timing would allow me to get home, get comfortable, and meet with Kim on the phone.

Soon, I began to see the benefits of having balance, and I arranged my schedule to allow for more God time.

Has work gotten so large in your life that it's starting to affect your relationships and your health? Scripture tells us to work for the Lord and not people—not your boss, but not yourself either. Work for the Lord, period. Burning yourself out and alienating others do not indicate a career given to the Lord. Set boundaries, include time for yourself and for serving others, and begin to gain a healthy balance.

Steps of Faith

Father, help me spend my time wisely and responsibly. Provide opportunities for me to rest and serve others.

Deeper Walk: Matthew 6:19-21

A Year of Thanks

Be thankful in all circumstances, for this is God's will
for you who belong to Christ Jesus.
1 Thessalonians 5:18

SARAH'S FACEBOOK STATUSES WERE often thought-provoking. Her first post on January 1 of this year was no different. "This year, I will give thanks." And throughout the year, Sarah often posted about various things she was grateful for: Jesus' sacrifice, family, friends, a sunrise, being spared from harm, birds chirping, chocolate, music, etc.

I told Sarah how uplifted I felt when reading her "grateful" posts. She shared that it wasn't always easy, but there was always something she could find, even in dark situations, that she could be grateful for. Even some of the seemingly insignificant things she posted about came from a place of enthrallment with God's vast creativity and attention to detail.

We went on to discuss how things had changed for her since seeking gratitude this past year. She noted a renewed perspective of unexpected blessings. And from that fresh perspective, she became more and more compelled to express her gratitude, not just in words, but through service and giving. In her year of thanks, she made tithing and giving to world missions a priority. And during school breaks, she started scheduling service projects with community ministries.

"The more I say thanks, the more I want to give and be a blessing to others," Sarah told me. "My year of gratitude has turned into my year of thanks and giving."

Many of us make goals and resolutions at the start of the year, but have you ever resolved to seek ways God wants you to serve Him in the coming twelve months? Now is a great time to sit with the Lord and prayerfully consider making the upcoming year all about gratitude. Keep a gratitude journal noting the things that come to mind to be thankful for and recording the changes God makes in your heart as you seek to praise Him in all things.

Steps of Faith

Father, I long to serve You in new ways. Awaken my heart to what You are doing around me so that I may join Your efforts and glorify Your name.

Deeper Walk: Psalm 118

Looking Back over the Year

Celebrate this Festival of Unleavened Bread, for it will remind you that I brought your forces out of the land of Egypt on this very day. This festival will be a permanent law for you; celebrate this day from generation to generation.

Exodus 12:17

WHEN I WAS GROWING UP, our church would get together at the end of every year to light a candle and remember the events from the year past. Afterward, we would pray, eat, and play games until well into the early-morning hours. I always looked forward to this service because it was interesting to hear what people experienced throughout the year—what happened, what they learned, and most significantly how God was faithful through each story. Year after year we met, and those stories of God's faithfulness built upon each other, which encouraged our faith and caused us to proclaim, "What a mighty God we serve!"

Many people encourage us not to look back but only to look ahead. But when we do that, we miss important and powerful lessons. Remembering and reflecting is so important that God encourages us to practice these disciplines. Throughout the Old Testament, we read again and again that God told His people to remember. He created celebrations, such as Passover and the Feast of Tabernacles, for His people to remember His faithfulness. He created the rainbow for us to remember His vow to us. And when an event happened at a certain place, the people named that well or that altar an appropriate name to help them remember what occurred there. When we remember, we see God's faithfulness and His hand over us—guiding, protecting, loving us.

As this year draws to a close and you think back to the events that happened, where do you see God's hand at work in your life? In what ways does that encourage or challenge you as you move into a new year? In what ways do you need to practice looking back and seeing God's faithfulness?

Steps of Faith

God, thank You for Your faithfulness to me! As I reflect on this past year, help me see clearly where You were and how You were working on my behalf. Let me hold those times close to my heart so I always remember that You are with me.

Deeper Walk: Leviticus 23

About Walk Thru the Bible

Walk Thru the Bible ignites passion for God's Word through innovative live events, inspiring biblical resources, and a global impact that changes lives worldwide . . . including yours.

Known for innovative methods and high-quality resources, we serve the whole body of Christ across denominational, cultural, and national lines. We partner with the local church worldwide to fulfill its mission, communicating the truths of God's Word in a way that makes the Bible readily accessible to anyone. Through our strong global network, we are strategically positioned to address the church's greatest need: developing mature, committed, and spiritually reproducing believers.

Our live events and small group curricula are taught in more than 50 languages by more than 80,000 people in more than 130 countries. More than 100 million devotionals have been packaged into daily magazines, books, and other publications that reach over five million people each year.

Wherever you are on your journey, we can help.

Walk Thru the Bible
www.walkthru.org
1.800.361.6131

THE BIBLE

It's...

- more than a book
- more than information
- more than black words on onion-skin pages.
- It's living and active and life-giving.

Take a walk thru the Bible today!
To learn more, visit
walkthru.org